# EXPLORING MICROSOFT® POWERPOINT 97

*Robert T. Grauer / Maryann Barber*

*University of Miami*

*Prentice Hall, Upper Saddle River, New Jersey 07458*

*Acquisitions Editor:* Carolyn Henderson
*Assistant Editor:* Audrey Regan
*Editorial Assistant:* Lori Cardillo
*Executive Marketing Manager:* Nancy Evans
*Editorial/Production Supervisor:* Greg Hubit
*Project Manager:* Lynne Breitfeller
*Senior Manufacturing Supervisor:* Paul Smolenski
*Manufacturing Coordinator:* Lisa DiMaulo
*Manufacturing Manager:* Vincent Scelta
*Senior Designer/Interior and Cover Design:* Suzanne Behnke
*Composition:* GTS Graphics


A Simon & Schuster Company
Upper Saddle River, New Jersey 07458



ISBN 0-13-754235-6

Prentice-Hall International (UK) Limited, London
Prentice-Hall of Australia Pty. Limited, Sydney
Prentice-Hall Canada Inc., Toronto
Prentice-Hall Hispanoamericana, S.A., Mexico
Prentice-Hall of India Private Limited, New Delhi
Prentice-Hall of Japan, Inc., Tokyo
Simon & Schuster Asia Pte. Ltd., Singapore
Editora Prentice-Hall do Brasil, Ltda., Rio de Janeiro

Printed in the United States of America

10 9 8 7 6 5 4 3 2 1

# EXPLORING MICROSOFT®
# POWERPOINT 97

# CONTENTS

# 2

## Creating a Presentation: Content, Formatting, and Animation 49



# 3

## Enhancing a Presentation: The Web and Other Resources 91

*To Marion, Benjy, Jessica, and Ellie*

*—Robert Grauer*

*To Frank, Jessica, and My Parents*

*—Maryann Barber*

# PREFACE

We are proud to announce the third edition of the *Exploring Windows* series in conjunction with the release of Microsoft Office 97. There is a separate book for each major application—*Word 97, Excel 97, Access 97,* and *PowerPoint 97*—as well as a book on Windows 95, and, eventually, Windows 97. There are also two combined texts, *Exploring Microsoft Office 97 Professional, Volumes I* and *II. Volume I* contains the introductory chapters for each application, supplementary modules on Internet Explorer and Windows 95, and a PC Buying Guide. It is designed for the instructor who seeks to cover the basics of all Office applications in a single course, but who does not need the extensive coverage that is provided in the individual books. *Volume II* consists of the advanced chapters from each application and was developed for the rapidly emerging second course in PC applications. The complete set of titles appears on the back cover.

*Exploring Microsoft PowerPoint 97* is a revision of our existing book on *Microsoft PowerPoint for Windows 95.* It reflects new features in PowerPoint 97 such as the automatic spell check, Office Art, and support of the Web. In addition, we have revised the end-of-chapter material to include a greater number of practice exercises and case studies. The many exercises provide substantial opportunity for students to master the material while simultaneously giving instructors considerable flexibility in student assignments.

Our most significant change, however, is the incorporation of the Internet and World Wide Web throughout the text. Students learn Office applications as before, and in addition are sent to the Web as appropriate for supplementary exercises. Students can download the practice files (or "data disk") from the *Exploring Windows* home page (***www.prenhall.com/grauer***). This site also contains additional practice exercises and case studies, which can be downloaded to supplement the text. The icon at the left of this paragraph appears throughout the text whenever there is a Web reference.

Each book in the *Exploring Windows* series is accompanied by an Instructor's Resource Manual with solutions to all exercises, PowerPoint lectures, and the printed version of our test bank. (The Instructor's Resource Manual is available on a CD-ROM, which contains a Windows-based testing program.) Instructors can also use the Prentice Hall Computerized Online Testing System to prepare customized tests for their courses and may obtain Interactive Multimedia courseware as a further supplement.

The *Exploring Windows* series is part of the Prentice Hall custom binding program, enabling you to create your own text by selecting any module(s) in *Office Volume I* to suit the needs of a specific course. You could, for example, create a custom text consisting of the introductory (essential) chapters in Word, Excel, and Internet Explorer. You get exactly the material you need, and students realize a cost saving. You can also take advantage of our ValuePack program to shrink-wrap multiple books together. If, for example, you are teaching a course that covers Excel and Access, and you want substantial coverage of both applications, a ValuePack results in significant savings for the student.

We look forward to continuing to provide quality textbooks for all of your Microsoft Office requirements.

# FEATURES AND BENEFITS

***Exploring Microsoft PowerPoint 97*** is written for the computer novice and assumes no previous knowledge about Windows 95. A detailed supplement introduces the reader to the operating system and emphasizes the file operations he or she will need.

An introductory section on Microsoft Office 97 emphasizes the benefits of the common user interface. Although the text assumes no previous knowledge, some users may already be acquainted with another Office application, in which case they can take advantage of what they already know.

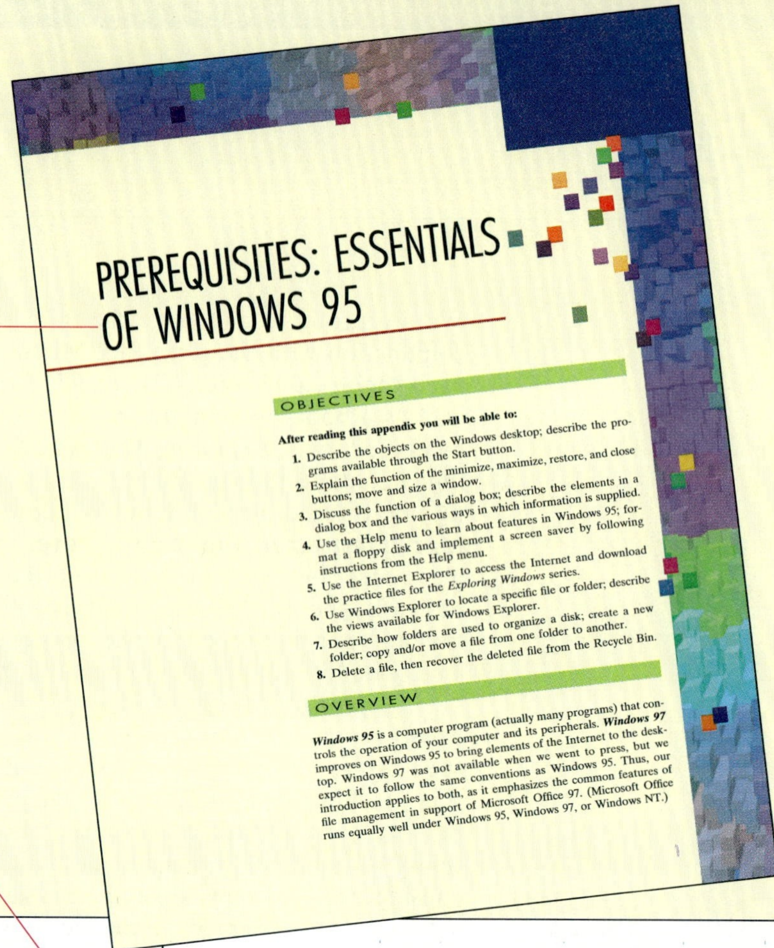

PREREQUISITES: ESSENTIALS OF WINDOWS 95

OBJECTIVES

**After reading this appendix you will be able to:**

1. Describe the objects on the Windows desktop; describe the programs available through the Start button.
2. Explain the function of the minimize, maximize, restore, and close buttons; move and size a window.
3. Discuss the function of a dialog box; describe the elements in a dialog box and the various ways in which information is supplied.
4. Use the Help menu to learn about features in Windows 95; format a floppy disk and implement a screen saver by following instructions from the Help menu.
5. Use the Internet Explorer to access the Internet and download the practice files for the *Exploring Windows* series.
6. Use Windows Explorer to locate a specific file or folder; describe the views available for Windows Explorer.
7. Describe how folders are used to organize a disk; create a new folder; copy and/or move a file from one folder to another.
8. Delete a file, then recover the deleted file from the Recycle Bin.

OVERVIEW

***Windows 95*** is a computer program (actually many programs) that controls the operation of your computer and its peripherals. ***Windows 97*** improves on Windows 95 to bring elements of the Internet to the desktop. Windows 97 was not available when we went to press, but we expect it to follow the same conventions as Windows 95. Thus, our introduction applies to both, as it emphasizes the common features of file management in support of Microsoft Office 97. (Microsoft Office runs equally well under Windows 95, Windows 97, or Windows NT.)

1

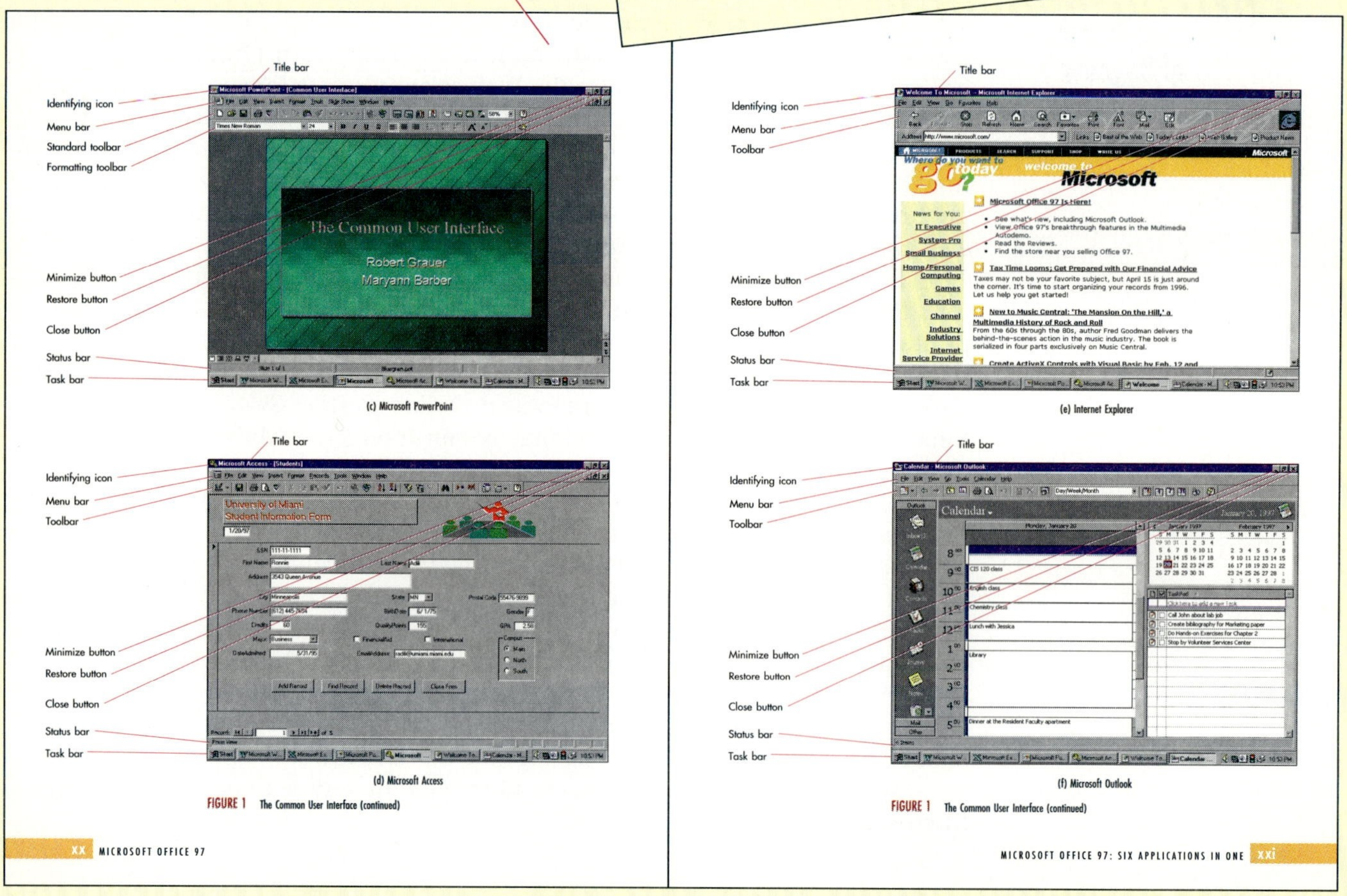



(c) Microsoft PowerPoint

(e) Internet Explorer

(d) Microsoft Access

(f) Microsoft Outlook

FIGURE 1 The Common User Interface (continued)

FIGURE 1 The Common User Interface (continued)

xx MICROSOFT OFFICE 97

MICROSOFT OFFICE 97: SIX APPLICATIONS IN ONE xxi

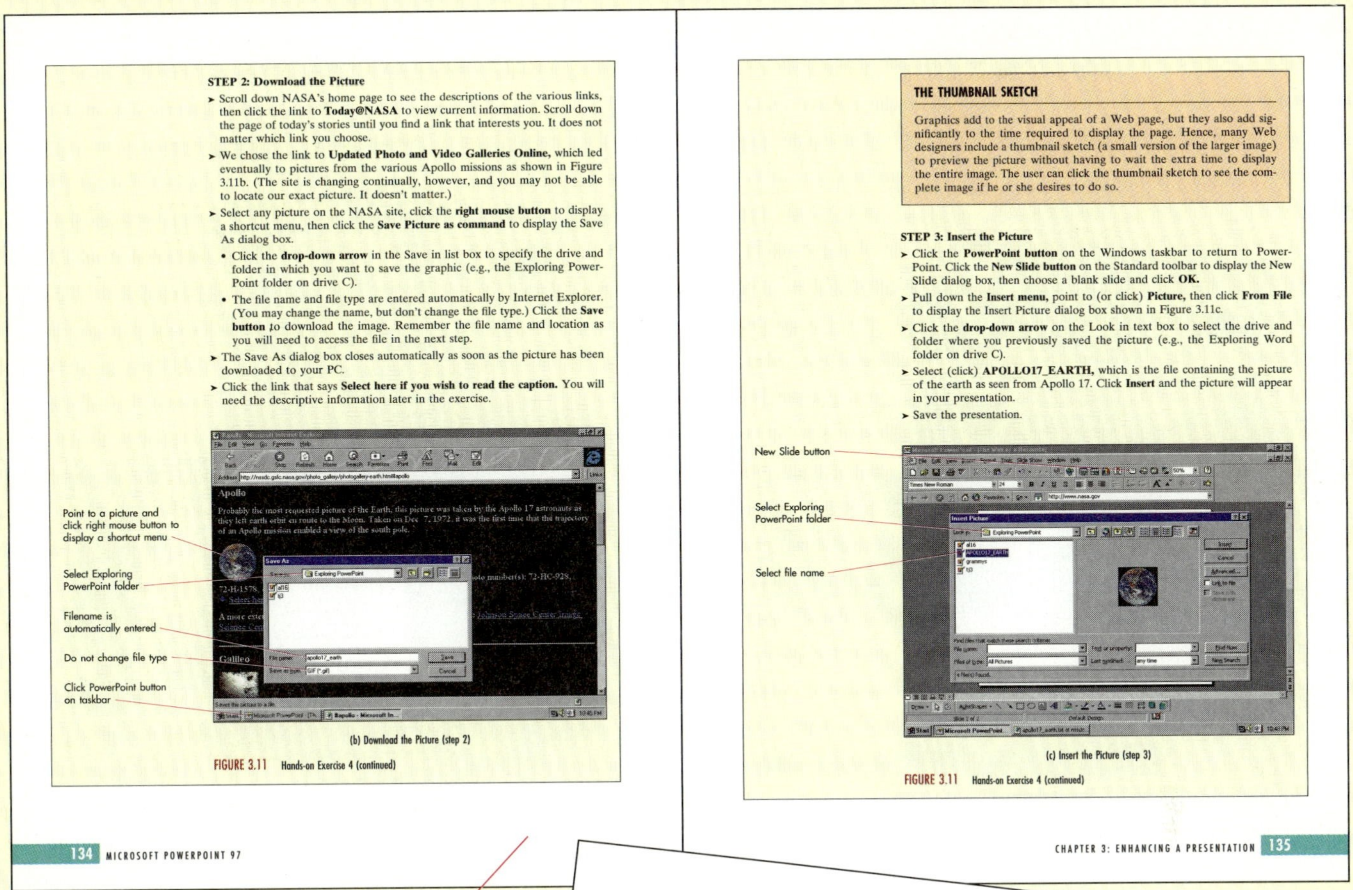

**STEP 2: Download the Picture**

- Scroll down NASA's home page to see the descriptions of the various links, then click the link to **Today@NASA** to view current information. Scroll down the page of today's stories until you find a link that interests you. It does not matter which link you choose.
- We chose the link to **Updated Photo and Video Galleries Online,** which led eventually to pictures from the various Apollo missions as shown in Figure 3.11b. (The site is changing continually, however, and you may not be able to locate our exact picture. It doesn't matter.)
- Select any picture on the NASA site, click the **right mouse button** to display a shortcut menu, then click the **Save Picture as command** to display the Save As dialog box.
  - Click the **drop-down arrow** in the Save in list box to specify the drive and folder in which you want to save the graphic (e.g., the Exploring PowerPoint folder on drive C).
  - The file name and file type are entered automatically by Internet Explorer. (You may change the name, but don't change the file type.) Click the **Save button** to download the image. Remember the file name and location as you will need to access the file in the next step.
- The Save As dialog box closes automatically as soon as the picture has been downloaded to your PC.
- Click the link that says **Select here if you wish to read the caption.** You will need the descriptive information later in the exercise.



(b) Download the Picture (step 2)

FIGURE 3.11 Hands-on Exercise 4 (continued)

134 MICROSOFT POWERPOINT 97

**THE THUMBNAIL SKETCH**

Graphics add to the visual appeal of a Web page, but they also add significantly to the time required to display the page. Hence, many Web designers include a thumbnail sketch (a small version of the larger image) to preview the picture without having to wait the extra time to display the entire image. The user can click the thumbnail sketch to see the complete image if he or she desires to do so.

**STEP 3: Insert the Picture**

- Click the **PowerPoint button** on the Windows taskbar to return to PowerPoint. Click the **New Slide button** on the Standard toolbar to display the New Slide dialog box, then choose a blank slide and click **OK.**
- Pull down the **Insert menu,** point to (or click) **Picture,** then click **From File** to display the Insert Picture dialog box shown in Figure 3.11c.
- Click the **drop-down arrow** on the Look in text box to select the drive and folder where you previously saved the picture (e.g., the Exploring Word folder on drive C).
- Select (click) **APOLLO17_EARTH,** which is the file containing the picture of the earth as seen from Apollo 17. Click **Insert** and the picture will appear in your presentation.
- Save the presentation.



(c) Insert the Picture (step 3)

FIGURE 3.11 Hands-on Exercise 4 (continued)

CHAPTER 3: ENHANCING A PRESENTATION 135

A total of 12 in-depth tutorials (hands-on exercises) guide the reader at the computer. Each tutorial is illustrated with large, full-color screen captures that are clear and easy to read. This example is taken from Chapter 3, which describes how to download resources from the Web for inclusion in a PowerPoint presentation.

FIGURE 3.3 What You Can Do with Clip Art

CHAPTER 3: ENHANCING A PRESENTATION 103

You don't have to be an artist to use the drawing tools within PowerPoint. Chapter 3 shows how to modify existing clip art to create new drawings to enliven your presentations.

b. Boldface and italicize the terms, *server, client,* and *browser* on slide 4. Boldface and italicize the acronyms, *HTTP, HTTPS, HTML,* and *TCP/IP* on slide 5.

c. Use Internet Explorer to go to your favorite Web page. Press the Print Screen key to capture the screen image of that page and copy it to the clipboard, then use the Windows 95 taskbar to switch to PowerPoint. Select the seventh slide, then click the Paste button on the Standard toolbar to paste the screen into the PowerPoint presentation. Size the image as appropriate.

d. Double click the WordArt image on the last slide to open the WordArt application. Change the words *Thank You* to *The End.* Change the style of the WordArt in any other way you see fit.

e. Print the slide miniatures six per page and submit them to your instructor as proof you did this exercise.

OLE

EXPLORING WWW

5. This problem is more difficult than the previous exercises as it asks you to create a presentation similar to the one in Figure 1.15. We have started the presentation for you in and have created the file *Chapter 1 Practice 5.* This presentation consists of three slides—a title slide and two slides containing an object and text.

a. Go to the White House Web site (www.whitehouse.com). Click the link to White House History & Tours, then click the link to the Presidents of the USA and select your favorite president(s). Point to the picture of the president, click the right mouse button to display a shortcut menu, then save the picture on your PC.

b. Use the Windows 95 taskbar to switch to PowerPoint, then double click the placeholder on slide two to add an object. Indicate that you are inserting the object from a file, click the Browse button, then select the file containing the president's picture.

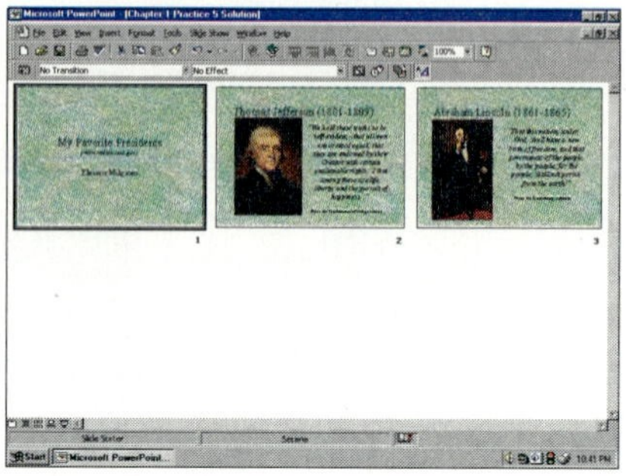

FIGURE 1.15 Screen for Practice Exercise 5



c. Return to the White House Web site, and click the link to a familiar quotation from your president, then copy that quotation to the appropriate slide in your presentation.

d. Create an appropriate title for this slide consisting of the president's name and years in office. Be sure to cite the source of the picture on this slide.

e. Repeat these steps for a second president.

f. Create a title slide for the presentation with your name somewhere on the slide. Print all three slides and submit them to your instructor as proof you did this exercise.

OLE

EXPLORING WWW

6. This exercise builds on the previous problem as it has you download pictures from the Internet for use in a presentation. Search the Web to select three landmarks, download the picture of each, then create a short presentation consisting of a title slide plus three additional slides similar to the one in Figure 1.16. This chapter did not tell you how to create a new presentation, but it's very straightforward as described below.

a. Start PowerPoint. If necessary, select the option button to create a blank presentation, then click OK to display the New Slide dialog box.

b. Choose the Title layout for your first slide. Enter the title of the presentation, *Landmarks Around the World,* and your name.

c. Click the new slide button to add a slide containing text and an object, then follow the instructions from the previous exercise.

d. Be sure to include an appropriate reference to the Web page where you obtained each picture.

e. Print the completed presentation for your instructor as proof you did this exercise.

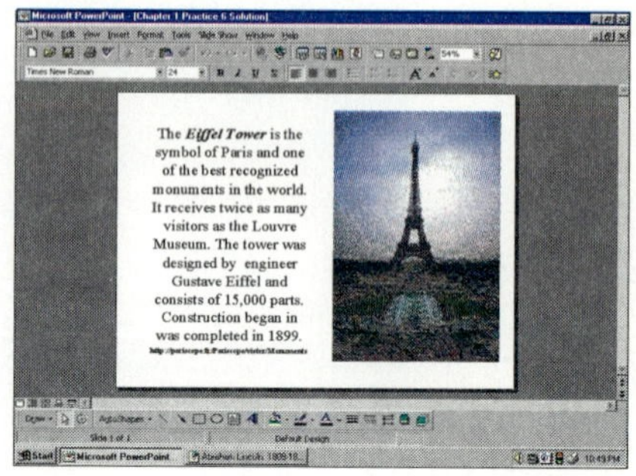


FIGURE 1.16 Screen for Practice Exercise 6



Every chapter contains a variety of assignments to avoid repetition from one semester to the next. The exercises vary in scope and difficulty and encourage students to create attractive documents. OLE and the Web are emphasized throughout the series.

Every chapter also contains a number of less-structured case studies to challenge the student. The Web icon appears throughout the text whenever the student is directed to the World Wide Web as a source of additional material.

CASE STUDIES

**Before and After**

As you already know, PowerPoint provides a set of drawing tools to develop virtually any type of illustration. Even if you are not artistic, you can use these tools to modify existing clip art and thus create new and very different illustrations. All it takes is a little imagination and a sense of what can be done. Choose any clip art image(s), then modify that image(s) to create an entirely different effect. Present your results in a three-slide presentation consisting of a title slide, a "before slide" showing the original image(s), and an "after slide" showing the modifications. Print the audience handouts for your presentation, three slides per page, and be sure to check the box to frame the slides. Ask your instructor to hold a class contest in which the class votes to determine the most creative application.

**Photographs versus Clip Art**

The right clip art can enhance a presentation, but there are times when clip art just won't do. It may be too juvenile or simply inappropriate. Photographs offer an alternative and are inserted into a presentation through the Insert Picture command. Once inserted into a presentation, photographs can be moved or sized just like any other Windows object. The CD-ROM version of the Clip Gallery contains a series of photographs. We invite you to explore these photographs, then report back to the class on their quality and cost.

**The National Debt**

EXPLORING WWW

The national debt is staggering—more than $5 trillion, or approximately $20,000 for every man, woman, and child in the United States. The annual budget is approximately $1.5 trillion, and Congress has yet to eliminate the deficit, which exceeds $100 billion annually.

Use the Internet to obtain exact figures for the current year, then use this information to create a presentation pleading for fiscal sanity. Do some additional research and obtain data on the budget, the deficit, and the national debt for the years 1945, 1967, and 1980. The numbers may surprise you. For example, how does the interest expense for the current year compare to the total budget in 1967 (at the height of the Viet Nam War)? To the total budget in 1945 (at the end of World War II)?

**File Compression**

EXPLORING WWW

Photographs add significantly to the appearance of a presentation, but they also add to its size. Accordingly, you might want to consider acquiring a file compression program to facilitate copying large files to a floppy disk in order to transport your presentations to and from school, home, or work. You can download an evaluation copy of the popular WinZip program at www.winzip.com. Investigate the subject of file compression, then submit a summary of your findings to your instructor.

Appendix B introduces the reader to the basics of multimedia. Students learn about hardware requirements, compression algorithms, and how to animate a presentation by incorporating sound and video files.

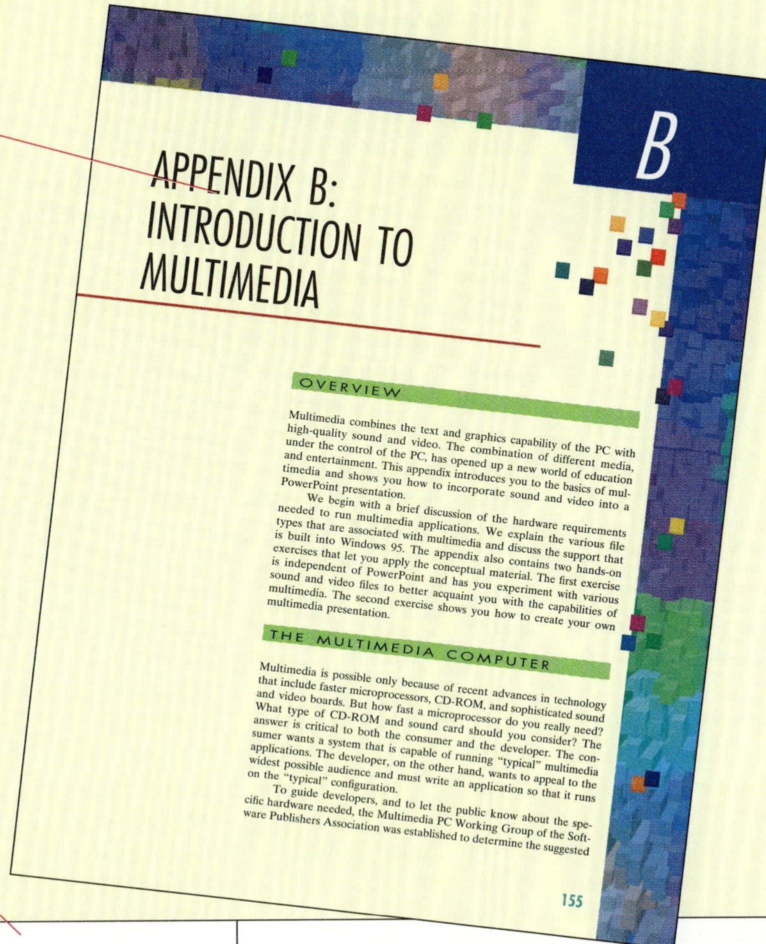

# APPENDIX B: INTRODUCTION TO MULTIMEDIA

B

## OVERVIEW

Multimedia combines the text and graphics capability of the PC with high-quality sound and video. The combination of different media, under the control of the PC, has opened up a new world of education and entertainment. This appendix introduces you to the basics of multimedia and shows you how to incorporate sound and video into a PowerPoint presentation.

We begin with a brief discussion of the hardware requirements needed to run multimedia applications. We explain the various file types that are associated with multimedia and discuss the support that is built into Windows 95. The appendix also contains two hands-on exercises that let you apply the conceptual material. The first exercise is independent of PowerPoint and has you experiment with various sound and video files to better acquaint you with the capabilities of multimedia. The second exercise shows you how to create your own multimedia presentation.

## THE MULTIMEDIA COMPUTER

Multimedia is possible only because of recent advances in technology that include faster microprocessors, CD-ROM, and sophisticated sound and video boards. But how fast a microprocessor do you really need? What type of CD-ROM and sound card should you consider? The answer is critical to both the consumer and the developer. The consumer wants a system that is capable of running "typical" multimedia applications. The developer, on the other hand, wants to appeal to the widest possible audience and must write an application so that it runs on the "typical" configuration.

To guide developers, and to let the public know about the specific hardware needed, the Multimedia PC Working Group of the Software Publishers Association was established to determine the suggested

155

Concepts are emphasized so that the reader appreciates the theory behind the application. Students are not just taught what to do, but are provided with the rationale for why they are doing it, and are able to extend the information to additional learning on their own.

interface. Thus, if you already use one Windows application, it is that much easier to learn PowerPoint because you can apply much of what you know. It's even easier if you use Microsoft Word, Excel, or Access, since there are over 100 commands that are common to the Microsoft Office.

The chapter begins by showing you an actual PowerPoint presentation so that you can better appreciate what you will be able to do. We describe the five PowerPoint views and the unique capabilities of each view. We show you how to add slides to, and delete slides from, an existing presentation, how to modify the text of a presentation; and how to add clip art. (We will show you how to create your own presentation in Chapter 2.) We also provide three hands-on exercises, in which you apply the conceptual material at the computer. The exercises are essential to the learn-by-doing philosophy we follow throughout the text, and it is through the exercises that you will truly master the material.

One final point, before we begin, is that while PowerPoint can help you create attractive presentations, the content and delivery are still up to you. It is important that you express yourself clearly and that you deliver the presentation effectively. The chapter ends with several suggestions to help you in this regard.

## A POWERPOINT PRESENTATION

A PowerPoint presentation consists of a series of slides such as those shown in Figure 1.1. Each slide contains different elements, including text, clip art, photographs and/or a chart. Nevertheless, the presentation has a consistent look from slide to slide with respect to its overall design and color scheme.

You might think that creating a presentation such as Figure 1.1 is difficult, but it isn't. It is remarkably easy, and that is the beauty of PowerPoint. In essence, PowerPoint allows you to concentrate on the *content* of a presentation without worrying about its *appearance.* You supply the text and supporting elements and leave the formatting to PowerPoint.

In addition to helping you create the presentation, PowerPoint provides a variety of ways to deliver it. You can show the presentation on a computer using animated transition effects as you move from one slide to the next. You can include sound in the presentation, provided your system has a sound card and speakers. You can also automate the presentation and distribute it on a disk for display at a convention booth or kiosk. If you cannot show the presentation on a computer, you can convert it to 35-mm slides or overhead transparencies.

PowerPoint gives you the ability to print the presentation in various ways to distribute to your audience. You can print one slide per page, or you can print miniature versions of each slide and can choose between two, three, or six slides per page. You can prepare speaker notes for yourself, consisting of a picture of each slide together with notes for its delivery. You can also print the entire presentation in outline form. Giving the audience a copy of the presentation (in any format) enables them to follow it more closely, and to take it home when the session is over.

**POLISH YOUR DELIVERY**

The speaker is still the most important part of any presentation, and a poor delivery will kill even the best presentation. Look at the audience as you speak to open communication and gain credibility. Don't read from a prepared script. Speak clearly and try to vary your delivery. Pause to emphasize key points and be sure the person in the last row can hear you.

2 MICROSOFT POWERPOINT 97

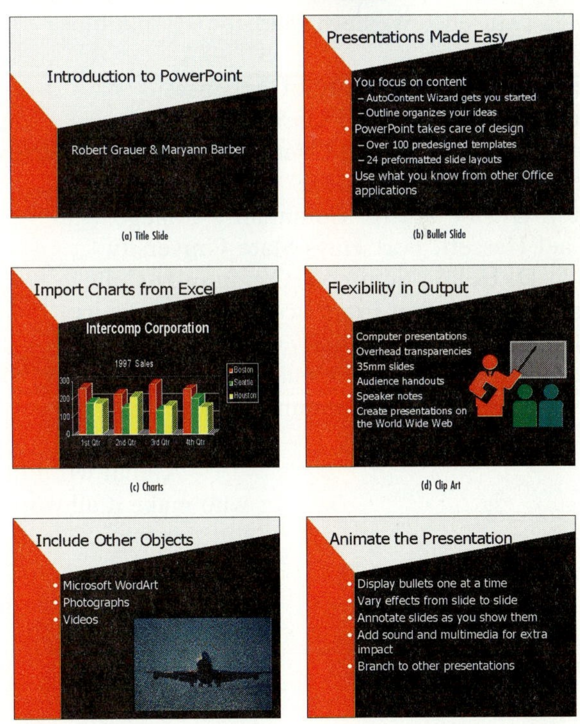


(a) Title Slide (b) Bullet Slide (c) Charts (d) Clip Art (e) Photographs (f) Animation

FIGURE 1.1 A PowerPoint Presentation

CHAPTER 1: INTRODUCTION TO POWERPOINT 3

## Acknowledgments

We want to thank the many individuals who helped bring this project to fruition. We are especially grateful to our editor at Prentice Hall, Carolyn Henderson, without whom the series would not have been possible. Cecil Yarbrough and Susan Hoffman did an outstanding job in checking the manuscript and proofs for technical accuracy. Suzanne Behnke developed the innovative and attractive design. John DeLara and David Nusspickel were responsible for our Web site. Carlotta Eaton of Radford University and Karen Vignare of Alfred University wrote the instructor manuals, and Dave Moles produced the CD. Paul Smolenski was manufacturing supervisor. Lynne Breitfeller was project manager. Greg Hubit was in charge of production and kept the project on target from beginning to end. Nancy Evans, our marketing manager at Prentice Hall, developed the innovative campaigns, which made the series a success. Lori Cardillo, editorial assistant at Prentice Hall, helped in ways too numerous to mention. We also want to acknowledge our reviewers who, through their comments and constructive criticism, greatly improved the *Exploring Windows* series.

Lynne Band, Middlesex Community College
Stuart P. Brian, Holy Family College
Carl M. Briggs, Indiana University School of Business
Kimberly Chambers, Scottsdale Community College
Alok Charturvedi, Purdue University
Jerry Chin, Southwest Missouri State University
Dean Combellick, Scottsdale Community College
Cody Copeland, Johnson County Community College
Larry S. Corman, Fort Lewis College
Janis Cox, Tri-County Technical College
Martin Crossland, Southwest Missouri State University
Paul E. Daurelle, Western Piedmont Community College
David Douglas, University of Arkansas
Carlotta Eaton, Radford University
Raymond Frost, Central Connecticut State University
James Gips, Boston College
Vernon Griffin, Austin Community College
Michael Hassett, Fort Hays State University
Wanda D. Heller, Seminole Community College
Bonnie Homan, San Francisco State University
Ernie Ivey, Polk Community College
Mike Kelly, Community College of Rhode Island
Jane King, Everett Community College
John Lesson, University of Central Florida
David B. Meinert, Southwest Missouri State University
Bill Morse, DeVry Institute of Technology
Alan Moltz, Naugatuck Valley Technical Community College
Kim Montney, Kellogg Community College
Kevin Pauli, University of Nebraska
Mary McKenry Percival, University of Miami
Delores Pusins, Hillsborough Community College
Gale E. Rand, College Misericordia
Judith Rice, Santa Fe Community College
David Rinehard, Lansing Community College
Marilyn Salas, Scottsdale Community College
John Shepherd, Duquesne University
Helen Stoloff, Hudson Valley Community College
Margaret Thomas, Ohio University
Mike Thomas, Indiana University School of Business
Suzanne Tomlinson, Iowa State University
Karen Tracey, Central Connecticut State University
Sally Visci, Lorain County Community College
David Weiner, University of San Francisco
Connie Wells, Georgia State University
Wallace John Whistance-Smith, Ryerson Polytechnic University
Jack Zeller, Kirkwood Community College

A final word of thanks to the unnamed students at the University of Miami, who make it all worthwhile. And most of all, thanks to you, our readers, for choosing this book. Please feel free to contact us with any comments and suggestions.

Robert T. Grauer
rgrauer@umiami.miami.edu
www.bus.miami.edu/~rgrauer
www.prenhall.com/grauer

Maryann Barber
mbarber@homer.bus.miami.edu
www.bus.miami.edu/~mbarber

# MICROSOFT OFFICE 97: SIX APPLICATIONS IN ONE

## OVERVIEW

Word processing, spreadsheets, and data management have always been significant microcomputer applications. The early days of the PC saw these applications emerge from different vendors with radically different user interfaces. WordPerfect, Lotus, and dBASE, for example, were dominant applications in their respective areas, and each was developed by a different company. The applications were totally dissimilar, and knowledge of one did not help in learning another.

The widespread acceptance of Windows 3.1 promoted the concept of a common user interface, which required all applications to follow a consistent set of conventions. This meant that all applications worked essentially the same way, and it provided a sense of familiarity when you learned a new application, since every application presented the same user interface. The development of a suite of applications from a single vendor extended this concept by imposing additional similarities on all applications within the suite.

This introduction will acquaint you with ***Microsoft Office 97*** and its four major applications—***Word, Excel, PowerPoint,*** and ***Access.*** The single biggest difference between Office 97 and its predecessor, Office 95, is that the Internet has become an integral part of the Office suite. Thus, we also discuss ***Internet Explorer,*** the Web browser included in Office 97, and ***Microsoft Outlook,*** the e-mail and scheduling program that is built into Office 97. The icon at the left of this paragraph appears throughout the text to highlight references to the Internet and enhance your use of Microsoft Office. Our introduction also includes the Clip Gallery, WordArt, and Office Art, three tools built into Microsoft Office that help you to add interest to your documents. And finally, we discuss Object Linking and Embedding, which enables you to combine data from multiple applications into a single document.

Our primary purpose in this introduction is to emphasize the similarities between the applications in Office 97 and to help you transfer your knowledge from one application to the next. You will find the same commands in the same menus. You will also recognize familiar toolbars and will be able to take advantage of similar keyboard shortcuts. You will learn that help can be obtained in a variety of ways, and that it is consistent in every application. Our goal is to show you how much you already know and to get you up and running as quickly as possible.

### TRY THE COLLEGE BOOKSTORE

Any machine you buy will come with Windows 95 (or Windows 97), but that is only the beginning since you must also obtain the application software you intend to run. Some hardware vendors will bundle (at no additional cost) Microsoft Office as an inducement to buy from them. If you have already purchased your system and you need software, the best place to buy Microsoft Office is the college bookstore, where it can be obtained at a substantial educational discount.

## MICROSOFT OFFICE 97

All Office applications share the ***common Windows interface*** with which you may already be familiar. (If you are new to Windows 95, then read the appendix on the "Essentials of Windows.") Microsoft Office 97 runs equally well under Windows 95, Windows 97, or Windows NT.

Figure 1 displays a screen from each major application in Microsoft Office—Word, Excel, PowerPoint, and Access. Our figure also includes screens from Internet Explorer and Microsoft Outlook, both of which are part of Office 97. Look closely at Figure 1, and realize that each screen contains both an application window and a document window, and that each document window has been maximized within the application window. The title bars of the application and document windows have been merged into a single title bar that appears at the top of the application window. The title bar displays the application (e.g., Microsoft Word in Figure 1a) as well as the name of the document (Web Enabled in Figure 1a) on which you are working.

All six screens in Figure 1 are similar in appearance even though the applications accomplish very different tasks. Each application window has an identifying icon, a menu bar, a title bar, and a minimize, maximize or restore, and a close button. Each document window has its own identifying icon, and its own minimize, maximize or restore, and close button. The Windows taskbar appears at the bottom of each application window and shows the open applications. The status bar appears above the taskbar and displays information relevant to the window or selected object.

Each major application in Microsoft Office uses a consistent command structure in which the same basic menus are found in all applications. The File, Edit, View, Insert, Tools, Window, and Help menus are present in all six applications. The same commands are found in the same menus. The Save, Open, Print, and Exit commands, for example, are contained in the File menu. The Cut, Copy, Paste, and Undo commands are found in the Edit menu.

The means for accessing the pull-down menus are consistent from one application to the next. Click the menu name on the menu bar, or press the Alt key plus the underlined letter of the menu name; for example, press Alt+F to pull down the File menu. If you already know some keyboard shortcuts in one application, there is a good chance that the shortcuts will work in another application. Ctrl+Home and Ctrl+End, for example, move to the beginning and end of a document, respectively. Ctrl+B, Ctrl+I, and Ctrl+U boldface, italicize, and underline text. Ctrl+X (the "X" is supposed to remind you of a pair of scissors), Ctrl+C, and Ctrl+V will cut, copy, and paste, respectively.

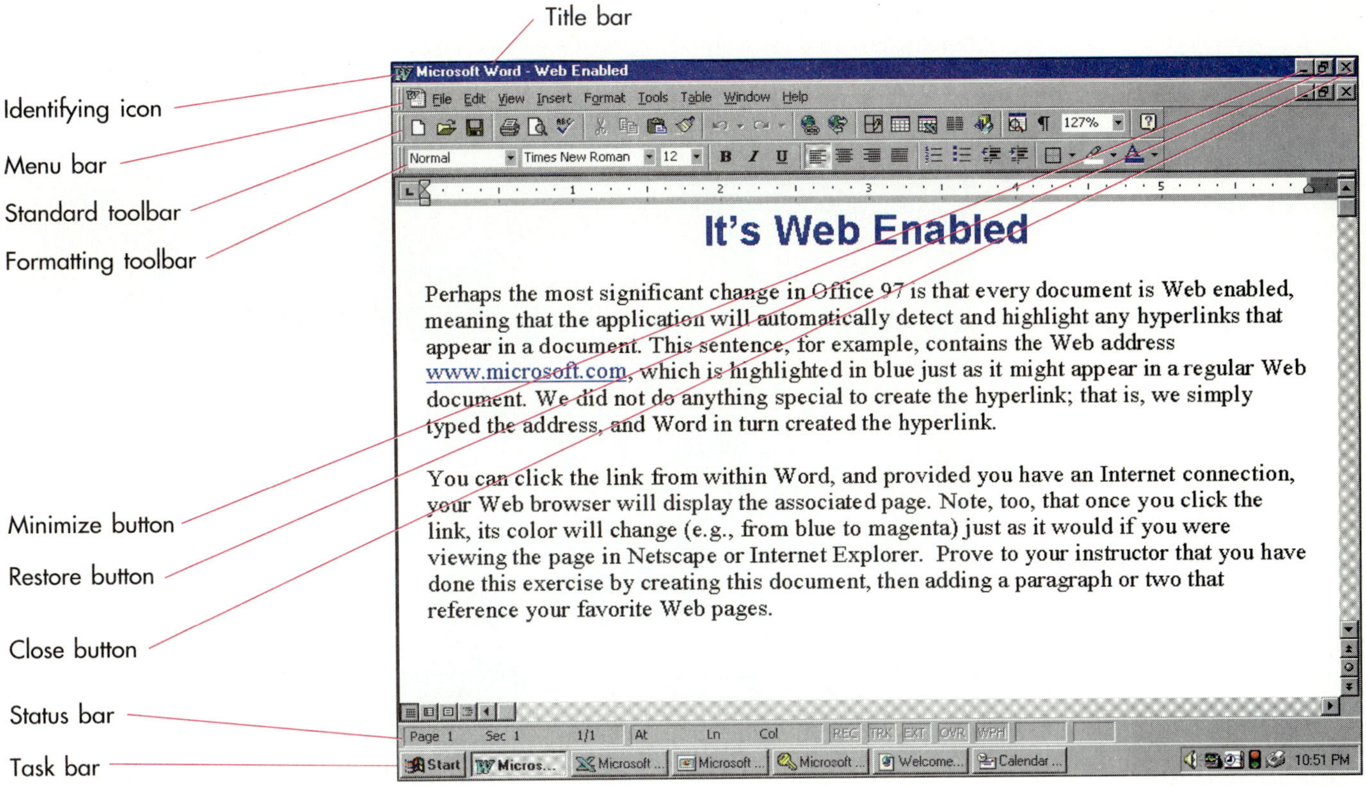


(a) Microsoft Word

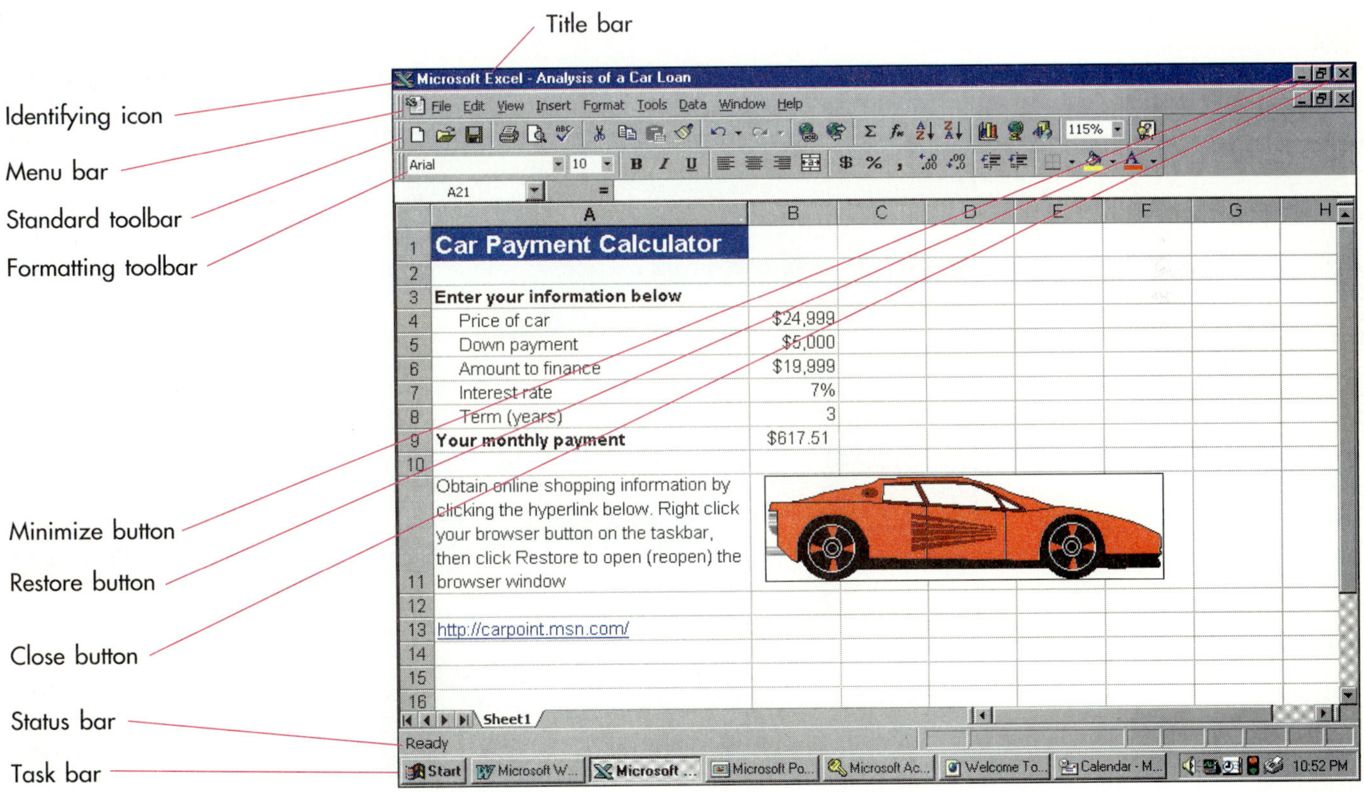


(b) Microsoft Excel

**FIGURE 1** The Common User Interface

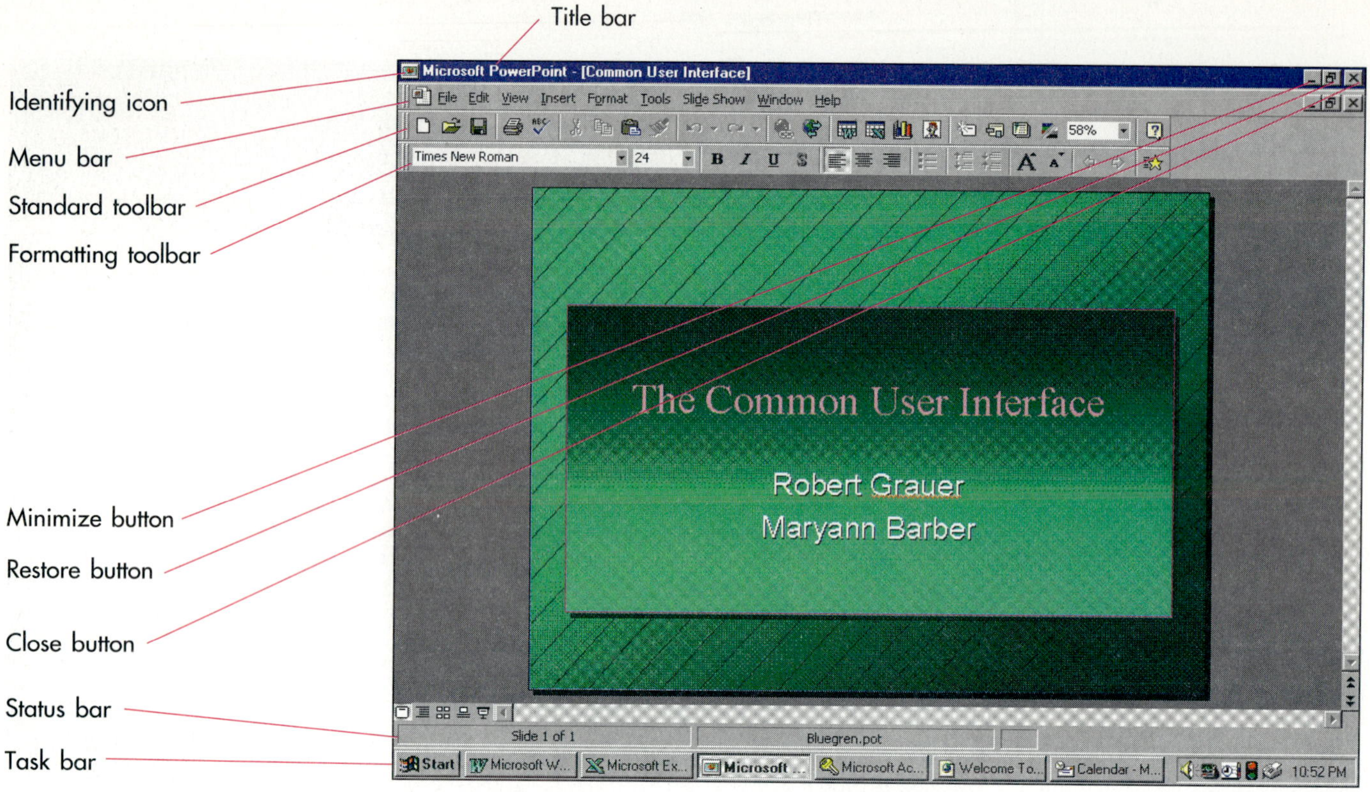


(c) Microsoft PowerPoint

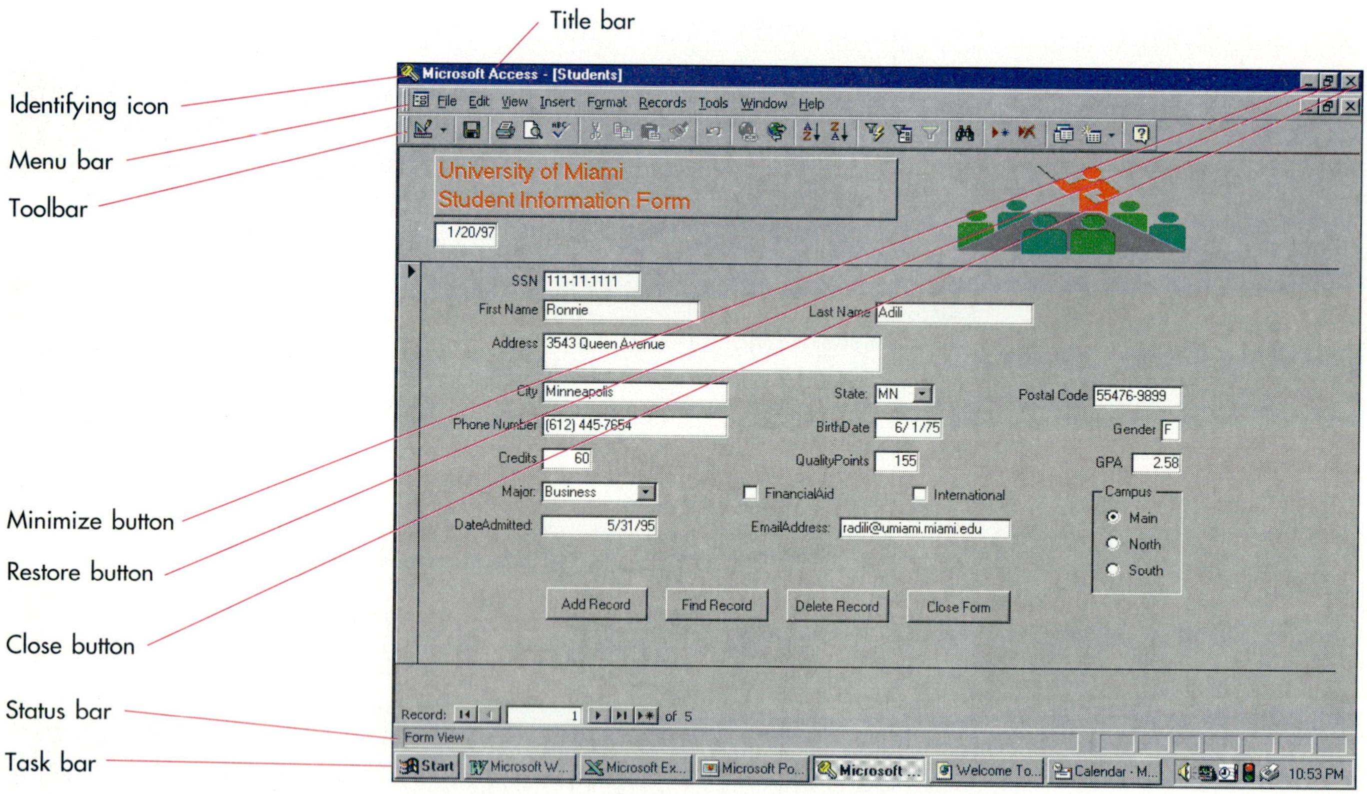


(d) Microsoft Access

**FIGURE 1** The Common User Interface (continued)

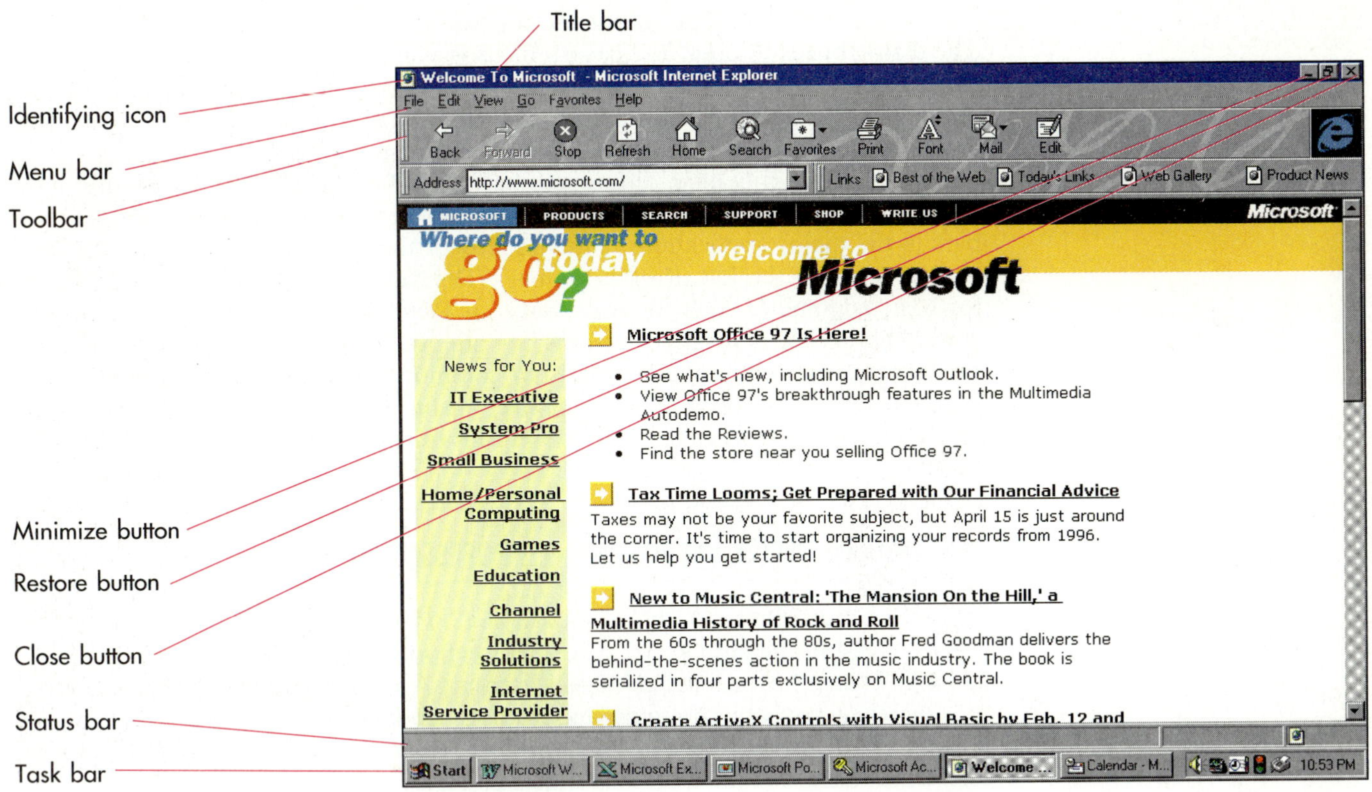


(e) Internet Explorer

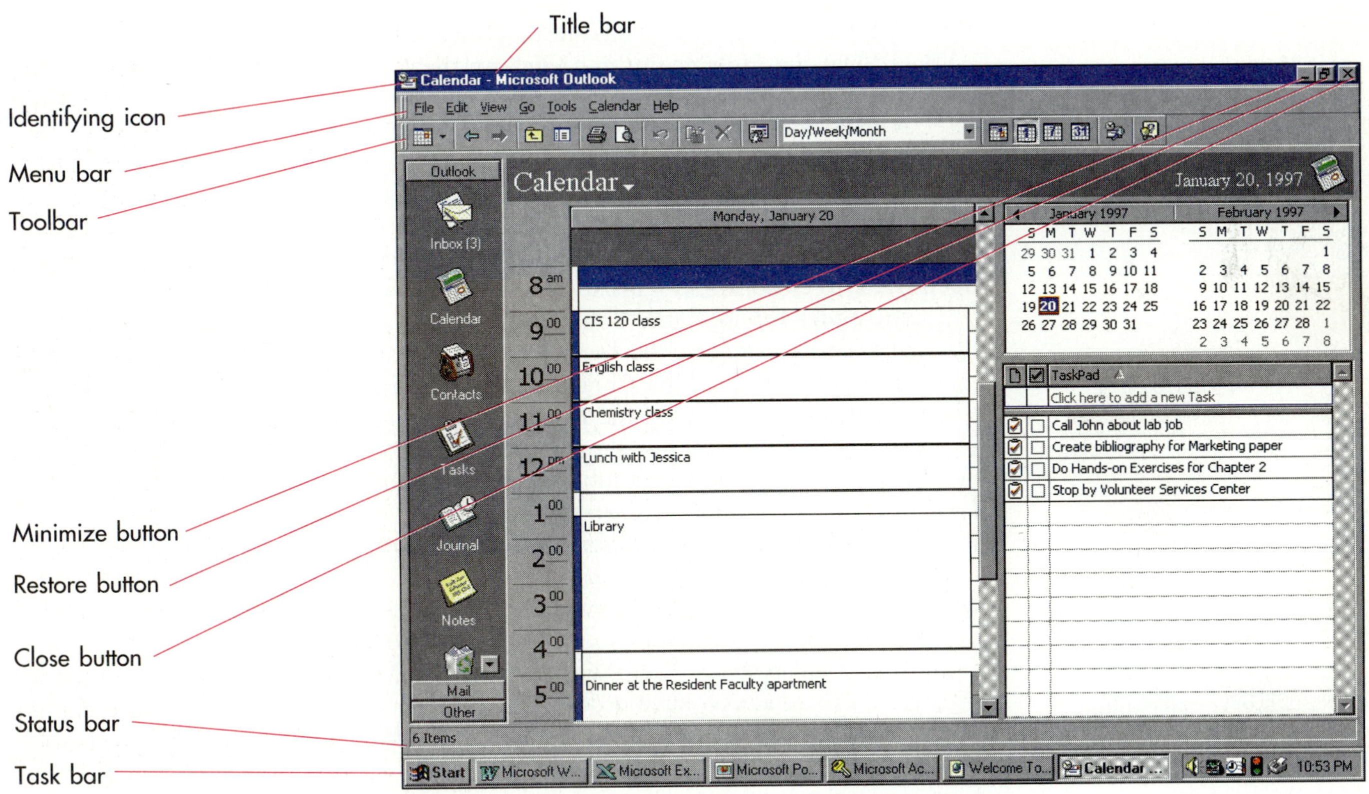


(f) Microsoft Outlook

**FIGURE 1** The Common User Interface (continued)

The four major applications use consistent (and often identical) dialog boxes. The dialog boxes to open and close a file, for example, are identical in every application. All four applications also share a common dictionary. The AutoCorrect feature (to correct common spelling mistakes) works identically in all four applications. The help feature also functions identically.

There are, of course, differences between the applications. Each application has unique menus and toolbars. Nevertheless, the Standard and Formatting toolbars in the major applications contain many of the same tools (especially the first several tools on the left of each toolbar). The ***Standard toolbar*** contains buttons for basic commands such as Open, Save, or Print. It also contains buttons to cut, copy, and paste, and these buttons are identical in all four applications. The ***Formatting toolbar*** provides access to common operations such as boldface or italics, or changing the font or point size; again, these buttons are identical in all four applications. ScreenTips are present in all applications.

**STANDARD OFFICE VERSUS OFFICE PROFESSIONAL**

Microsoft distributes both a Standard and a Professional edition of Office 97. Both versions include Word, Excel, PowerPoint, Internet Explorer, and Outlook. Office Professional also has Microsoft Access. The difference is important when you are shopping and you are comparing prices from different sources. Be sure to purchase the version that is appropriate for your needs.

## Help for Office 97

Several types of help are available in Office 97. The most basic is accessed by pulling down the Help menu and clicking the Contents and Index command to display the Help Contents window as shown in Figures 2a and 2b. (The Help screens are from Microsoft Word, but similar screens are available for each of the other applications.) The ***Contents tab*** in Figure 2a is analogous to the table of contents in an ordinary book. It displays the major topics in the application as a series of books that are open or closed. You can click any closed book to open it, which in turn displays additional books and/or help topics. Conversely, you can click any open book to close it and gain additional space on the screen.

The ***Index tab*** in Figure 2b is similar to the index of an ordinary book. Enter the first several letters of the topic to look up, such as "we" in Figure 2b. Help then returns all of the topics beginning with the letters you entered. Select the topic you want, then display the topic for immediate viewing, or print it for later reference. (The Find tab, not shown in Figure 2, contains a more extensive listing of entries than does the Index tab. It lets you enter a specific word, then it returns every topic that contains that word.)

The ***Office Assistant*** in Figure 2c is new to Office 97 and is activated by clicking the Office Assistant button on the Standard toolbar or by pressing the F1 function key. The Assistant enables you to ask a question in English, then it returns a series of topics that attempt to answer your question.

EXPLORING WWW

Additional help can be obtained from the Microsoft Web site as shown in Figure 2d, provided you have access to the Internet. The easiest way to access the site is to pull down the Help menu from any Office application, click Microsoft on the Web, then click Online Support. This, in turn, will start the Internet Explorer and take you to the appropriate page on the Web, where you will find the most current information available as well as the most detailed support. You can, for example, access the same knowledge base as that used by Microsoft support engineers when you call for technical assistance.

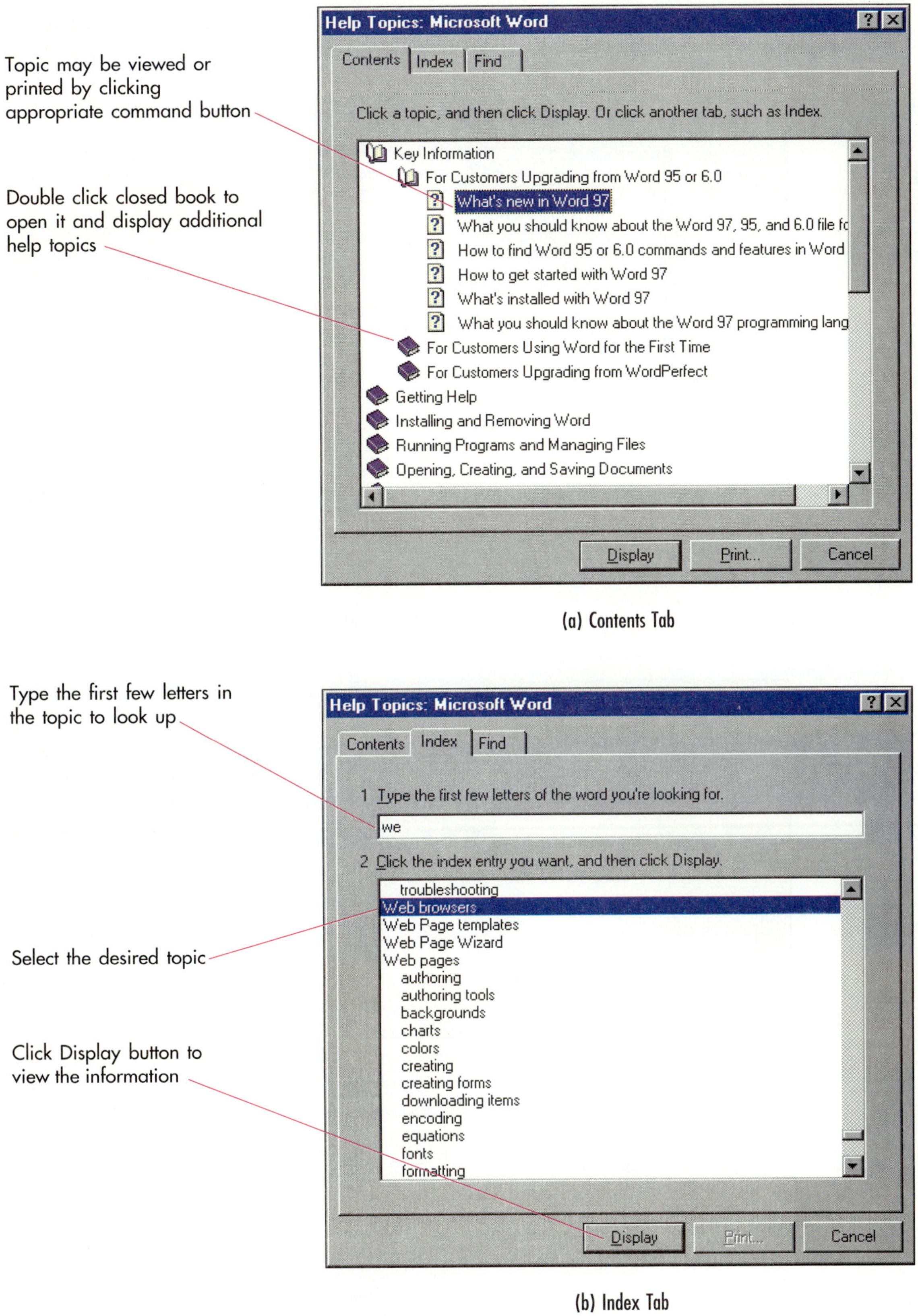


**FIGURE 2** Help with Microsoft Office

Help screen contains links to additional information

Click any topic to display the help screen

Enter your question, then click the Search button

Office Assistant (other images are available)

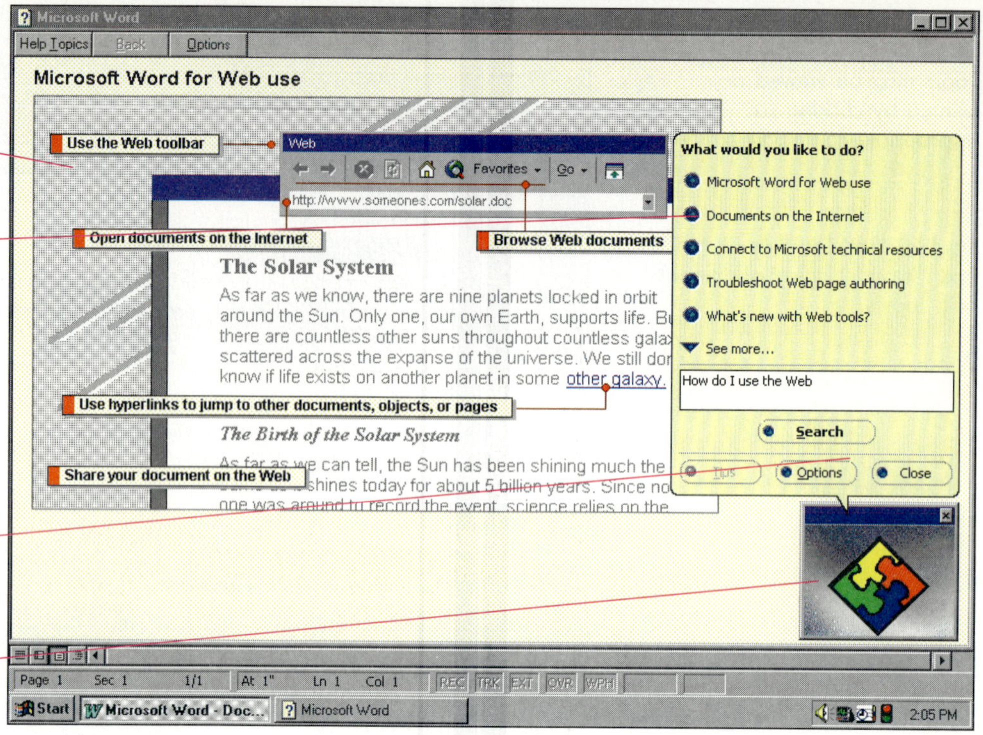


(c) The Office Assistant

Internet Explorer opens automatically

Web address

Link to Frequently Asked Questions

Click the link to desired information

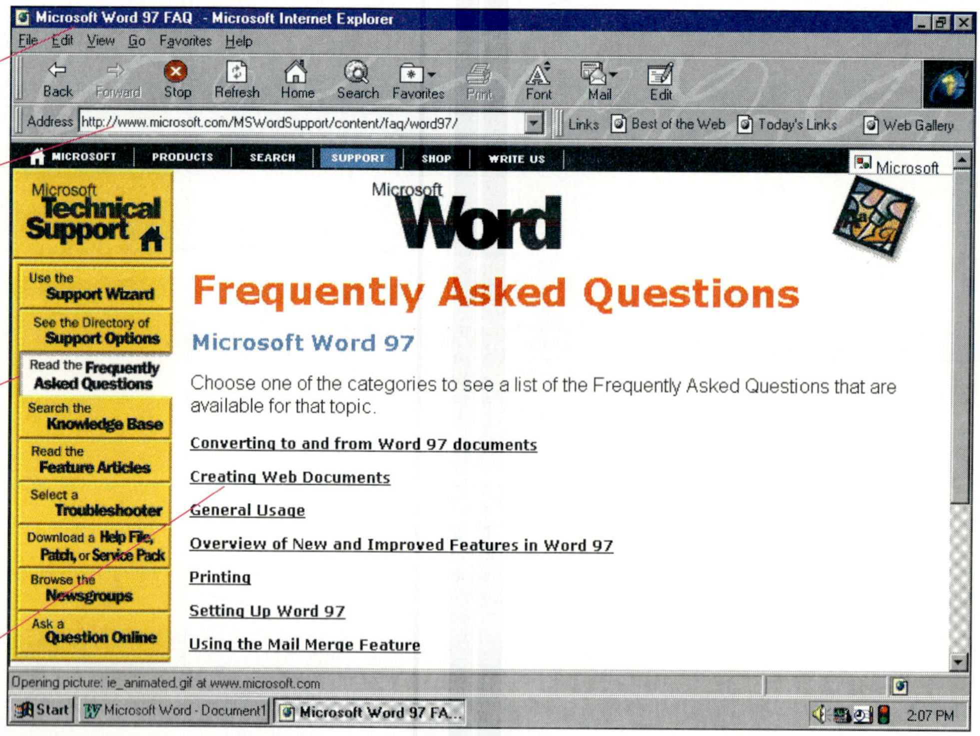


(d) Microsoft Online

FIGURE 2 Help with Microsoft Office (continued)

## Office Shortcut Bar

The ***Microsoft Office Shortcut Bar*** provides immediate access to each application within Microsoft Office. It consists of a row of buttons and can be placed anywhere on the screen. The Shortcut Bar is anchored by default on the right side of the desktop, but you can position it along any edge, or have it "float" in the middle of the desktop. You can even hide it from view when it is not in use.

Figure 3a displays the Shortcut Bar as it appears on our desktop. The buttons that are displayed (and the order in which they appear) are established through the Customize dialog box in Figure 3b. Our Shortcut Bar contains a button for each Office application, a button for the Windows Explorer, and a button for Bookshelf Basics.

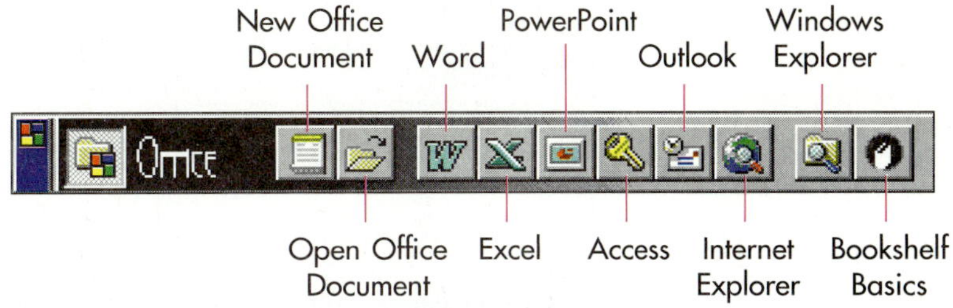


(a) Office Shortcut Bar

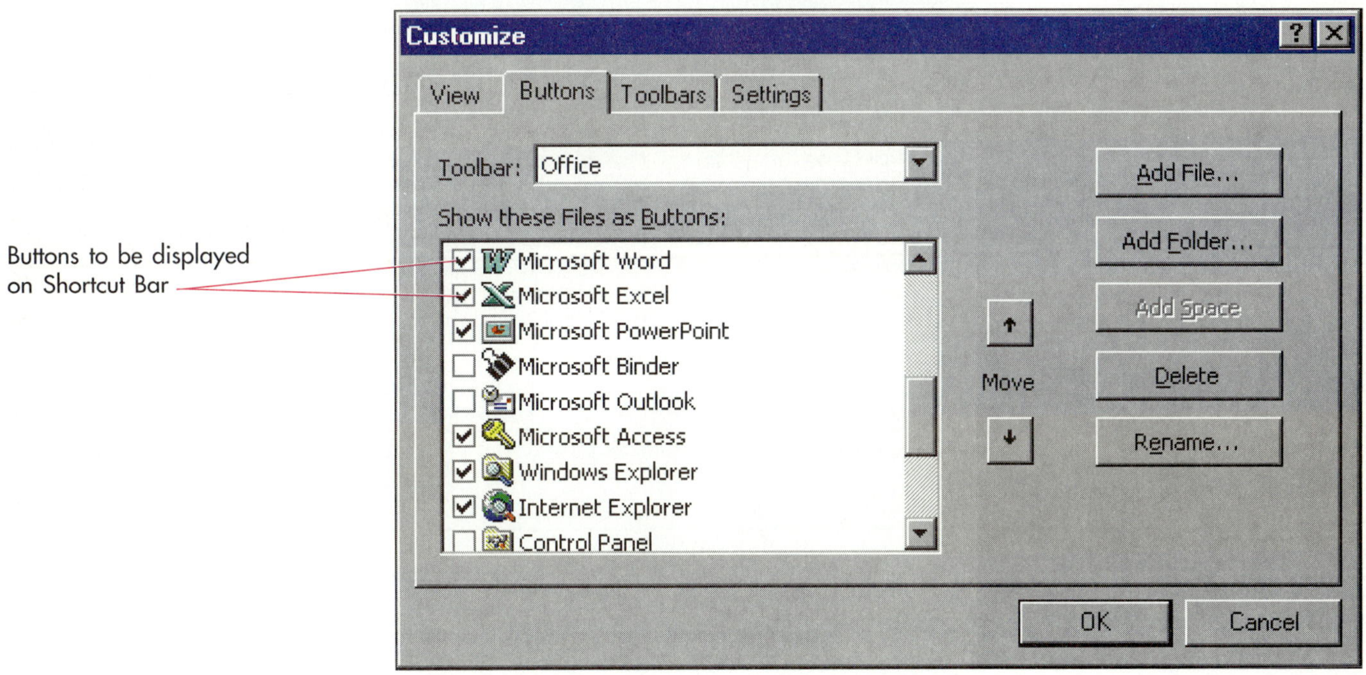


(b) Customize Dialog Box

FIGURE 3 Microsoft Office Shortcut Bar

## Docucentric Orientation

Our Shortcut Bar contains two additional buttons: to open an existing document and to start a new document. These buttons are very useful and take advantage of the "docucentric" orientation of Microsoft Office, which lets you think in terms

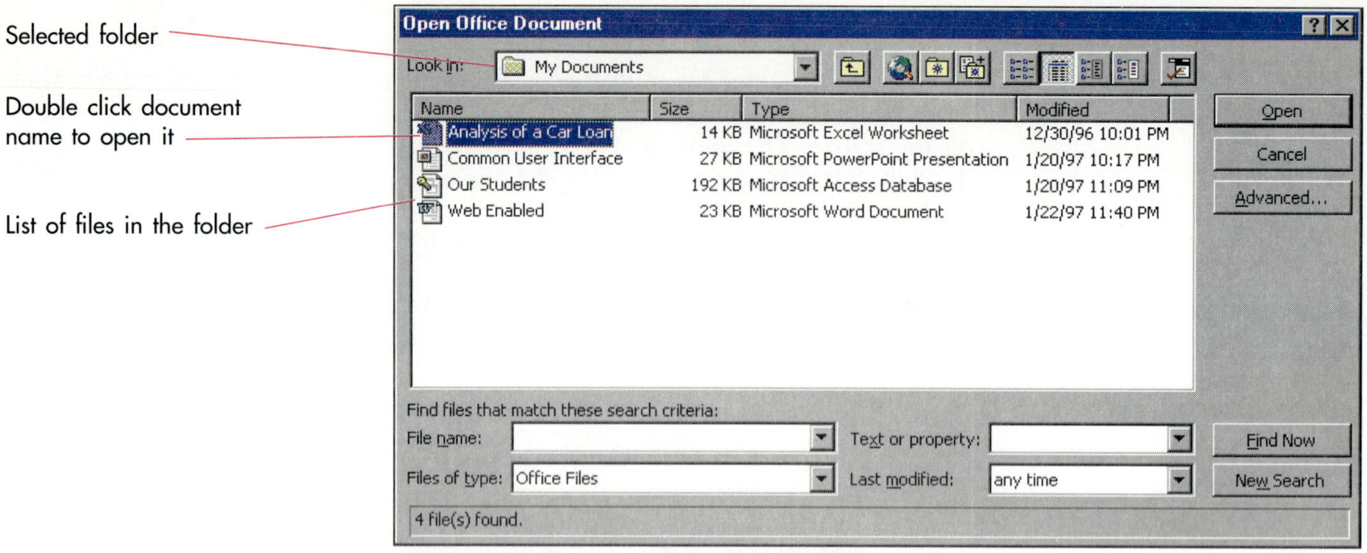


(a) Open an Existing Document

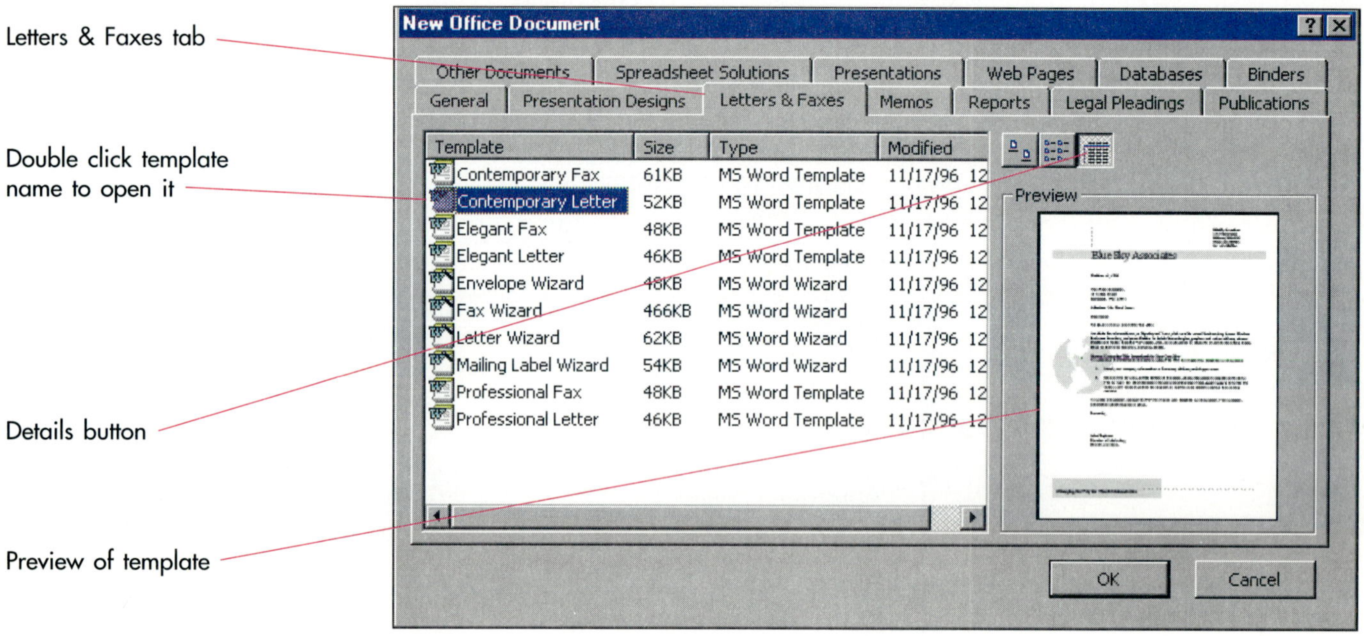


(b) Start a New Document

FIGURE 4 Document Orientation

of a document rather than the associated application. You can still open a document in traditional fashion, by starting the application (e.g., clicking its button on the Shortcut Bar), then using the File Open command to open the document. It's easier, however, to locate the document, then double click its icon, which automatically loads the associated program.

Consider, for example, the Open dialog box in Figure 4a, which is displayed by clicking the Open a Document button on the Shortcut Bar. The Open dialog box is common to the major Office applications, and it works identically in each application. The My Documents folder is selected in Figure 4a, and it contains four documents of various file types. The documents are displayed in the Details view, which shows the document name, size, file type, and date and time the document was last modified. To open any document—for example, "Analysis of a Car Loan"—just double click its name or icon. The associated application (Microsoft Excel in this example) will be started automatically; and it, in turn, will open the selected workbook.

The "docucentric" orientation also applies to new documents. Click the Start a New Document button on the Office Shortcut Bar, and you display the New dialog box in Figure 4b. Click the tab corresponding to the type of document you want to create, such as Letters & Faxes in Figure 4b. Change to the Details view, then click (select) various templates so that you can choose the one most appropriate for your purpose. Double click the desired template to start the application, which opens the template and enables you to create the document.

### CHANGE THE VIEW

The toolbar in the Open dialog box contains buttons to display the documents within the selected folder in one of several views. Click the Details button to switch to the Details view and see the date and time the file was last modified, as well as its size and type. Click the List button to display an icon representing the associated application, enabling you to see many more files than in the Details view. The Preview button lets you see a document before you open it. The Properties button displays information about the document, including the number of revisions.

## SHARED APPLICATIONS AND UTILITIES

Microsoft Office includes additional applications and shared utilities, several of which are illustrated in Figure 5. The ***Microsoft Clip Gallery*** in Figure 5a has more than 3,000 clip art images and almost 150 photographs, each in a variety of categories. It also contains a lesser number of sound files and video clips. The Clip Gallery can be accessed from every Office application, most easily through the Insert Picture command, which displays the Clip Gallery dialog box.

The ***Microsoft WordArt*** utility adds decorative text to a document, and is accessed through the Insert Picture command from Word, Excel, or PowerPoint. WordArt is intuitive and easy to use. In essence, you choose a style for the text from among the selections in the dialog box of Figure 5b, then you enter the specific text in a second dialog box (which is not shown in Figure 5). It's fun, it's easy, and you can create some truly dynamite documents that will add interest to a document.

***Office Art*** consists of a set of drawing tools that is found on the Drawing toolbar in Word, Excel, or PowerPoint. You don't have to be an artist—all it takes is a little imagination and an appreciation for what the individual tools can do. In Figure 5c, for example, we began with a single clip art image, copied it several times within the PowerPoint slide, then rotated and colored the students as shown. We also used the AutoShapes tool to add a callout for our student.

***Microsoft Bookshelf Basics*** contains three of the nine books available in the complete version of Microsoft Bookshelf (which is an additional cost item). The *American Heritage Dictionary,* the *Original Roget's Thesaurus,* and the *Columbia Dictionary of Quotations* are provided at no charge. An excerpt from the *American Heritage Dictionary* is illustrated in Figure 5d. Enter the word you are looking for in the text box on the left, then read the definition on the right. You can click the sound icon and hear the pronunciation of the word.

(a) Microsoft Clip Gallery

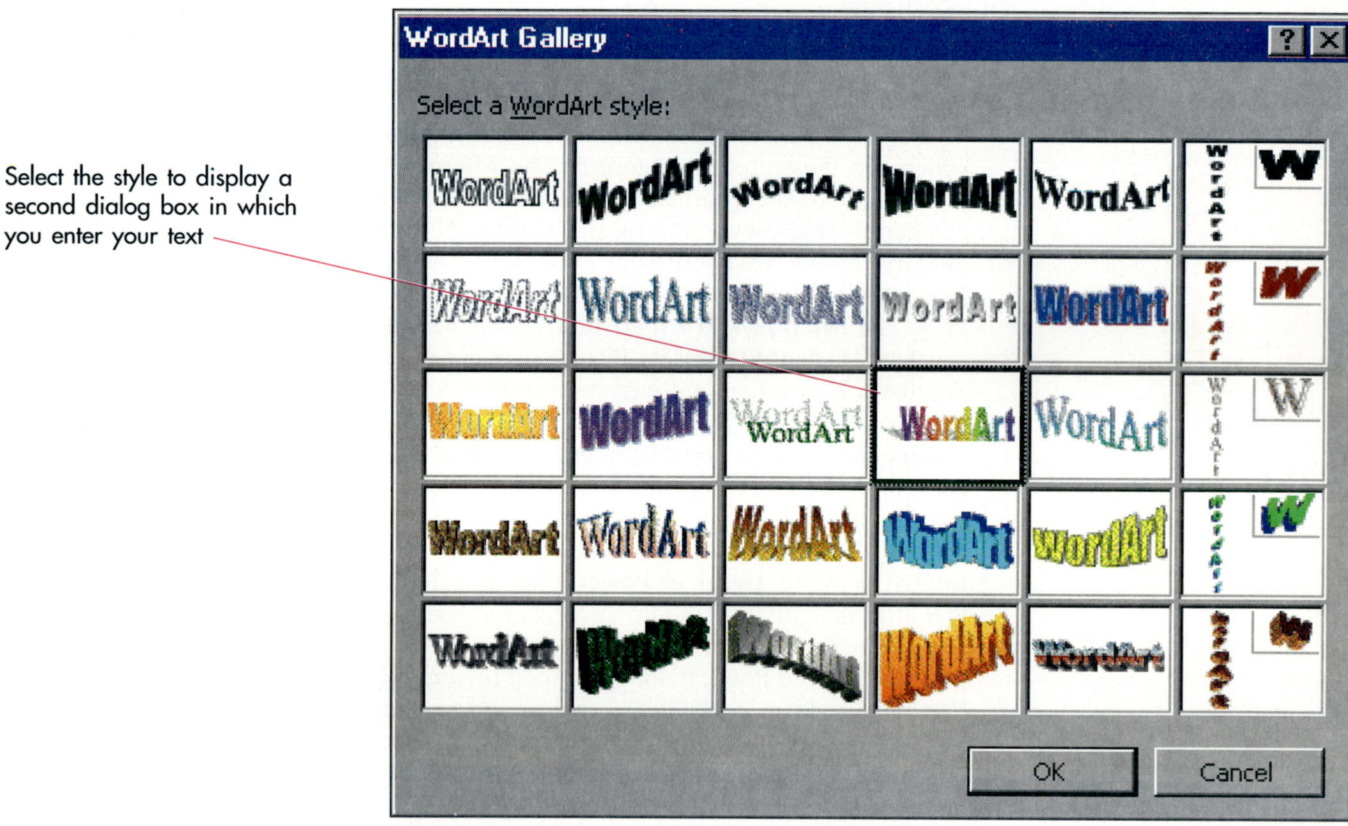


(b) WordArt

**FIGURE 5** Shared Applications

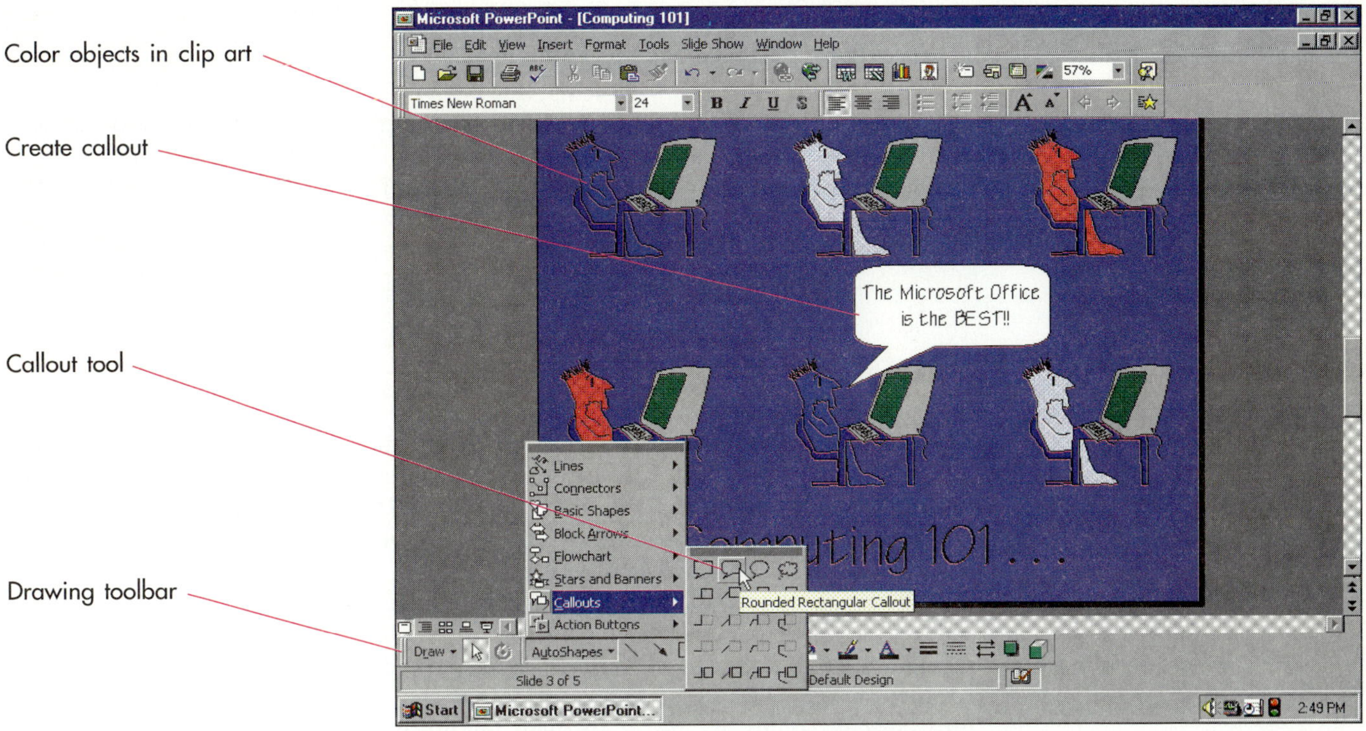


(c) Office Art

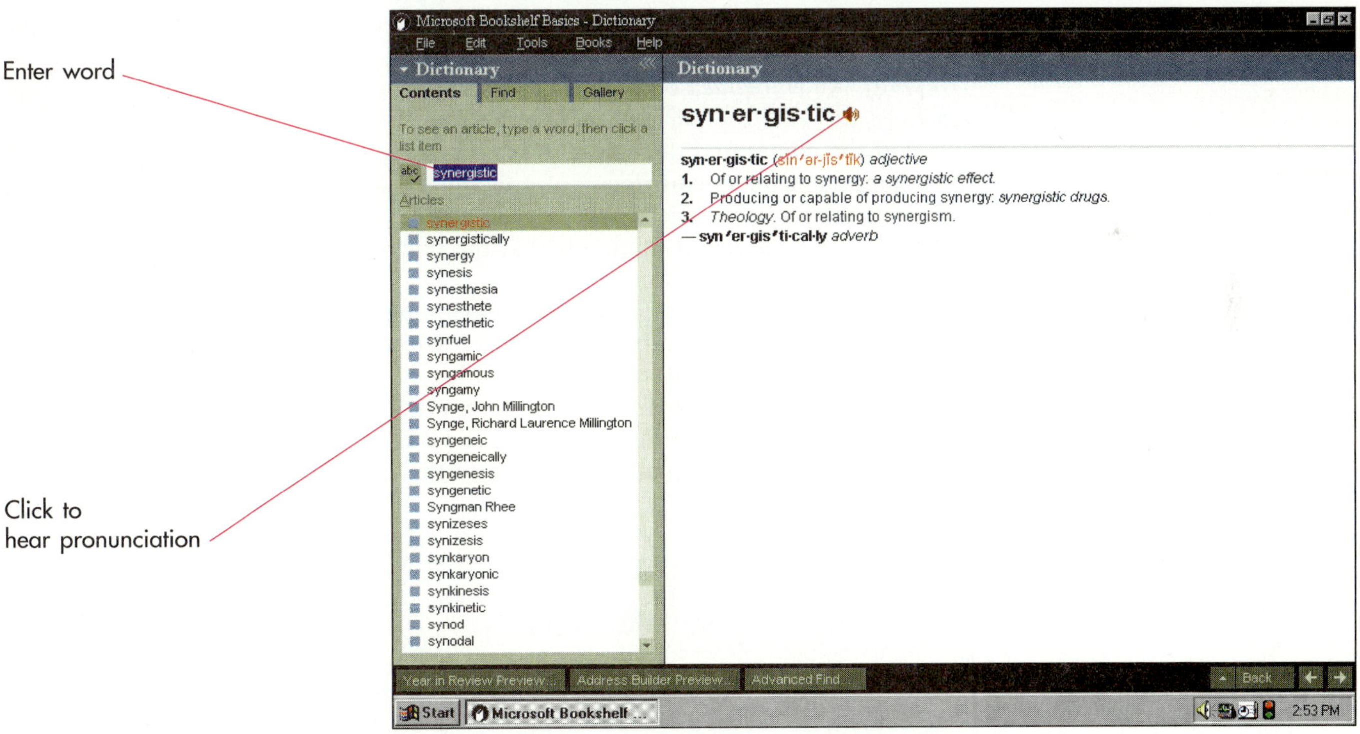


(d) Bookshelf Basics

**FIGURE 5** Shared Applications (continued)

### THE OTHER SHARED APPLICATIONS

Microsoft Office includes several additional applications whose functions can be inferred from their names. The Equation Editor, Organization Chart, Data Map, and Graph utilities are accessed through the Insert Object command. All of these applications are straightforward and easy to use as they follow the common user interface and provide online help.

## OBJECT LINKING AND EMBEDDING

The applications in Microsoft Office are thoroughly integrated with one another. They look alike and they work in consistent fashion. Equally important, they share information through a technology known as ***Object Linking and Embedding (OLE),*** which enables you to create a ***compound document*** containing data (objects) from multiple applications.

The compound document in Figure 6 was created in Word, and it contains objects (a worksheet and a chart) that were created in Excel. The letterhead uses a logo that was taken from the Clip Gallery, while the name and address of the recipient were drawn from an Access database. The various objects were inserted into the compound document through linking or embedding, which are actually two very different techniques. Both operations, however, are much more sophisticated than simply pasting an object, because with either linking or embedding, you can edit the object by using the tools of the original application.

The difference between linking and embedding depends on whether the object is stored within the compound document (***embedding***) or in its own file (***linking***). An *embedded object* is stored in the compound document, which in turn becomes the only user (client) of that object. A *linked object* is stored in its own file, and the compound document is one of many potential clients of that object. The compound document does not contain the linked object per se, but only a representation of the object as well as a pointer (link) to the file containing the object. The advantage of linking is that the document is updated automatically if the object changes.

The choice between linking and embedding depends on how the object will be used. Linking is preferable if the object is likely to change and the compound document requires the latest version. Linking should also be used when the same object is placed in many documents so that any change to the object has to be made in only one place. Embedding should be used if you need to take the object with you (to a different computer) and/or if there is only a single destination document for the object.

### OBJECT LINKING AND EMBEDDING

Object Linking and Embedding (OLE) enables you to create a compound document containing objects (data) from multiple Windows applications. OLE is one of the major benefits of working in the Windows environment, but it would be impossible to illustrate all of the techniques in a single discussion. Accordingly, we have created the icon at the left to help you identify the many examples of object linking and embedding that appear throughout the Exploring Windows series.

# Office of Residential Living

University of Miami • P.O. Box 248904 • Coral Gables, FL 33124

January 10, 1998

Mr. Jeffrey Redmond, President
Dynamic Dining Services
4329 Palmetto Lane
Miami, FL 33157

Dear Jeff,

As per our conversation, occupancy is projected to be back up from last year. I have enclosed a spreadsheet and chart that show the total enrollment for the past four school years. Please realize, however, that the 1997–1998 figures are projections, as the Spring 1998 numbers are still incomplete. The final 1997–1998 numbers should be confirmed within the next two weeks. I hope that this helps with your planning. If you need further information, please contact me at the above address.

**Dorm Occupancy**

| | 94-95 | 95-96 | 96-97 | 97-98 |
|---|---|---|---|---|
| Beatty | 330 | 285 | 270 | 250 |
| Broward | 620 | 580 | 620 | 565 |
| Graham | 450 | 397 | 352 | 420 |
| Rawlings | 435 | 470 | 295 | 372 |
| Tolbert | 550 | 554 | 524 | 635 |
| Totals | 2385 | 2286 | 2061 | 2242 |

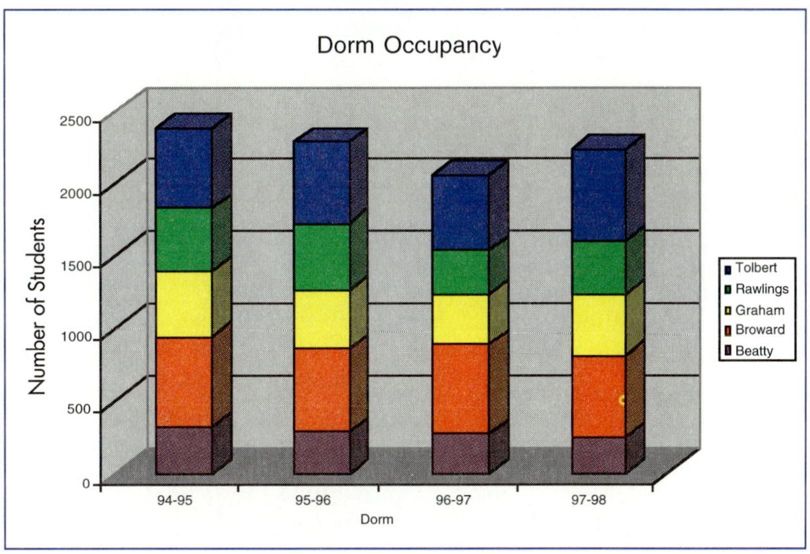


FIGURE 6 A Compound Document

## SUMMARY

The common user interface requires every Windows application to follow a consistent set of conventions and ensures that all applications work basically the same way. The development of a suite of applications from a single vendor extends this concept by imposing additional similarities on all applications within the suite.

Microsoft distributes both a Standard and a Professional edition of Office 97. Both versions include Word, Excel, PowerPoint, Internet Explorer, and Outlook. Office Professional also has Microsoft Access. The single biggest difference between Office 97 and its predecessor, Office 95, is that the Internet has become an integral part of the Office suite.

Help for all Office applications is available in a variety of formats. The Help Contents window provides access to a Contents and Index tab in which you look up specific topics. The Office Assistant enables you to ask a question in English. Still additional help is available from the Microsoft Web site, provided you have access to the Internet.

Microsoft Office includes several additional applications and shared utilities that can be used to add interest to a document. The Clip Gallery has more than 3,000 clip art images, 150 photographs, and a lesser number of sound files and video clips. WordArt enables you to create decorative text, while Office Art consists of a powerful set of drawing tools.

The Microsoft Office Shortcut Bar provides immediate access to each application in Microsoft Office. The Shortcut Bar is fully customizable with respect to the buttons it displays, its appearance, and its position on the desktop. The Open a Document and Start a New Document buttons enable you to think in terms of a document rather than the associated application.

Object Linking and Embedding (OLE) enables you to create a compound document containing data (objects) from multiple applications. Linking and embedding are different operations. The difference between the two depends on whether the object is stored within the compound document (embedding) or in its own file (linking).

## KEY WORDS AND CONCEPTS

- Common Windows interface
- Compound document
- Contents tab
- Docucentric orientation
- Embedding
- Formatting toolbar
- Index tab
- Internet Explorer
- Linking
- Microsoft Access
- Microsoft Bookshelf Basics
- Microsoft Clip Gallery
- Microsoft Excel
- Microsoft Office Professional
- Microsoft Office Shortcut Bar
- Microsoft Outlook
- Microsoft PowerPoint
- Microsoft Standard Office
- Microsoft Word
- Microsoft WordArt
- Object Linking and Embedding (OLE)
- Office Art
- Office Assistant
- Online help
- Shared applications
- Standard toolbar

7

# INTRODUCTION TO POWERPOINT: PRESENTATIONS MADE EASY

## OBJECTIVES

**After reading this chapter you will be able to:**

1. Describe the common user interface; give several examples of how PowerPoint follows the same conventions as other Microsoft applications.
2. Start PowerPoint; open, modify, and view an existing presentation.
3. Describe the various ways to print a presentation.
4. List the views in PowerPoint; describe the unique features of each view.
5. Use the Outline view to add slides to, and/or delete slides from, an existing presentation and/or to modify the text on an existing slide.
6. Add clip art to an existing slide.
7. Use the Rehearse Timings feature to time a presentation.
8. Describe the Meeting Minder, Slide Navigator, and Pen; explain how these tools are used to enhance a presentation.

## OVERVIEW

This chapter introduces you to PowerPoint, one of the four major applications in the Professional version of Microsoft Office (Microsoft Word, Microsoft Excel, and Microsoft Access are the other three). In essence, PowerPoint helps you to create a professional presentation without relying on others. It enables you to deliver a presentation on the computer (or via 35-mm slides or overhead transparencies) and to print that presentation in a variety of formats.

PowerPoint is easy to learn because it is a Windows application and follows all of the conventions associated with the common user interface. Thus, if you already use one Windows application, it is that much easier to learn PowerPoint because you can apply much of what you know. It's even easier if you use Microsoft Word, Excel, or Access, since there are over 100 commands that are common to the Microsoft Office.

The chapter begins by showing you an actual PowerPoint presentation so that you can better appreciate what you will be able to do. We describe the five PowerPoint views and the unique capabilities of each view. We show you how to add slides to, and delete slides from, an existing presentation, how to modify the text of a presentation; and how to add clip art. (We will show you how to create your own presentation in Chapter 2.) We also provide three hands-on exercises, in which you apply the conceptual material at the computer. The exercises are essential to the learn-by-doing philosophy we follow throughout the text, and it is through the exercises that you will truly master the material.

One final point, before we begin, is that while PowerPoint can help you create attractive presentations, the content and delivery are still up to you. It is important that you express yourself clearly and that you deliver the presentation effectively. The chapter ends with several suggestions to help you in this regard.

## A POWERPOINT PRESENTATION

A PowerPoint presentation consists of a series of slides such as those shown in Figure 1.1. Each slide contains different elements, including text, clip art, photographs and/or a chart. Nevertheless, the presentation has a consistent look from slide to slide with respect to its overall design and color scheme.

You might think that creating a presentation such as Figure 1.1 is difficult, but it isn't. It is remarkably easy, and that is the beauty of PowerPoint. In essence, PowerPoint allows you to concentrate on the *content* of a presentation without worrying about its *appearance.* You supply the text and supporting elements and leave the formatting to PowerPoint.

In addition to helping you create the presentation, PowerPoint provides a variety of ways to deliver it. You can show the presentation on a computer using animated transition effects as you move from one slide to the next. You can include sound in the presentation, provided your system has a sound card and speakers. You can also automate the presentation and distribute it on a disk for display at a convention booth or kiosk. If you cannot show the presentation on a computer, you can convert it to 35-mm slides or overhead transparencies.

PowerPoint gives you the ability to print the presentation in various ways to distribute to your audience. You can print one slide per page, or you can print miniature versions of each slide and can choose between two, three, or six slides per page. You can prepare speaker notes for yourself, consisting of a picture of each slide together with notes for its delivery. You can also print the entire presentation in outline form. Giving the audience a copy of the presentation (in any format) enables them to follow it more closely, and to take it home when the session is over.

### POLISH YOUR DELIVERY

The speaker is still the most important part of any presentation, and a poor delivery will kill even the best presentation. Look at the audience as you speak to open communication and gain credibility. Don't read from a prepared script. Speak clearly and try to vary your delivery. Pause to emphasize key points and be sure the person in the last row can hear you.

(a) Title Slide

(b) Bullet Slide

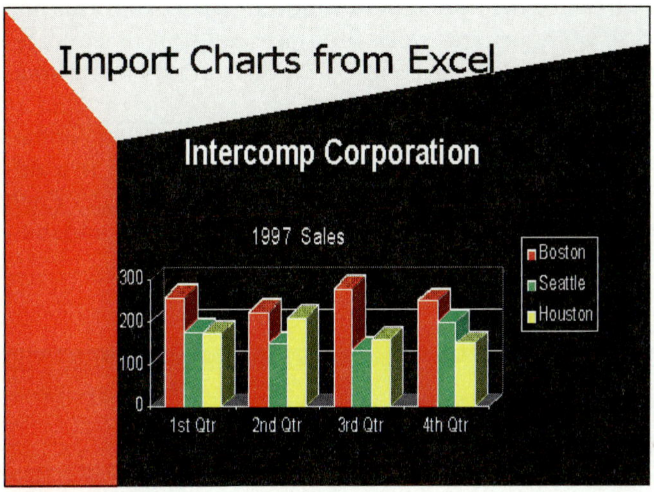


(c) Charts

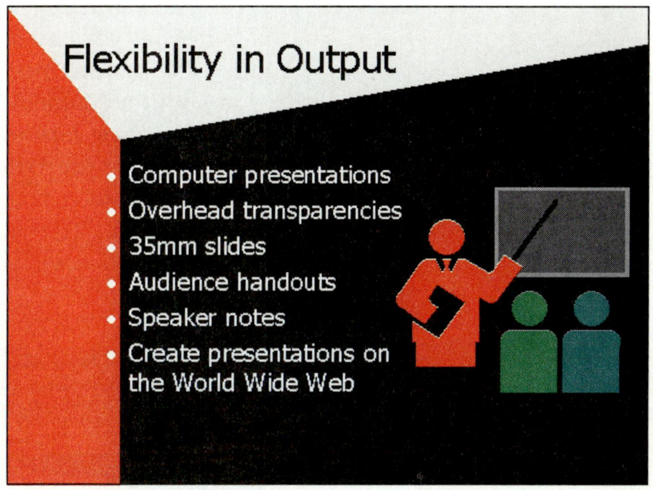


(d) Clip Art

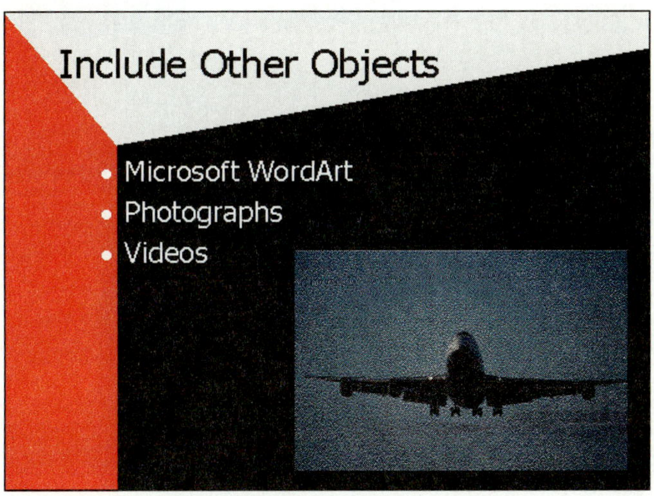


(e) Photographs

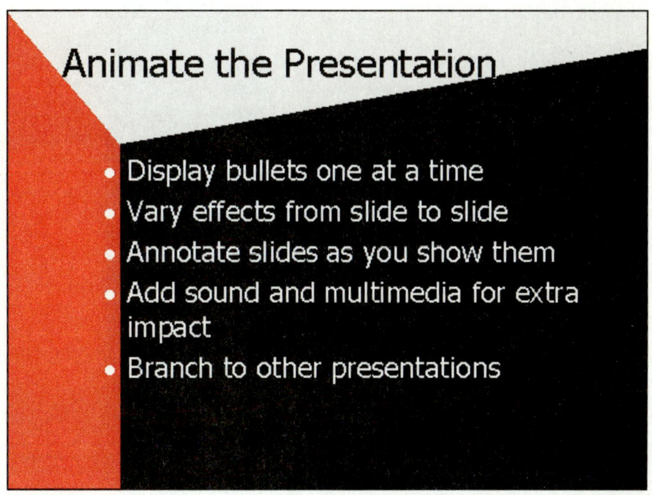


(f) Animation

**FIGURE 1.1** A PowerPoint Presentation

The desktop in Figure 1.2 should look somewhat familiar, even if you have never used PowerPoint, because PowerPoint shares the common user interface that is present in every Windows application. You should recognize, therefore, the two open windows in Figure 1.2—the application window for PowerPoint and the document window for the current presentation.

Each window has its own Minimize, Maximize (or Restore), and Close buttons. Both windows have been maximized, and thus the title bars have been merged into a single title bar that appears at the top of the application window. The title bar indicates the application (Microsoft PowerPoint) as well as the name of the presentation (Introduction to PowerPoint) on which you are working.

A ***menu bar*** appears immediately below the title bar. The Standard and Formatting toolbars appear below the menu bar. S***croll bars*** appears at the right and bottom of the document window. The Windows 95 taskbar appears at the bottom of the screen and shows the open applications—Microsoft PowerPoint, Word, and Excel. The taskbar enables you to switch from one application to the next by clicking the appropriate button.

The ***status bar*** at the bottom of the application window displays information about what you are seeing and doing as you work on a presentation. It indicates the slide you are working on (e.g., Slide 1 in Figure 1.2), or it provides information about a command you have selected.

The ***view buttons*** are located to the left of the horizontal scroll bar, immediately above the Drawing toolbar, and are used to switch between the five different views of a presentation. (The Slide view is displayed in Figure 1.2.) Each view offers a different way of looking at a presentation and has unique capabilities. PowerPoint views are discussed later in the chapter.

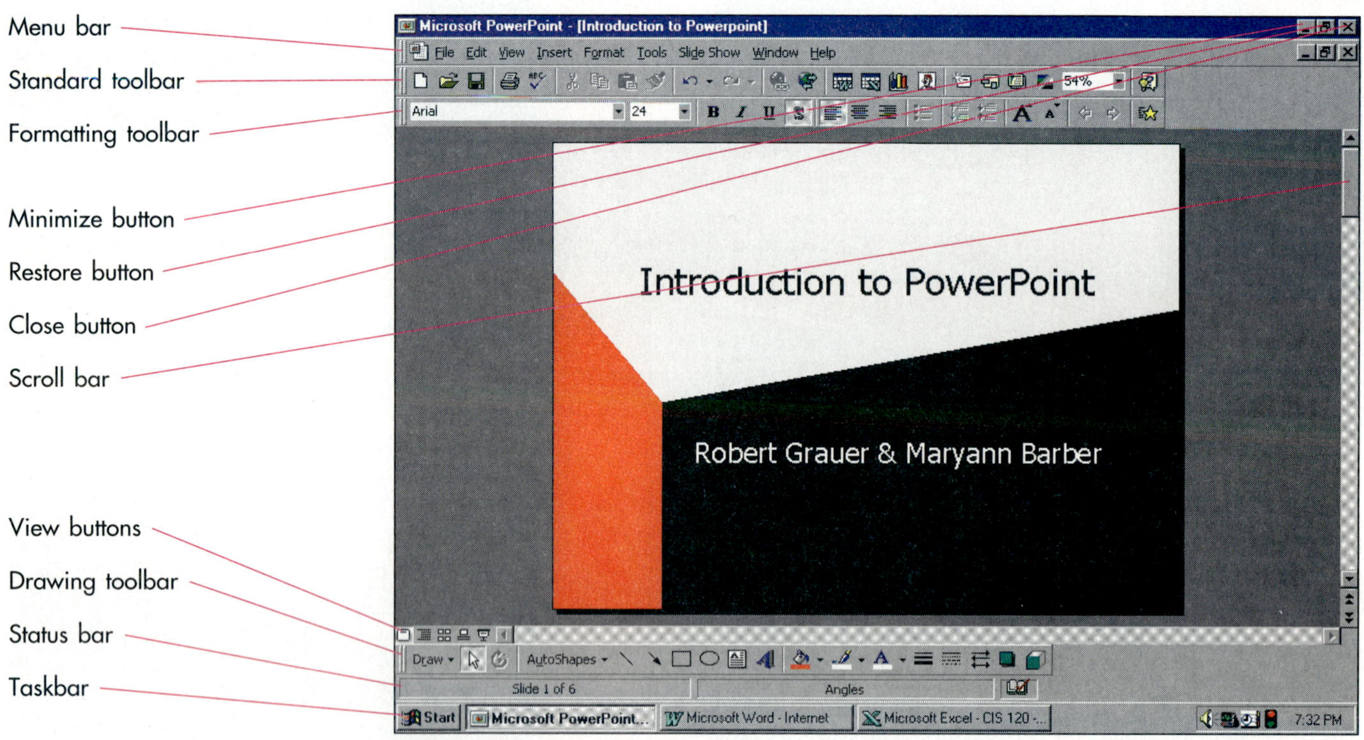


**FIGURE 1.2** The PowerPoint Window

## Toolbars

The Standard and Formatting toolbars are similar to those in Word and Excel, and you may recognize several buttons from those applications. The ***Standard toolbar*** appears immediately below the menu bar and contains buttons for the most basic commands in PowerPoint—for example, opening, saving, and printing a presentation. The ***Formatting toolbar,*** under the Standard toolbar, provides access to formatting operations such as boldface, italics, and underlining. The ***Drawing toolbar*** appears at the bottom of the window and contains various tools with which to modify the slide.

As with all other Microsoft applications, you can point to any button on any toolbar and PowerPoint will display the name of the button, which indicates its function. You can also gain an overall appreciation for the toolbars by considering the buttons in groups, as shown in Figure 1.3.

Remember, too, that while PowerPoint is designed for a mouse, it provides keyboard equivalents for almost every command. You may at first wonder why there are so many different ways to do the same thing, but you will come to recognize the many options as part of PowerPoint's charm. The most appropriate technique depends on personal preference, as well as the specific situation.

If, for example, your hands are already on the keyboard, it is faster to use the keyboard equivalent. Other times, your hand will be on the mouse and that will be the fastest way. It is not necessary to memorize anything, nor should you even try; just be flexible and willing to experiment. The more you do, the easier it will be!

## The File Menu

The ***File menu*** is a critically important menu in virtually every Windows application. It contains the ***Save command*** to save a presentation to disk and the ***Open command*** to retrieve (open) the presentation at a later time. The File menu also contains the ***Print command*** to print a presentation, the ***Close command*** to close the current presentation but continue working in PowerPoint, and the ***Exit command*** to quit PowerPoint altogether.

The Save command copies the presentation that is currently being edited (i.e., the presentation in memory) to disk. The Save dialog box appears the first time a presentation is saved so that you can specify the file name and other required information. All subsequent executions of the Save command save the presentation under the assigned name, replacing the previously saved version with the new version.

The file name (e.g., *My First Presentation* in Figure 1.4a) can be up to 255 characters in length and may contain both spaces and commas. The Save dialog box also requires the drive (and folder) in which the file is to be saved, as well as the file type, which determines the application the file is associated with. (Longtime DOS users will remember the three-character extension at the end of a file name, such as PPT to indicate a PowerPoint presentation. The extension is generally hidden in Windows 95, according to options set through the View menu in My Computer or the Windows Explorer.

The Open command brings a copy of a previously saved presentation into memory, enabling you to show, edit, and/or print the presentation. The Open command displays the Open dialog box in which you specify the file to retrieve. You indicate the drive (and the folder) that contains the file, as well as the type of file you want to retrieve. PowerPoint will then list all files of that type on the designated drive (and folder), enabling you to open the file you want.

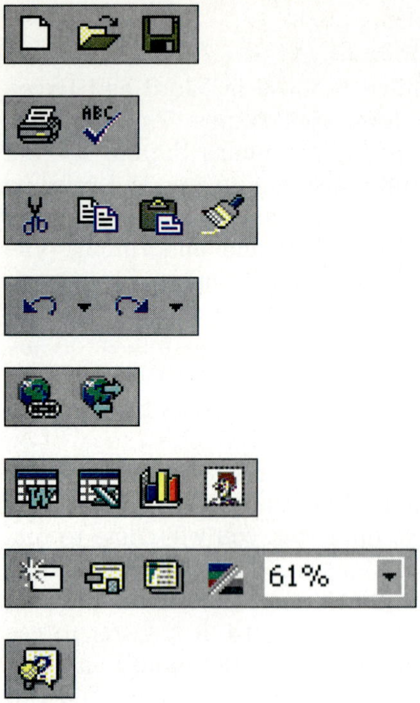


Starts a new document, opens an existing document, or saves the document to disk

Prints the document or checks the spelling in the document

Cuts or copies the selection to the clipboard; pastes the clipboard contents; copies the format of the selected text

Undoes or redoes a previously executed command

Inserts a hyperlink or displays the Web toolbar

Inserts a Microsoft Word table, a Microsoft Excel worksheet, a graph, or a clip art image

Inserts a new slide, applies a new slide layout, applies a design template, changes the display to black and white, or changes the zoom percentage

Starts the Office Assistant

(a) Standard Toolbar

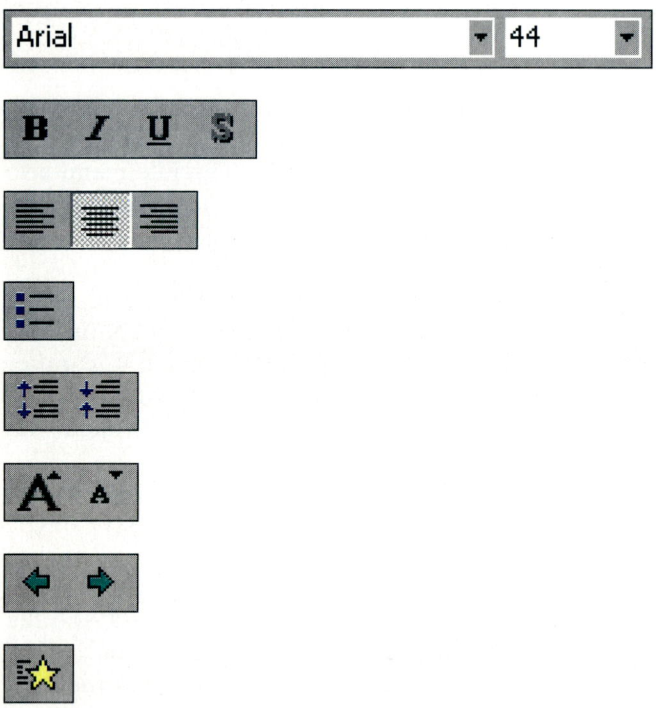


Changes the font or point size

Toggles boldface, italics, underline, or shadow on and off

Aligns left, center, or right

Toggles bullets on and off

Increases or decreases the paragraph spacing

Increases or decreases the font size

Promotes or demotes text

Applies animation effects

(b) Formatting Toolbar

**FIGURE 1.3** Toolbars

The Save and Open commands work in conjunction with one another. The Save dialog box in Figure 1.4a, for example, saves the file *My First Presentation* onto the disk in the Exploring PowerPoint folder. The Open dialog box in Figure 1.4b brings that file back into memory so that you can work with the file, after which you can save the revised file for use at a later time.

The ***Save As*** command saves a presentation under a different name, and is useful when you want to retain a copy of the original presentation prior to making changes. The original presentation is kept on disk under its original name. A copy of the presentation is saved under a new name and remains in memory. All subsequent editing is done on the new presentation.

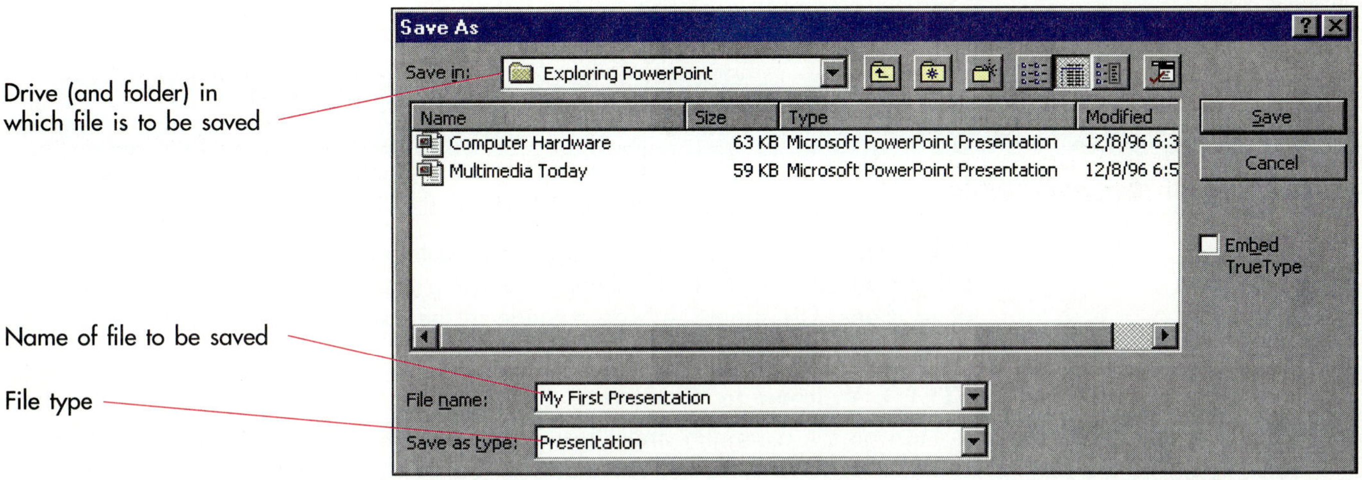


(a) File Save Dialog Box

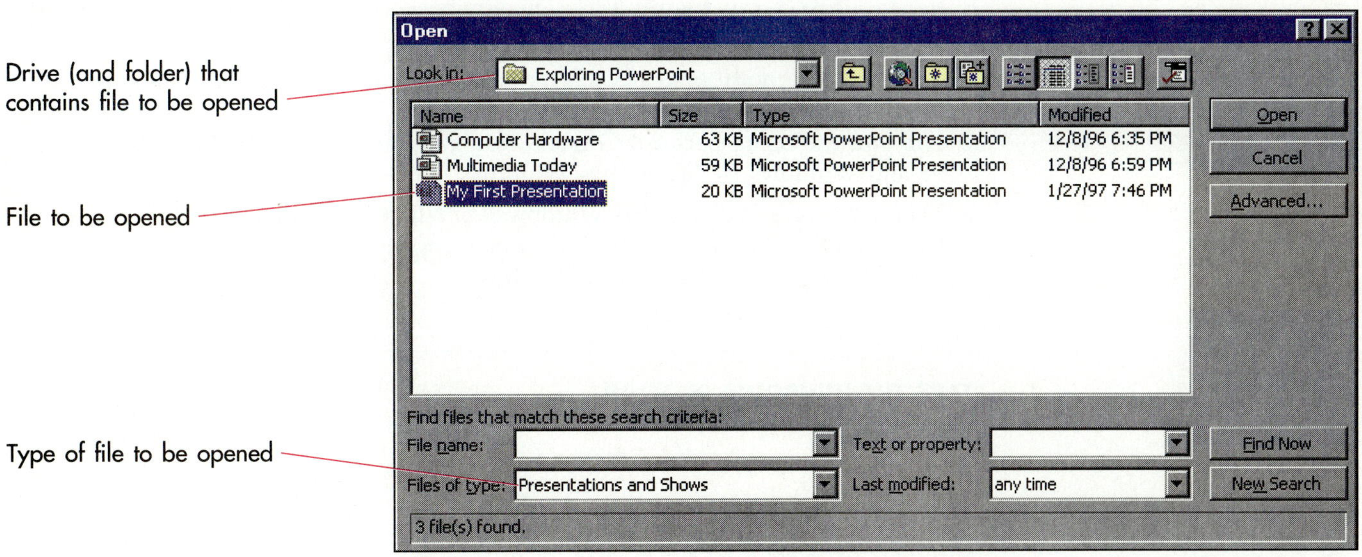


(b) File Open Dialog Box

**FIGURE 1.4** The Save and Open Commands

## LEARNING BY DOING

We believe strongly in learning by doing, and thus there comes a point where you must sit down at the computer if the discussion is to have real meaning. The exercise introduces you to the practice files or data disk that is available from your instructor and/or our Web site. The data disk contains the presentations referenced in the hands-on exercises throughout the text and enables you to build on the presentations we supply.

The following exercise has you open the presentation that was shown earlier in Figure 1.1. The exercise has you change the title slide to include your name, then directs you to view the presentation on the computer and to print the corresponding audience handouts. It's fun, it's easy, and it will give you a better appreciation for PowerPoint.

## HANDS-ON EXERCISE 1

### *Introduction to PowerPoint*

**Objective:** To start PowerPoint, open an existing presentation, and modify the text on an existing slide. To show an existing presentation and print handouts of its slides. Use Figure 1.5 as a guide in the exercise.

**STEP 1: Welcome to Windows**

- Turn on the computer and all of its peripherals. The floppy drive should be empty prior to starting your machine. This ensures that the system starts by reading from the hard disk, which contains the Windows files, as opposed to a floppy disk, which does not.
- Your system will take a minute or so to get started, after which you should see the desktop in Figure 1.5a. Do not be concerned if the appearance of your desktop is different from ours.
- You may see additional objects on the desktop in Windows 95 and/or the active desktop content in Windows 97. It doesn't matter which operating system you are using because Office 97 runs equally well under both Windows 95 and Windows 97 (as well as Windows NT).
- You may see a Welcome to Windows 95/Windows 97 dialog box with command buttons to take a tour of the operating system. If so, click the appropriate button(s) or close the dialog box.

**TAKE THE WINDOWS 95 TOUR**

Windows 95 may greet you with a Welcome window that contains a command button to take you on a 10-minute tour. Click the command button and enjoy the show. If you do not see the Welcome window when you start Windows 95, click the Start button, click Run, type WELCOME in the Open text box, and press enter. Windows 97 was not available when we went to press, but we expect it to have a similar option.

Click the Start button

(a) Welcome to Windows 95 (step 1)

**FIGURE 1.5** Hands-on Exercise 1

**STEP 2: Obtain the Practice Files**

- We have created a series of practice files for you to use throughout the text. Your instructor will make these files available to you in a variety of ways:
  - You can download the files from our Web site if you have access to the Internet and World Wide Web (see boxed tip).
  - The files may be on a network drive, in which case you use the Windows Explorer to copy the files from the network to a floppy disk.
  - There may be an actual "data disk" that you are to check out from the lab in order to use the Copy Disk command to duplicate the disk
- Check with your instructor for additional information.

### DOWNLOAD THE PRACTICE FILES

You can download the practice files for any book in the *Exploring Windows* series from Bob Grauer's home page (www.bus.miami.edu/~rgrauer). Use any Web browser to get to Bob's page, then click the link to the *Exploring Windows* series where you choose the appropriate book and download the file. Be sure to read the associated "read me" file, which provides additional information about downloading the file.

**STEP 3: Start PowerPoint**

- Click the **Start button** to display the Start menu. Slide the mouse pointer over the various menu options and notice that each time you point to a submenu, its items are displayed; i.e., you can point rather than click a submenu.
- Point to (or click) the **Programs menu,** then click **Microsoft PowerPoint** to start the program and display the screen in Figure 1.2b. Close the Office Assistant if it appears.
- Click the **option button** to **Open an Existing Presentation,** the click **OK.** (If you do not see the PowerPoint dialog box, pull down the **File menu** and click **Open,** or click the **Open button** on the Standard toolbar.)

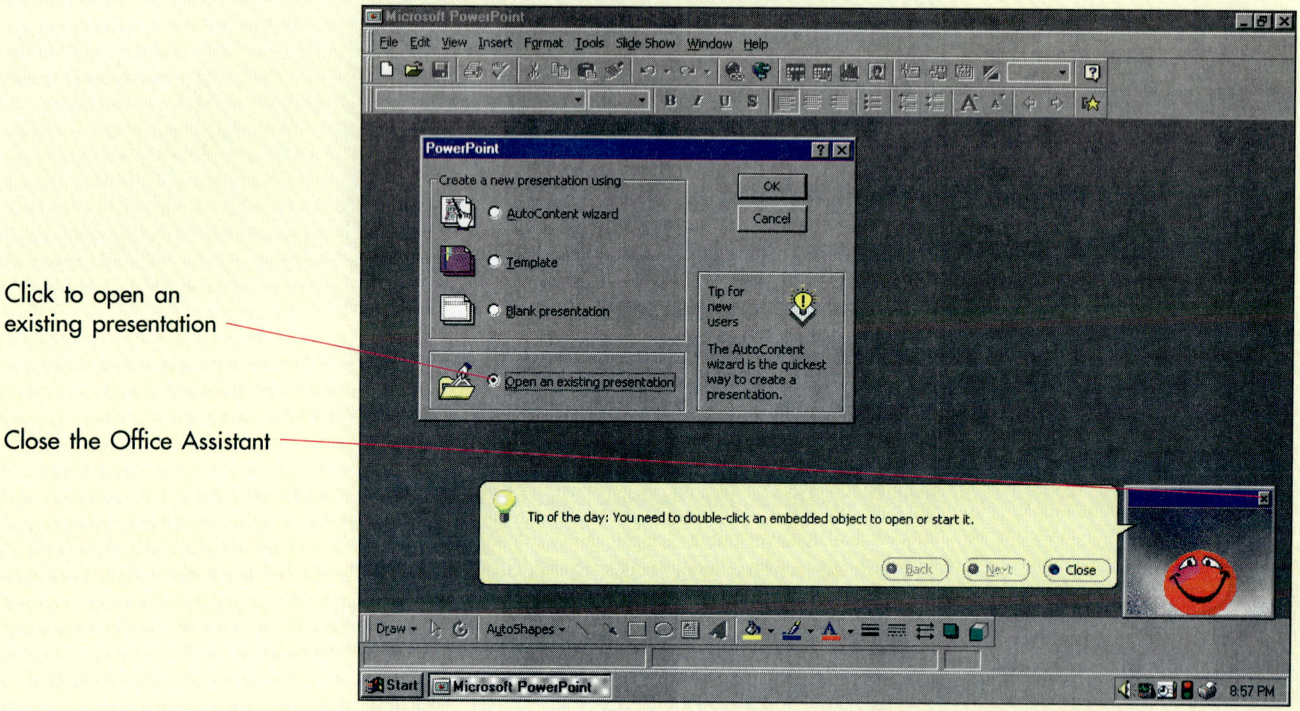


(b) Start PowerPoint (step 3)

**FIGURE 1.5** Hands-on Exercise 1 (continued)

### CHOOSE YOUR OWN ASSISTANT

You can choose your own personal assistant from one of several available images. Click the Office Assistant button on the Standard toolbar to display the Assistant, click the options button to display the Office Assistant dialog box, click the Gallery tab, then click the Next button repeatedly to cycle through the available images. Click OK to select the image and close the dialog box.

**STEP 4: Open a Presentation**

- You should see an Open dialog box similar to the one in Figure 1.5c. Click the **Details button** to change to the Details view. If necessary, click and drag the vertical border between columns to increase (or decrease) the size of a column.
- Click the **drop-down arrow** on the Look In list box. Click the appropriate drive, drive C or drive A, depending on the location of your data. Double click the **Exploring PowerPoint folder** to make it the active folder (the folder from which you will retrieve and into which you will save the presentation).
- Click **Introduction to PowerPoint** to select the presentation. Click the **Open button** to open the presentation and begin the exercise.

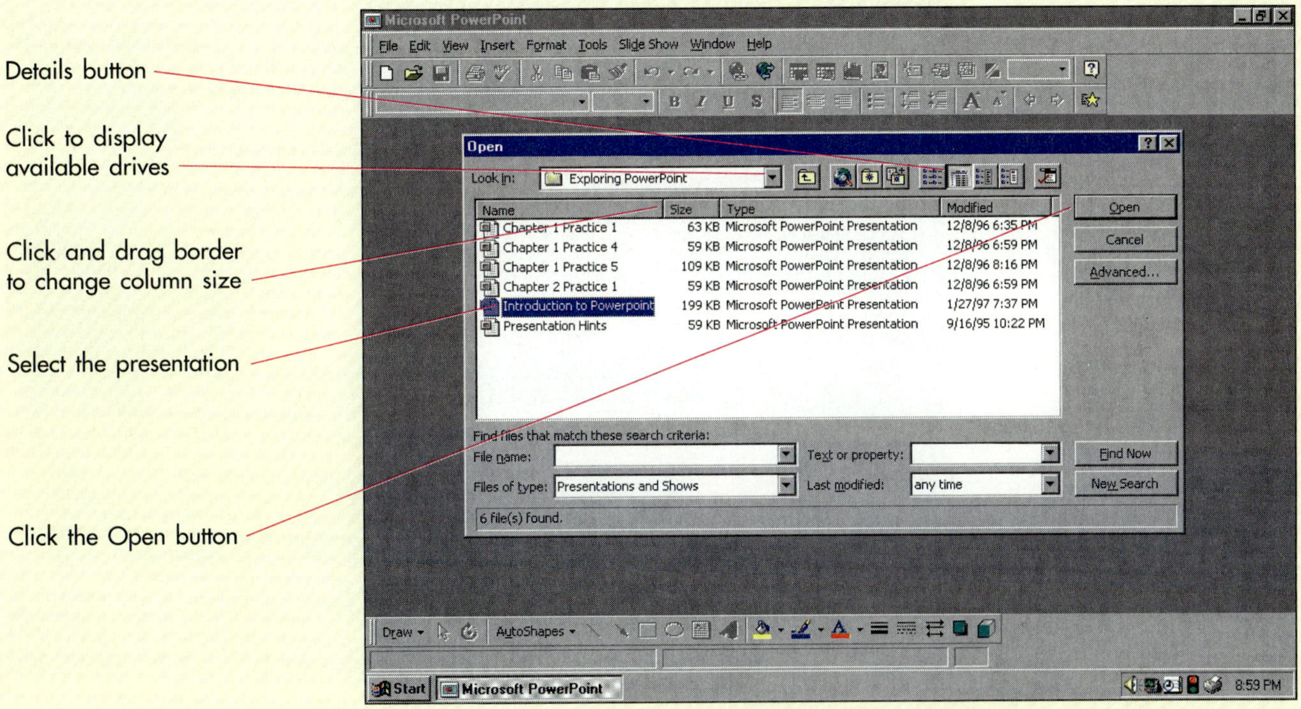


(c) Open an Existing Presentation (step 4)

**FIGURE 1.5** Hands-on Exercise 1 (continued)

### A VERY USEFUL TOOLBAR

The Open and Save dialog boxes display similar toolbars with several common buttons. Click the Details button to switch to the Details view and see the date and time the file was last modified, as well as its size. Click the List button to display an icon for each file, enabling you to see many more files at the same time than in the Details view. The Properties button displays information about the presentation, including the author's name and number of revisions.

**STEP 5: The Save As Command**

- If necessary, click the **Maximize button** in the application window so that PowerPoint takes the entire desktop. Click the **Maximize button** in the document window (if necessary) so that the document window is as large as possible.
- Pull down the **File menu.** Click **Save As** to display the dialog box shown in Figure 1.5d. Enter **Finished Introduction** as the name of the new presentation. (A file name may contain up to 255 characters; blanks are permitted.)
- Click the **Save button.** Press the **Esc key** or click the **Close button** if you see a Properties dialog box.

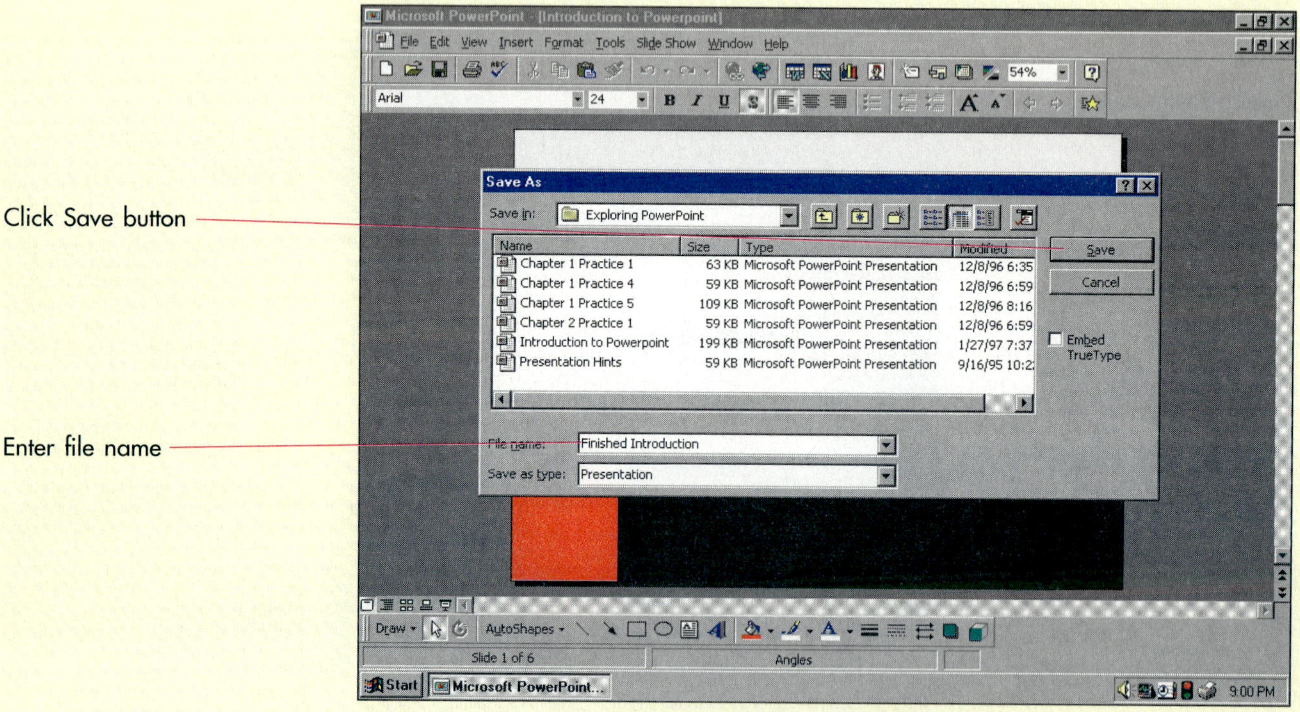


(d) The Save As Command (step 5)

**FIGURE 1.5** Hands-on Exercise 1 (continued)

### DIFFERENT FILE TYPES

The file format for PowerPoint 97 is incompatible with the format for PowerPoint 95. The newer release (PowerPoint 97) can open a presentation created in its predecessor (PowerPoint 95), but the reverse is not possible; that is, you cannot open a presentation created in PowerPoint 97 in PowerPoint 95. You can, however, use the Save As command in PowerPoint 97 to specify the PowerPoint 95 file type, enabling you to create a presentation in the new release and read it in the old (although you will lose any formatting unique to PowerPoint 97).

- There are now two identical copies of the file on disk: "Introduction to PowerPoint," which is the original presentation that we supplied, and "Finished Introduction," which you just created. The title bar shows the latter name, as it is the presentation currently in memory.

**STEP 6: Modify a Slide**

- Press and hold the left mouse button as you drag the mouse over the presenters' names (Robert Grauer and Maryann Barber). Release the mouse.
- The names should be highlighted (selected) as shown in Figure 1.5e. The selected text is the text that will be affected by the next command.
- Type your name, which automatically replaces the selected text. Click outside the placeholder to deselect it.

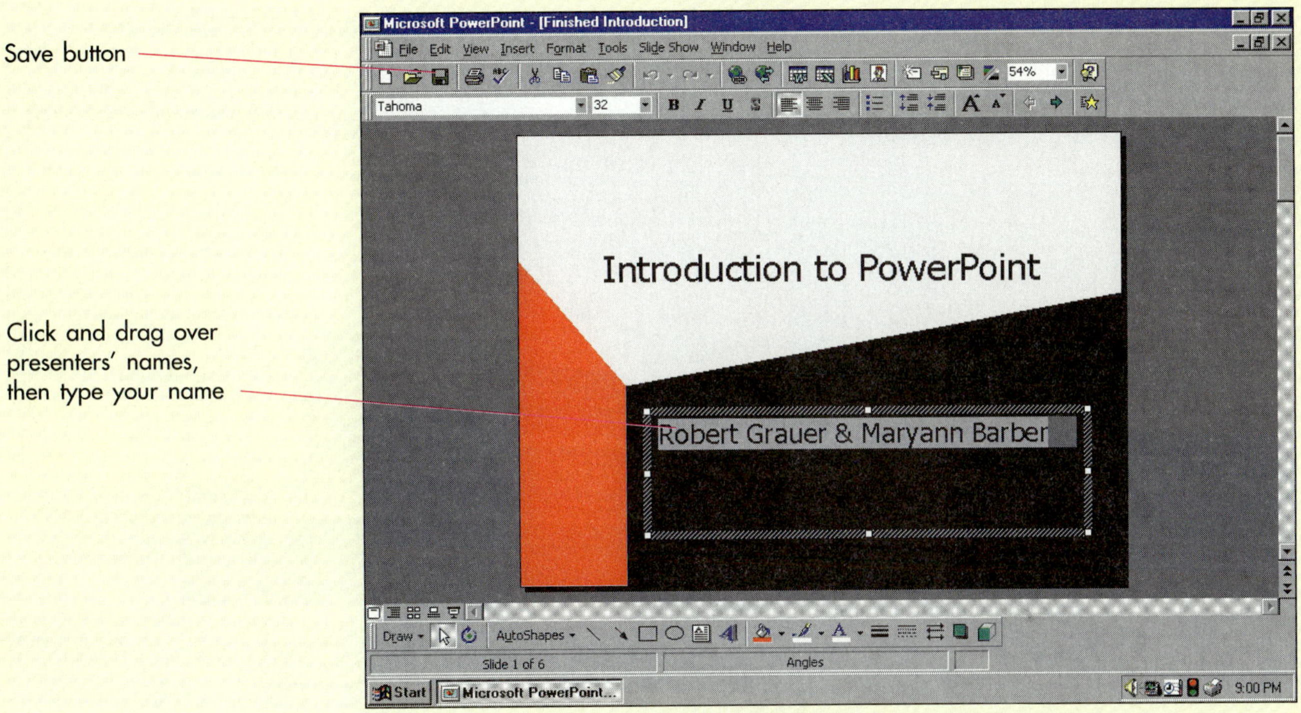


(e) Modify a Slide (step 6)

**FIGURE 1.5** Hands-on Exercise 1 (continued)

### THE AUTOMATIC SPELL CHECK

A red wavy line under a word indicates that the word is misspelled, or in the case of a proper name, that the word is spelled correctly but is not in the dictionary. In either event, point to the underlined word and click the right mouse button to display a shortcut menu. Select the appropriate spelling from the list of suggestions, ignore it, or add the word to the supplementary dictionary. To enable (disable) the automatic spell check, pull down the Tools menu, click the Options command, click the Spelling tab, then check (clear) the option to check spelling as you type.

**STEP 7: The Office Assistant**

- Click the **Office Assistant button** on the Standard toolbar to display the Office Assistant. (You may see a different character than the one we have selected.)
- Enter your question—for example, **How do I show a presentation?**—as shown in Figure 1.5f, then click the **Search button** to look for the answer.
- The size of the balloon expands as the Assistant suggests several topics that may be appropriate to answer your question.
- Select the topic, **Start a slide show**, which in turn displays a help screen with detailed information. Read the help screen, then close the Help Window.
- Close the Office Assistant.

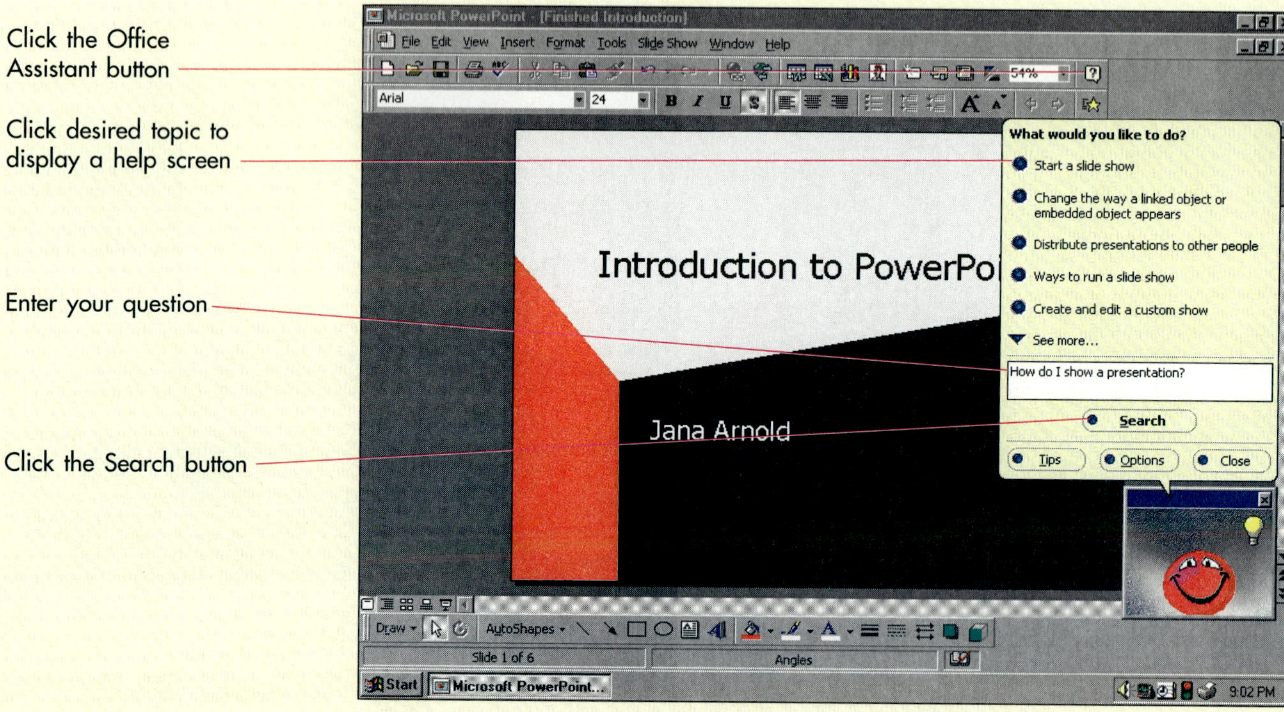


(f) The Office Assistant (step 7)

**FIGURE 1.5** Hands-on Exercise 1 (continued)

### TIP OF THE DAY

You can set the Office Assistant to greet you with a "Tip of the Day" whenever you start PowerPoint. If the Office Assistant is not visible, click the Office Assistant button on the Standard toolbar to start the Assistant, then click the Options button to display the Office Assistant dialog box. Click the Options tab, check the Show the Tip of the Day at startup box, then click OK. The next time you start PowerPoint, you will be greeted by the Assistant who will offer you a tip of the day.

**STEP 8: Show the Presentation**

- Pull down the **View menu** and click **Slide Show.**
- The presentation will begin with the first slide as shown in Figure 1.5g. You should see your name on the slide because of the modification you made in the previous step.
- Click the mouse to move to the second slide, which comes into the presentation from the left side of your monitor. (This is one of several transition effects available to add interest to a presentation.) Click the mouse again to move to the next (third) slide, which also comes in from the top of the screen.
- Continue to view the show until you come to the end of the presentation:
  - You can press the **Esc key** at any time to cancel the show and return to the PowerPoint window.
  - The last slide (Animate the Presentation) utilizes a build effect, which requires you to continue to click the mouse as you display each bullet.
- Click the left mouse button a final time to return to the regular PowerPoint window.

Your name should be displayed on the slide

(g) Print the Presentation (step 8)

**FIGURE 1.5** Hands-on Exercise 1 (continued)

**STEP 9: Print the Presentation**

- Pull down the **File menu.** Click **Print** to display the Print dialog box in Figure 1.5h.
  - Click the **down arrow** in the **Print What** drop-down list box.

- Scroll to, then click **Handouts (6 slides per page)** as shown in Figure 1.5h.
- Check the box to **Frame Slides.**
- Check that the **All option button** is selected under Print range.

➤ Click the **OK command button** to print the handouts for the presentation.

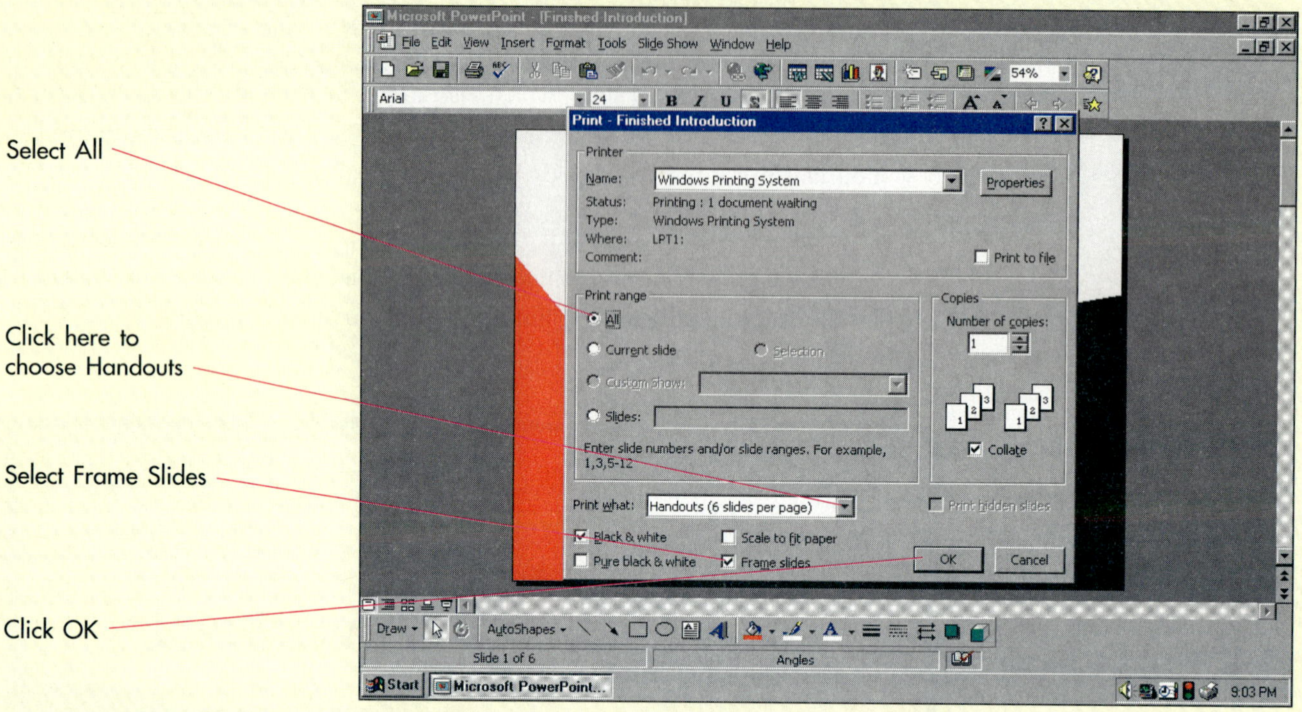


(h) Print the Presentation (step 9)

FIGURE 1.5 Hands-on Exercise 1 (continued)

> **THE COMMON USER INTERFACE**
>
> One of the most significant benefits of the Windows environment is the common user interface, which provides a sense of familiarity when you begin to learn a new application. In other words, once you know one Windows application, it will be that much easier for you to learn PowerPoint, because all applications work basically the same way. The benefits are magnified if you use other applications in Microsoft Office. Indeed, if you use either Word or Excel, you already know more than 100 commands in PowerPoint.

**STEP 10: Exit PowerPoint**

➤ Pull down the **File menu.** Click **Close** to close the presentation but remain in PowerPoint. Click **Yes** if asked whether to save the changes.

➤ Pull down the **File menu.** Click **Exit** to exit PowerPoint if you do not want to continue with the next exercise at this time.

## FIVE DIFFERENT VIEWS

PowerPoint offers five different views in which to create, modify, and show a presentation. Figure 1.6 shows the five views for the introductory presentation from the first exercise. Each view represents a different way of looking at the presentation, and each view has unique capabilities. Some views display only a single slide, whereas others show multiple slides, making it easy to organize the presentation. You can switch back and forth between the views by clicking the appropriate view button at the bottom of the presentation window.

The ***Slide view*** in Figure 1.6a displays one slide at a time and enables all operations for that slide. You can enter, delete, or format text. You can draw or add objects such as a graph, clip art, or an organization chart. The ***Drawing Toolbar*** is displayed by default in this view.

The ***Slide Sorter view*** in Figure 1.6b displays multiple slides on the screen (each slide is in miniature) and lets you see the overall flow of the presentation. You can change the order of a presentation by clicking and dragging a slide from one position to another. You can delete a slide by clicking the slide and pressing the Del key. You can also set transition and/or animation effects on each slide to add interest to the presentation. The Slide Sorter view has its own toolbar, which is discussed in Chapter 2 in conjunction with creating animation effects.

The ***Outline view*** in Figure 1.6c shows the presentation in outline form. You can see all of the text on every slide, but you cannot see the graphic elements that may be present on the individual slides. You can, however, open a ***slide miniature*** to see the current slide within the Outline view.) The Outline view is the fastest way to enter or edit text, in that you type directly into the outline. You can copy and/or move text from one slide to another. You can also rearrange the order of the slides within the presentation. The Outline view has its own toolbar and is discussed more fully in Chapter 2.

The ***Notes Page view*** in Figure 1.6d lets you create speaker's notes for some or all of the slides in a presentation. These notes do not appear when you show the presentation, but can be printed prior to the presentation to help you remember what you want to say about each slide.

The ***Slide Show view*** displays the slides one at a time as an electronic presentation on the computer. The show may be presented manually, where you click the mouse to move from one slide to the next. The presentation can also be shown automatically, where each slide stays on the screen for a predetermined amount of time, after which the next slide appears automatically. Either way, the slide show may contain transition effects from one slide to the next as was demonstrated in the first hands-on exercise.

The easiest way to switch from one view to another is by clicking the appropriate view button. The buttons are displayed in the lower-left part of the screen (above the status bar) in all views except the Slide Show view.

### POWERPOINT VIEWS

PowerPoint has five different views of a presentation, each with unique capabilities. Anything you do in one view is automatically reflected in the other views. If, for example, you rearrange the slides in the Slide Sorter view, the new arrangement is reflected in the Outline view. In similar fashion, if you add or format text in the Outline view, the changes are also made in the Slide view.

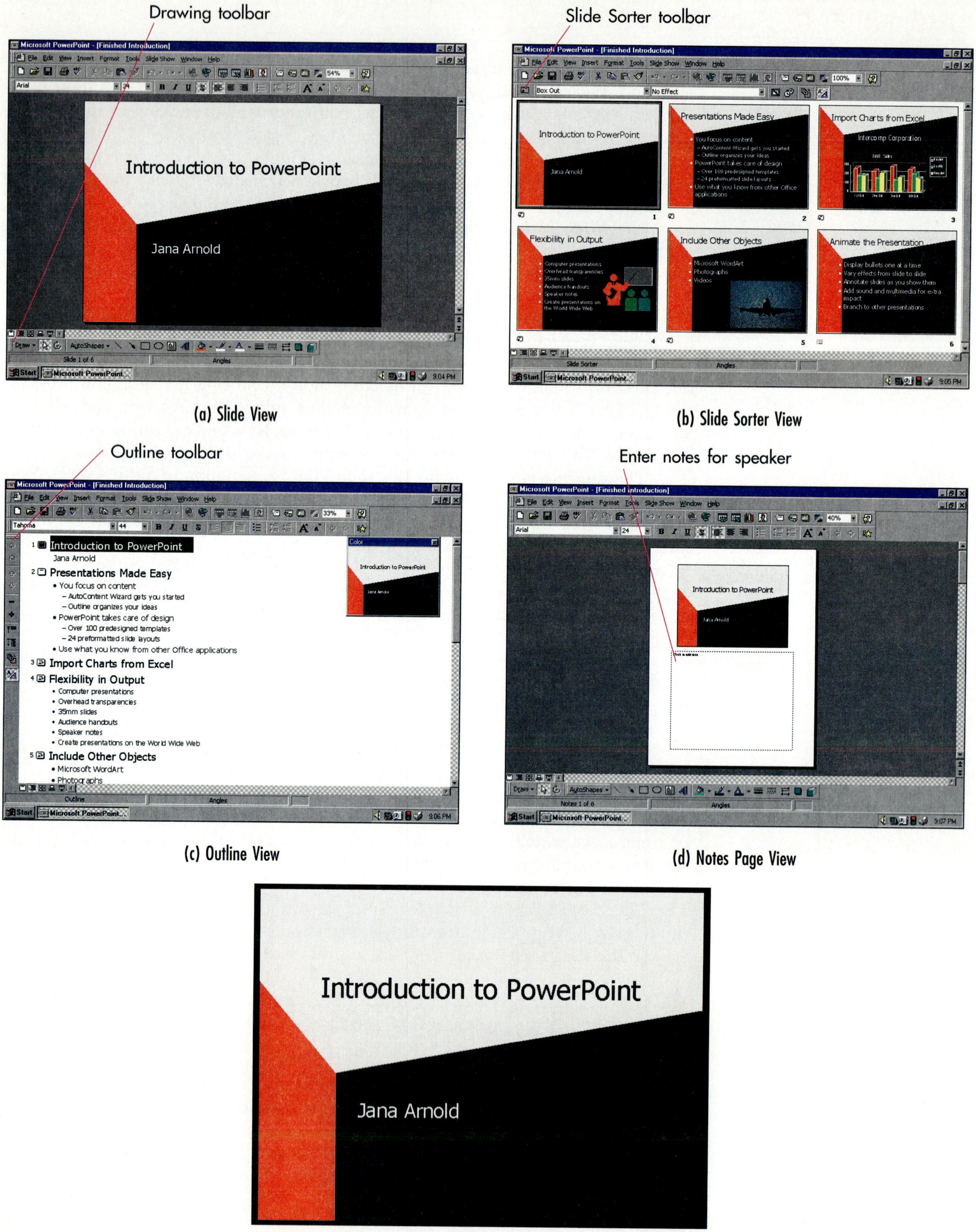


(a) Slide View

(b) Slide Sorter View

(c) Outline View

(d) Notes Page View

(e) Slide Show View

**FIGURE 1.6** PowerPoint Views

## ADDING AND DELETING SLIDES

Slides are added to a presentation by using one of 24 predefined slide formats known as ***AutoLayouts.*** Pull down the Insert menu and click the ***New Slide command*** to display the dialog box in Figure 1.7a, then choose the type of slide you want. (The slide will be added to the presentation immediately after the current slide.)

Figure 1.7a depicts the addition of a bulleted slide with ***clip art.*** The user chooses the desired layout, then clicks the OK command button to switch to the slide view in Figure 1.7b. The AutoLayout contains ***placeholders*** for the various

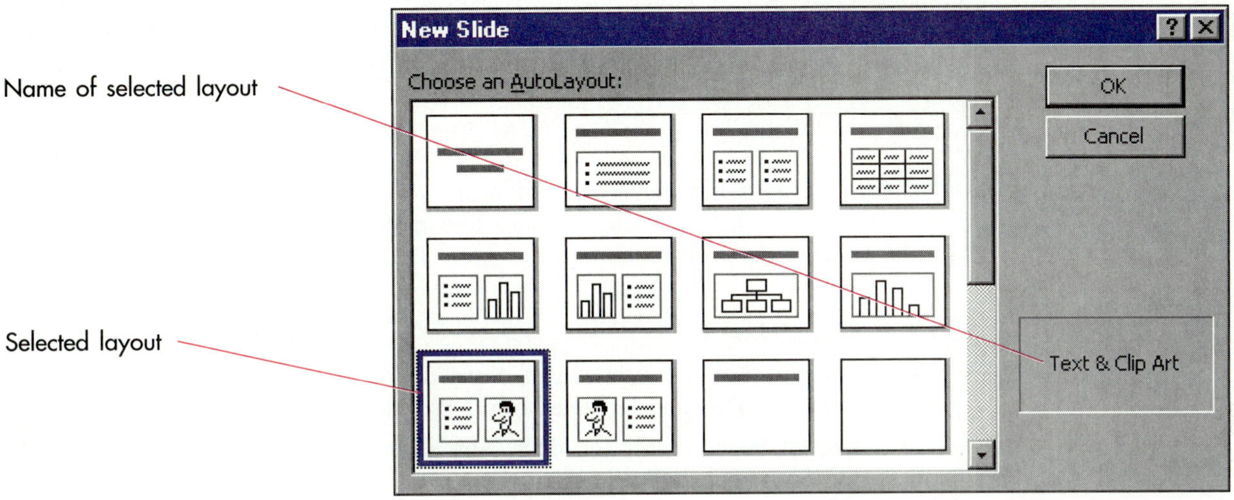


(a) AutoLayout

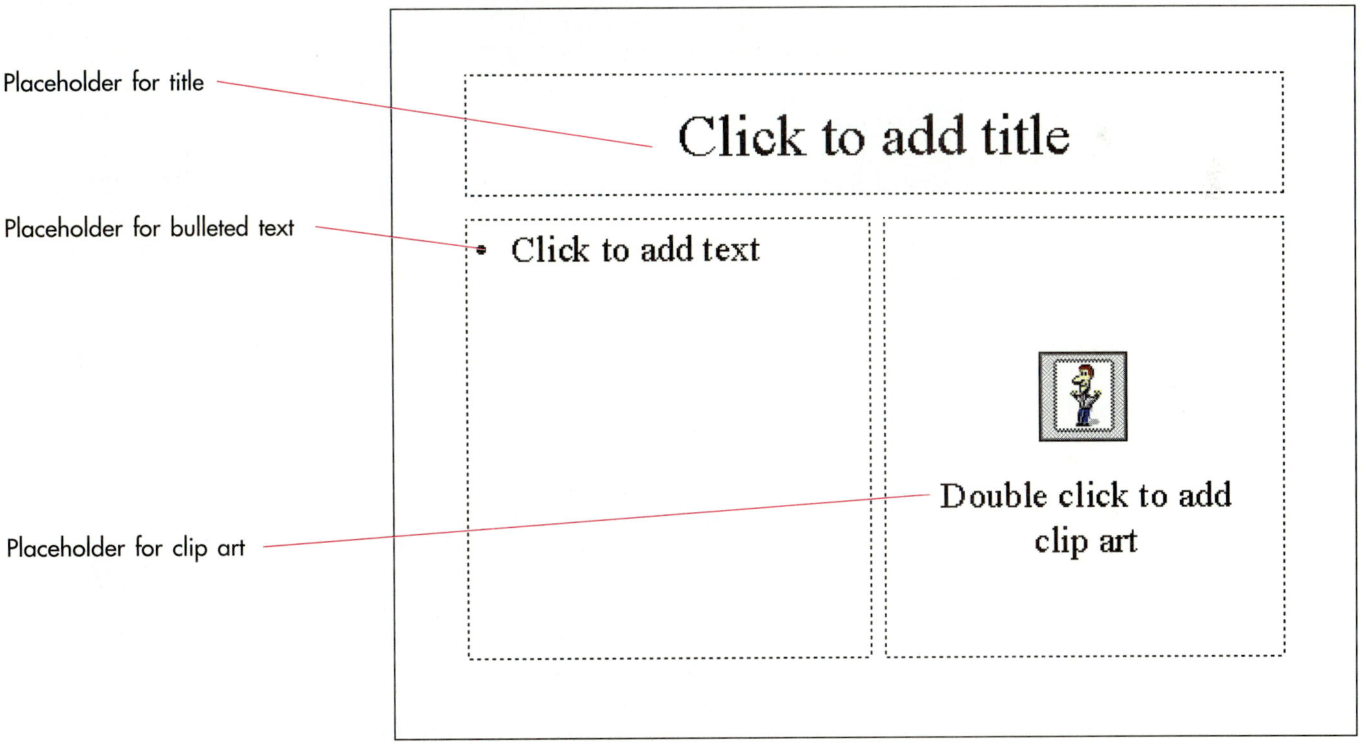


(b) Placeholders

**FIGURE 1.7** Adding a Slide

objects on the slide to position them properly. There are three placeholders in Figure 1.7b—one for the title, one for the bulleted text, and one for the clip art. Just follow the directions on the slide by clicking the appropriate placeholder to add the title or text, or double clicking to add the clip art. It's that easy, as you will see in the exercise that follows shortly.

You can delete a slide from any view except the Slide Show view. To delete a slide from the Slide or Notes Page view, select the slide by making it the current slide, pull down the Edit menu, and choose the Delete Slide command. To delete a slide from the Slide Sorter or Outline view, select the slide, then press the Del key.

## HANDS-ON EXERCISE 2

### *PowerPoint Views*

**Objective:** To switch between the different views while modifying a presentation; to use the Microsoft Clip Gallery and add clip art to a slide; to add a slide to an existing presentation. Use Figure 1.8 as a guide in the exercise.

**STEP 1: Add a New Slide**

- Start PowerPoint. Follow the instructions from step 4 in the previous exercise to open the **Finished Introduction** presentation.
- Pull down the **Insert menu** and click **New slide** (or click the **New Slide button** on the Standard toolbar). You will see the New Slide dialog box in Figure 1.8a.

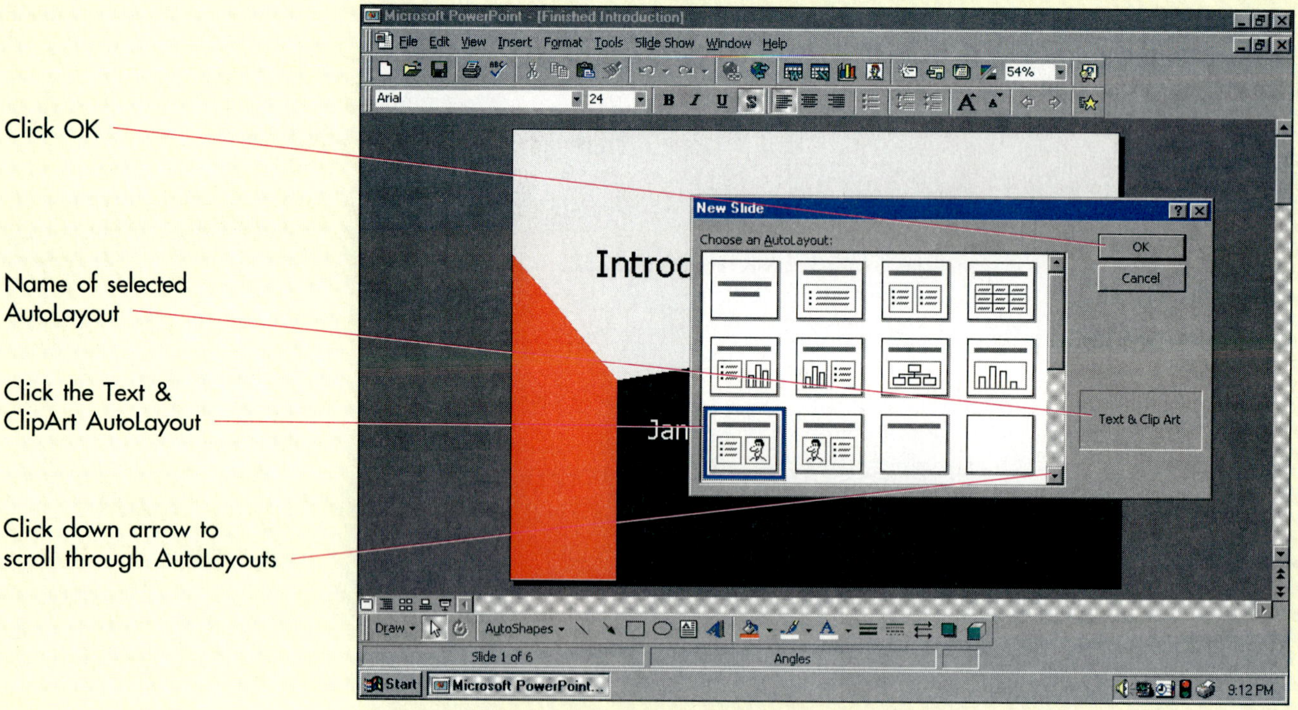


(a) Add a New Slide (step 1)

**FIGURE 1.8** Hands-on Exercise 2

- ➤ Click the **down arrow** on the vertical scroll bar to scroll through AutoLayouts within PowerPoint.
- ➤ Select (click) the **Text & Clip Art layout** as shown in the figure. (The name of the selected layout appears in the lower-right corner of the dialog box.) Click the **OK command button.**

### THE MOST RECENTLY OPENED FILE LIST

The easiest way to open a recently used presentation is to select the presentation directly from the File menu. Pull down the File menu, but instead of clicking the Open command, check to see if the presentation appears on the list of the most recently opened presentations located at the bottom of the menu. If so, you can click the presentation name rather than having to make the appropriate selections through the Open dialog box.

**STEP 2: Click Here**

- ➤ Click the **placeholder** where it says **Click to add title** in Figure 1.8b. Type **The Microsoft Clip Gallery** as the title of the slide.
- ➤ Click the **placeholder** where it indicates **Click to add text.** Type **Choose from many different categories** as the first bullet. Press **enter** to move to the next bullet.

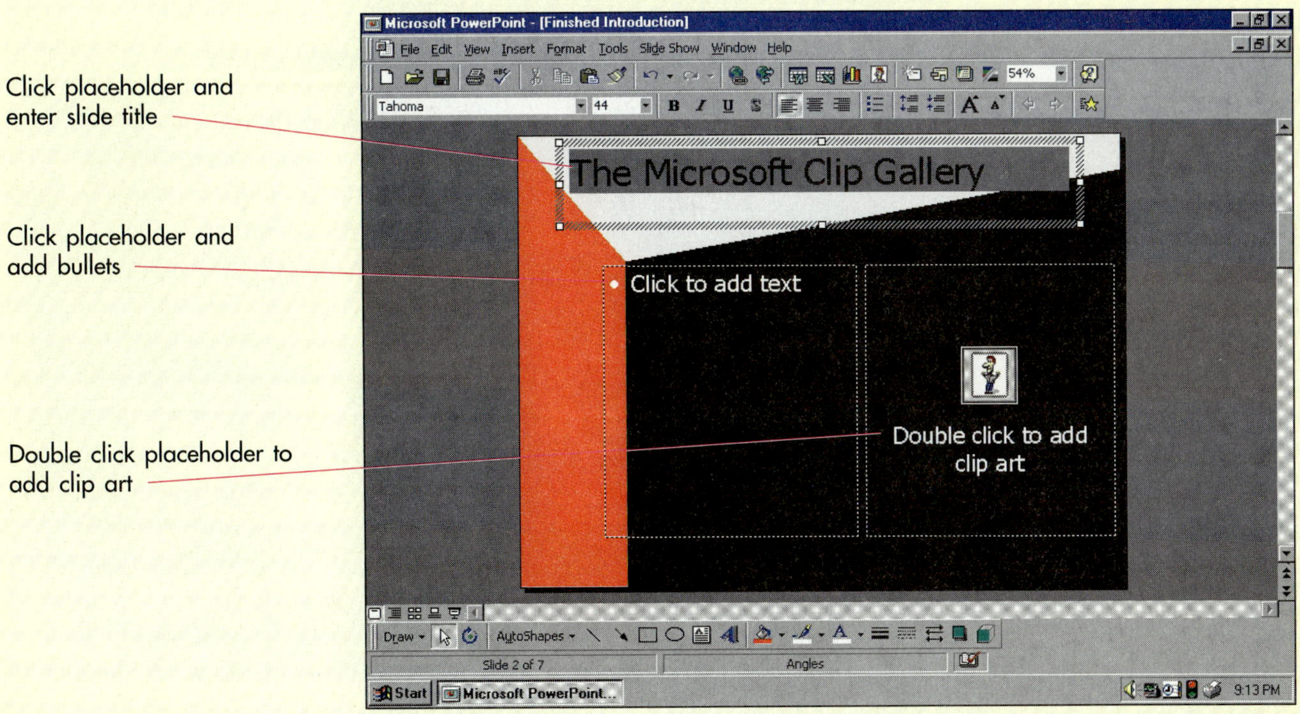


(b) Click Here (step 2)

**FIGURE 1.8** Hands-on Exercise 2 (continued)

- Press **Tab** to indent the next bullet one level. Type **Cartoons.** Press **enter** to move to the next bullet.
- You do *not* have to press the Tab key because PowerPoint automatically aligns each succeeding bullet under the previous bullet. Type **Maps.** Press **enter** to move to the next bullet.
- Type **People.** Press **enter** to move to the next bullet.

➤ Press **Shift+Tab** to move the new bullet one level to the left. Enter **ValuPack on CD contains more than 3,000 images** as the final bullet. Do *not* press the enter key or else you will create another bullet.

### BULLETS AND THE TAB (SHIFT+TAB) KEY

Bullets are entered one after another simply by typing the text of a bullet and pressing the enter key. A new bullet appears automatically under the previous bullet. Press the Tab key to indent the new bullet or press Shift+Tab to move the bullet back one level to the left.

**STEP 3: Add Clip Art**

➤ Double click the **placeholder** for the **clip art.** You will see the Clip Gallery dialog box shown in Figure 1.8c (although you may not see all of the categories listed in the figure).

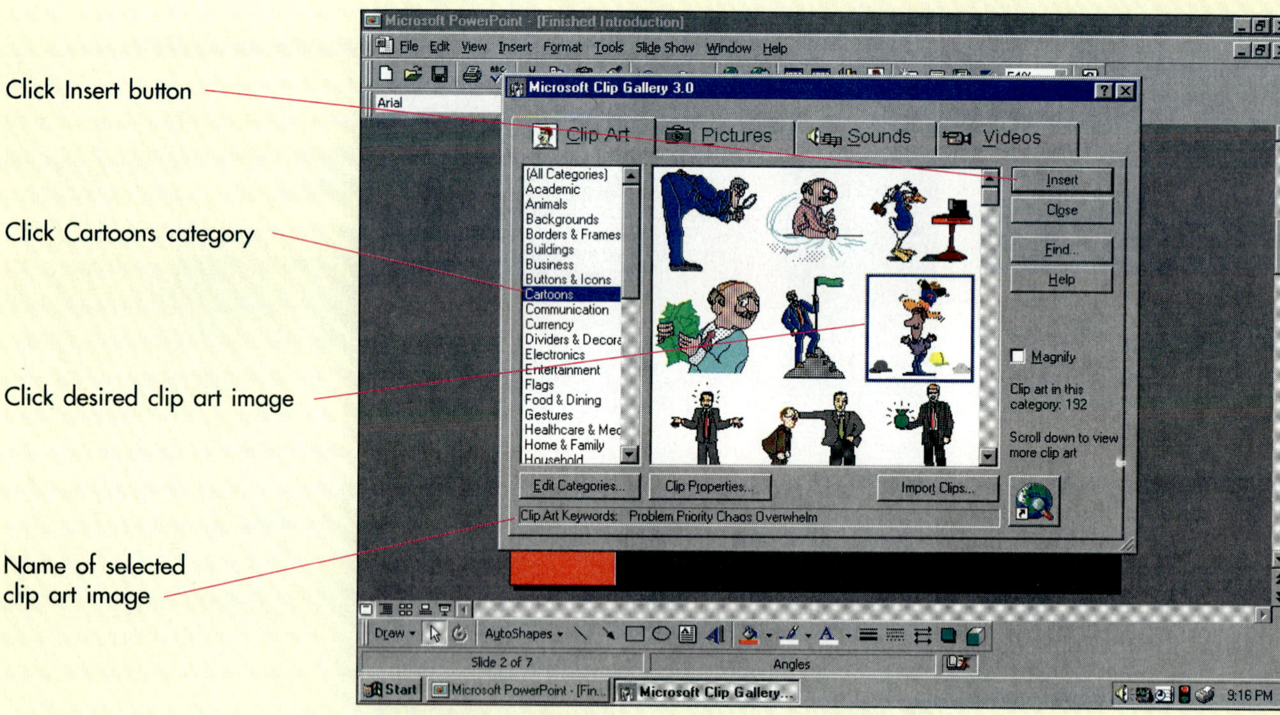


(c) The ClipArt Gallery (step 3)

**FIGURE 1.8** Hands-on Exercise 2 (continued)

➤ Click the **ClickArt tab.** Click the **Cartoons** ategory. If necessary, click the **down arrow** on the scroll bar to scroll through the available cartoons until you see the image you want.

➤ Select (click) the **Problem Priority** cartoon as shown in Figure 1.8c. Click the **Insert button** to insert the clip art onto the slide.

### ADDITIONAL CLIP ART

The Microsoft Clip Gallery contains over 100MB of data consisting of more than 3,000 clip art images, 144 photographs, 28 sounds, and 20 video clips. Only a fraction of these are installed with Microsoft Office, but you can access the additional objects from the Office CD at any time. You can also install some or all of the objects on your hard disk, provided you have sufficient space. Start the Windows Explorer, then open the ClipArt folder on the Office CD. Double click the Setup icon to start the Setup Wizard, then follow the on-screen instructions to install the additional components you want.

**STEP 4: Select-Then-Do**

➤ You should see the completed slide in Figure 1.8d. Click and drag to select the number 3,000.

- Click the **Bold button** on the Formatting toolbar to boldface the selected text.

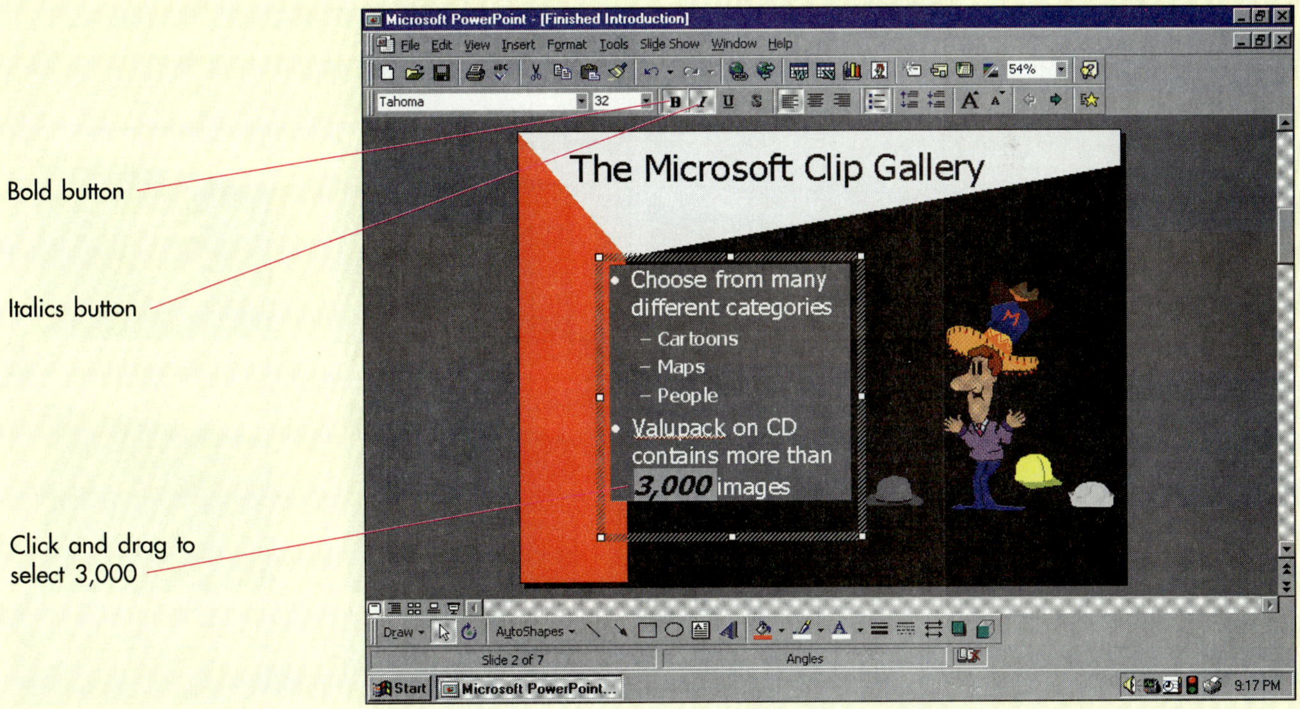


(d) Select-Then-Do (step 4)

FIGURE 1.8 Hands-on Exercise 2 (continued)

- Click the **Italic button** on the Formatting toolbar to italicize the selected text.
- Click the **Increase font size button** on the Formatting toolbar to increase the size of the selected text.

➤ Click outside the text area to deselect the text to see the results. Save the presentation.

> **SELECT-THEN-DO**
>
> All editing and formatting operations take place within the context of select-then-do; that is, you select a block of text, then you execute the command to operate on that text. Selected text is affected by any subsequent operation; for example, clicking the Boldface or Italic button changes the selected text to boldface or italics, respectively. In similar fashion, pressing the Del key deletes the selected text. And finally, the fastest way to replace existing text is to select the text, then type a new entry while the text is still selected. Selected text remains highlighted until you click elsewhere on the slide.

**STEP 5: The Slide Sorter View**

➤ Pull down the **View menu** and click **Slide Sorter** (or click the **Slide Sorter View button** on the status bar). This changes to the Slide Sorter view in Figure 1.8e.

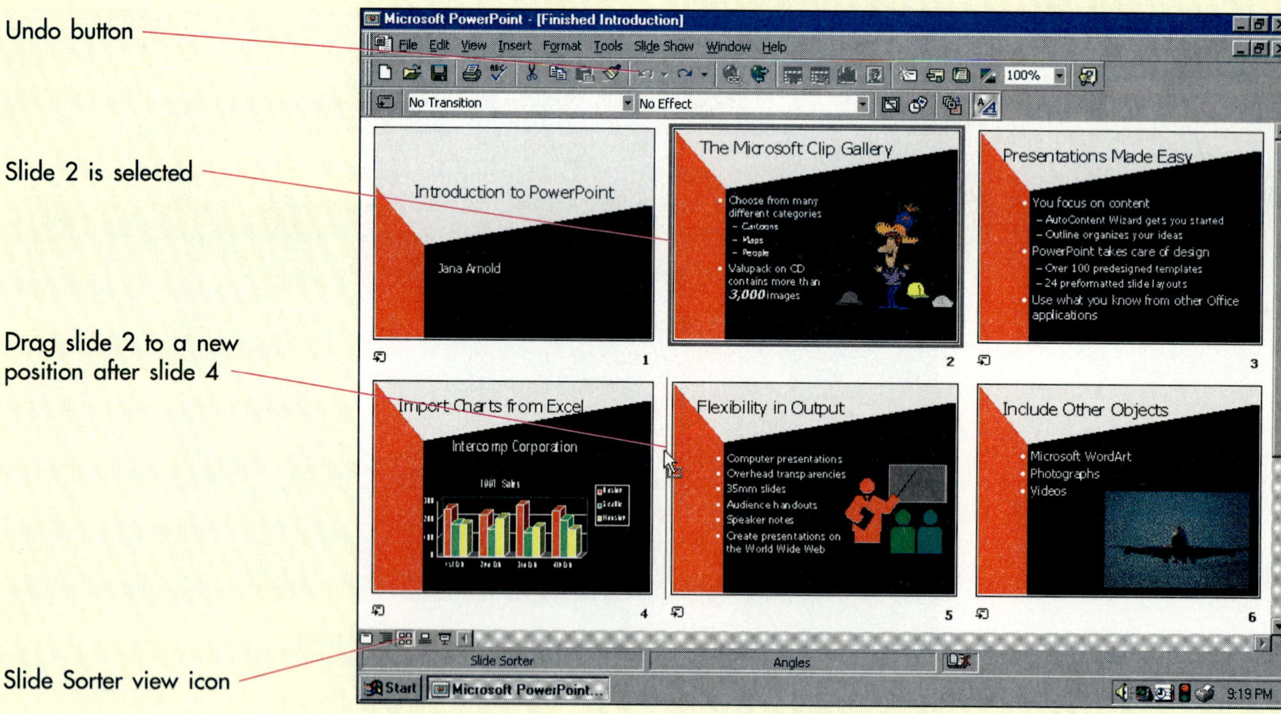


(e) Slide Sorter View (step 5)

**FIGURE 1.8** Hands-on Exercise 2 (continued)

- Slide 2 (the slide you just created) is already selected as indicated by the heavy border around the slide.
- Click and drag slide 2 and move it after slide 4. (A vertical line appears in the presentation as you drag the slide to indicate where it will be placed.)
- Release the mouse. The existing slides are automatically renumbered to reflect the new sequence.
- Pull down the **Edit menu** and click **Undo Drag and Drop** (or click the **Undo button** on the Standard toolbar). The slide containing the clip art goes back to its original position.
- Click and drag slide 2 and move it after slide 4.
- Save the presentation.

### MULTIPLE-LEVEL UNDO

The Undo command reverses (undoes) the most recent command. The command is executed from the Edit menu or more easily by clicking the Undo button on the Standard toolbar. Each click of the Undo button reverses one command; that is, click the Undo button and you reverse the last command. Click the Undo button a second time and you reverse the previous command. The Redo command works in reverse and undoes the most recent Undo command (i.e., it redoes the command you just undid). The maximum number of Undo commands (the default is 20) is set through the Tools menu. Pull down the Tools menu, click Options, click the Edit tab, then enter the desired number.

**STEP 6: The Outline View**

- Click the **Outline View button** on the status bar to change to the Outline view in Figure 1.8f. Press **Ctrl+End** to move to the end of the outline. Press **enter.** Press **Shift+Tab** to begin a new slide:
  - Type **Five Different Views** (the title of the slide). Press **enter.**
  - Press the **Tab key** to indent one level. Type **Slide view** as shown in Figure 1.8f. Press **enter** to move to the next bullet.
  - Type **Outline view.** Press **enter.**
  - Type **Slide Sorter view.** Press **enter.**

### SLIDE MINIATURES

The Outline view displays the text of the presentation, but not the graphic elements. You can, however, open a slide miniature window to display these elements from within the Outline view. The slide miniature is shown by default but can be toggled on and off by pulling down the View menu and checking (clearing) the Slide Miniature command.

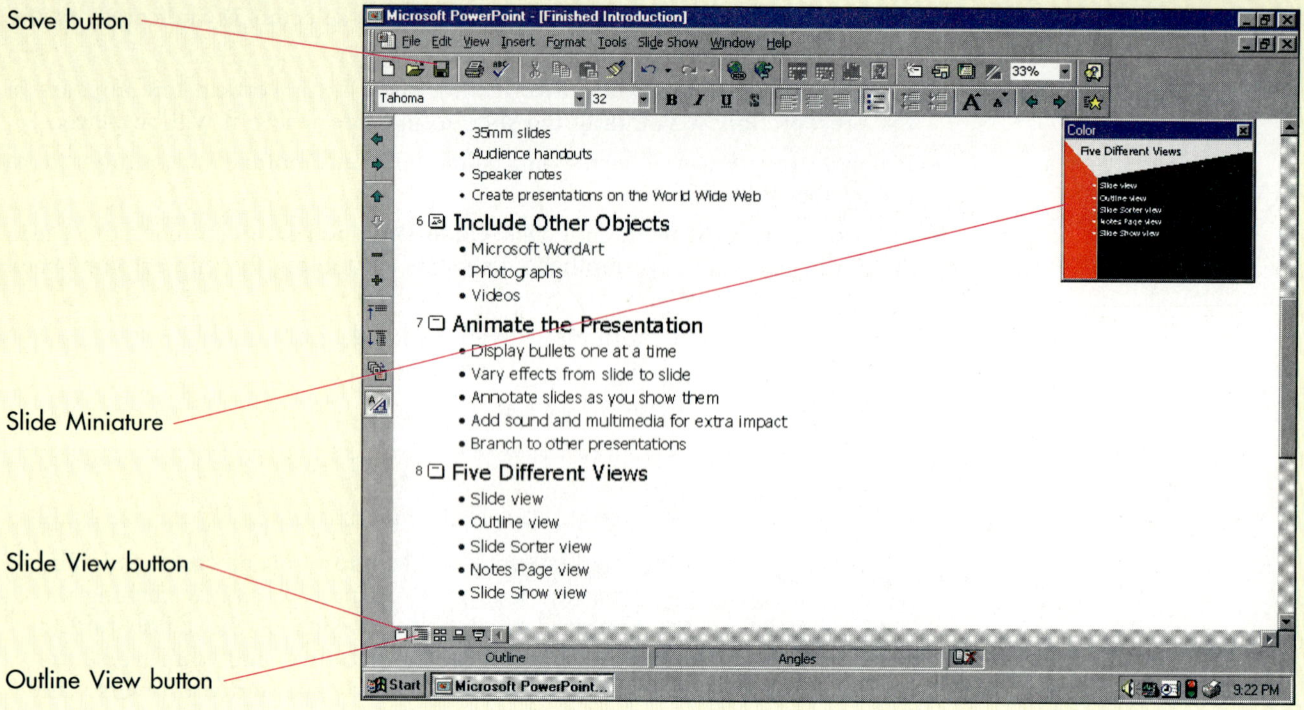


(f) Outline View (step 6)

FIGURE 1.8 Hands-on Exercise 2 (continued)

- Type **Notes Page view.** Press **enter.**
- Type **Slide Show view.**

➤ The slide is complete. Click the **Save button** on the Standard toolbar to save the presentation.

**STEP 7: The Slide View**

➤ Click the **Slide View button** to change to the Slide view as shown in Figure 1.8g. You should see the Slide view of the slide created in the previous step.

➤ Click the **Previous Slide button** on the vertical scroll bar (or press the **PgUp key**) to move to the previous slide (slide 7) in the presentation.

➤ Click the **Next Slide button** on the vertical scroll bar (or press the **PgDn key**) to move to the next slide (slide 8).

### THE SLIDE ELEVATOR

PowerPoint uses the scroll box (common to all Windows applications) in the vertical scroll bar as an elevator to move up and down within the presentation. Click and drag the elevator to go to a specific slide; as you drag, you will see a ScreenTip indicating the slide you are about to display. Release the mouse when you see the number (title) of the slide you want.

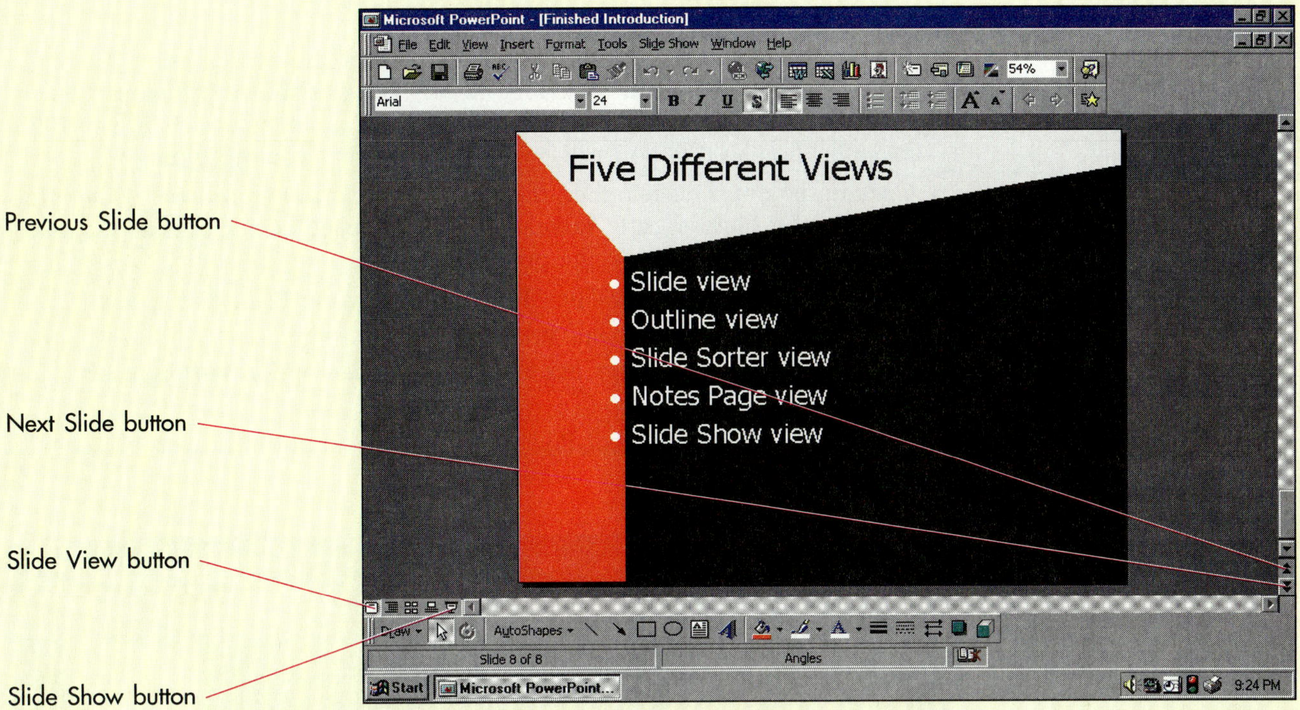


(g) Slide View (step 7)

**FIGURE 1.8** Hands-on Exercise 2 (continued)

**STEP 8: The Slide Show View**

➤ Press **Ctrl+Home** to move to the beginning of the presentation. Click the **Slide Show button** to view the presentation as follows:

- Click the **left mouse button** (or press the **PgDn key**) to move forward in the presentation. Continue to click the left mouse button to move from one slide to the next.
- Click the **right mouse button** and click **Previous** from the shortcut menu (or press the **PgUp key**) to move backward in the presentation.
- Press the **Esc key** at any time to quit the presentation and return to the Slide view.

### TRANSITIONS AND ANIMATIONS

Transitions add interest and variety to a presentation by changing the way in which you progress from one slide to the next. Slides may move onto the screen from the left or right, be uncovered by horizontal or vertical blinds, fade, dissolve, etc. Animations may also be applied to individual bullets to display the bullets one at a time with a variety of special effects (e.g., a letter at a time accompanied by the sound of a typewriter.) Transitions and animations are further described in Chapter 2.

**STEP 9: The Notes Page View**

- Press **Ctrl+Home** to move to the beginning of the presentation. Click the **Notes Page View button** to change to this view, as shown in Figure 1.8h. (If necessary, click the **down arrow** on the Zoom Control box to change to **100%** magnification so that you will be able to see what you are typing.)
- Click in the **notes placeholder,** then enter the text in Figure 1.8h. (The information is for the presenter rather than the audience.) Click outside the placeholder to deselect it. Save the presentation.
- Pull down the **File menu.** Click **Print** to display the Print dialog box.
- Click the **down arrow** in the **Print What** drop-down list box. Scroll so that you can click **Notes Page.** Click the **Current Slide option button** to print just this slide. Click **OK.**
- Close the presentation. Exit PowerPoint if you do not want to continue with the next exercise.

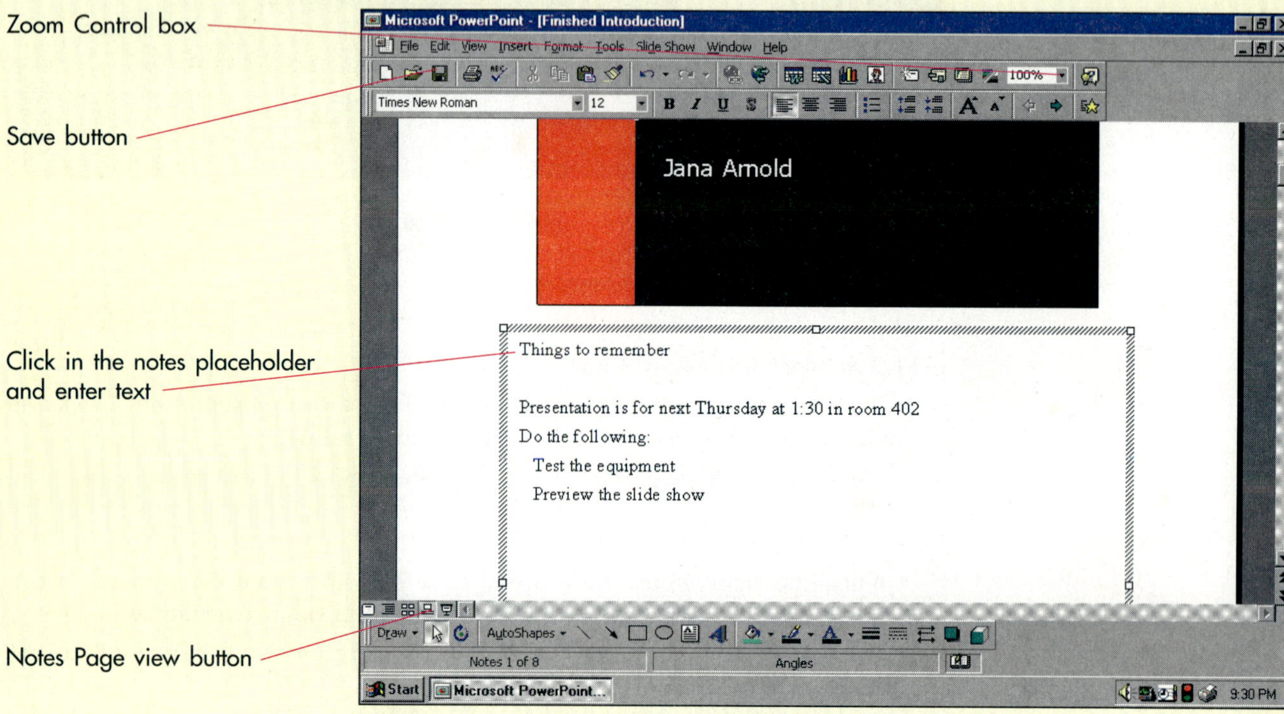


(h) Notes Page View (step 9)

FIGURE 1.8 Hands-on Exercise 2 (continued)

### ADD SPEAKER NOTES IN ANY VIEW

You do not have to be in the Notes Page view in order to add notes to a slide. Go to any view (other than Notes Page), pull down the View menu, click Speaker Notes to display the Speaker Notes dialog box, add your note, then close the dialog box. Change to the Notes Page view and your note will appear. The advantage of the Speaker Notes dialog box is that you can continue to develop your presentation without having to leave a slide to add a note.

## SLIDE SHOW TOOLS

PowerPoint can help you create an attractive presentation, but it is up to you to deliver the presentation effectively. Accordingly, PowerPoint provides a series of Slide Show tools to help you accomplish this goal. The tools can be accessed from any slide during the slide show by clicking the right mouse button to display a shortcut menu. The tools are discussed briefly in conjunction with the presentation in Figure 1.9, then illustrated in detail in a hands-on exercise.

### Rehearse Timings

The Slide Show view in Figure 1.9a displays a presentation consisting of five slides. It is similar to the Slide Show view shown earlier in the chapter, but with one significant difference. Look carefully under the slides and you will see a number preceded by a colon (e.g., :30 under slide 1) corresponding to the amount of time the presenter intends to devote to the slide. The timings were entered through the ***Rehearse Timings*** feature that enables you to time your presentation. This feature is extremely valuable because it provides a sense of timing as you practice your presentation. (The Rehearse Timings feature can also be used to automate a presentation so that each slide will be shown for the set time, after which the next slide will appear automatically.)

#### PRACTICE MAKES PERFECT

You have worked hard to gain the opportunity to present your ideas. Be prepared! You cannot bluff your way through a presentation. Practice aloud several times, preferably under the same conditions as the actual presentation. Everyone is nervous, but the more you practice, the more confident you will be.

### Action Items

Questions arise during any presentation, suggestions are given, and action items are developed. The ***Meeting Minder*** enables you to keep track of these items as they occur and to summarize them at the end of the presentation. The slide in Figure 1.9b, for example, is not part of the original presentation (it does not appear in the Slide Sorter view) but is created *during* the presentation, as explained in the hands-on exercise.

Note, too, the annotation that has been added to the Action Items slide. The mouse pointer has changed from an arrow to a pencil, changing the effect of the mouse to an annotation tool. This enables you to click anywhere on the slide in order to ***annotate the slide*** as shown in Figure 1.9b.

#### ARRIVE EARLY

You need time to gather your thoughts and set up the presentation. Start PowerPoint and open the presentation prior to beginning. Be sure you have your notes. Check that water is available for you during the presentation. Try to relax. Greet the audience as they come in.

Time allotted to slide with Rehearse Timings feature

Icon indicates a hidden slide

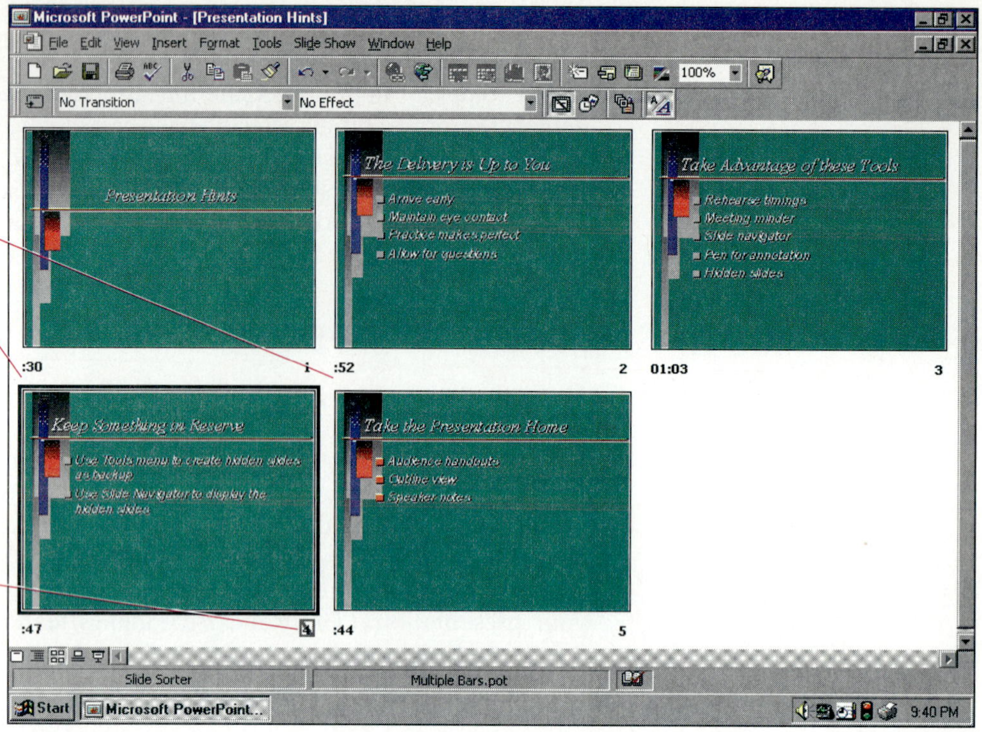


(a) Timings and Hidden Slides

Action Items slide created during presentation through Meeting Minder

Annotation added to slide

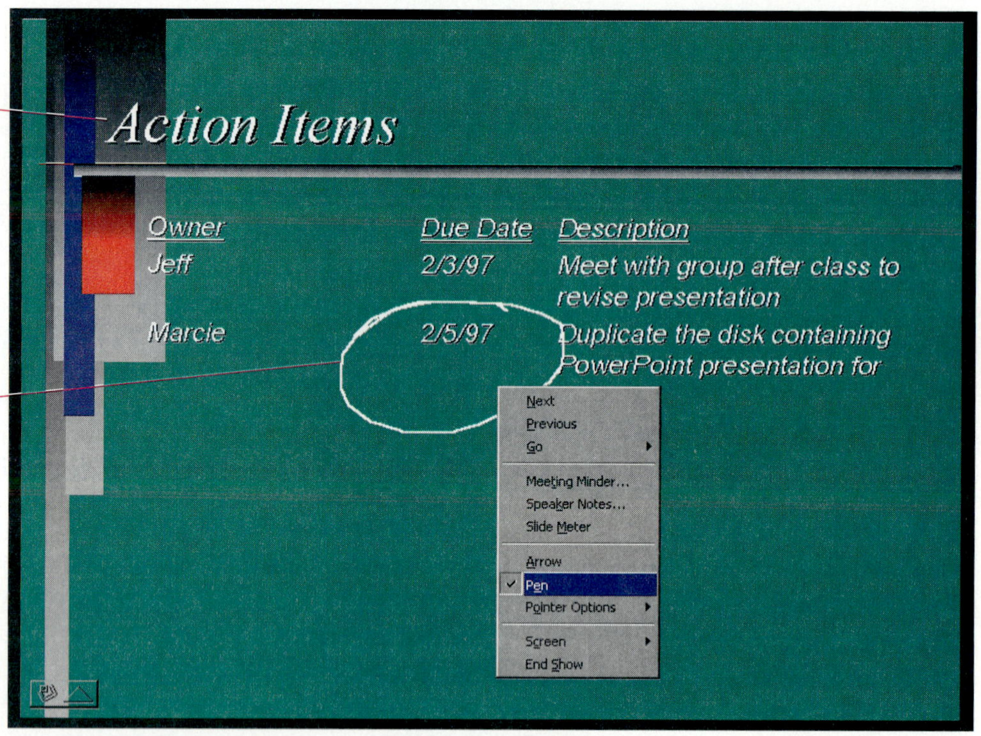


(b) Action Items and Annotation

**FIGURE 1.9** Slide Show

## Hidden Slides

The icon under slide number 4 in Figure 1.9a indicates that it is a ***hidden slide.*** The slide is contained within the presentation, but the presenter has elected not to display the slide in the slide show. This is a common practice among experienced speakers who anticipate probing questions that may arise during the presentation. The presenter prefers not to address the topic initially and elects to hide the slide. The presenter can, however, access the slide during the show (through the ***Slide Navigator***) should it become necessary.

> **BE FLEXIBLE**
>
> Every presentation begins with its slides in a specific order. Each audience is different, however, and you may find it necessary to change the order, to jump to a later slide, or to return to an earlier slide. You may also find it necessary to display a hidden slide, a slide that you kept in reserve should a specific question arise. Be flexible and use the Slide Navigator to respond appropriately to questions from the audience.

## HANDS-ON EXERCISE 3

### *Slide Show Tools*

**Objective:** To use the Rehearse Timings feature to time a presentation; to hide a slide, then use the Slide Navigator to display that slide on demand; to use the Meeting Minder to create a list of action items during a presentation; and to annotate a slide for emphasis. Use Figure 1.10 as a guide in the exercise.

**STEP 1: Open the Existing Presentation**

- Start PowerPoint. Open **Presentation Hints** in the **Exploring PowerPoint folder** as shown in Figure 1.10a. Click where indicated to add your name to the title slide.
- Pull down the **File menu,** click the **Save As command** to display the Save As dialog box, then save the presentation as **Finished Presentation Hints.** (Press the **Esc key** or click the **Close button** if you see a Properties dialog box after saving the file.)

> **CHANGE THE DEFAULT FOLDER**
>
> The default folder is the folder where PowerPoint retrieves (saves) presentations unless it is otherwise instructed. To change the default folder, pull down the Tools menu, click Options, click the Advanced tab, then enter the name of the default folder (for example, C:\Exploring PowerPoint) in the Default File Location text box. Click OK. The next time you execute the Open command, PowerPoint looks in this folder.

Click to add your name to the slide

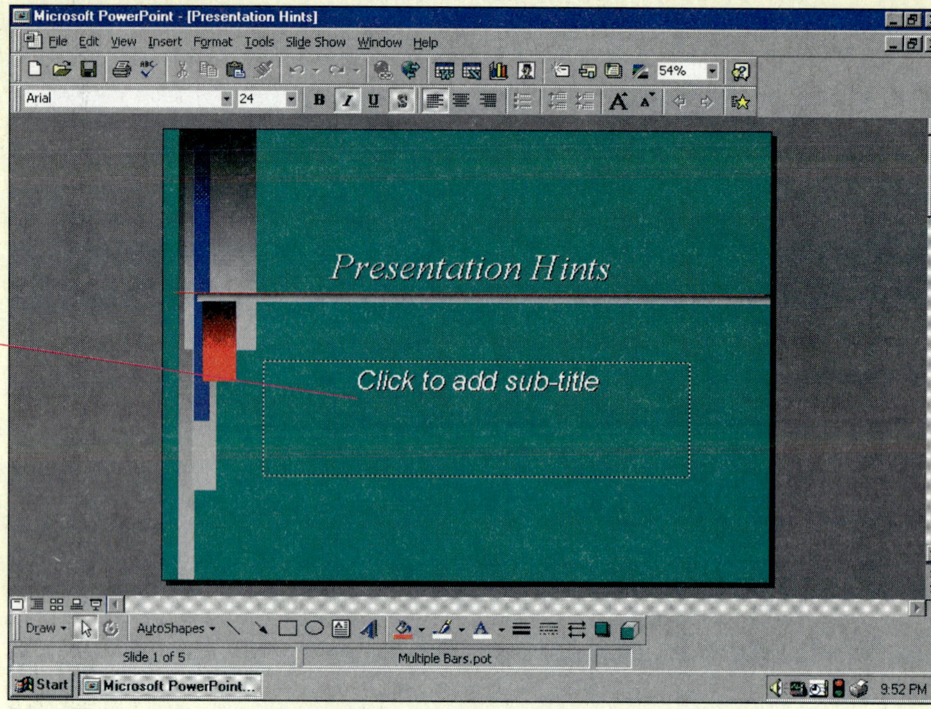


(a) Open the Presentation (step 1)

**FIGURE 1.10** Hands-on Exercise 3

**STEP 2: Hide a Slide**

- Click the **Slide Sorter View button** (or pull down the **View menu** and click **Slide Sorter**).
- If necessary, click the **down arrow** on the Zoom Control box to zoom to 100%. The slides are larger and easier to read as shown in Figure 1.10b.
- Point to slide 4 (Keep Something in Reserve), then click the **right mouse button** to select the slide and simultaneously display a shortcut menu.
- Click **Hide Slide** as shown in Figure 1.10b. The menu closes and a hidden slide icon is displayed under slide 4. The slide remains in the presentation, but it will *not* be displayed during the slide show.
- The Hide Slide command functions as a toggle switch. Click the command once and the slide is hidden. Click the command a second time and the slide is no longer hidden.
- Save the presentation. Click on the first slide, then lick the **Slide Show button** to move quickly through the presentation.
- You will not see the slide titled Keep Something in Reserve because it has been hidden. (You can still access this slide through the Slide Navigator as described in step 5.)

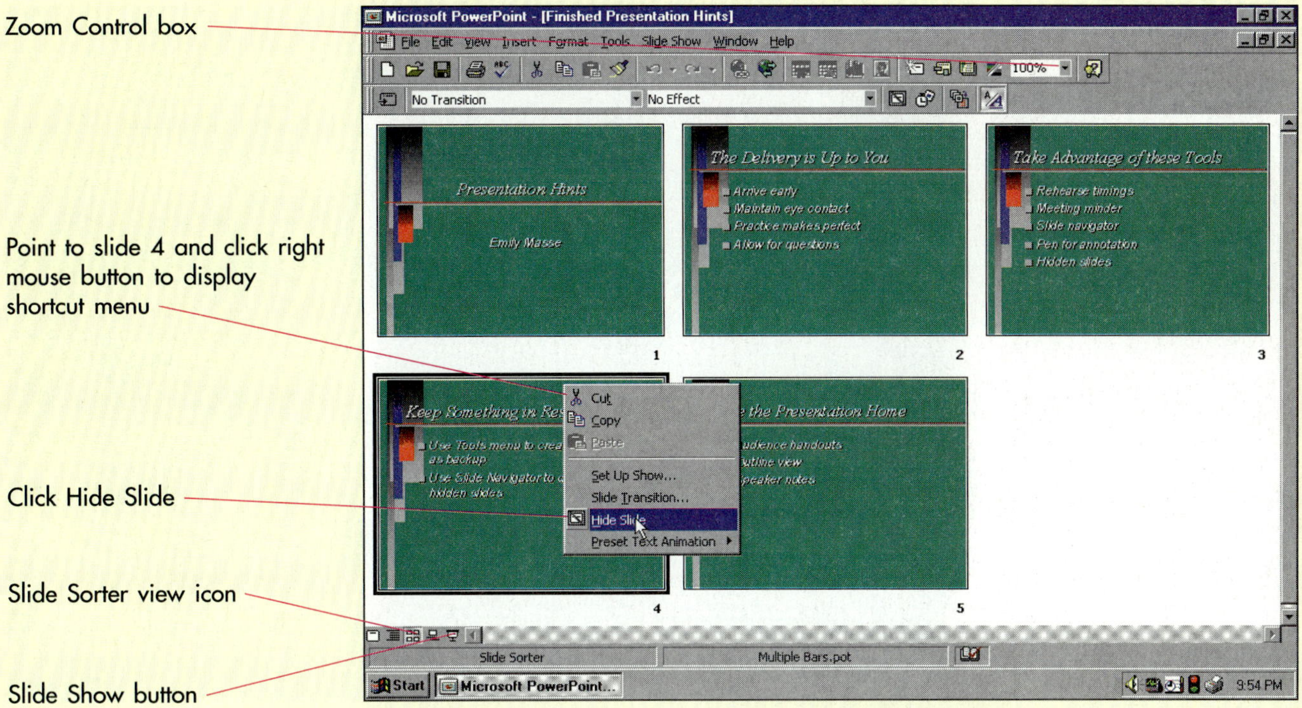


(b) Hide a Slide (step 2)

**FIGURE 1.10** Hands-on Exercise 3 (continued)

> **MOVING WITHIN THE PRESENTATION**
>
> Ctrl+Home and Ctrl+End are universal Windows shortcuts that move to the beginning or end of a document. Not only do the techniques work in PowerPoint, but they work in four of the five views (the Slide Show view is the exception). The shortcuts are quite valuable as you develop a presentation because you often need to move to the first or last slide.

**STEP 3: Rehearse the Presentation**

- Press **Ctrl+Home** to return to the first slide. Pull down the **Slide Show menu** and click **Rehearse Timings.**
- The first slide appears in the Slide Show view, and the Rehearsal dialog box is displayed in the lower-right corner of the screen. Speak as though you were presenting the slide, then click the mouse to register the elapsed time for that slide and move to the next slide.
- The second slide in the presentation should appear as shown in Figure 1.10c. Speak as though you were presenting the slide and note the times that appear in the dialog box. The cumulative time appears on the left (1 minute and 6 seconds). The time for this specific slide (39 seconds) is shown at the right.
  - Click the **Repeat button** to redo the timing for the slide.
  - Click the **Pause button** to (temporarily) stop the clock. Click the **Pause button** a second time to resume the clock.
  - Click the **Next Slide button** to record the timing and move to the next slide.

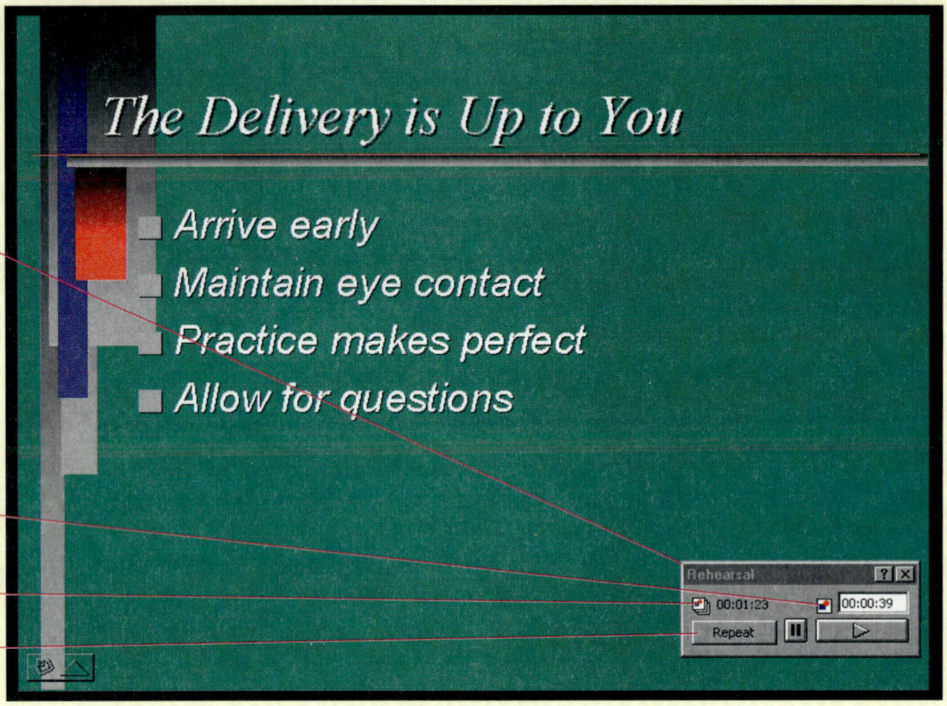


(c) Rehearse Timings (step 3)

**FIGURE 1.10** Hands-on Exercise 3 (continued)

- Continue rehearsing the show until you reach the end of the presentation.
- You should see a dialog box at the end of the presentation that indicates the total time of the slide show. Click **Yes** when asked whether you want to record the new timings. Click **Yes** when asked whether you want to review the timings in the Slide Sorter view.
- PowerPoint returns to the Slide Sorter view and records the timings under each slide (except for the hidden slide). Note, too, the hidden icon under the fourth slide.

**STEP 4: The Meeting Minder**

- Click the **first slide** (or press **Ctrl+Home**) to move to the beginning of the presentation. Click the **Slide Show button** to show the presentation.
- You should see the title slide as shown in Figure 1.10d. Point anywhere on the slide and click the **right mouse button** to display a shortcut menu.
- Click **Meeting Minder** to display the Meeting Minder dialog box, then click the **Action Items tab** as shown in Figure 1.10d.
- Enter the first action item in Figure 1.10d. Press the **Tab key** to move to the Assigned To box to enter a person's name. Enter a Due Date, then click the **Add button** to complete the task. Enter a second action item of your own choosing. Click **OK** to close the dialog box.
- Click the mouse to move from one slide to the next (you can enter an action item from any slide) until you reach the end of the presentation (the slide titled Action Items). A new slide has been created containing the action items you just supplied. Leave this slide on the screen.

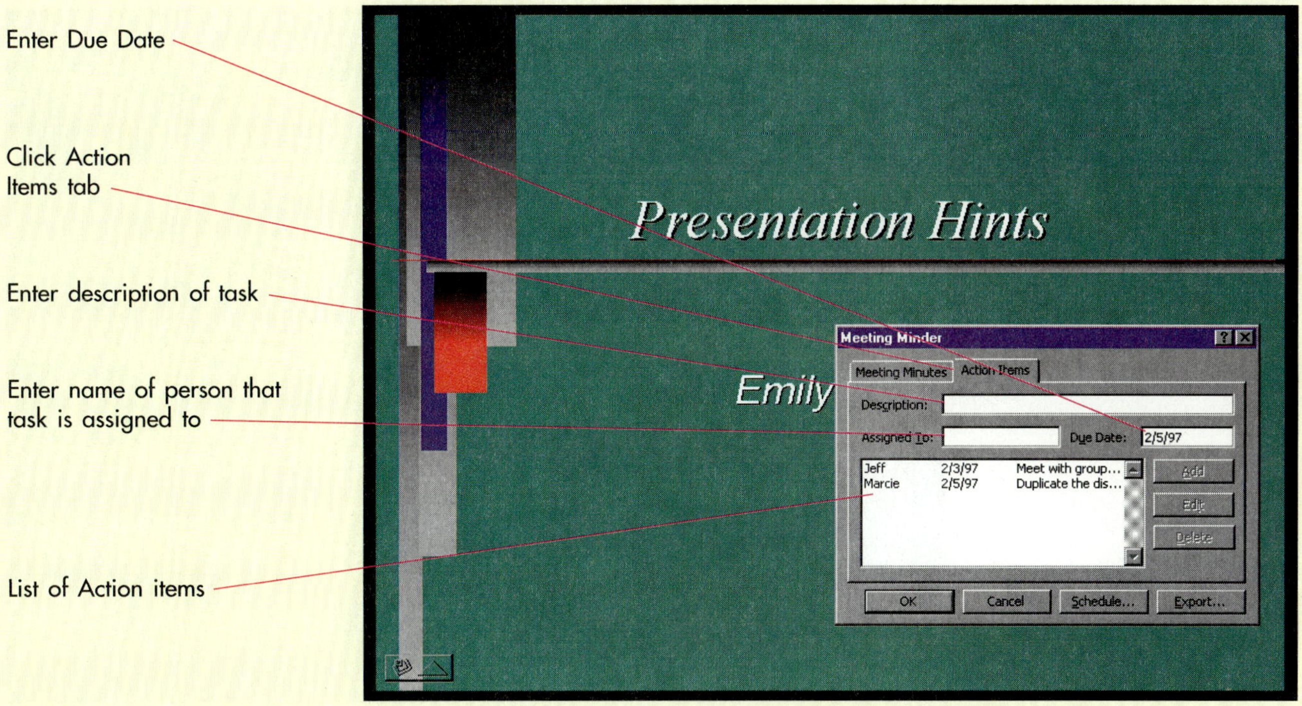


(d) Meeting Minder (step 4)

**FIGURE 1.10** Hands-on Exercise 3 (continued)

## QUESTIONS AND ANSWERS (Q & A)

Indicate at the beginning of your talk whether you will take questions during the presentation or collectively at the end. Announce the length of time that will be allocated to questions. Rephrase all questions so the audience can hear, then use the Slide Navigator to return to the appropriate slide in order to answer the question. Rephrase hostile questions in a neutral way and try to disarm the challenger by paying a compliment. If you don't know the answer, say so.

**STEP 5: The Slide Navigator**

- You should be positioned on the last slide (Action Items). Click the **right mouse button** to display a shortcut menu, click **Go,** then click **Slide Navigator** to display the Slide Navigator dialog box as shown in Figure 1.10e.
- The titles of all slides (including the hidden slide) are displayed in the Slide Navigator dialog box. The number of the hidden slide, however, is enclosed in parentheses to indicate it is a hidden slide.
- Select (click) the **hidden slide,** then click the **Go To button** to display this slide.

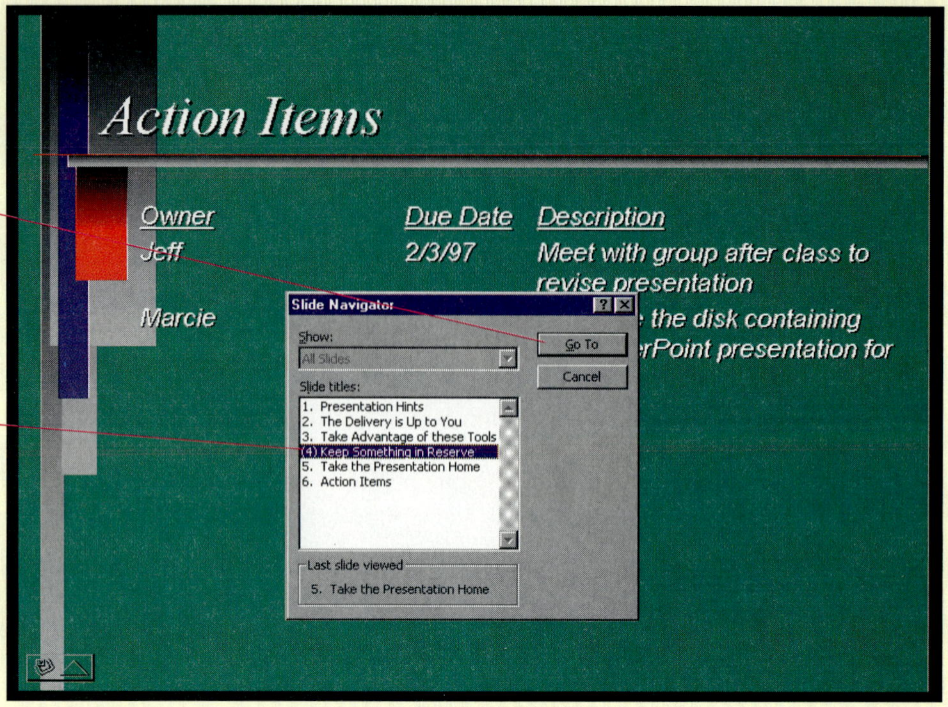


(e) Slide Navigator (step 5)

**FIGURE 1.10** Hands-on Exercise 3 (continued)

> **BACK UP IMPORTANT FILES**
>
> We cannot overemphasize the importance of adequate backup. Hard disks die, files are accidentally deleted or lost, and viruses may infect a system. It takes only a few minutes to copy your data files to a floppy disk, so do it now. You will thank us when (not if) you lose an important file and wish you had another copy.

**STEP 6: Annotate a Slide**

- You should see the slide in Figure 1.10f. Click the **right mouse button** to display the shortcut menu containing the Slide Show tools. Click **Pen.** The mouse pointer changes from an arrow to a pencil.
- Click and drag on the slide to annotate the slide as shown in Figure 1.10f. The annotation is temporary and will be visible only as long as you display the slide.
- Press **N** (or the **PgDn key**) to move to the next slide, then press **P** (or the **PgUp key**) to return to the previous slide. The annotation is gone.
- Click the **right mouse button,** point to (or click) **Pointer Options,** point to (or click) **Pen Color,** then choose (click) a different color. The mouse pointer automatically changes to the pen, and you can annotate the slide in the new color.

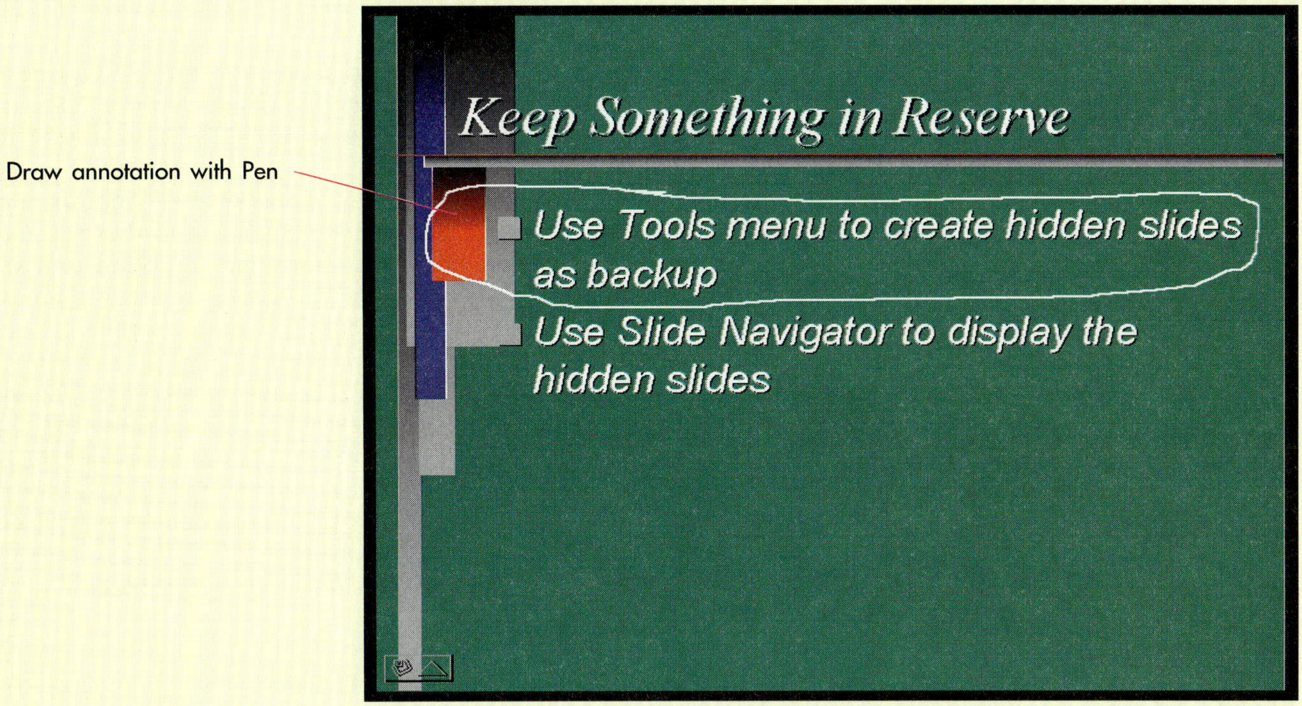


(f) Annotate a Slide (step 6)

**FIGURE 1.10** Hands-on Exercise 3 (continued)

### THE PEN AND THE ARROW

The shortcut menu can be used to toggle the mouse pointer between the Pen and the arrow, but we find various other shortcuts easier. For example, press Ctrl+P or Ctrl+A at any time to change to the pencil or an arrow, respectively. You can also press the Esc key to return the mouse to a pointer after using it as a Pen. And finally, you can use the keyboard to move to a different slide, which automatically resets the mouse to the pointer.

**STEP 7: End the Show**

- Click the **right mouse button** to display the shortcut menu, then click **End Show** to end the presentation.
- Pull down the **File menu.** Click **Print** to produce the Print dialog box. Click the **arrow** in the **Print What** drop-down list box. Click **Handouts (6 slides per page).** Check the boxes for **Frame Slides** and **Print Hidden Slides.**
- Check that the **All option button** is selected under Print Range. You will print every slide in the presentation, including the hidden slide and the slide containing the action items. Click **OK.**
- Pull down the **File menu** and click **Exit** to leave PowerPoint. Click **Yes** when asked whether to save the changes to the presentation.

## SUMMARY

A PowerPoint presentation consists of a series of slides with a consistent design and color scheme. A PowerPoint presentation may be delivered on a computer, via overhead transparencies or 35-mm slides, and/or printed in a variety of formats.

The PowerPoint window contains the basic elements of any Windows application. The benefits of the common user interface are magnified further if you are familiar with other applications in the Microsoft Office such as Word or Excel. PowerPoint is designed for a mouse, but it provides keyboard equivalents for almost every command. Toolbars provide still another way to execute the most frequent operations.

PowerPoint has five different views, each with unique capabilities. The Slide view displays one slide at a time and enables all operations on that slide. The Slide Sorter view displays multiple slides on one screen (each slide is in miniature) and lets you see the overall flow of the presentation. The Outline view shows the presentation text in outline form and is the fastest way to enter or edit text. The Notes Page view enables you to create speaker's notes for use in giving the presentation. The Slide Show view displays the slides one at a time with transition and animation effects for added interest.

Slides are added to a presentation using one of 24 predefined slide formats known as AutoLayouts. Each AutoLayout contains placeholders for the different objects on the slide. A slide may be deleted from a presentation in any view except the Slide Show view.

PowerPoint includes several slide show tools to help you enliven a presentation. The Rehearse Timings feature enables you to time and/or automate a presentation. The Slide Navigator enables you to branch directly to any slide, including hidden slides. The Pen lets you annotate a slide for added emphasis. The Meeting Minder enables you to create a list of action items.

Although PowerPoint helps to create attractive presentations, you are still the most important element in delivering the presentation. The chapter ended with several hints on how to rehearse and present presentations effectively.

## KEY WORDS AND CONCEPTS

Action items
Animation effects
Annotating a slide
AutoLayout
Clip art
Close command
Drawing toolbar
Elevator
Exit command
File menu
Formatting toolbar
Hidden slide
Meeting Minder
Menu bar
New Slide command
Notes Page view
Open command
Outline view
Pen
Placeholders
Print Command
Redo command
Rehearse Timings
Save command
ScreenTip
Slide miniature
Slide Navigator
Slide Show view
Slide Sorter view
Slide view
Standard toolbar
Status bar
Transition effects
Undo command
View buttons

# MULTIPLE CHOICE

1. How do you save changes to a PowerPoint presentation?
   (a) Pull down the File menu and click the Save command
   (b) Click the Save button on the Standard toolbar
   (c) Both (a) and (b)
   (d) Neither (a) nor (b)
2. Which toolbars are displayed by default in all views?
   (a) The Standard toolbar
   (b) The Formatting toolbar
   (c) Both (a) and (b)
   (d) Neither (a) nor (b)
3. Which view displays multiple slides on a single screen?
   (a) Outline view
   (b) Slide Sorter view
   (c) Both (a) and (b)
   (d) Neither (a) nor (b)
4. Which view displays multiple slides and also shows the graphical elements in each slide?
   (a) Outline view (with slide miniature displayed)
   (b) Slide Sorter view
   (c) Both (a) and (b)
   (d) Neither (a) nor (b)
5. Which view lets you delete a slide?
   (a) Outline view
   (b) Slide Sorter view
   (c) Both (a) and (b)
   (d) Neither (a) nor (b)
6. Which of the following can be printed in support of a PowerPoint presentation?
   (a) Audience handouts
   (b) Speaker's notes
   (c) An outline
   (d) All of the above
7. Which menu contains the Undo command?
   (a) File menu
   (b) Edit menu
   (c) Tools menu
   (d) Format menu
8. Ctrl+Home and Ctrl+End are keyboard shortcuts that move to the beginning or end of the presentation in the:
   (a) Outline view
   (b) Slide Sorter view
   (c) Slide view
   (d) All of the above

9. The predefined slide formats in PowerPoint are known as:
   (a) Views
   (b) AutoLayouts
   (c) Audience handouts
   (d) Speaker notes
10. Which menu contains the command to print a presentation?
    (a) The Tools menu
    (b) The File menu
    (c) The View menu
    (d) The Edit menu
11. The Open command:
    (a) Brings a presentation from disk into memory
    (b) Brings a presentation from disk into memory, then erases the presentation on disk
    (c) Stores the presentation in memory on disk
    (d) Stores the presentation in memory on disk, then erases the presentation from memory
12. The Save command:
    (a) Brings a presentation from disk into memory
    (b) Brings a presentation from disk into memory, then erases the presentation on disk
    (c) Stores the presentation in memory on disk
    (d) Stores the presentation in memory on disk, then erases the presentation from memory
13. Which of the following is true about hidden slides?
    (a) Hidden slides are invisible in every view
    (b) Hidden slides cannot be accessed during a slide show
    (c) Both (a) and (b)
    (d) Neither (a) nor (b)
14. Which view displays timings for individual slides after the timings have been established by rehearsing the presentation?
    (a) Slide view
    (b) Outline view
    (c) Slide Sorter view
    (d) All of the above
15. Which of the following is true about annotating a slide?
    (a) The annotations are permanent and cannot be erased
    (b) The annotations are entered by using the pen during the slide show
    (c) Both (a) and (b)
    (d) Neither (a) nor (b)

**ANSWERS**

|  |  |  |
|---|---|---|
| **1.** c | **6.** d | **11.** a |
| **2.** c | **7.** b | **12.** c |
| **3.** c | **8.** d | **13.** d |
| **4.** c | **9.** b | **14.** c |
| **5.** c | **10.** b | **15.** b |

# Practice with Microsoft PowerPoint 97

**1.** Figure 1.11 displays the Outline view of a presentation that was created by one of our students in a successful job search.

a. Open the *Chapter 1 Pratice 1* presentation in the set of practice files (it is found in the Exploring PowerPoint folder), then modify the presentation to reflect your personal data.

b. Print the title slide as a cover page for your assignment.

c. Print the revised audience handouts (six per page) and submit them to your instructor.

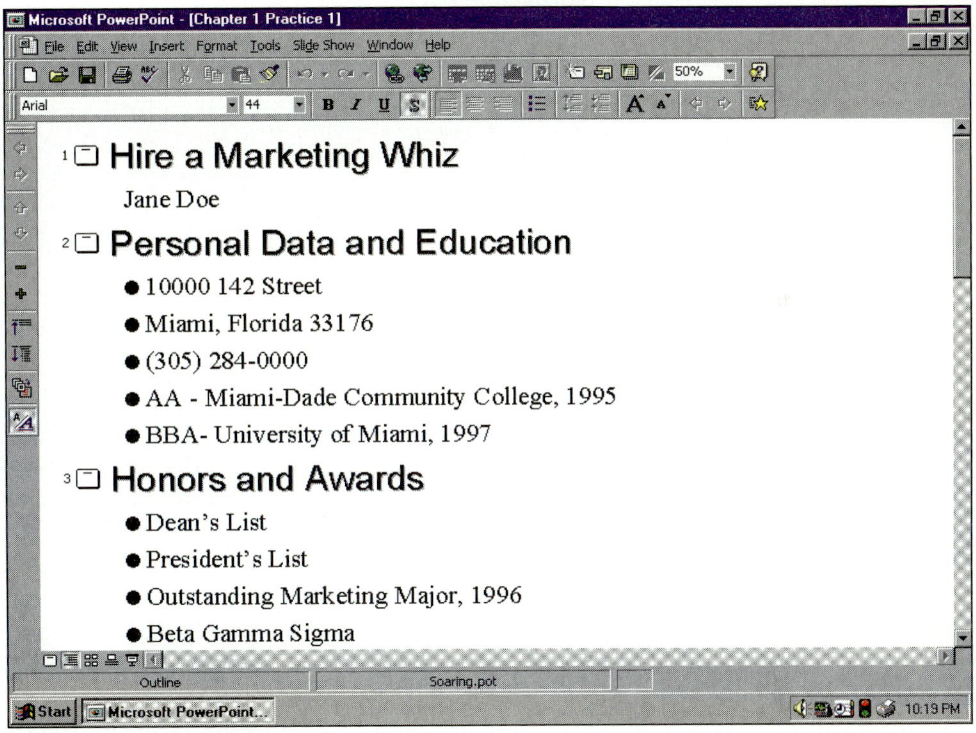


**FIGURE 1.11** Screen for Practice Exercise 1

**2.** Ready-made presentations: The most difficult part of a presentation is getting started. PowerPoint anticipates the problem and provides general outlines on a variety of topics as shown in Figure 1.12.

a. Pull down the File menu, click New, click the Presentations tab (if necessary), then click the Details button so that your screen matches Figure 1.12.

b. Select Recommending a Strategy (Standard) as shown in Figure 1.12. Click OK to open the presentation.

c. Change to the Outline view so that you can see the text of the overall presentation, which is general in nature and intended for any type of strategy. Modify the presentation to develop a strategy for doing well in this class.

d. Add your name to the title page.

e. Print the presentation in miniature and submit it to your instructor.

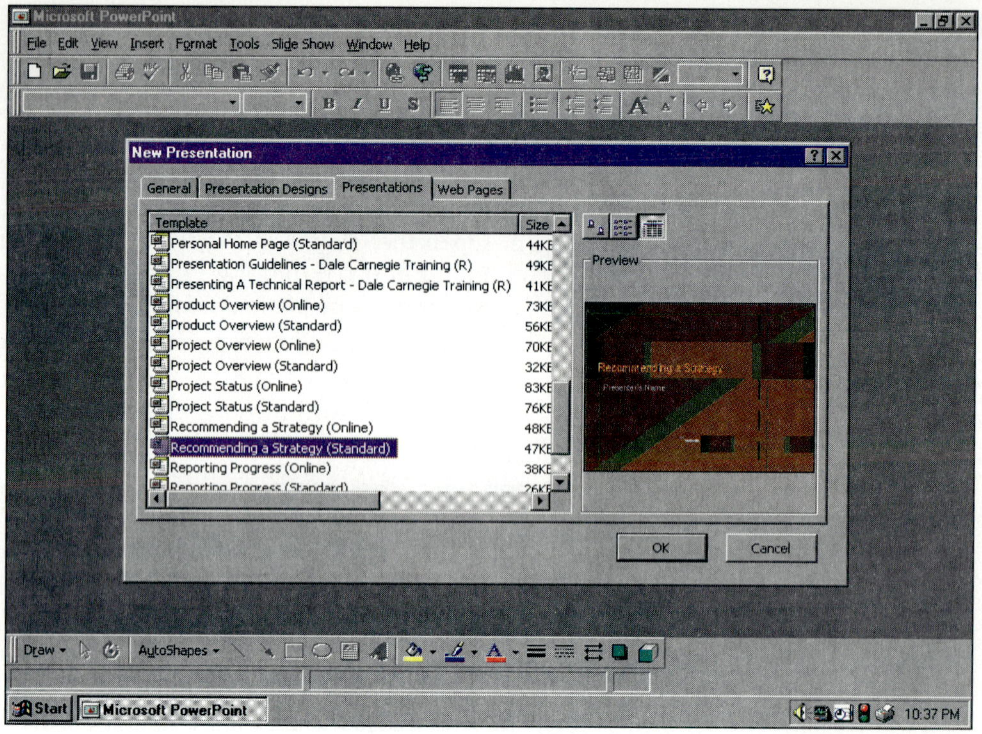


**FIGURE 1.12** Screen for Practice Exercise 2

3. The Send To command enables you to import a presentation into a Word document as shown in Figure 1.13. The command combines audience handouts with speaker notes to display several slides on one page with notes for each. It also gives you the option to link the slides to the Word document, so that if a slide changes, the Word document is updated automatically. (The document is not, however, updated to reflect the insertion or deletion of slides.)
   a. Do Hands-on Exercises 1 and 2 as described in the hands-on exercises in the chapter, then retrieve the Finished Introduction presentation as the basis of this problem.
   b. Click the Black and White view button on the Standard toolbar. Pull down the File menu, click the Send To command, then click Microsoft Word.
   c. Click the option button for the type of document you want (e.g., Notes Next to Slide so that you will create Figure 1.13 at the end of this exercise).
   d. Click the option button to Paste Link the slides to a Word document, then click OK. PowerPoint will create a document similar to the one in Figure 1.13. Be patient, for this step takes time, especially on a non-Pentium machine.
   e. Change to the Page Layout view in Word and zoom to Two Pages. Click in the cell next to each slide (the Word document is a table) and enter an appropriate comment.
   f. Save and print the document just as you would any other document in Microsoft Word.
   g. Submit the finished document to your instructor as proof that you did this exercise.

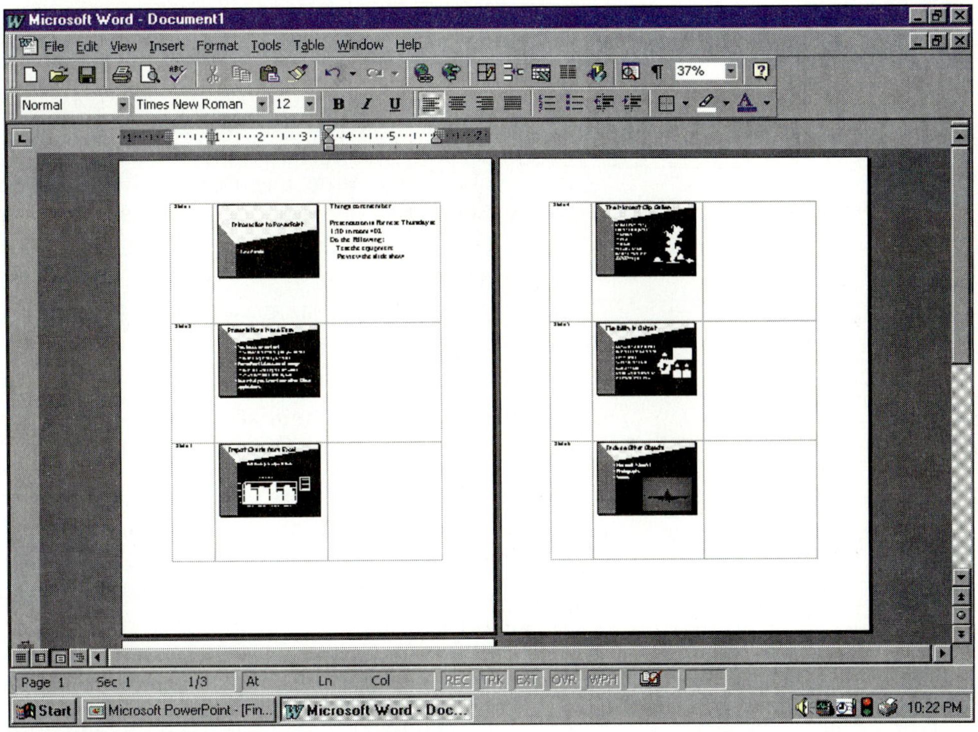


FIGURE 1.13 Screen for Practice Exercise 3

4. A partially completed version of the presentation in Figure 1.14 can be found in the file *Chapter 1 Practice 4.* Open the presentation, then make the following changes:

   a. Add your name and e-mail address on the title page.

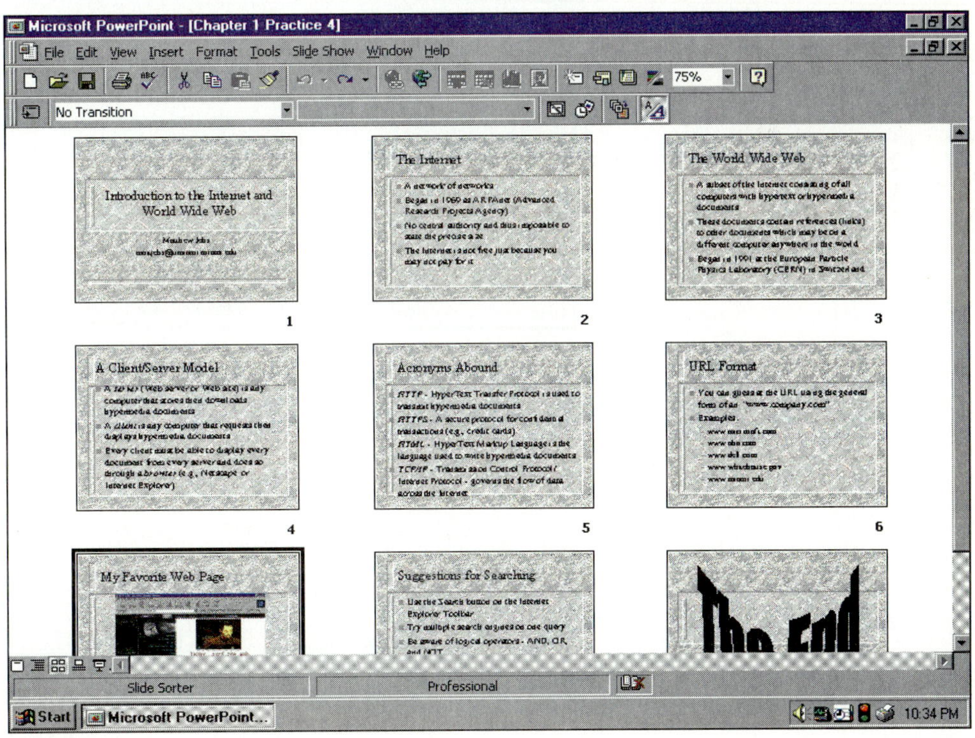


FIGURE 1.14 Screen for Practice Exercise 4

b. Boldface and italicize the terms, *server, client,* and *browser* on slide 4. Boldface and italicize the acronyms, *HTTP, HTTPS, HTML,* and *TCP/IP* on slide 5.

c. Use Internet Explorer to go to your favorite Web page. Press the Print Screen key to capture the screen image of that page and copy it to the clipboard, then use the Windows 95 taskbar to switch to PowerPoint. Select the seventh slide, then click the Paste button on the Standard toolbar to paste the screen into the PowerPoint presentation. Size the image as appropriate.

d. Double click the WordArt image on the last slide to open the WordArt application. Change the words *Thank You* to *The End.* Change the style of the WordArt in any other way you see fit.

e. Print the slide miniatures six per page and submit them to your instructor as proof you did this exercise.

**5.** This problem is more difficult than the previous exercises as it asks you to create a presentation similar to the one in Figure 1.15. We have started the presentation for you in and have created the file *Chapter 1 Practice 5.* This presentation consists of three slides—a title slide and two slides containing an object and text.

a. Go to the White House Web site (www.whitehouse.gov). Click the link to White House History & Tours, then click the link to the Presidents of the USA and select your favorite president(s). Point to the picture of the president, click the right mouse button to display a shortcut menu, then save the picture on your PC.

b. Use the Windows 95 taskbar to switch to PowerPoint, then double click the placeholder on slide two to add an object. Indicate that you are inserting the object from a file, click the Browse button, then select the file containing the president's picture.

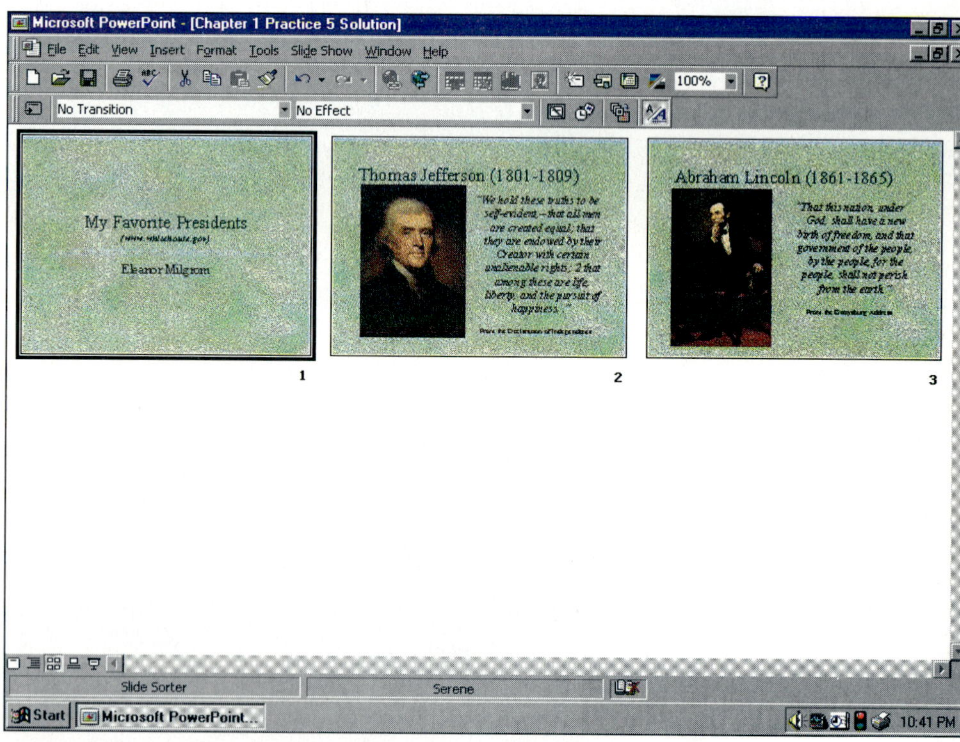


FIGURE 1.15 Screen for Practice Exercise 5

c. Return to the White House Web site, and click the link to a familiar quotation from your president, then copy that quotation to the appropriate slide in your presentation.

d. Create an appropriate title for this slide consisting of the president's name and years in office. Be sure to cite the source of the picture on this slide.

e. Repeat these steps for a second president.

f. Create a title slide for the presentation with your name somewhere on the slide. Print all three slides and submit them to your instructor as proof you did this exercise.

6. This exercise builds on the previous problem as it has you download pictures from the Internet for use in a presentation. Search the Web to select three landmarks, download the picture of each, then create a short presentation consisting of a title slide plus three additional slides similar to the one in Figure 1.16. This chapter did not tell you how to create a new presentation, but it's very straightforward as described below.

   a. Start PowerPoint. If necessary, select the option button to create a blank presentation, then click OK to display the New Slide dialog box.

   b. Choose the Title layout for your first slide. Enter the title of the presentation, *Landmarks Around the World,* and your name.

   c. Click the new slide button to add a slide containing text and an object, then follow the instructions from the previous exercise.

   d. Be sure to include an appropriate reference to the Web page where you obtained each picture.

   e. Print the completed presentation for your instructor as proof you did this exercise.

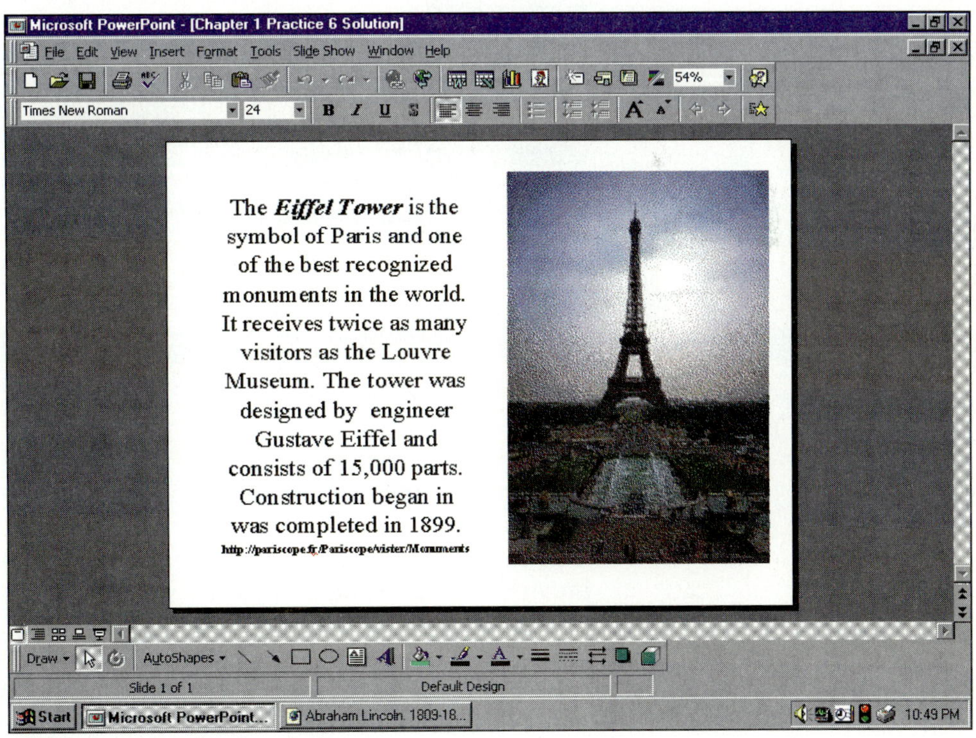


**FIGURE 1.16** Screen for Practice Exercise 6

7. The subject of a PowerPoint presentation is limited only by your imagination. Use any Internet search engine to locate information about your favorite singer or recording group, then download information about that person or group to create a presentation of four to six slides. Follow the instructions in the previous problems with respect to creating a new presentation and incorporating a picture from the Web. (Be sure to include the reference to the appropriate Web page.)

   Figure 1.17 displays one of the slides in our presentation about LeAnn Rimes. Print your presentation in miniature (six slides per page) and submit it to your instructor as proof you did this exercise.

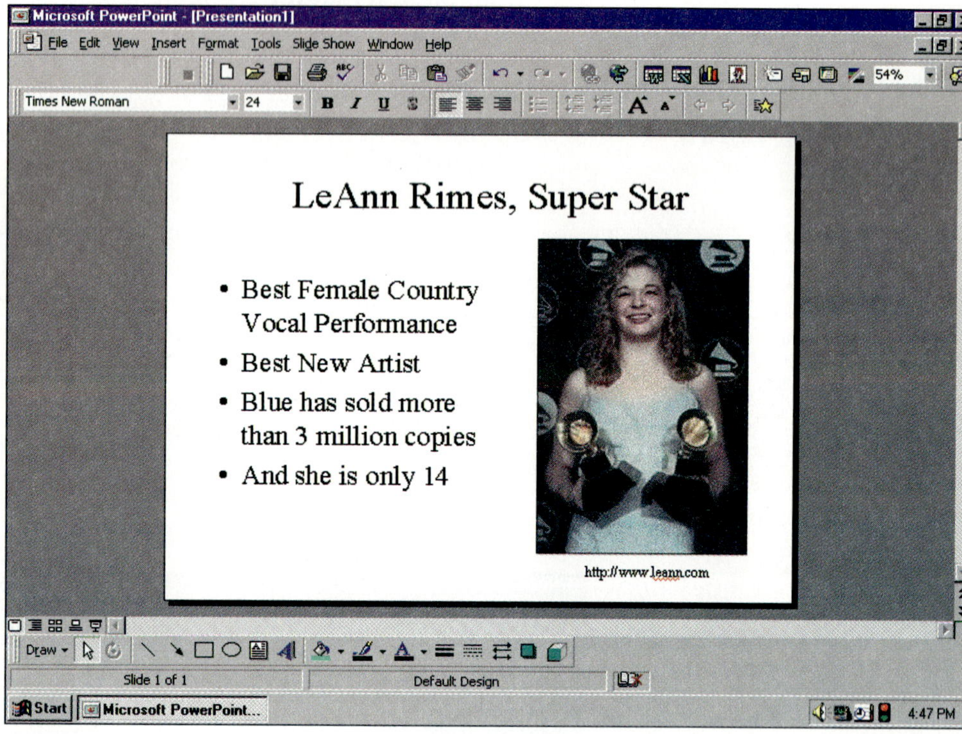


**FIGURE 1.17** Screen for Practice Exercise 7

# CASE STUDIES

## Planning for Disaster

This case has nothing to do with presentations per se, but it is perhaps the most important case of all, as it deals with the question of backup. Do you have a backup strategy? Do you even know what a backup strategy is? This is a good time to learn, because sooner or later you will need to recover a file. The problem always seems to occur the night before an assignment is due. You accidentally erased a file, are unable to read from a floppy disk, or worse yet, suffer a hardware failure in which you are unable to access the hard drive. The ultimate disaster is the disappearance of your computer, by theft or natural disaster (e.g.,

Hurricane Andrew, the floods in the Midwest, or the Los Angeles earthquake). Describe in 250 or fewer words the backup strategy you plan to implement in conjunction with your work in this class.

## Slides To Go

You have created the perfect presentation and are scheduled to deliver it next week. The presentation looks great on your PC, but you have to deliver the presentation without the aid of a computer. How do you create 35-mm slides or overhead transparencies as an alternative to the slide show? It's much easier than you think as PowerPoint provides access to the Genigraphics Corporation through the Send command on the File menu. Use the Genigraphics Wizard to determine what can be done, then call the company (an 800 number is provided) to determine the exact costs for a 20-slide presentation. Summarize your findings in a one-page report to your instructor.

## Clip Art

Clip art—you see it all the time, but where do you get it, and how much does it cost? A limited number of images are installed automatically with PowerPoint, but you will quickly grow tired of this selection. Additional clip art is available on the ValuPack, and we recommend that you install this clip art to your hard drive (assuming you have the space). Scan the computer magazines and find at least two sources for additional clip art. Return to class with specific information on price and the nature of the clip art. You might also research the availability of photographs, as opposed to clip art.

## Microsoft Online

Exploring WWW

Help for Microsoft PowerPoint is available from a variety of sources. You can consult the Office Assistant or you can pull down the Help menu to display the Help Contents and Index. Both techniques were illustrated in the chapter. In addition, you can go to the Microsoft Web site to obtain more recent, and often more detailed, information. You will find answers to the most frequently asked questions and you can access the same Knowledge Base used by Microsoft support engineers. Experiment with various sources of help, then submit a summary of your findings to your instructor. Try to differentiate between the various techniques and suggest the most appropriate use for each.

## The ValuPack and PowerPoint Central

The CD version of Microsoft Office contains a ValuPack folder that contains additional resources for PowerPoint. You will find extra clip art, videos, sound clips, graphic effects, templates, and tips for creating a presentation. You can access the ValuPack folder through the PowerPoint Central command on the Tools menu which opens a presentation describing these resources. Go through the presentation, then write a short summary for your instructor describing what is available.

# 2

# CREATING A PRESENTATION: CONTENT, FORMATTING, AND ANIMATION

## OBJECTIVES

**After reading this chapter you will be able to:**

1. Use the Outline view to create and edit a presentation; display and hide text within the Outline view.
2. Check the spelling in a presentation.
3. Apply a design template to a presentation.
4. Add transition effects to the slides in a presentation; apply animation effects to the bullets and graphical objects in a specific slide.
5. Modify the template of an existing presentation by changing its color scheme and/or background shading.
6. Explain the role of masters in formatting a presentation; modify the slide master to include a company name.
7. Explain how the AutoContent Wizard facilitates the creation of a presentation.

## OVERVIEW

There are in essence two independent steps to creating a PowerPoint presentation. You must develop the content, and you must format the presentation. PowerPoint lets you do the steps in either order, but we suggest you start with the content. Both steps are iterative in nature, and you are likely to go back and forth many times before you are finished.

We begin the chapter by showing you how to enter the text of a presentation in the Outline view. We show you how to move and copy text within a slide (or from one slide to another) and how to rearrange the order of the slides within the presentation. We describe how the AutoContent Wizard facilitates the creation of a presentation. We also illustrate the use of the Spell Check and AutoCorrect features that are common to all Office applications.

The chapter also shows you how to format a presentation using one of many professionally designed templates that are supplied with PowerPoint. The templates control every aspect of a presentation, from the formatting of the text to the color scheme of the slides. We describe how to change the template and/or how to vary a color scheme. We show you how to add transition and animation effects to individual slides to enhance a presentation as it is given on a computer. The chapter also shows you how to fine-tune a presentation by changing the slide master to include a corporate logo (or other text) on every slide.

### CRYSTALLIZE YOUR MESSAGE

Every presentation exists to deliver a message, whether it's to sell a product, present an idea, or provide instruction. Decide on the message you want to deliver, then write the text for the presentation. Edit the text to be sure it is consistent with your objective. Then, and only then, should you think about formatting, but always keep the message foremost in your mind.

## CREATING A PRESENTATION

The text of a presentation can be developed in the Slide view or the Outline view or a combination of the two. You can begin in the Outline view, switch to the Slide view to see how a particular slide will look, return to the Outline view to enter the text for additional slides, and so on. We prefer the Outline view because it displays the text for many slides at once. It also enables you to change the order of slides and to move and copy text from one slide to another.

### The Outline View

Figure 2.1 displays the outline of the presentation we will develop in this chapter. The outline shows the title of each slide, followed by the text on that slide. (Graphic elements such as clip art and charts are not visible in the Outline.) Each slide is numbered, and the numbers adjust automatically for the insertion or deletion of slides as you edit the presentation.

A ***slide icon*** appears between the number and title of the slide. The icon is subtly different, depending on the slide layout. In Figure 2.1, for example, the same icon appears next to slides 1 through 6 and indicates the slides contain only text. A different icon appears next to slide 7 and indicates the presence of a graphic element, such as clip art.

Each slide begins with a title, followed by bulleted items, which are indented one to five levels corresponding to the importance of the item. The main points appear on level one. Subsidiary items are indented below the main point to which they apply. Any item can be ***promoted*** to a higher level or ***demoted*** to a lower level, either before or after the text is entered.

Consider, for example, slide 4 in Figure 2.1a. The title of the slide, *Develop the Content*, appears immediately after the slide number and icon. The first bullet, *Use the Outline view,* is indented one level under the title, and it in turn has two subsidiary bullets. The next main bullet, *Review the flow of ideas,* is moved back to level one, and it, too, has two subsidiary bullets.

The outline is (to us) the ideal way to create and edit the presentation. The ***insertion point*** marks the place where new text is entered; this is established by

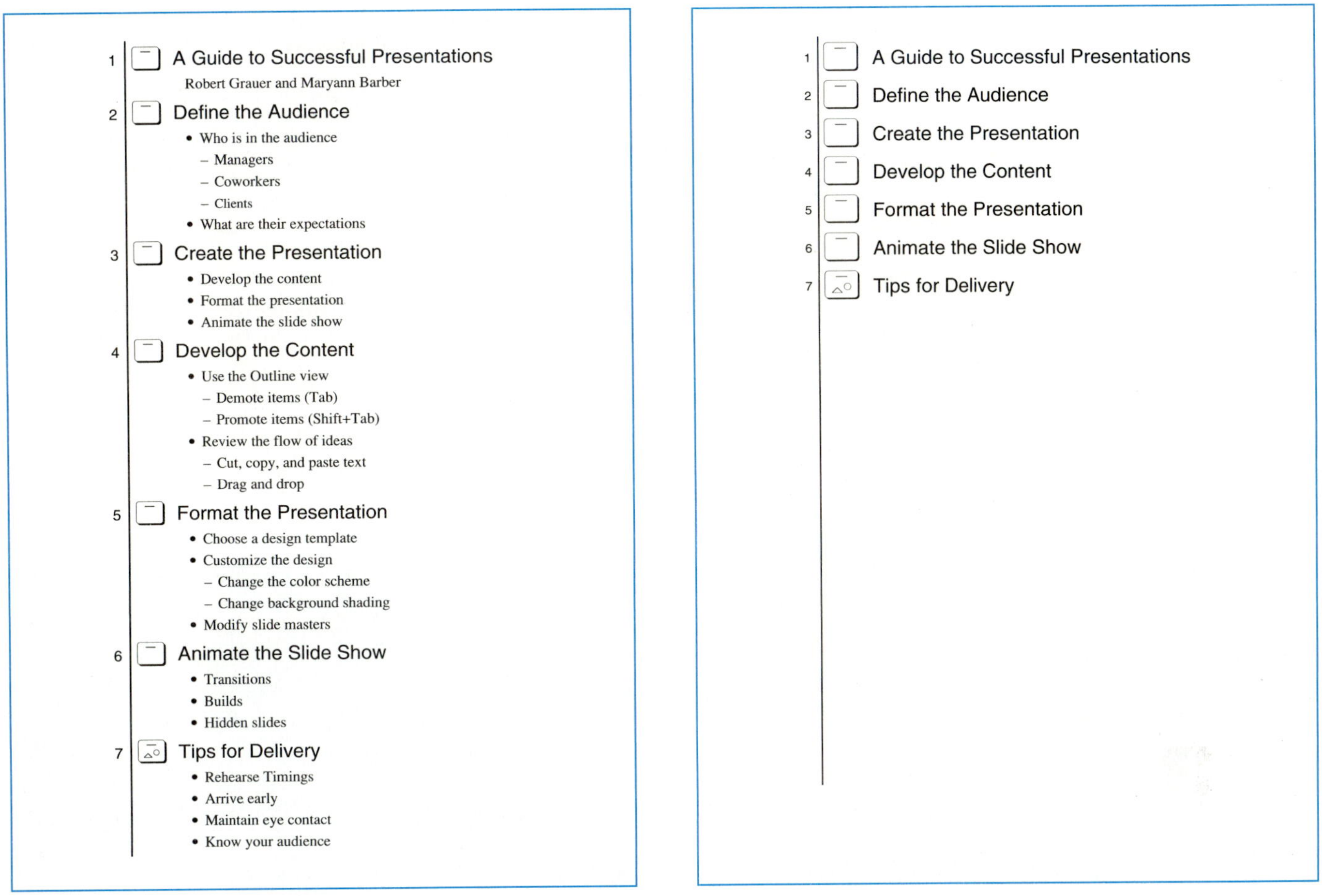


(a) The Expanded Outline

(b) The Collapsed Outline

**FIGURE 2.1** The Outline View

clicking anywhere in the outline. (The insertion point is automatically placed at the title of the first slide in a new presentation.) To enter text, click in the outline to establish the insertion point, then start typing. Press enter after typing the title of a slide or after entering the text of a bulleted item, which starts a new slide or bullet, respectively. The new item may then be promoted (by pressing **Shift+Tab**) or demoted (by pressing **Tab**) as necessary.

Editing is accomplished through the same techniques used in other Windows applications. For example, you can use the Cut, Copy, and Paste commands in the Edit menu (or the corresponding buttons on the Standard toolbar) to move and copy selected text, or you can simply drag and drop text from one place to another.

Figure 2.1b displays a collapsed view of the outline, which displays only the title of each slide. The advantage to this view is that you can see more slides on the screen at the same time, making it easier to move slides within the presentation. The slides are expanded or collapsed by using the appropriate tool on the Outline toolbar as described in a hands-on exercise. (The ***Outline toolbar*** appears automatically when you switch to the Outline view. As with the Standard and Formatting toolbars in Chapter 1, a ScreenTip will appear when you point to a button to describe its function.)

Text is formatted by using the select-then-do approach common to Word and Excel; that is, you select the text, then you execute the appropriate command or click the appropriate button. The selected text remains highlighted and is affected by all subsequent commands until you click elsewhere in the outline.

# TEMPLATES

PowerPoint enables you to concentrate on the content of a presentation without concern for its appearance. You focus on what you are going to say, and trust in PowerPoint to format the presentation attractively. The formatting is implemented automatically by selecting one of the many templates that are supplied with PowerPoint.

A ***template*** is a design specification that controls every element in a presentation. It specifies the color scheme for the slides and the arrangement of the different elements (placeholders) on each slide. It determines the formatting of the text, the fonts that are used, and the size and placement of the bulleted text.

Figure 2.2 displays the title slide of a presentation in four different templates. Just choose the template you like, and PowerPoint formats the entire presentation according to that template. And don't be afraid to change your mind. You can use the Format menu at any time to select a different template and change the look of your presentation.

FIGURE 2.2 Templates

# HANDS-ON EXERCISE 1

## *Creating a Presentation*

**Objective:** To create a presentation by entering text in the Outline view; to check a presentation for spelling errors; and to apply a design template to a presentation. Use Figure 2.3 as a guide in the exercise.

### STEP 1: Create a New Presentation

- Start PowerPoint. Close the Office Assistant if it appears. (You can reopen the Assistant at any time by clicking its button on the Standard toolbar.)
- Click the **option button** to create a new presentation using a **Blank Presentation**. Click **OK**.
- You should see the **New Slide** dialog box in Figure 2.3a with the AutoLayout for the title slide already selected. Click **OK** to create a title slide and simultaneously close the New Slide dialog box.
- If necessary, click the **Maximize buttons** in both the application and document windows so that PowerPoint takes the entire desktop and the current presentation is as large as possible. Both Maximize buttons will be replaced with Restore buttons as shown in Figure 2.3a.

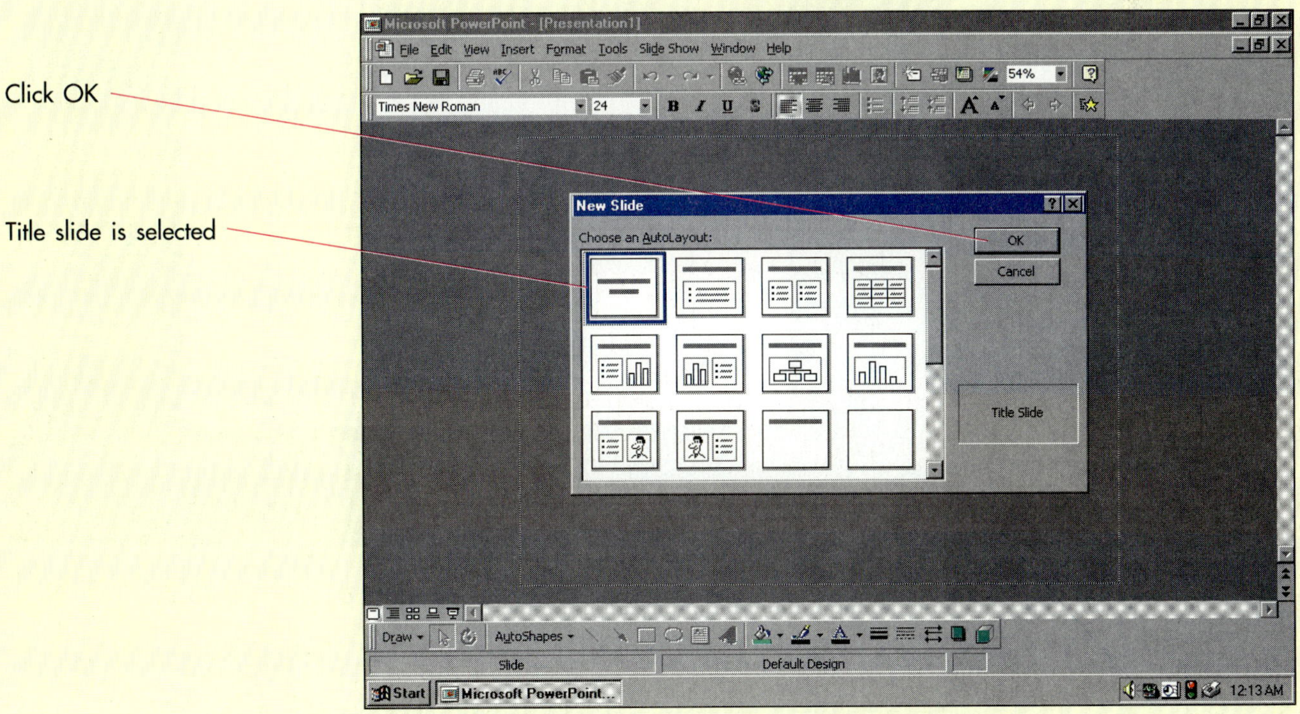


(a) Start PowerPoint (step 1)

**FIGURE 2.3** Hands-on Exercise 1

## CONTENT, CONTENT, AND CONTENT

It is much more important to focus on the content of the presentation than to worry about how it will look. Start with the AutoContent Wizard (described later in the chapter) or with a blank presentation in the Outline view. Save the formatting for last. Otherwise you will spend too much time changing templates and too little time developing the text.

**STEP 2: Create the Title Slide**

- Click anywhere in the box containing **Click to add title**, then type the title, **A Guide to Successful Presentations** as shown in Figure 2.3b. The title will automatically wrap to a second line.
- Click anywhere in the box containing **Click to add sub-title** and enter your name. Click outside the sub-title placeholder when you have entered your name.

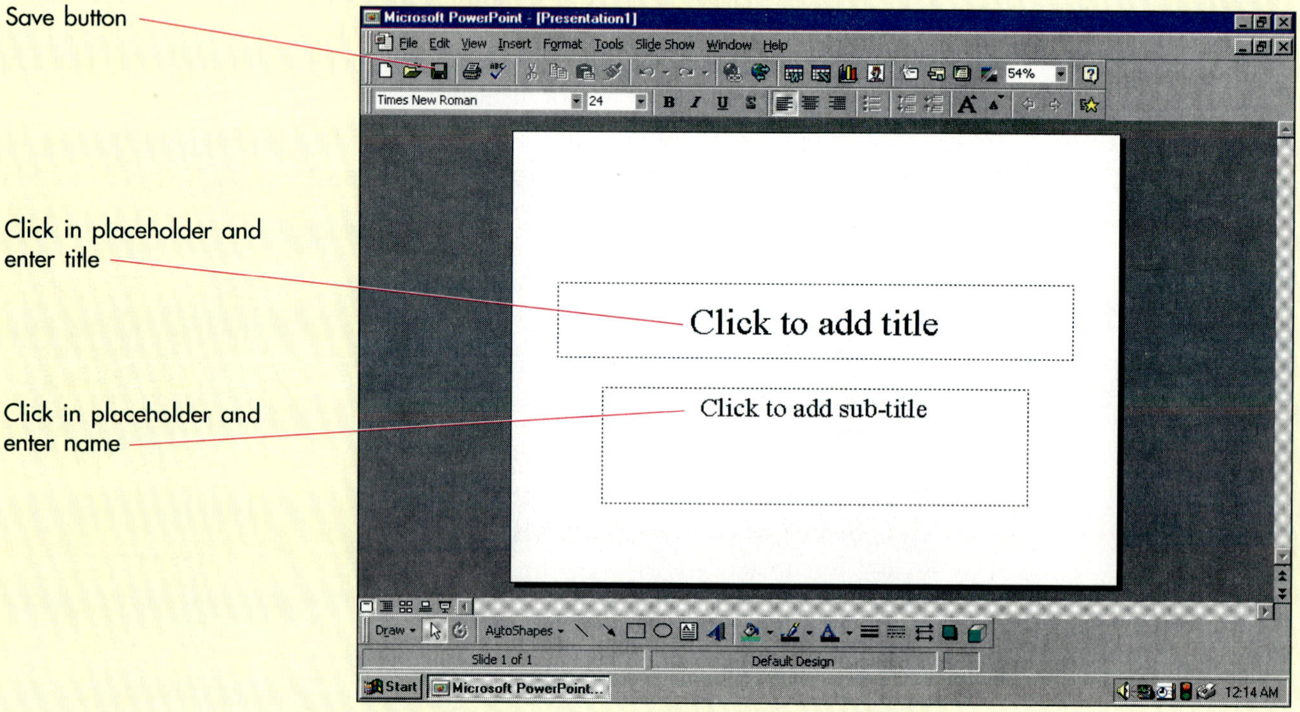


(b) Create the Title Slide (step 2)

**FIGURE 2.3** Hands-on Exercise 1 (continued)

## THE DEFAULT PRESENTATION

PowerPoint supplies a default presentation containing the specifications for color (a plain white background with black text), formatting, and AutoLayouts. The default presentation is selected automatically when you work on a blank presentation, and it remains in effect until you choose a different template.

**STEP 3: Save the Presentation**

- Pull down the **File menu** and click **Save** (or click the **Save button** on the Standard toolbar). You should see the Save dialog box in Figure 2.3c. If necessary, click the **Details button**.
- To save the file:
  - Click the **drop-down arrow** on the Save In list box.
  - Click the appropriate drive, drive C or drive A, depending on whether or not you installed the data disk on your hard drive.
  - Double click the **Exploring PowerPoint folder,** to make it the active folder (the folder in which you will save the document).
  - Enter **My First Presentation** as the name of the presentation.
  - Click **Save** or press the **enter key.** Click **Cancel** or press the **Esc key** if you see the Properties dialog box. The title bar changes to reflect the name of the presentation.

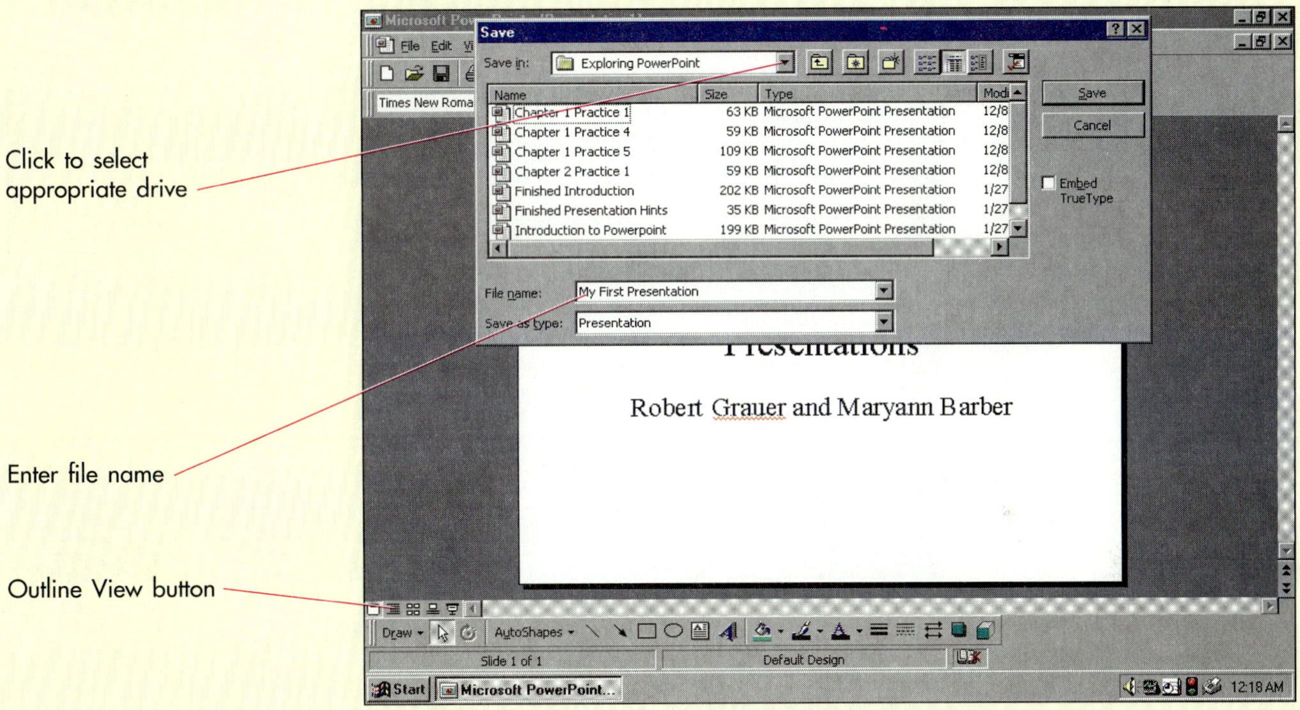


(c) The Save Command (step 3)

FIGURE 2.3 Hands-on Exercise 1 (continued)

**STEP 4: Create the Presentation**

- Click the **Outline view button** above the status bar to change to the Outline view. Your presentation at this point contains only the title slide.
- Pull down the **View menu** and (if necessary) toggle **Slide miniature** on.
- Click the **New Slide button** on the **Standard toolbar**. Select the **Bulleted List** AutoLayout. Click OK. The icon for slide 2 will appear in the outline. Type **Define the Audience** as the title of the slide and press **enter.**
- Press the **Tab key** (or click the **Demote button** on the Outline toolbar) to enter the first bullet. Type **Who is in the audience** and press **enter.**

➤ Press the **Tab key** (or click the **Demote button** on the Outline toolbar) to enter the second-level bullets.

- Type **Managers.** Press **enter.**
- Type **Coworkers.** Press **enter.**
- Type **Clients.** Press **enter.**

➤ Press **Shift+Tab** (or click the **Promote button** on the Outline toolbar) to return to the first-level bullets.

- Type **What are their expectations.** Press **enter.**

➤ Press **Shift+Tab** to enter the title of the third slide. Type **Tips for Delivery.** Add the remaining text for this slide and for slide 4 as shown in Figure 2.3d.

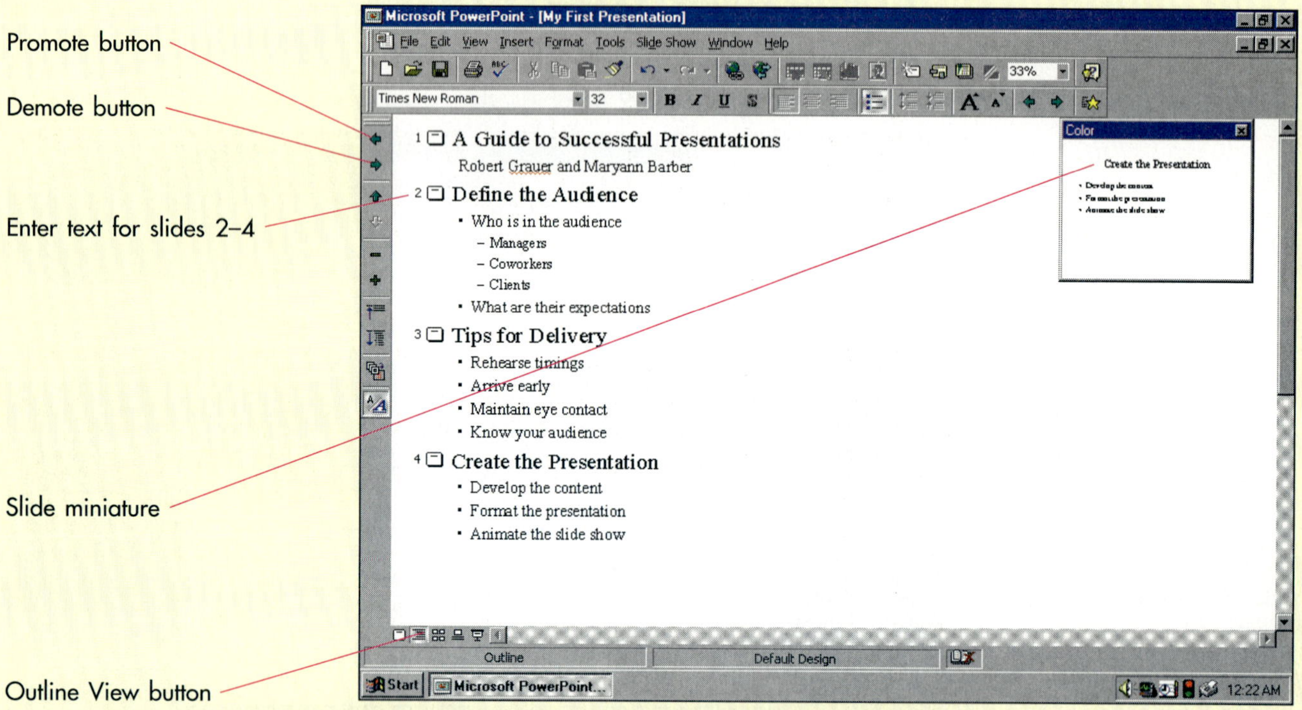


(d) Create the Presentation (step 4)

FIGURE 2.3 Hands-on Exercise 1 (continued)

## JUST KEEP TYPING

The easiest way to enter the text for a presentation is in the Outline view. Just type an item, then press enter to move to the next item. You will be automatically positioned at the next item on the same level, where you can type the next entry. Continue to enter text in this manner. Press the Tab key as necessary to demote an item (move it to the next lower level). Press Shift+Tab to promote an item (move it to the next higher level).

### STEP 5: The Spell Check

- Enter the title of the fifth slide as **Develop teh Content** (deliberately misspelling the word “the”). Try to look at the monitor as you type to see the AutoCorrect feature (common to all Office applications) in action. PowerPoint will correct the misspelling and change *teh* to *the.*
- If you did not see the correction being made, click the arrow next to the Undo button on the Standard toolbar and undo the last several actions. Click the arrow next to the Redo button and redo the corrections in order to see the error and subsequent auto correction.
- Enter the text of the remaining slides as shown in Figure 2.3e. Do *not* press enter after entering the last bullet on the last slide or else you will add a blank bullet.
- Click the **Spelling button** on the Standard toolbar to check the presentation for spelling:
  - The result of the Spell Check will depend on how accurately you entered the text of the presentation. We deliberately misspelled the word “Transitions” in the last slide.
  - Continue to check the document for spelling errors. Click **OK** when PowerPoint indicates it has checked the entire presentation.
- Click the **Save button** on the Standard toolbar to save the presentation.

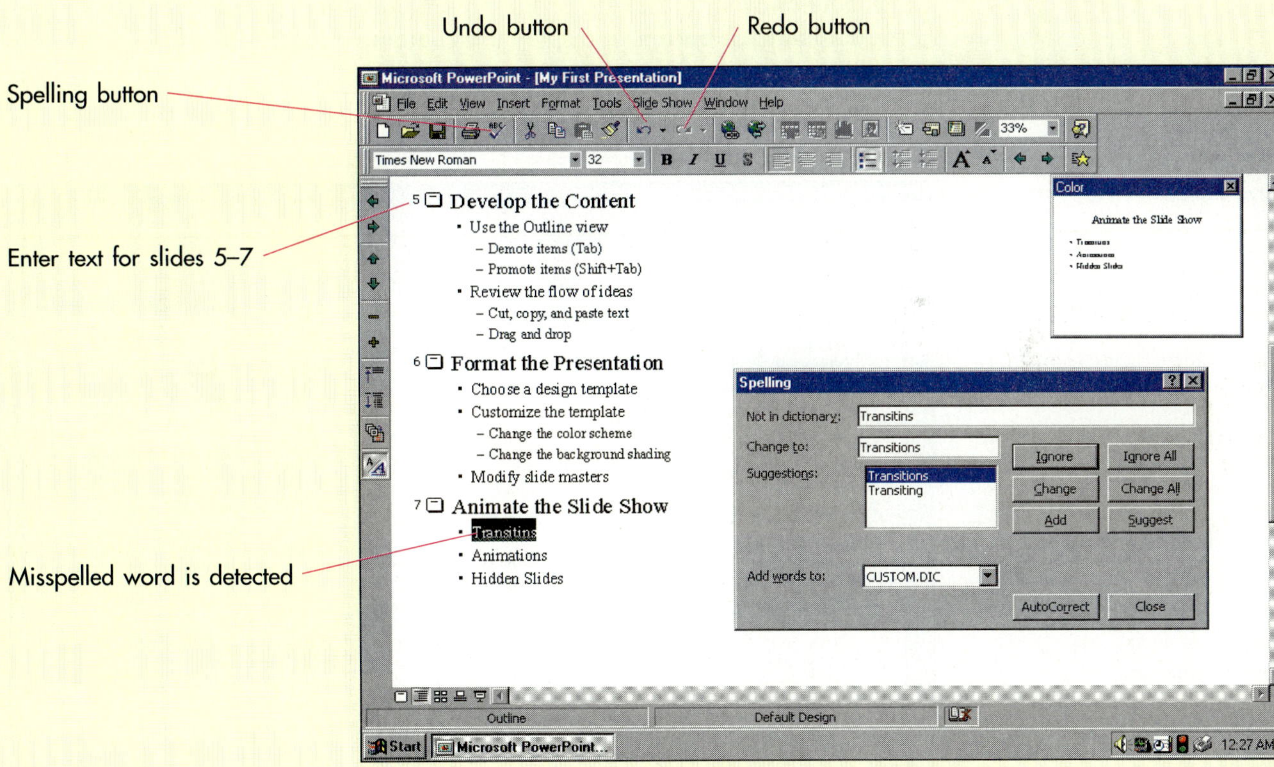


(e) The Spell Check (step 5)

**FIGURE 2.3** Hands-on Exercise 1 (continued)

### CREATE YOUR OWN SHORTHAND

Use the AutoCorrect feature, which is common to all Office applications, to expand abbreviations such as "usa" for United States of America. Pull down the Tools menu, click AutoCorrect, then type the abbreviation in the Replace text box and the expanded entry in the With text box. Click the Add command button, then click OK to exit the dialog box and return to the document. The next time you type usa in a presentation, it will automatically be expanded to United States of America.

**STEP 6: Drag and Drop**

- Press **Ctrl+Home** to move to the beginning of the presentation. Click the **Collapse All button** on the Outline toolbar to collapse the outline as shown in Figure 2.3f.
- Click the **icon** for **slide 3** (Tips for Delivery). The slide is selected and its title is highlighted. Point to the **slide icon** (the mouse pointer changes to a four-headed arrow), then click and drag to move the slide to the end of the presentation. Release the mouse.
- All of the slides have been renumbered. The slide titled Tips for Delivery has been moved to the end of the presentation and appears as slide 7. Click the **Expand All button** to display the contents of each slide. Click anywhere in the presentation to deselect the last slide.
- Click the **Save button** on the Standard toolbar to save the presentation.

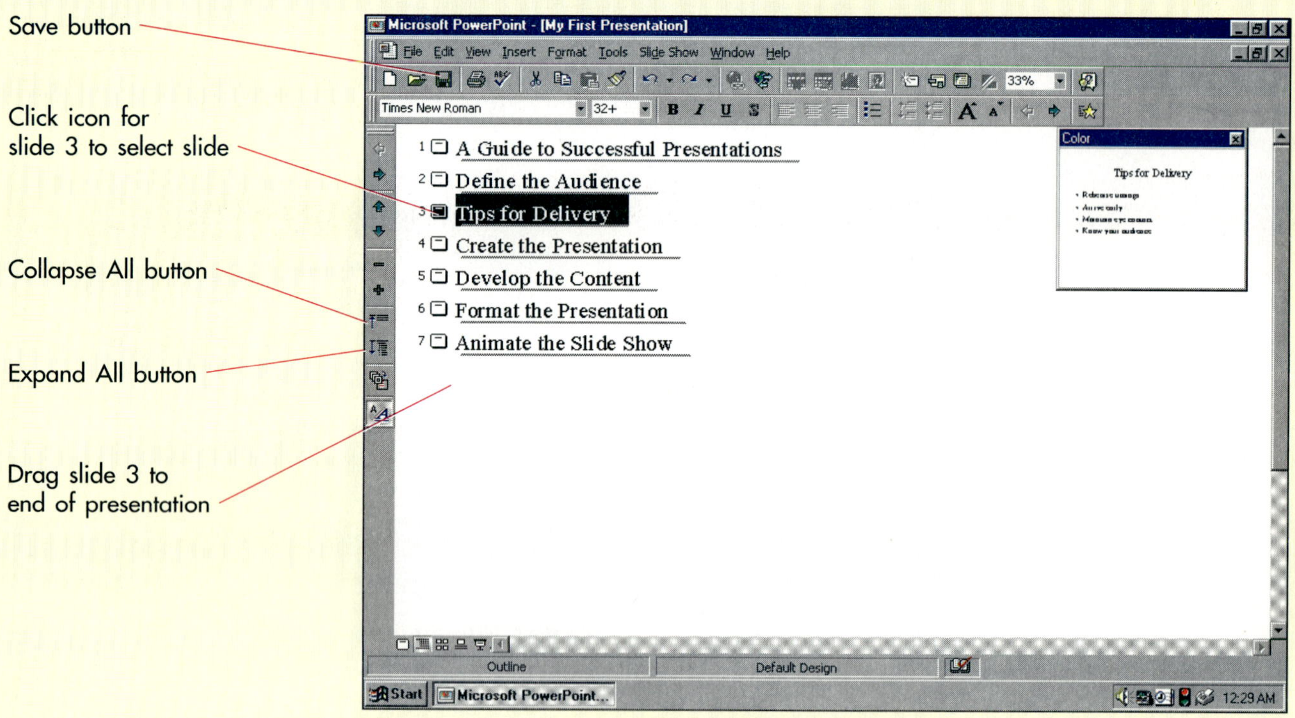


(f) Drag and Drop (step 6)

**FIGURE 2.3** Hands-on Exercise 1 (continued)

## SELECTING SLIDES IN THE OUTLINE VIEW

Click the slide icon or the slide number next to the slide title to select the slide. PowerPoint will select the entire slide (including its title, text, and any other objects that are not visible in the Outline view). Click the first slide, then press and hold the Shift key as you click the ending slide to select a group of sequential slides. Press Ctrl+A to select the entire outline. You can use these techniques to select multiple slides regardless of whether the outline is collapsed or expanded. The selected slides can be copied, moved, or deleted as a unit.

**STEP 7: Choose a Design Template**

➤ Pull down the **Format menu** and click **Apply Design** (or click the **Apply Design button** on the Standard toolbar) to display the dialog box in Figure 2.3g:

- The **Presentation Designs folder** should appear automatically in the List box. If it doesn't, change to this folder, which is contained within the Templates folder within the Microsoft Office Folder, which in turn is in the Programs Folder on drive c.
- **Presentation Templates** should be selected in the Files of Type list box. If it isn't, click the **drop-down arrow** to change to this file type.
- The **Preview view** should be selected. If it isn't, click the **Preview button** so that you can preview the selected template.
- Scroll through the available designs to select (click) the **Fireball template** as shown in Figure 2.3g. Click **Apply** to close the dialog box.

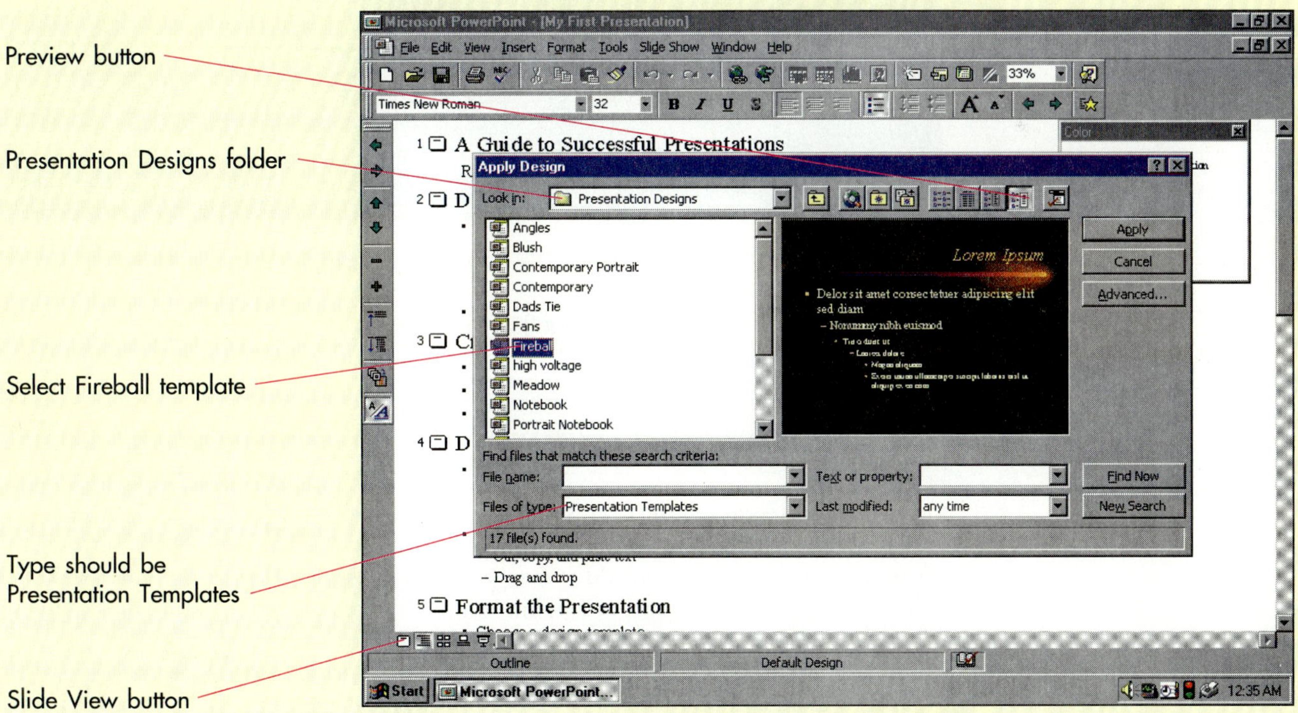


(g) Apply a Design Template (step 7)

**FIGURE 2.3** Hands-on Exercise 1 (continued)

➤ You are still in the Outline view. The slide miniature, if open, will show the selected template. You can also click the **Slide View button** to change to the Slide view to see that the template has been applied. Save the presentation.

**STEP 8: View the Presentation**

➤ Press **Ctrl+Home** to move to the beginning of the presentation. Click the **Slide Show button** on the status bar to view the presentation as shown in Figure 2.3h.

- To move to the next slide: Click the **left mouse button,** type the letter **N,** or press the **PgDn key.**
- To move to the previous slide: Type the letter **P,** or press the **PgUp key.**

➤ Continue to move from one slide to the next until you come to the end of the presentation and are returned to the Slide view.

➤ Exit PowerPoint if you do not want to continue with the next exercise.

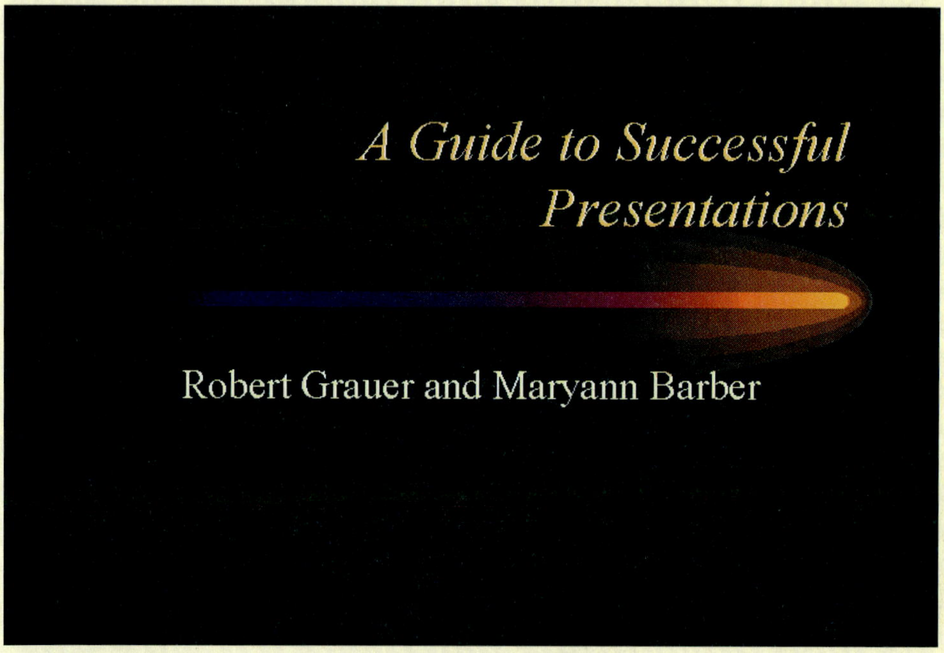


(h) View the Presentation (step 8)

**FIGURE 2.3** Hands-on Exercise 1 (continued)

### TIPS FROM THE OFFICE ASSISTANT

The Office Assistant indicates it has a suggestion by displaying a lightbulb. Click the lightbulb to display the tip, then click the Back or Next buttons as appropriate to view additional tips. The Assistant will not, however, repeat a tip from an earlier session unless you reset it at the start of a new session. This is especially important in a laboratory situation where you are sharing a computer with many students. To reset the tips, click the Assistant to display a balloon asking what you want to do, click the Options button, click the Options tab, then click the button to Reset My Tips.

## CREATING A SLIDE SHOW

You develop the content of a presentation, then you format it attractively using a PowerPoint template. The most important step is yet to come—the delivery of the presentation to an audience, which is best accomplished through a computerized slide show (as opposed to using overhead transparencies or 35-mm slides). The computer becomes the equivalent of a slide projector, and the presentation is called a slide show.

PowerPoint can help you add interest to the slide show in two ways, transitions and animation effects. ***Transitions*** control the way in which one slide moves off the screen and the next slide appears. ***Animation effects*** vary the way in which objects on a slide appear during the presentation.

Transitions are created through the Slide Transition command in the Slide Show menu, which displays the dialog box in Figure 2.4a. The drop-down list box enables you to choose the transition effect. Slides may move on to the screen from the left or right, be uncovered by horizontal or vertical blinds, fade, dissolve, and so on. The dialog box also enables you to set the speed of the transition and/or to preview the effect.

Animation enables the bulleted items to appear one at a time with each successive mouse click. The effect is created through the Custom Animation command in the Slide Show menu, which displays the dialog box of Figure 2.4b. Each bullet can appear with its own transition effect. You can make the bullets appear one word or one letter at a time. You can specify that the bullets appear in reverse order (i.e., the bottom bullet first), and you can dim each bullet as the next one appears. You can even add sound and make the bullets appear in conjunction with a round of applause.

Transitions and animation effects can also be created from the Slide Sorter toolbar as shown in Figure 2.4c. As with the other toolbars, a ScreenTip is displayed when you point to a button on the toolbar.

### ANIMATE THE OTHER OBJECTS

An animation effect can be applied to any object on a slide although it is used most frequently with bulleted text. You can create a special effect by animating another object, such as a piece of clip art or a chart. Point to the object, click the right mouse button to display a shortcut menu, then click the Custom Animations command to display a dialog box in which you choose the desired effect(s).

## AUTOLAYOUTS

Every slide in a presentation is created according to one of 24 predefined slide formats known as AutoLayouts. The AutoLayout determines the objects that will appear on a slide (e.g., text, clip art, a chart, or other object) and specifies the placement for those objects. (Any text entered through the Outline view is automatically formatted according to the Bulleted List AutoLayout.)

What if, however, you want to add a graphic element, such as clip art (or a chart) to a bulleted slide that was created initially from the Outline view? The easiest way to do this is to change to the Slide view, then change the AutoLayout of the slide from a Bulleted List to one containing text and clip art (or text and a chart). This procedure is illustrated in steps 1 and 2 of the next hands-on exercise.

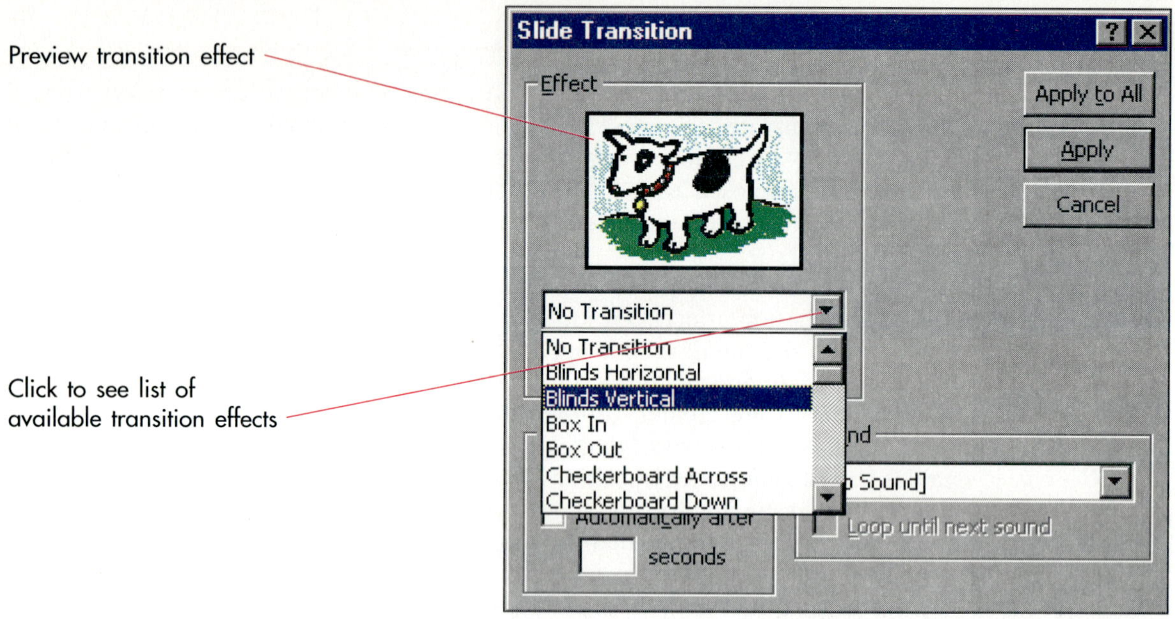


(a) Transitions

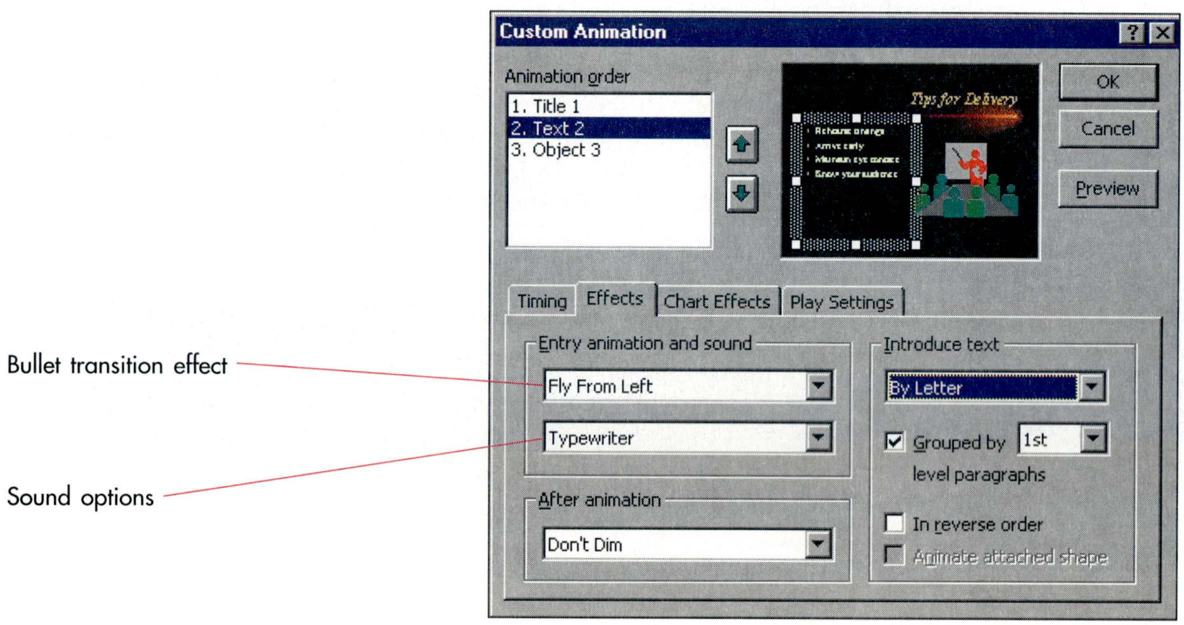


(b) Animation Effects

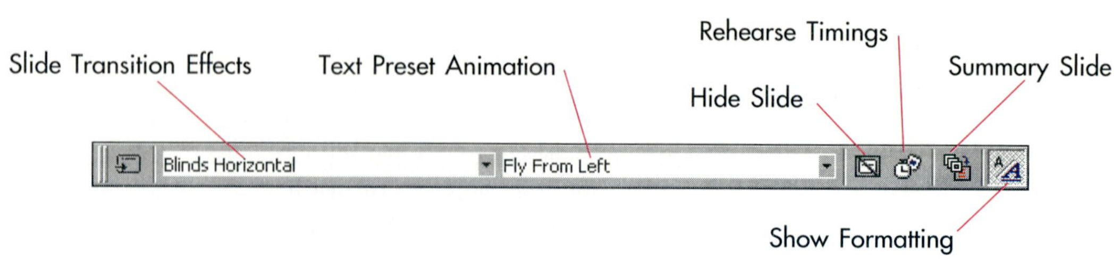


(c) Slide Sorter Toolbar

FIGURE 2.4 Transitions and Animation Effects

# HANDS-ON EXERCISE 2

## *Animating the Presentation*

**Objective:** To change the layout of an existing slide; to establish transition and animation effects. Use Figure 2.5 as a guide in the exercise.

### STEP 1: Change the AutoLayout

- Start PowerPoint and open **My First Presentation** from the previous exercise. If necessary, switch to the **Slide view.** Press **Ctrl+End** to move to the last slide as shown in Figure 2.5a, which is currently a bulleted list.
- Pull down the **Format menu** and click **Slide Layout** (or click the **Slide Layout button** on the Standard toolbar).
- Choose the **Text and Clip Art layout** as shown in Figure 2.5a. Click the **Apply command button** to change the slide layout.

Click Apply

Click Text & Clip Art AutoLayout

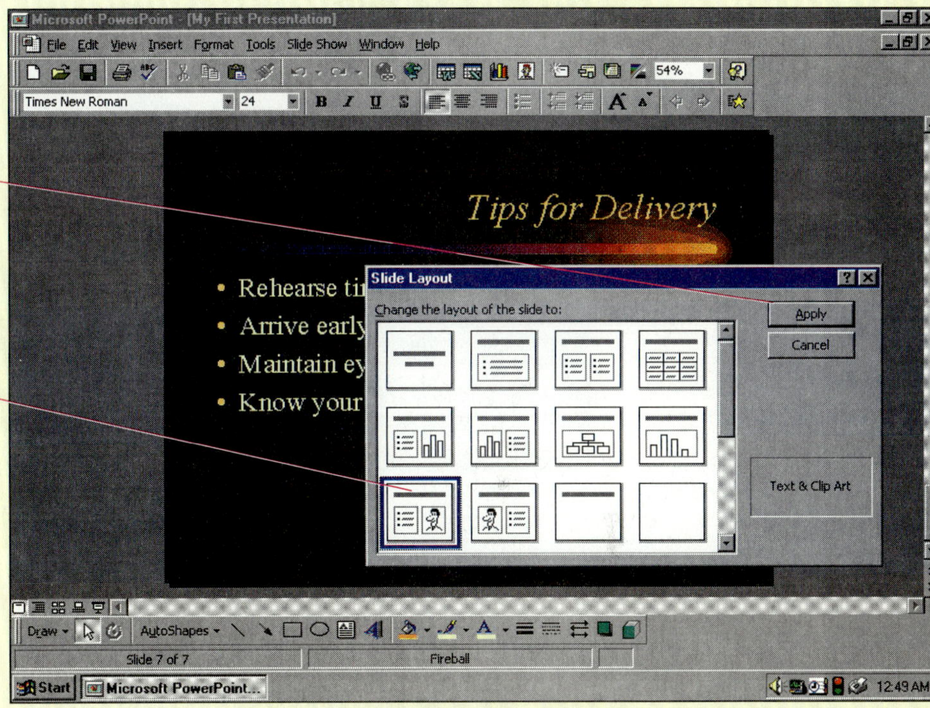


(a) Change the AutoLayout (step 1)

**FIGURE 2.5** Hands-on Exercise 2

> **THE DOCUMENTS SUBMENU**
>
> One of the fastest ways to get to a recently used document, regardless of the application, is through the Windows 95 Start menu, which includes a Documents submenu containing the last 15 documents that were opened. Click the Start button, click (or point to) the Documents submenu, then click the document you wish to open (e.g., My First Presentation) if it appears on the submenu.

**STEP 2: Add the Clip Art**

- Double click the **placeholder** on the slide to add clip art. You will see the Microsoft Clip Gallery dialog box as shown in Figure 2.5b (although you may not see all of the categories listed in the figure).
- Click the **Clip Art tab.** Select the **Academic category**. Click the **down arrow** to scroll through the available images until you can select the image in Figure 2.5b. Click **Insert** to add the clip art to the slide.
- Save the presentation.

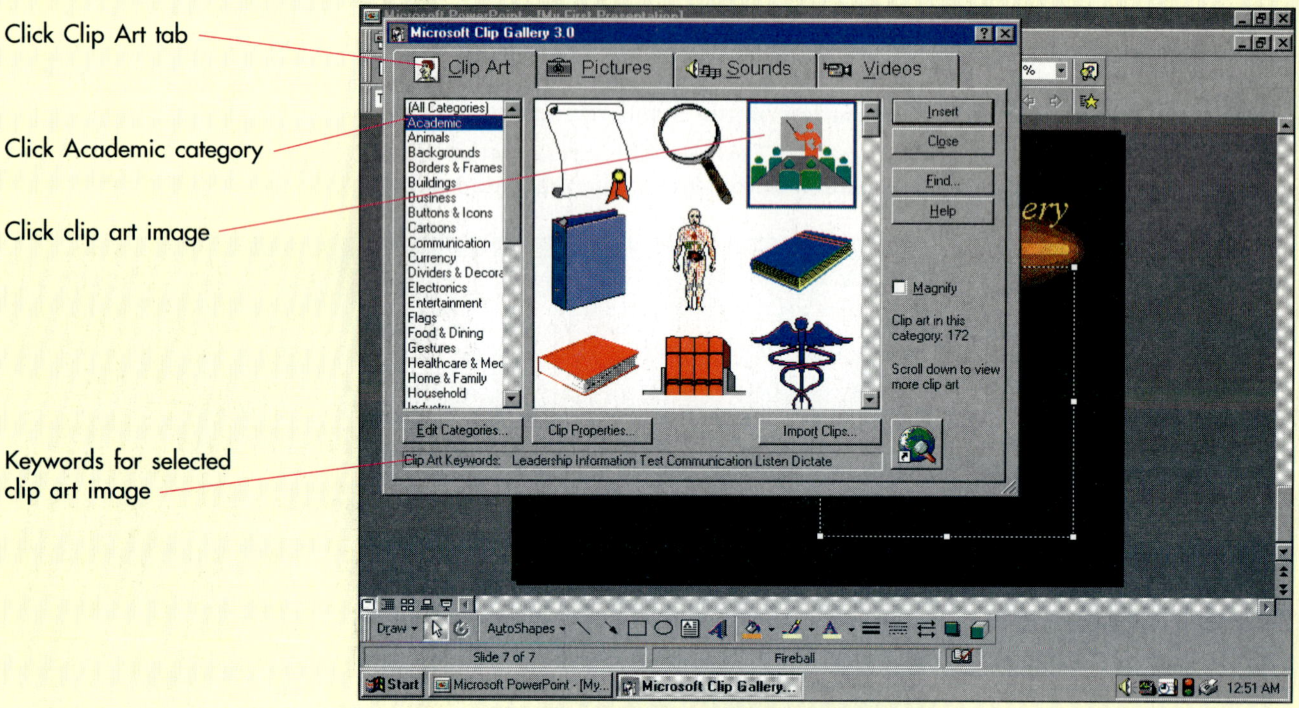


(b) Add the Clip Art (step 2)

**FIGURE 2.5** Hands-on Exercise 2 (continued)

## FIND THE RIGHT CLIP ART

The Find button within the Clip Gallery enables you to search for specific images. Open the Clip Gallery, then click the Find button to display the Find Clip dialog box. Click in the Keyword text box, then enter a key word (e.g., communication) that describes the clip art you want. Click the Find Now button, and the Clip Gallery will search for images that match the description. Be sure to have the Office CD-ROM available, or install the additional clip art to your hard drive.

**STEP 3: Add Transition Effects**

- Click the **Slide Sorter View button** to change to the Slide Sorter view as shown in Figure 2.5c. The number of slides you see at one time depends on the resolution of your monitor and the zoom percentage.
- Press **Ctrl+Home** to select the first slide. Pull down the **Slide Show menu,** then click **Slide Transition** to display the dialog box in Figure 2.5c. Click the **down arrow** on the Effect list box, then click the **Blinds Vertical** effect. You will see the effect displayed on the sample slide (dog) in the effect preview area. If you miss the effect, click the **dog** (or the **key**) to repeat the effect.
- Click **Apply** to accept the transition and close the dialog box. A slide icon appears under slide 1, indicating a transition effect.
- Point to slide 2, click the **right mouse button** to display a shortcut menu, then click the **Slide Transition command.** Choose **Checkerboard Across.** Click the **Slow option button.** Click **Apply** to close the dialog box.

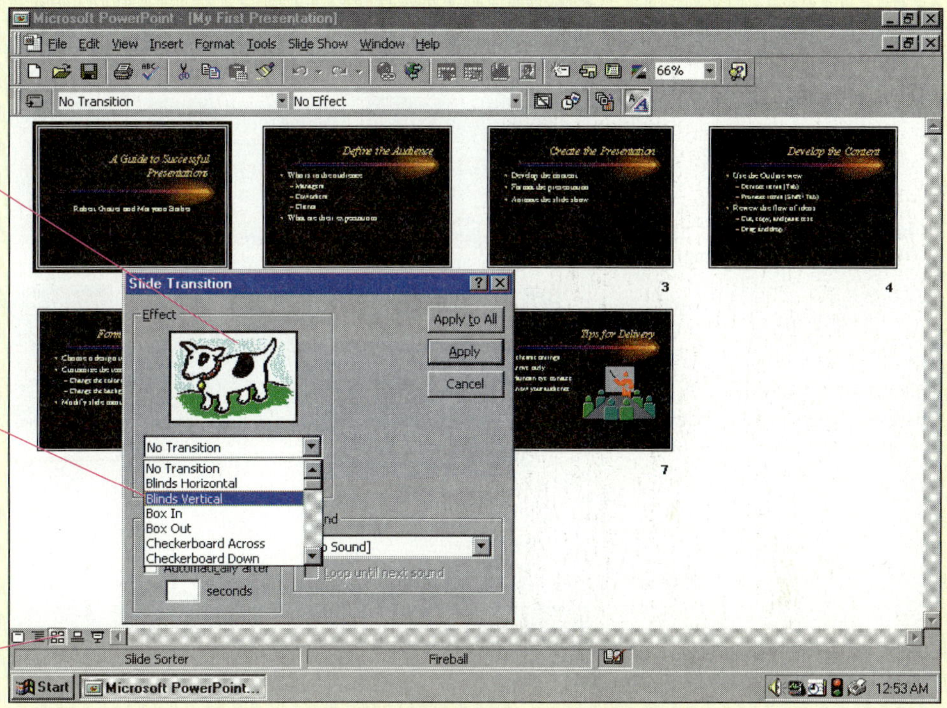


(c) Add Transition Effects (step 3)

**FIGURE 2.5** Hands-on Exercise 2 (continued)

## CHANGE THE MAGNIFICATION

Click the down arrow on the Zoom Control box to change the display magnification, which in turn controls the size of individual slides. The higher the magnification, the easier it is to read the text of an individual slide, but the fewer slides you see at one time. Conversely, changing to a smaller magnification decreases the size of the individual slides, but enables you to see more of the presentation.

**STEP 4: Create a Summary Slide**

- Pull down the **Edit menu** and press **Select All** to select every slide in the presentation. (Alternatively, you can also press and hold the **Shift key** as you click each slide in succession.)
- Click the **Summary Slide button** on the Slide Sorter toolbar to create a summary slide containing a bullet with the title of each selected slide. The new slide appears at the beginning of the presentation as shown in Figure 2.5d.
- Click and drag the **Summary slide** to the end of the presentation. (As you drag the slide, the mouse pointer changes to include the outline of a miniature slide and a vertical line appears to indicate the new position of the slide.)
- Release the mouse. The Summary slide has been moved to the end of the presentation and the slides are renumbered automatically.
- Save the presentation.

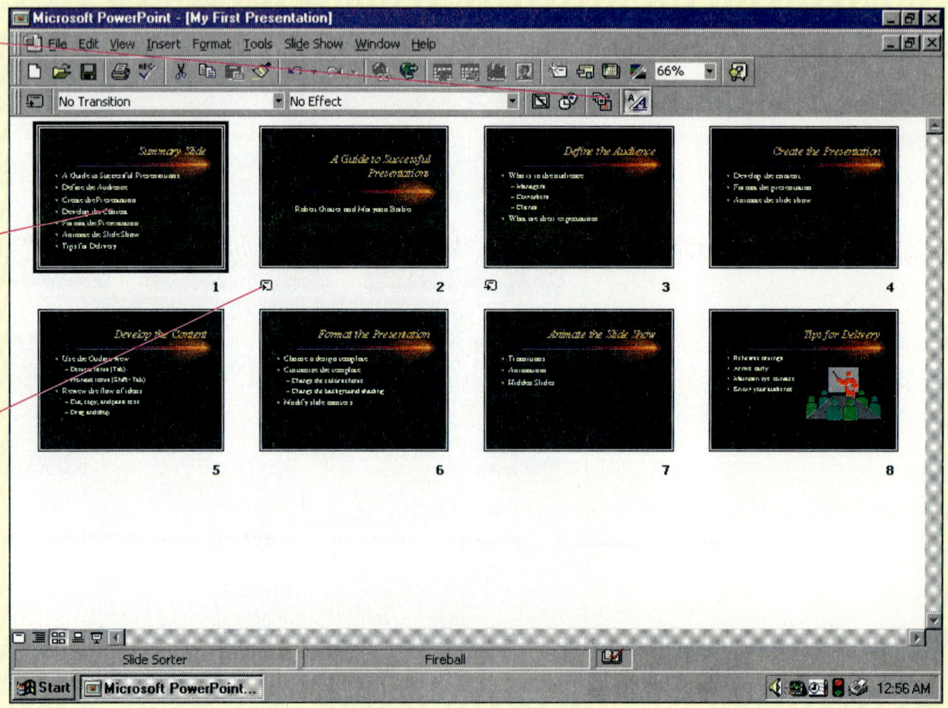


(d) Create a Summary Slide (step 4)

**FIGURE 2.5** Hands-on Exercise 2 (continued)

## SELECTING MULTIPLE SLIDES

You can apply the same transition or animation effect to multiple slides with a single command. Change to the Slide Sorter view, then select the slides by pressing and holding the Shift key as you click the slides. Use the Slide Show menu or the Slide Sorter toolbar to choose the desired transition or animation effect when all the slides have been selected. Click anywhere in the Slide Sorter view to deselect the slides and continue working.

**STEP 5: Create the Animation Effects**

- Double click the Summary slide to select the slide and simultaneously change to the Slide view. Click anywhere within the title to select the title.
- Pull down the **Slide Show menu**, click **Preset Animation** to display a cascade menu, then click **Typewriter** to display the title with this effect during the slide show.
- Click anywhere within the bulleted text to select the bulleted text (and deselect the title). Pull down the **Slide Show menu** and select **Custom Animation** to display the dialog box in Figure 2.5e.
- Click the **Effects tab.** Click the first **drop-down arrow** under Entry animation and sound to display the entry transitions. Click **Fly From Left**.
- Click the **drop-down arrow** to show the Introduce Text effects and select **All at Once.** Click the **drop-down arrow** for sound effects, then scroll until you can select **Screeching Brakes**.
- Check that the title appears first within the animation order. If not, select the title, then click the up arrow to move it ahead of the text. Click **OK** to close the dialog box. Click outside the placeholder to deselect it.
- Pull down the **Slide Show menu** a second time. Click **Animation Preview** to display the slide miniature window to see (and hear) the animation effect. Close the miniature window. Save the presentation.

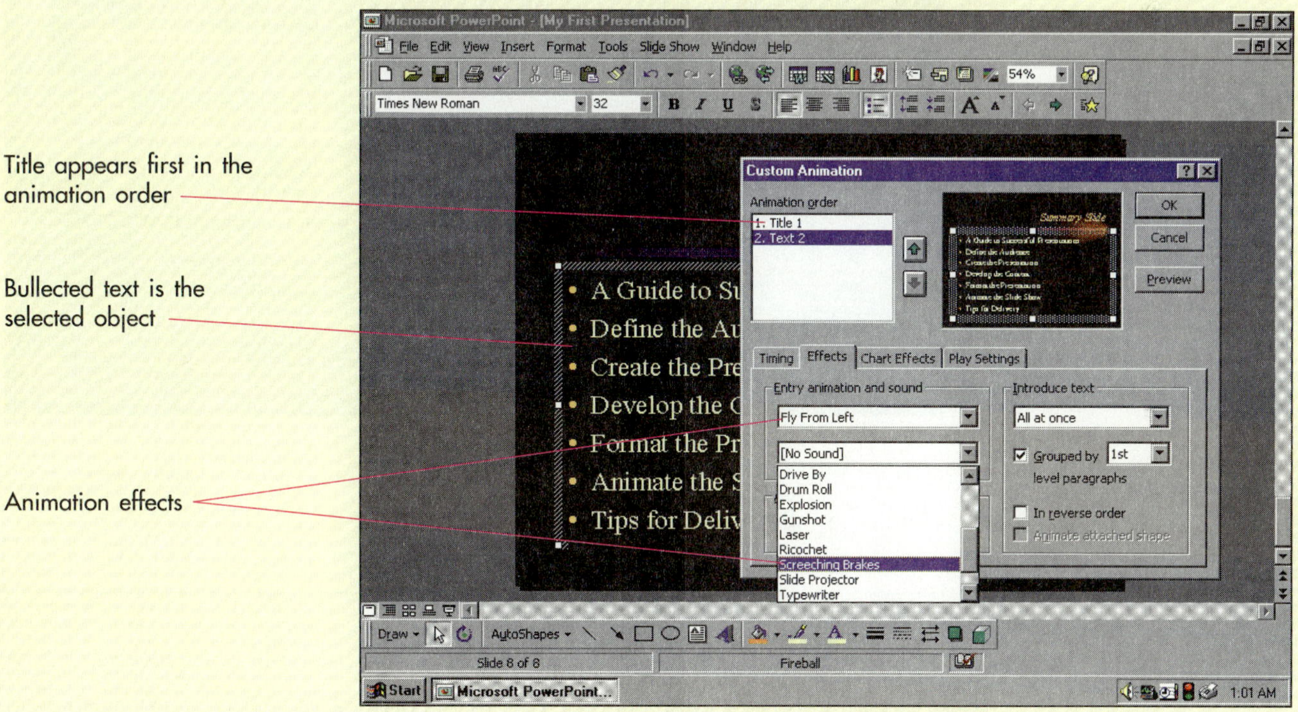


(e) Create Animation Effects (step 5)

**FIGURE 2.5** Hands-on Exercise 2 (continued)

**STEP 6: Show the Presentation**

- Press **Ctrl+Home** to return to the first slide, then click the **Slide Show button** to view the presentation. You should see the opening slide in Figure 2.5f.
- Click the **left mouse button** to move to the next slide (or to the next bullet on the current slide when animation is in effect).
- Click the **right mouse button** to display the shortcut menu and return to the previous slide (or to the previous bullet on the current slide when a build is in effect).
- Continue to view the presentation until you come to the end. Click the left mouse button a final time to return to the regular PowerPoint window.
- Exit PowerPoint if you do not want to continue with the next exercise.

(f) Show the Presentation

**FIGURE 2.5** Hands-on Exercise 2 (continued)

### THE MEETING MINDER

The Meeting Minder enables you to keep track of action items as they occur during a presentation and to summarize them at the end of the presentation. Click the right mouse button at any time to display a shortcut menu, click Meeting Minder, then click the Action Items tab in the Meeting Minder dialog box. Enter the description assigned to Due Date for each item, click OK to close the dialog box, then continue through the slide show. An Action Items slide will appear at the end of the presentation with the items you added during the show.

One of the hardest things about creating a presentation is getting started. You have a general idea of what you want to say, but the words do not come easily to you. The AutoContent Wizard offers a potential solution. It asks you a series of questions, then it uses your answers to suggest a presentation. The presentation is not complete, but it does provide an excellent beginning.

The AutoContent Wizard is accessed through the New command in the File menu and is illustrated in Figure 2.6. The Wizard prompts you for the type of presentation in Figure 2.6a, for output options in Figure 2.6b, and for additional information in Figure 2.6c. The Wizard then has all the information it needs and proceeds to create a presentation for you. It even chooses a design template as illustrated by the title slide in Figure 2.6d. The template contains a color scheme and custom formatting to give your presentation a certain "look." You can change the design at any time to give your presentation a completely different look while retaining its content.

The real benefit of the Wizard, however, is the outline shown in Figure 2.6e, which corresponds to the topic you selected earlier (Marketing Plan). The outline is very general, as it must be, but it provides the essential topics to include in your presentation. You work with the outline provided by the AutoContent Wizard just as you would with any other outline. You can type over existing text, add or delete slides, move slides around, promote or demote items, and so on. In short, you don't use the AutoContent outline exactly as it is presented; instead you use the outline as a starting point, then modify it to fit the needs of your presentation.

The presentation created by the AutoWizard is based on one of several presentations that are provided with PowerPoint. You can use the Wizard as just described, or you can bypass the Wizard entirely and select the outline directly from the New command in the File menu. Either way you wind up with a professional presentation with respect to design and content. Naturally, you have to modify the content to fit your needs, but you have jump-started the creative process. You simply open the presentation, then you modify the existing text as necessary, while retaining the formatting in the selected template.

Figure 2.7 displays the title slides of several sample presentations that are included with PowerPoint. The presentations vary considerably in content and design. There is a presentation for a creativity session in Figure 2.7a, a business plan in Figure 2.7b, and even a presentation to communicate bad news in Figure 2.7c. The presentation in Figure 2.7d is one of several developed by the Dale Carnegie Foundation and is designed to thank a speaker. The presentations in Figure 2.7e and 2.7f are for an employee orientation and a Who's Who corporate list. Animation and branching are also built into several of the presentations. Look carefully at the Business Plan in Figure 2.7b, which contains a series of buttons that link directly to other slides in the presentation.

### CHOOSE AN APPROPRIATE DESIGN

A design should enhance a presentation without calling attention to itself. It should be consistent with your message, and as authoritative or informal as the situation demands. Choosing the right template requires common sense and good taste. What works in one instance will not necessarily work in another. You would not, for example, use the same template to proclaim a year-end bonus as you would to announce a fourth-quarter loss and impending layoffs.

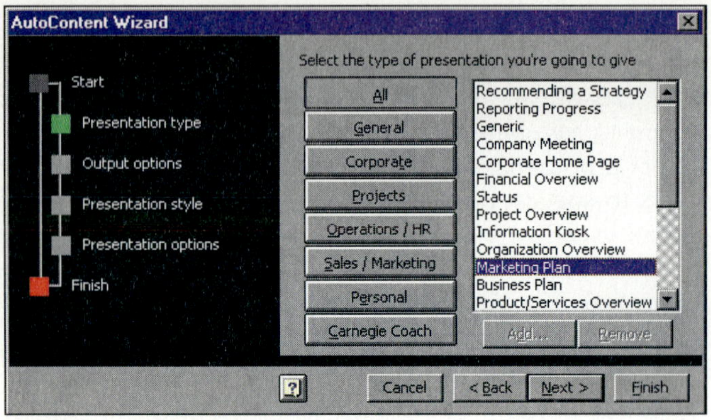


(a) Presentation Type

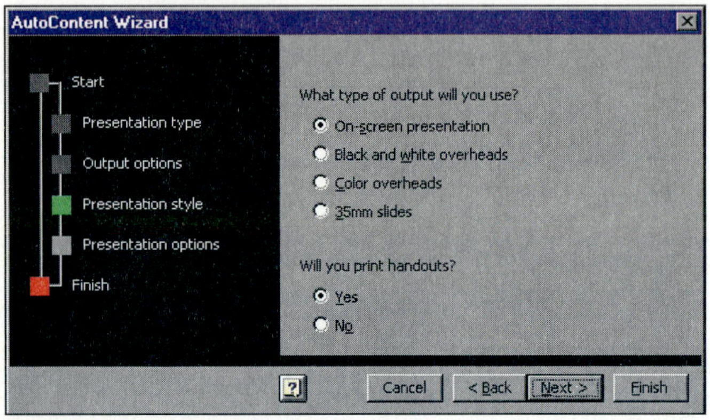


(b) Presentation Style

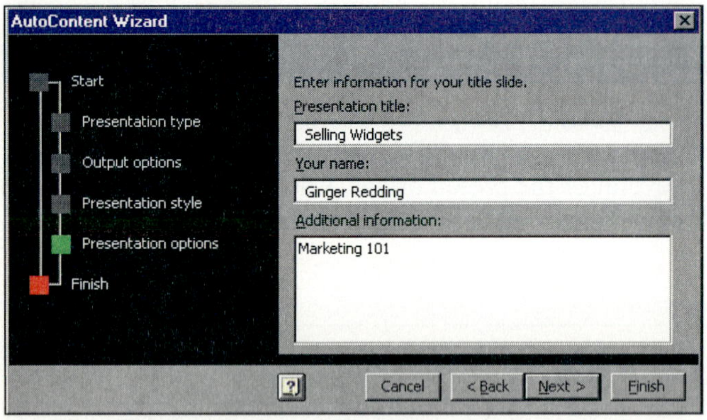


(c) Presentation Options

(d) Title Slide and Selected Template

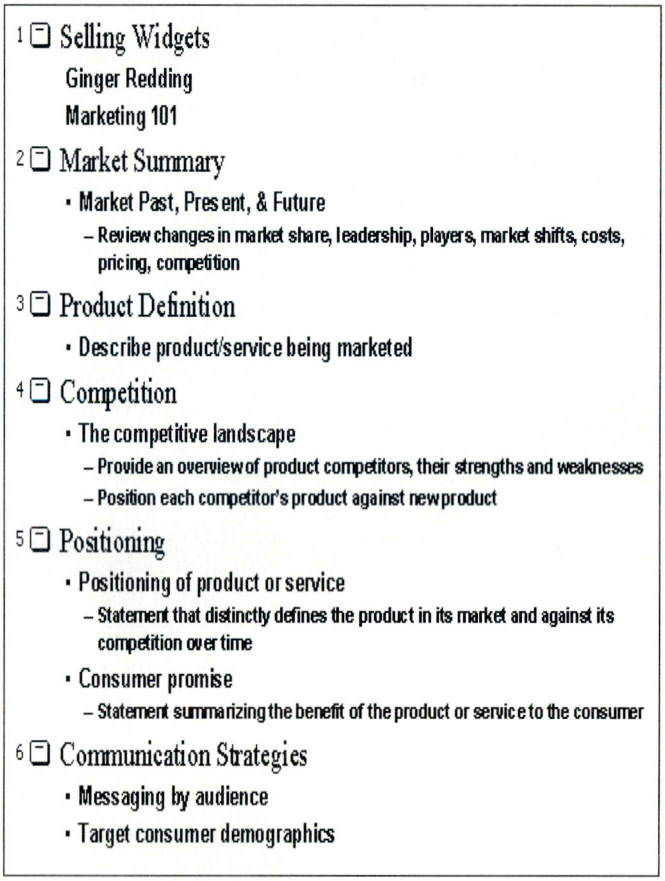


(e) Suggested Outline (additional slides not shown)

**FIGURE 2.6** The AutoContent Wizard

(a) Creativity Session

(b) Business Plan

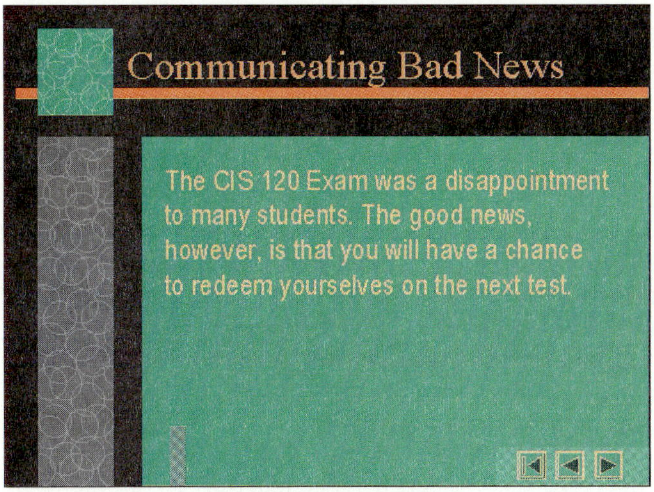


(c) Communicating Bad News

(d) Thanking a Speaker

(e) Employee Orientation

(f) Who's Who

**FIGURE 2.7** Suggested Presentations

A template is a design specification that controls every aspect of a presentation. It specifies the background design, the formatting of the text, the fonts and colors that are used, and the design, size, and placement of the bullets. You can change the look of a presentation at any time by applying a different template. Changing from one template to another changes the appearance of the presentation in every way, while maintaining the content.

What if, however, you want to make subtle changes to the template? In other words, you are content with the overall design, but you want to change one or more of its elements. You don't want a radical change, but you want to fine-tune the presentation by modifying its color scheme and/or background shading. Or perhaps you want to add a consistent element to every slide, such as a corporate name or logo.

## The Color Scheme

A ***color scheme*** is a set of eight balanced colors that is associated with a template. It consists of a background color, a color for the title of each slide, a color for lines and text, and five additional colors to provide accents to different elements, such as shadows and fill colors. Each template has a default color scheme, which is applied when the template is selected. Each template also has a set of alternate color schemes from which to choose.

Figure 2.8a displays the title slide of a presentation. The Fans template is selected and the default color scheme is in effect. Figure 2.8b displays the Color Scheme dialog box (which is accessed through the Format menu) with the suggested color schemes for this template. To choose one of the other color schemes, select the color scheme, then click the Apply All command button to apply the new color scheme to the entire presentation.

You have additional flexibility in that you can change any of the individual colors within a color scheme. Select the desired color scheme, click the Custom tab, select the color you wish to change (e.g., the color of the Title Text), then click the Change Color command button as shown in Figure 2.8c. Figure 2.8d displays the title slide after the color scheme has been changed to green, then further customized by changing the color of the title text to bright yellow.

### SLIDES VERSUS TRANSPARENCIES

Choose the color scheme in conjunction with the means of delivery. Light backgrounds work best for overhead transparencies, whereas dark backgrounds are preferable for computer presentations and 35-mm slides. This suggestion is presented in the Color Scheme dialog box itself (as can be seen in Figure 2.8b). We urge you to look for similar tips as you use other PowerPoint features.

## The Background Shading

The ***Background command*** in the Format menu changes the background color and/or shading of a slide, enabling you to truly fine-tune a presentation. Figure 2.9a displays the title slide of a presentation using the Soaring template. This design incorporates background shading that goes from blue to black as you go from left to right on the slide. The shading is built into the template according to the Shaded Fill dialog box in Figure 2.9b.

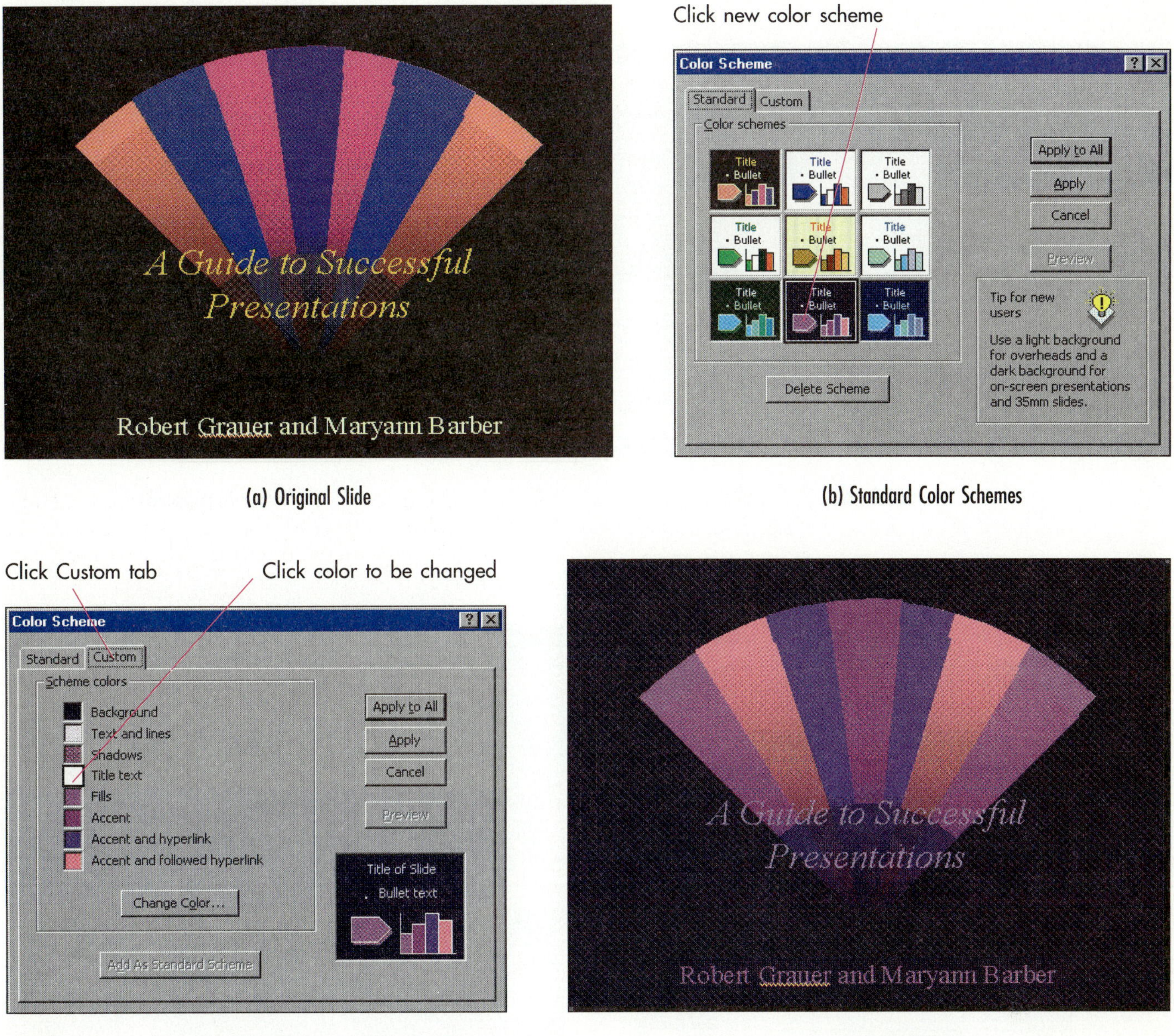


(a) Original Slide

(b) Standard Color Schemes

(c) Custom Colors

(d) Modified Slide

**FIGURE 2.8** Changing the Color Scheme

Figure 2.9c changes the parameters within the Fill Effects dialog box to use a single color (blue) and a horizontal shading pattern. Again, you have additional flexibility in that you can change the variation in color by dragging the scroll box from dark to light or vice versa. You can also choose from one of four variations of horizontal shading. The modified title slide is shown in Figure 2.9d.

## PowerPoint Masters

One of the best ways to customize a presentation is to add a unifying element to each slide, such as a corporate name or logo. You could add the element to every slide, but that would be unnecessarily tedious. It is much easier to use the View menu to add the element to the ***slide master,*** which defines the formatting and other elements that appear on the individual slides. Any change to the slide master is automatically reflected in every slide (except for the title slide).

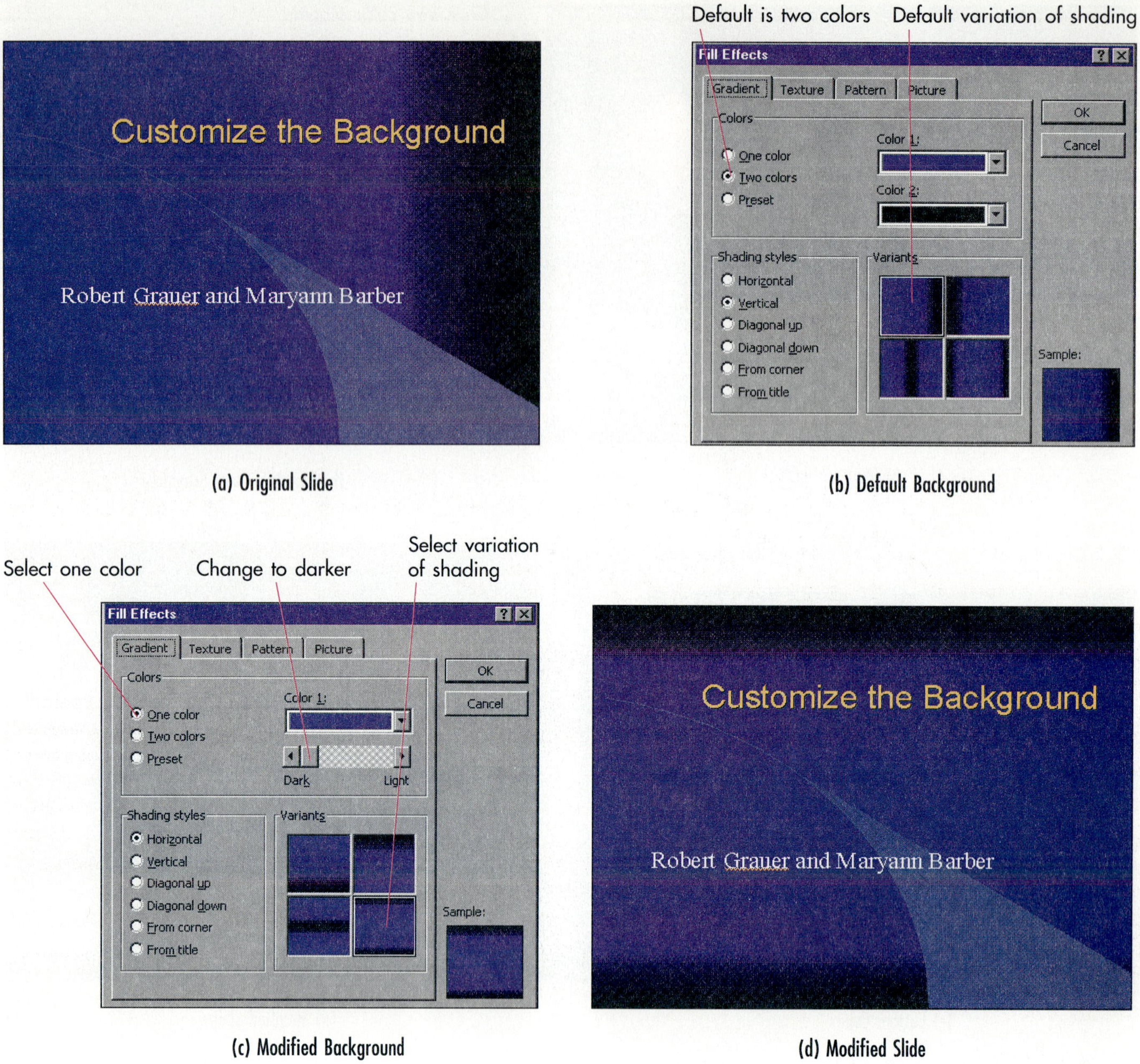


**FIGURE 2.9** Customize the Background

Consider, for example, the slide master shown in Figure 2.10, which contains a placeholder for the title of the slide and a second placeholder for the bulleted text. The slide master also contains additional placeholders at the bottom of the slide for the date, footer, and slide number. Change the position and/or content of any of these elements on the master slide, and the corresponding element will be changed throughout the presentation. Thus, you could add the name of the organization in the footer area of the master slide, and have it appear on every slide in the presentation. In similar fashion, any change to the font, bullets, font color, point size, or alignment within a placeholder would also carry through to all of the individual slides.

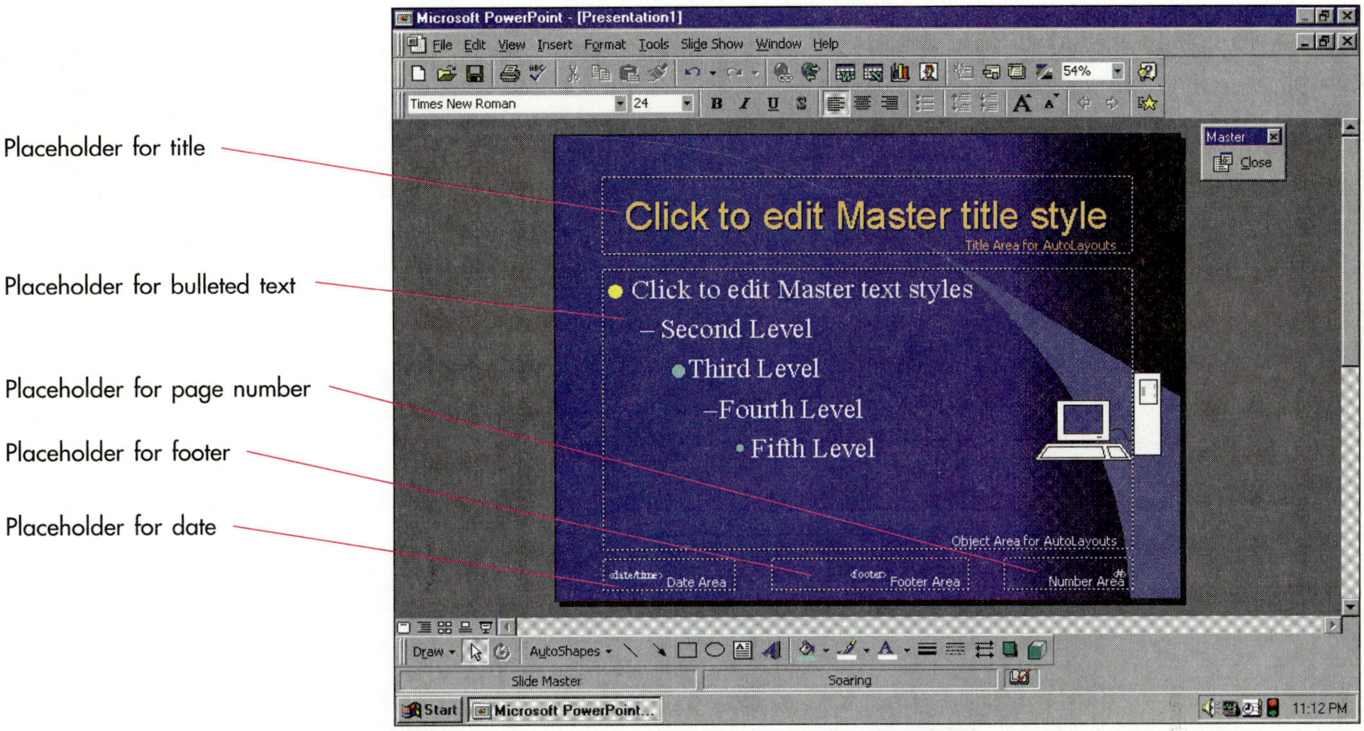


**FIGURE 2.10** The Slide Master

The slide master is modified by using commands from the appropriate menu or toolbar. The easiest way to place a logo on the slide master (such as the small computer in Figure 2.10) is to click the Insert Clip Art button on the Standard toolbar. This in turn displays the Microsoft Clip Gallery dialog box, in which you select the desired clip art. Once the clip art has been added to the slide master, you can click and drag its sizing handles to move and size the clip art like any other Windows object. Every slide in the presentation will contain the clip art image that was added to the slide master.

## HANDS-ON EXERCISE 3

### *Fine-Tuning a Presentation*

**Objective:** To create a presentation based on an existing PowerPoint presentation; to experiment with different color schemes and custom backgrounds. Use Figure 2.11 as a guide in the exercise.

#### SET A TIME LIMIT

We warn you—it's addictive and it can be very time consuming. Yes, it's fun to experiment with different color schemes and backgrounds, but it is all too easy to spend too much time fine-tuning the design by changing its color scheme or background shading. Concentrate on the content of your presentation rather than its appearance. Impose a limit on the amount of time you will spend on formatting. End the session when the limit is reached.

**STEP 1: Open an Existing Presentation**

- ➤ Start PowerPoint. Pull down the **File menu**, click **New** to display the New Presentations dialog box, then click the **Presentations tab.**
- ➤ Click the **Details button** so that you can see the title of each presentation more clearly. Scroll until you can select the **Reporting Progress (Standard)** presentation as shown in Figure 2.11a.
- ➤ Click **OK** to open the presentation. Save the presentation as **Reporting Progress.**

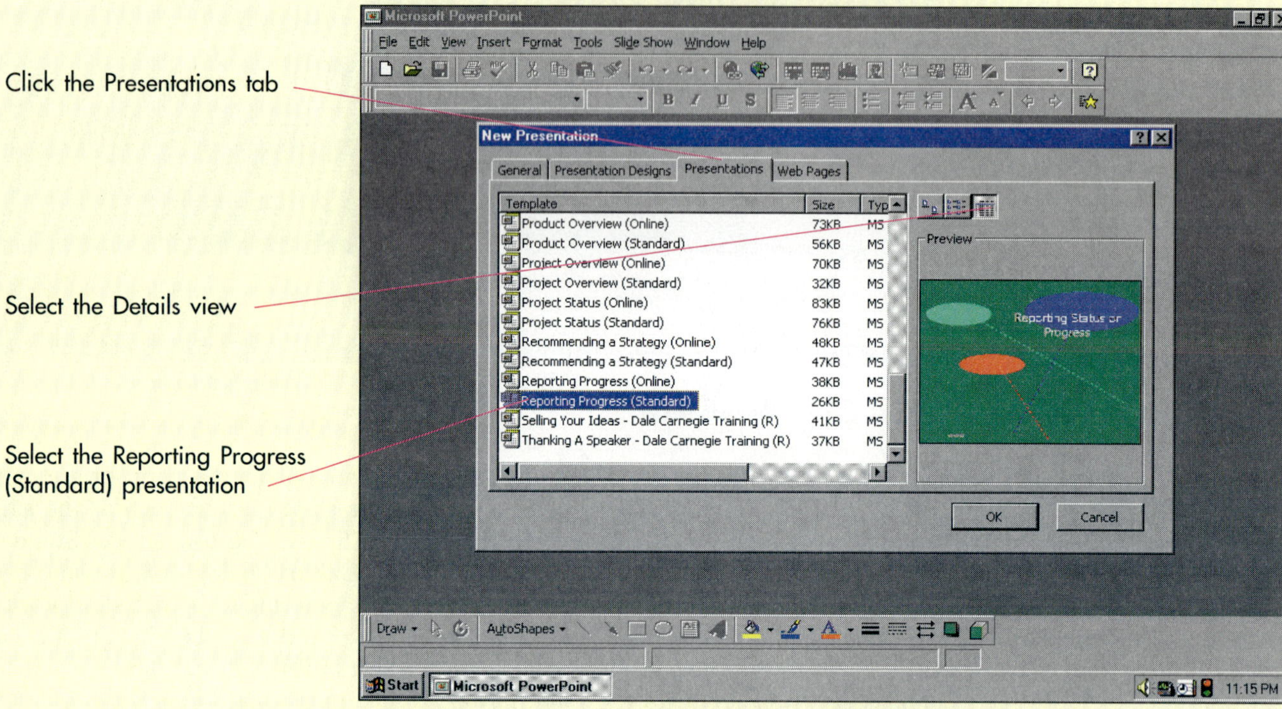


(a) Open the Presentation (step 1)

FIGURE 2.11 Hands-on Exercise 3

**EXTRA PRESENTATIONS**

The standard PowerPoint installation contains 38 suggested presentations on a variety of subjects. The variety is not as great as you might expect since many of the presentations come in both a standard and an online (Web) version, effectively halving the selection. Twenty-six additional presentations (on 13 topics) are available in the ValuPack folder on the CD-ROM. (Select the ValuPack folder, select the Template folder, then open the Presentation folder.) Ask your instructor for information about these additional presentations.

**STEP 2: Modify the Outline**

- Change to the **Outline view.** If necessary, pull down the **View menu** and toggle the **Slide Miniature** on as shown in Figure 2.11b.
- Change the entry on the title slide to **Reporting Progress.** Press the **enter key** at the end of the title to move to a new line. Press **Tab** to indent one level. Enter the names of your group (e.g., Tom, Dick, and Harry).
- Scroll through the nine slides, which are included in the default presentation. The outline is very general, as it must be, but it provides the essential topics to report the progress for your study group. Change the text as appropriate.
- Save the presentation.

Enter the names of your group

Slide Miniature shows slide as it is created or modified

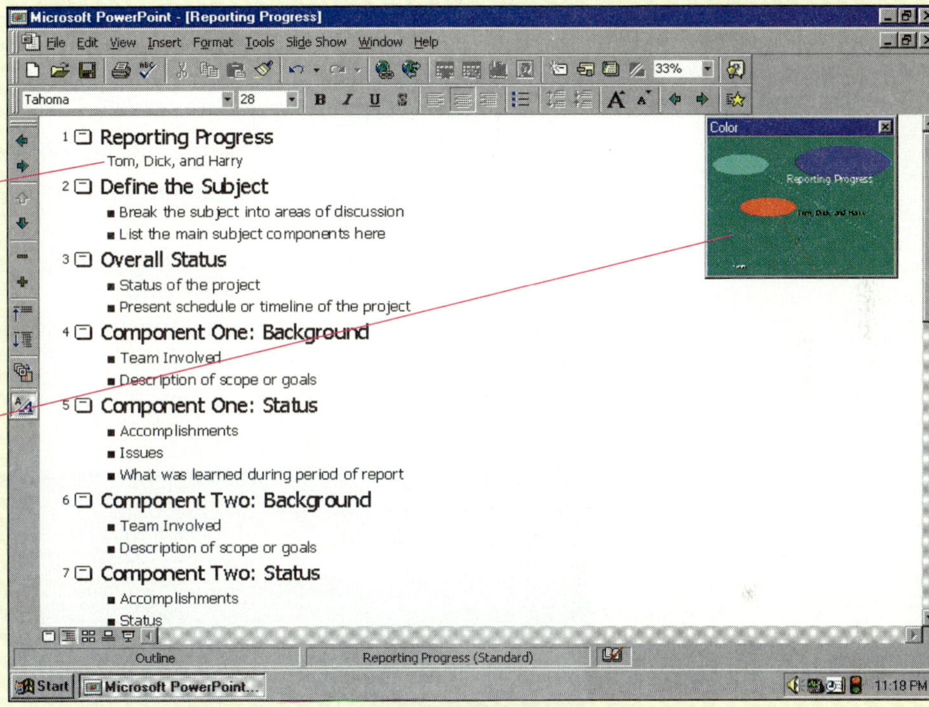


(b) Modify the Outline (step 2)

**FIGURE 2.11** Hands-on Exercise 3 (continued)

> **ADDING CLIP ART**
>
> The easiest way to add clip art to a bulleted list is to change to the Slide view, then change the AutoLayout of the slide. Click the Slide Layout button on the Standard toolbar, choose the AutoLayout with Text and Clip Art, and click the Apply command button. Double click the clip art placeholder on the slide, then select the desired image from the Microsoft Clip Gallery.

**STEP 3: Change the Slide Master**

- Pull down the **View menu,** click **Master,** then click **Slide Master** to display the slide master as shown in Figure 2.11c. (The Header and Footer dialog box is not yet visible.)
- Click the **dashed lines** surrounding the number area at the bottom right of the slide to select this element. Press the **Del key** to delete this element.
- Click the **dashed lines** surrounding the footer area at the bottom left of the slide, then click and drag the footer to the right side of the slide as shown in Figure 2.11c.
- Pull down the **View menu.** Click **Header and Footer** to display the Header and Footer dialog box:
  - The **Date and Time** check box is selected. Click the option button to **Update Automatically.**
  - Select the **Footer** check box, then enter the name of your school as shown in Figure 2.11c.
  - Check the box to suppress the display on the title slide.
  - Click the **Apply to All command button** to accept these settings and close the dialog box.
- Click the **Slide view button** on the status bar, then press the **PgDn key** once or twice to move from slide to slide. You should see today's date and the name of your school at the bottom of each slide except for the title slide. (Press **Ctrl+Home** to view the title slide.)
- Save the presentation.

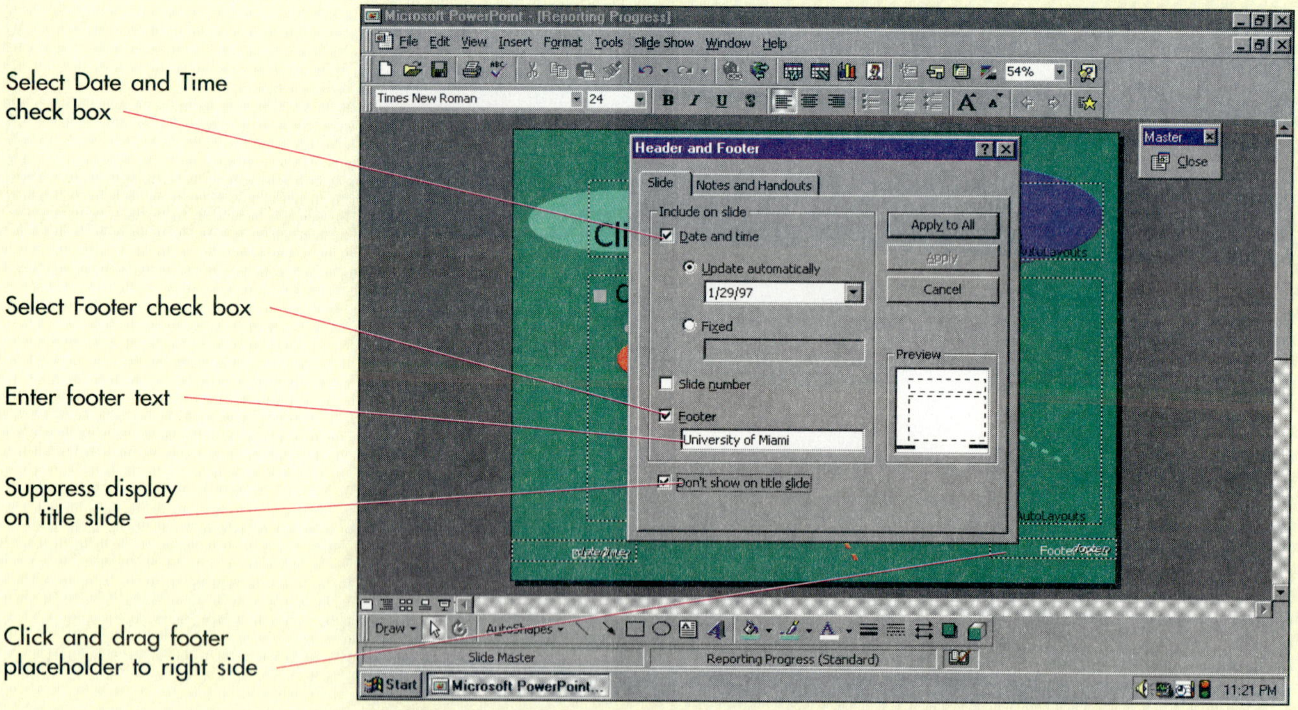


(c) Modify the Slide Master (step 3)

**FIGURE 2.11** Hands-on Exercise 3 (continued)

### THE VIEW BUTTONS AND THE SHIFT KEY

The Slide View button provides the fastest way to change to the slide master. Select any slide other than the title slide, then press and hold the Shift key as you click the Slide View button above the status bar to display the slide master. You can also press and hold the Shift key as you click the Slide Sorter or Outline View button to customize the Handout master.

**STEP 4: Change the Color Scheme**

- Change to the **Slide Sorter view.** You should see a footer (containing the name of your school) on every slide except the title slide, as shown in Figure 2.11d.
- Pull down the **Format menu.** Click **Slide Color Scheme** to display the Color Scheme dialog box. Select a different color scheme (e.g., blue), then click the **Apply to All button** to change the color scheme of every slide.

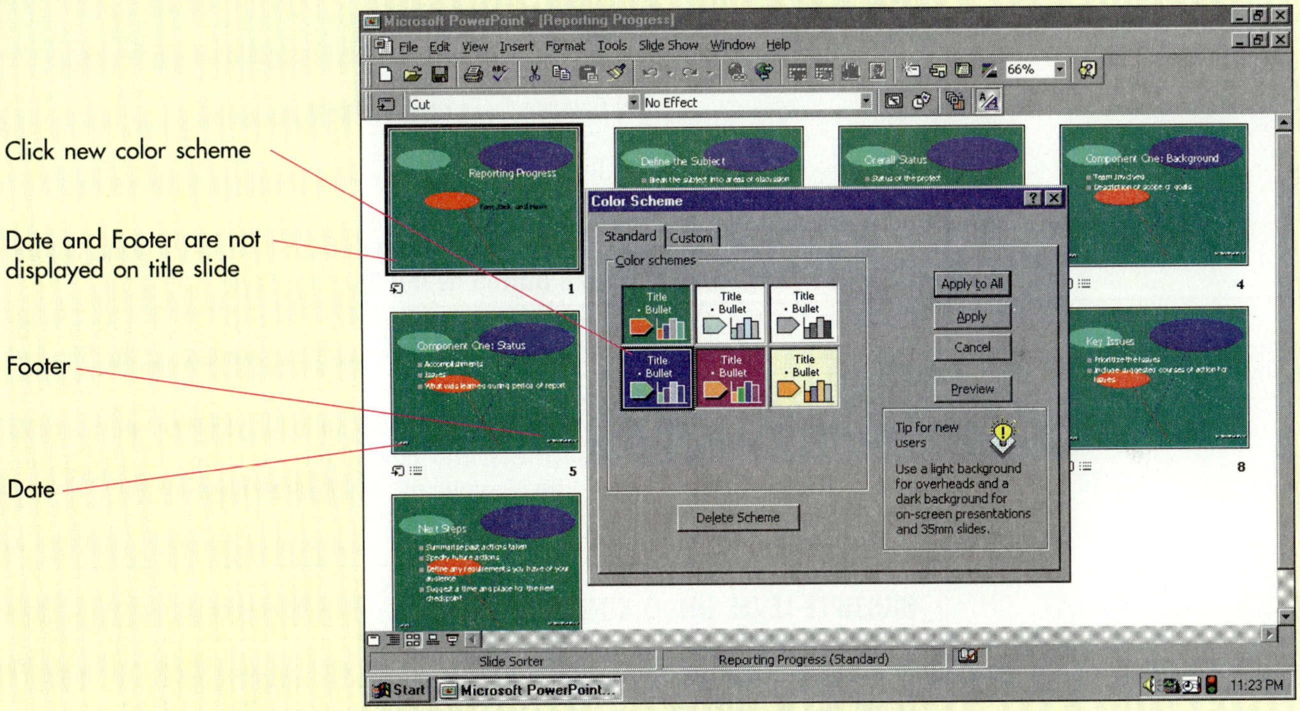


(d) Change the Color Scheme (step 4)

FIGURE 2.11 Hands-on Exercise 3 (continued)

**STEP 5: Customize the Background**

- Pull down the **Format menu.** Click **Background** to display the Background dialog box in Figure 2.11e.
- Click the **drop-down arrow** to display the various types of backgrounds, then click **Fill Effects** to display the Fill Effects dialog box in Figure 2.11e.

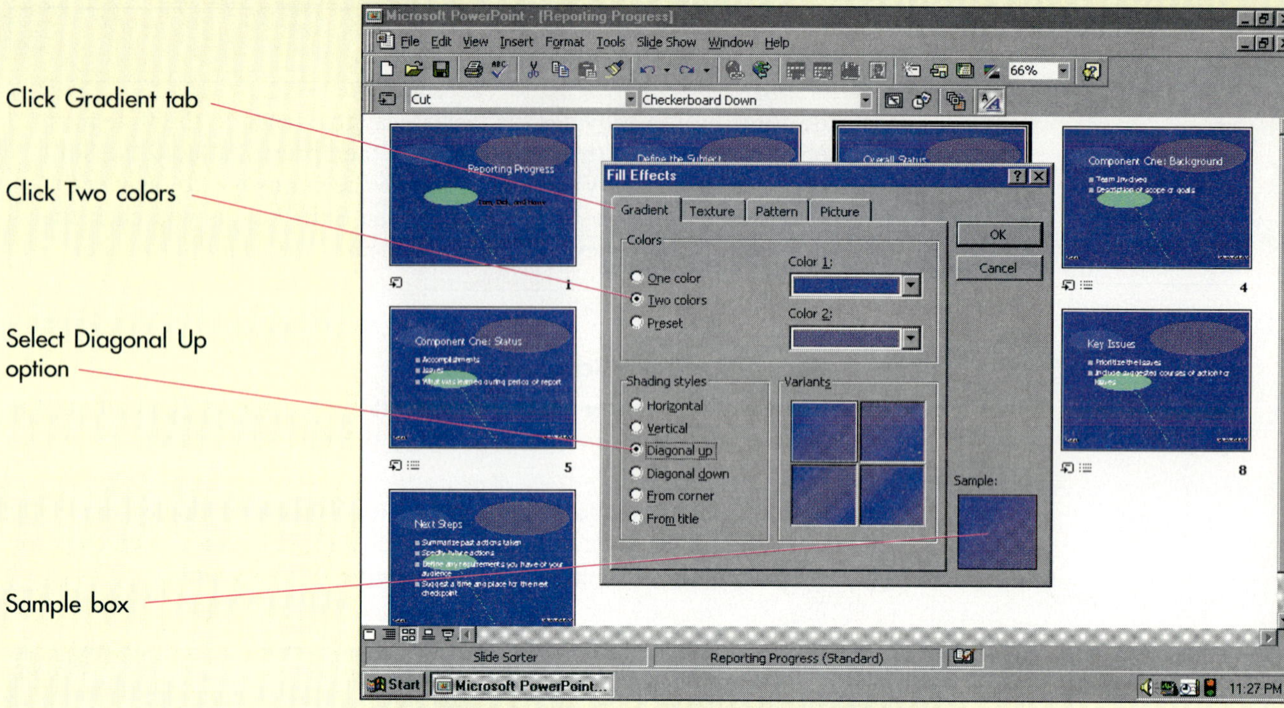


(e) Customize the Background (step 5)

**FIGURE 2.11** Hands-on Exercise 3 (continued)

- If necessary, click the **Gradient tab.** Click the option button for **Two colors.** Click the **Diagonal Up option button** as the Shading Style. Click OK.
- You can see the effect of these changes in the Sample box. Experiment with additional changes, then click **OK** to accept the changes and close the Shaded Fill dialog box.
- Click **Apply to All** to apply the changes to all slides and close the Custom Background dialog box. Use the **Undo command** to return to the initial design if you are disappointed with your modification.

## MULTIPLE-LEVEL UNDO COMMAND

The Undo command reverses (undoes) the most recent command. The command is executed from the Edit menu or more easily by clicking the Undo button on the Standard toolbar. Each click of the Undo button reverses one command; that is, click the Undo button and you reverse the last command. Click the Undo button a second time and you reverse the previous command. The Redo button works in reverse and undoes the most recent Undo command (i.e., it redoes the command you just undid). The maximum number of Undo commands (the default is 20) is set through the Tools menu. Pull down the Tools menu, click Options, click the Advanced tab, then enter the desired number.

**STEP 6: Print the Audience Handouts**

- Pull down the **File menu.** Click **Print** to display the Print dialog box in Figure 2.11f. Set the print options to match those in the figure:
  - Click the **All option button** as the print range.
  - Click the **down arrow** on the Print What list box to select **Handouts (6 slides per page).**
  - Check the boxes to **Frame Slides** and print in Black and White.
  - Click **OK**.
- Submit the audience handouts to your instructor as proof that you did the exercise. Save the presentation.
- Exit PowerPoint. Congratulations on a job well done.

## PRINT THE OUTLINE

You can print the outline of a presentation and distribute it to the audience in the form of a handout. This enables the audience to follow the presentation as it is delivered and gives them an ideal vehicle on which to take notes. Pull down the File menu, click Print, then choose Outline view from the Print What list box. Be sure you know the expected size of the audience so that you will have an adequate number of handouts.

Print all slides

Print audience handouts

Frame individual slides

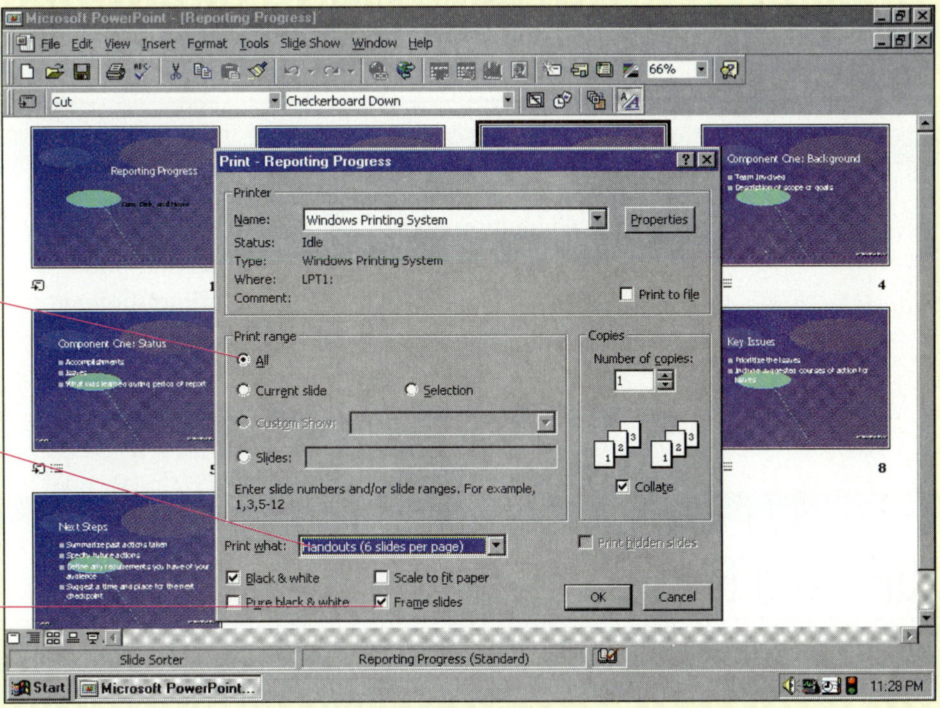


(f) Prepare the Audience Handouts (step 6)

FIGURE 2.11 Hands-on Exercise 3 (continued)

## SUMMARY

There are in essence two independent steps to creating a PowerPoint presentation. You must develop the content, and you must format the presentation. Both steps are iterative in nature, and you are likely to go back and forth many times before you are finished.

The text of a presentation can be developed from the Slide view or the Outline view or a combination of the two. The Outline view is easier because it displays the contents of many slides at once, enabling you to see the overall flow of your ideas. You can change the order of the slides and/or move text from one slide to another as necessary. Text can be entered continually in the outline, then promoted or demoted so that it appears on the proper level in the slide.

A template is a design specification that controls every aspect of a presentation. It specifies the formatting of the text, the fonts and colors that are used, and the design, size, and placement of the bullets.

Transitions and animation effects can be added to a presentation for additional interest. Transitions control the way in which one slide moves off the screen and the next slide appears. Animation effects are used to display the individual elements on a single slide.

The design of a presentation can be customized by modifying its color scheme or background shading. The slide master enables you to add a unifying element to every slide, such as a corporate name or logo.

The AutoContent Wizard facilitates the creation of a new presentation. The Wizard asks a series of questions, then it uses your answers to suggest a presentation based on one of several general presentations included within PowerPoint. The end result of the Wizard is an outline based on the topic you selected. The outline is very general, as it must be, but it provides the essential topics to include in your presentation. It is the best way we know to jump-start the creation process.

## KEY WORDS AND CONCEPTS

- Animation effect
- AutoContent Wizard
- AutoCorrect
- Background command
- Color scheme
- Demote
- Insertion point
- Outline toolbar
- Promote
- Slide icon
- Slide master
- Slide Sorter toolbar
- Summary slide
- Template
- Transition

# MULTIPLE CHOICE

1. Which view displays multiple slides while letting you change the text in a slide?
   (a) Outline view
   (b) Slide Sorter view
   (c) Both (a) and (b)
   (d) Neither (a) nor (b)

2. Where will the insertion point be after you complete the text for a bullet in the Outline view and press the enter key?
   (a) On the next bullet at the same level of indentation
   (b) On the next bullet at a higher level of indentation
   (c) On the next bullet at a lower level of indentation
   (d) Impossible to determine

3. Which of the following is true?
   (a) Shift+Tab promotes an item to the next higher level
   (b) Tab demotes an item to the next lower level
   (c) Both (a) and (b)
   (d) Neither (a) nor (b)

4. Which of the following is true about the Outline view?
   (a) The position of a slide may be changed by dragging its icon
   (b) All slides display the identical icon regardless of content
   (c) Both (a) and (b)
   (d) Neither (a) nor (b)

5. What advantage, if any, is there to collapsing the Outline view so that only the slide titles are visible?
   (a) More slides are displayed at one time, making it easier to rearrange the slides in the presentation
   (b) Transition and animation effects can be added
   (c) Graphic objects become visible
   (d) All of the above

6. Which of the following is true regarding transition and animation effects?
   (a) Every slide must have the same transition effect
   (b) Every bullet must have the same animation effect
   (c) Both (a) and (b)
   (d) Neither (a) nor (b)

7. The AutoContent Wizard provides suggested presentations for:
   (a) Communicating bad news
   (b) Selling a product, service, or idea
   (c) Both (a) and (b)
   (d) Neither (a) nor (b)

8. Which of the following is true?
   (a) Slides can be added to a presentation after a template has been chosen
   (b) The template can be changed after all of the slides have been created
   (c) Both (a) and (b)
   (d) Neither (a) nor (b)

9. What is the easiest way to add a corporate name to every slide (except the title slide) in the presentation?
   (a) Add the information to the handout master
   (b) Add the information to the slide master
   (c) Both (a) and (b)
   (d) Neither (a) nor (b)

10. Which of the following can be changed after a slide has been created?
    (a) Its layout and transition effect
    (b) Its position within the presentation
    (c) Both (a) and (b)
    (d) Neither (a) nor (b)

11. Which view enables you to select multiple slides?
    (a) Outline view
    (b) Slide sorter view
    (c) Both (a) and (b)
    (d) Neither (a) nor (b)

12. Which applications in Microsoft Office support the AutoCorrect feature?
    (a) PowerPoint
    (b) Word
    (c) Excel
    (d) All of the above

13. How do you move to the next slide during a slide show?
    (a) Click the left mouse button
    (b) Type the letter N
    (c) Press the PgDn key
    (d) All of the above

14. Which of the following is the best way to create a Summary slide?
    (a) Pull down the Insert menu and click the Summary Slide command
    (b) Pull down the Slide Show menu and click the Summary Slide command
    (c) Insert a new slide, then manually type the headings of all existing slides onto the new slide
    (d) Select all slides in the Slide Sorter view, then click the Summary Slide button on the Slide Sorter toolbar

15. Which of the following can be changed without changing the template?
    (a) The color scheme and background shading
    (b) The slide master
    (c) Both (a) and (b)
    (d) Neither (a) nor (b)

## ANSWERS

| | | |
|---|---|---|
| **1.** a | **6.** d | **11.** c |
| **2.** a | **7.** c | **12.** d |
| **3.** c | **8.** c | **13.** d |
| **4.** a | **9.** b | **14.** d |
| **5.** a | **10.** c | **15.** c |

# Practice with Microsoft PowerPoint 97

1. Figure 2.12 displays the title slide of a presentation that can be found in the Exploring PowerPoint folder on the data disk. Much of the presentation has been created for you, but there are several finishing touches that need to be made:
   a. Open the existing presentation titled *Chapter 2 Practice 1,* then save it as *Chapter 2 Practice 1 Solution* so that you can return to the original presentation if necessary.
   b. Replace our name with your name on the title slide.
   c. Move the slide on Modems after the one on Multimedia Requirements.
   d. Delete the slide on The PC, Then and Now.
   e. Add a slide at the end of the presentation on software that should be considered in addition to Windows 95 and the Microsoft Office.
   f. Change the layout of slide 7 to a Two-column Text slide. Modify the text as necessary for the new layout.
   g. Select a different design template.
   h. Print the completed presentation in both outline and handout form. Submit both to your instructor.

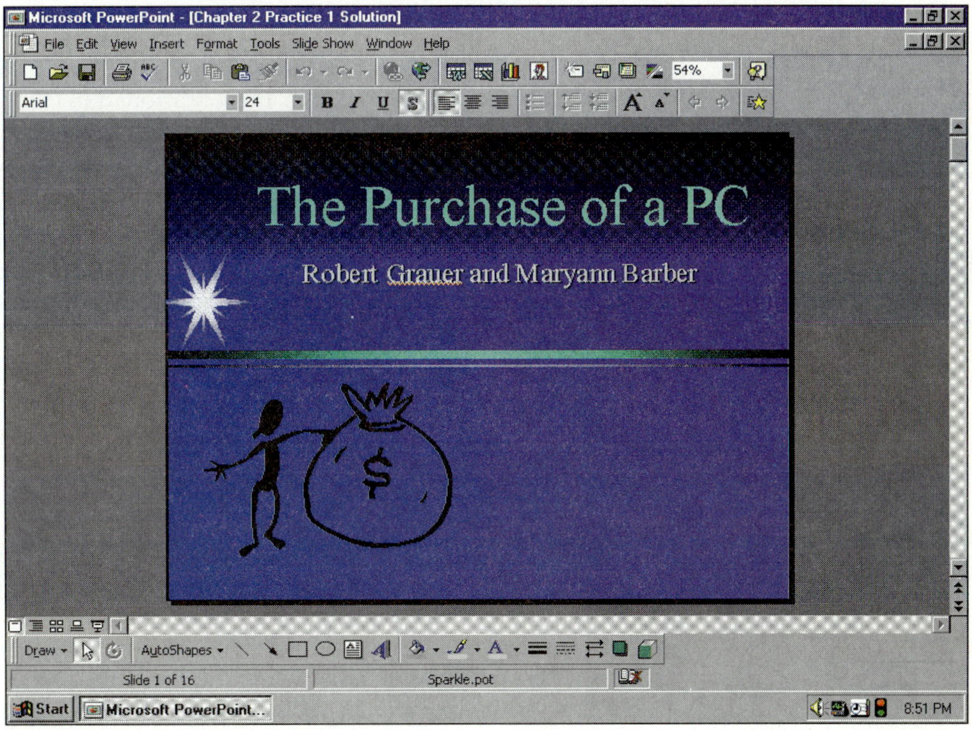


**FIGURE 2.12** Screen for Practice Exercise 1

2. Figure 2.13 displays a very general outline for a presentation. The outline can be accessed through the AutoContent Wizard or directly through the File New command.

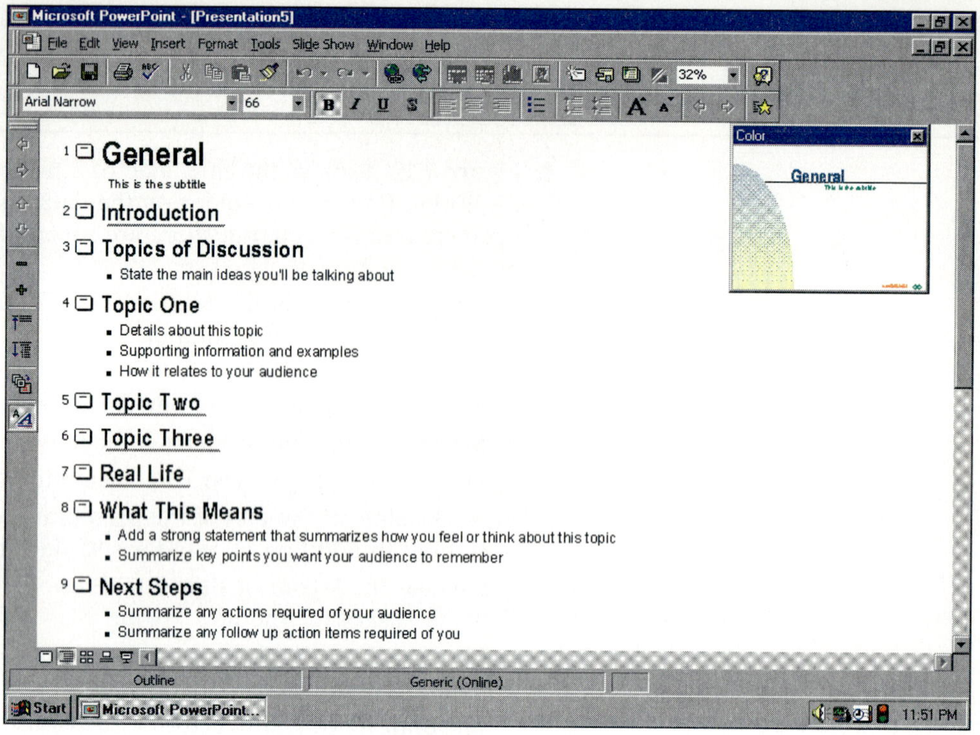


FIGURE 2.13 Screen for Practice Exercise 2

a. Pull down the File menu, click New to display the New Presentation dialog box, click the Presentations tab, then double click the Generic (standard) presentation.
b. Change to the Outline view to display the presentation in Figure 2.13. (Some slides have been collapsed in our outline as can be seen by the underlined slide titles.)
c. Choose any topic you like, then prepare a presentation on that topic using the outline provided. You need not follow the outline exactly, but it should provide a good beginning. The completed presentation should contain from six to ten slides.
d. Apply a new (different) design template to the completed presentation.
e. Print the completed presentation in both outline and miniature slide form. Submit both handouts to your instructor.

3. Figure 2.14 displays the Slide Sorter view of a presentation to sell an idea or product. The template is available in the ValuPack folder on the CD-ROM. (The complete path is ValuPack\Template\Present. Change the file type to Presentation Templates, then select the Sell_S template.) Assume that you have been appointed the Director of Marketing for a national corporation, then modify the presentation as follows:
   a. Change the title slide to reflect the product you wish to sell.
   b. Modify the remaining slides to reflect your sales strategy. You can change the slide layout and content.
   c. Use the Header and Footer command in the View menu to print today's date on every slide except the title slide.
   d. Modify the Slide master to include uniform clip art in the lower right corner of each slide (except the title slide).

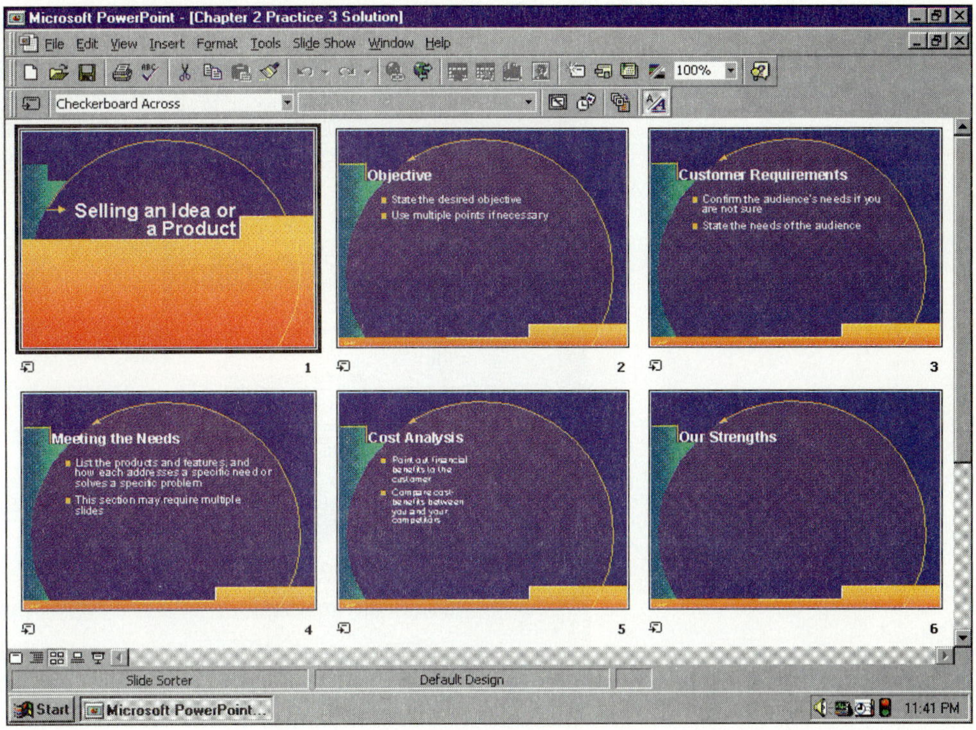


FIGURE 2.14 Screen for Practice Exercise 3

e. View the slide show of the completed presentation. Slide transitions are built into the presentation as can be seen by viewing the transition icon under each slide.

f. Print the completed presentation in slide miniature form and submit the printout to your instructor.

4. The potential uses of PowerPoint are limited only by your imagination. Figure 2.15, for example, displays an award certificate that was created using the drawing tools within Microsoft Office. The template is found in the Certificate Online presentation in the ValuPack folder on the CD-ROM.

   a. Modify the existing template to award yourself for your efforts in this class.

   b. Use the existing slide as the basis for three additional awards for real people in any category. Experiment with the various animation effects. It's best if you have a sound card so you can hear the sound of applause as the certificate is displayed.

   c. Print the completed presentation and submit it to your instructor.

5. The presentation in Figure 2.16 is one of several provided by Dale Carnegie & Associates. Use the AutoContent Wizard to select the Presentation Guidelines presentation. (Alternatively, you can pull down the File menu, click New to display the New Presentation dialog box, click the Presentations tab, then double click Presentation Guidelines from the list of available presentations.)

   a. Go to the first slide in the presentation, then switch to the Slide Show view and view the entire presentation.

   b. Print the presentation in Outline view or Slide Miniatures (six slides per page) and keep it as a guide. This is a valuable reference, which you can use the next time you have to deliver a presentation.

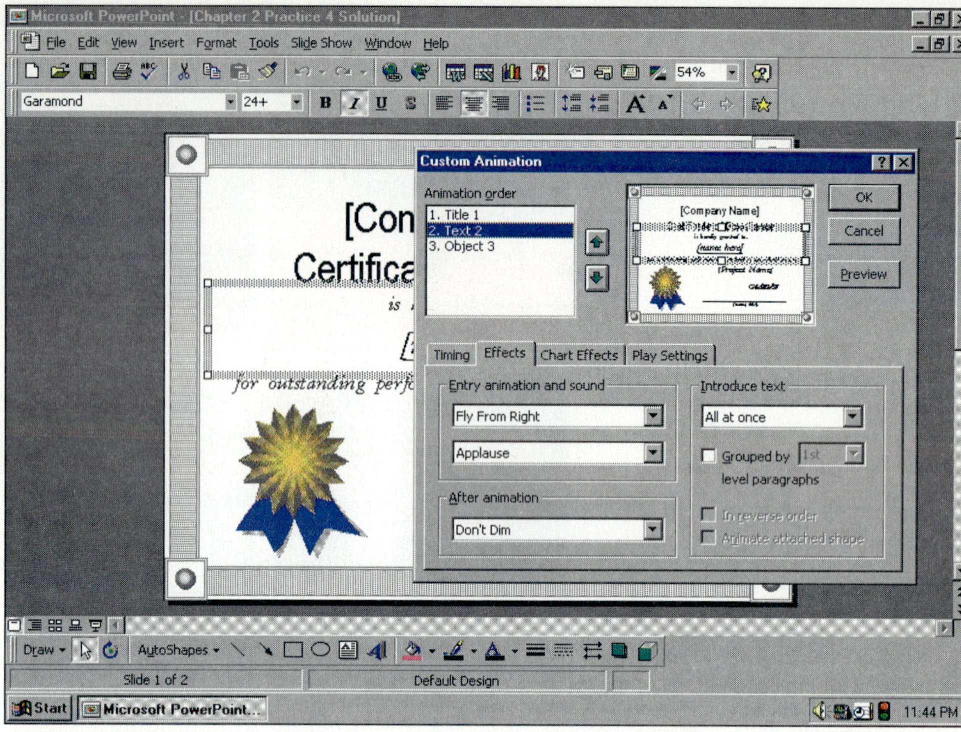


**FIGURE 2.15** Screen for Practice Exercise 4

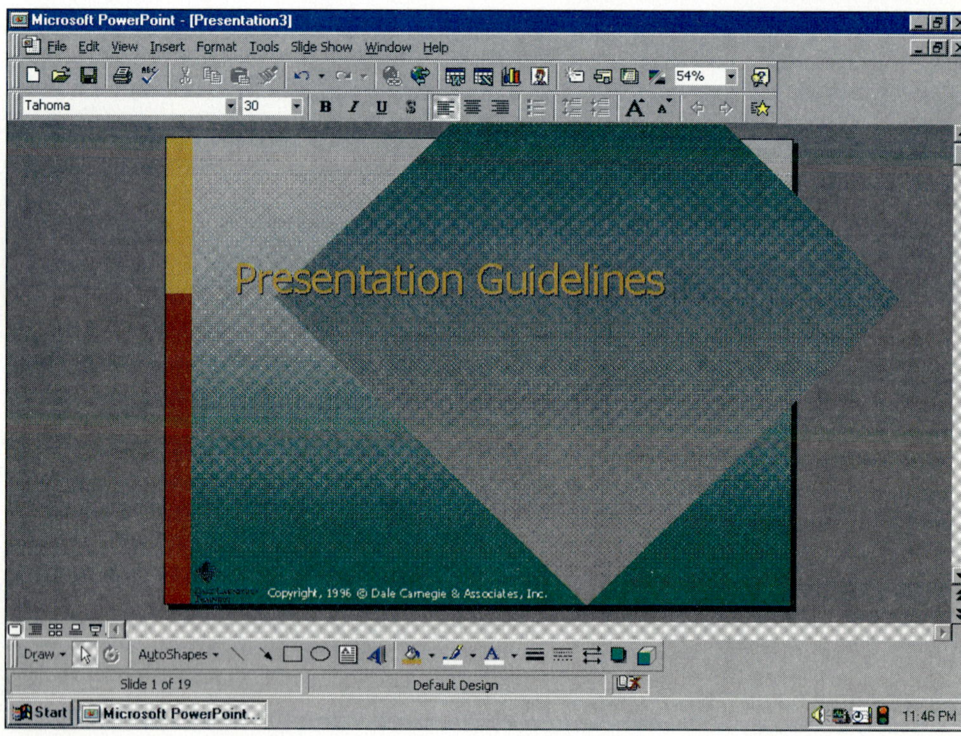


**FIGURE 2.16** Screen for Practice Exercise 5

6. Figure 2.17 displays the Outline view of a presentation for a Creativity Session. (The template is available in the ValuPack folder on the CD-ROM. The complete path is ValuPack\Template\Present. Change the file type to Presentation Templates, then select the Brain__S template.) Ask your

instructor to divide the class into groups of three or four students each. Each group is given the assignment of creating a presentation to attract publicity for a political issue of interest to you and your classmates. Your group has a meeting scheduled for next Monday, at which point you are to decide on the issue and an associated strategy. Modify the text of the Creativity Session to facilitate the upcoming meeting.

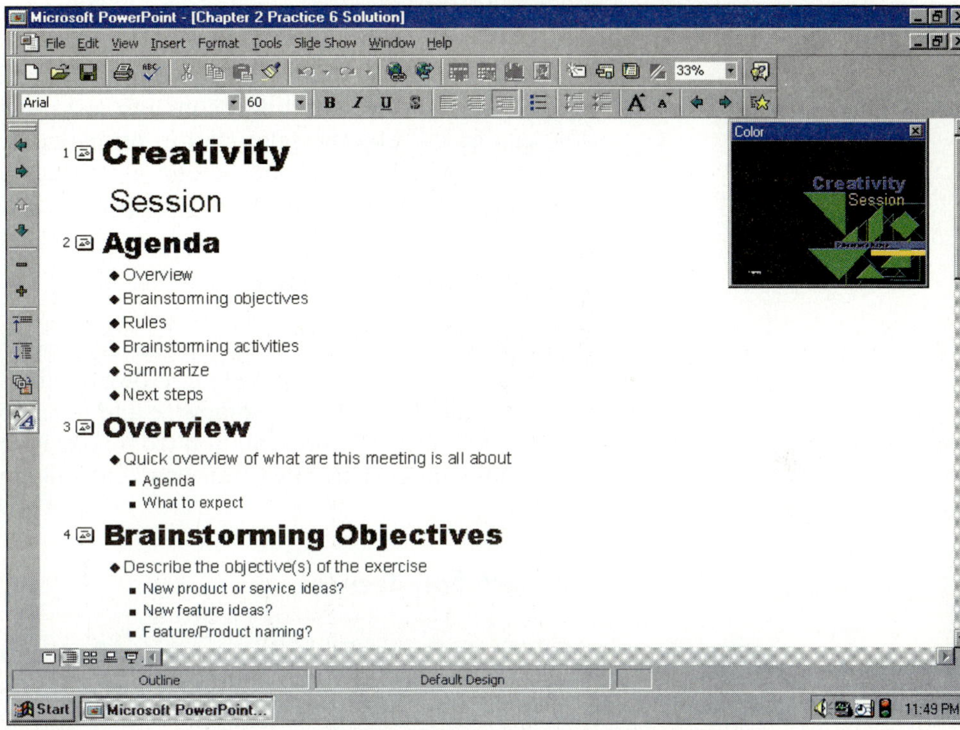


FIGURE 2.17 Screen for Practice Exercise 6

# CASE STUDIES

## Be Creative

One interesting way of exploring the potential of presentation graphics is to imagine how it might have been used by historical figures had it been available. Choose any historical figure or current personality and create at least a six-slide presentation. You could, for example, show how Columbus might have used PowerPoint to request funding from Queen Isabella, or how Elvis Presley might have pleaded for his first recording contract. The content of your presentation should be reasonable, but you don't have to spend an inordinate amount of time on research. Just be creative and use your imagination. Use clip art as appropriate, but don't overdo it. Place your name on the title slide as technical adviser.

## The Annual Report

EXPLORING WWW

Corporate America spends a small fortune to produce its annual reports, which are readily available to the public. Choose any company and obtain a copy of its most recent annual report. Use your imagination on how best to obtain the data.

You might try a stockbroker, the 800 directory, or even the Internet. Use the information in the annual report as the basis for a PowerPoint presentation. PowerPoint is one step ahead of you and offers a suggested financial report through the AutoContent Wizard.

## Director of Marketing

Congratulations on your appointment as Director of Marketing. The company that hired you has 50 sales representatives across the United States. Laptop computers have just been ordered for the entire sales staff and will be delivered at next week's annual sales meeting. Your job is to prepare a PowerPoint presentation that can be used by the sales staff in future sales calls. It's short notice, but it is a critical assignment. Use the Selling a Product template provided by the AutoContent Wizard as the basis for your presentation.

## Take It on the Road

Your presentation looks great on the desktop, but you have to deliver it to an audience of 50, too many people to crowd around your machine. Fortunately, however, you have a notebook computer and a generous budget. What equipment do you need to show the presentation from your notebook computer? How much will the equipment cost to buy? Can you rent the equipment instead, and if so, from whom?

## An Ad for Travel

The Clip Gallery includes the maps and flags of many foreign countries as well as maps of all 50 states and pictures of many landmarks. It's an excellent beginning, but why limit yourself as you can obtain additional resources on the Web. Design a six-slide presentation for a place you want to visit, in the United States or abroad. Print the miniatures of your presentation six slides to a page. Collect the assignments, then ask your instructor to hold a contest to select the most appealing document. It's fun, it's easy, and it's educational. Bon voyage!

3

# ENHANCING A PRESENTATION: THE WEB AND OTHER RESOURCES

## OBJECTIVES

**After reading this chapter you will be able to:**

1. Use Microsoft Graph to create and edit a graph within a presentation.
2. Use the Drawing toolbar to modify existing clip art; describe the function of at least four different drawing tools.
3. Use Microsoft Organization Chart to embed an organization chart into a presentation.
4. Use Microsoft WordArt to embed a WordArt object into a presentation.
5. Link an Excel worksheet to a PowerPoint presentation.
6. Distinguish between linking and embedding; explain how in-place editing is used to modify an embedded object.
7. Embed a sound file into a PowerPoint presentation.
8. Describe the Internet and World Wide Web; explain how to display the Web toolbar in PowerPoint.
9. Download a photograph from the Web and include it in a PowerPoint presentation.

## OVERVIEW

Thus far we have focused on presentations that consisted largely of text. PowerPoint also enables you to include a variety of visual elements that add impact to your presentation. You can add clip art or photographs from within PowerPoint through the Microsoft Clip Gallery, or you can include these elements from other sources. You can use the supplementary applications that are included with Microsoft Office to add graphs, organization charts, and WordArt. You can insert objects created in other applications, such as a worksheet from Microsoft Excel or a table from Microsoft Word. And best of all, you can download resources from the World Wide Web for inclusion in a PowerPoint presentation.

We begin by introducing Microsoft Graph, an application that creates (and modifies) a graph based on data in an associated datasheet. We show you how to use the Drawing toolbar to modify existing clip art and/or develop original images, even if you are not artistic by nature. We describe how to create special text effects through WordArt, how to create organization charts, and how to include sound in a presentation. We describe the Internet and World Wide Web, explain how to display the Web toolbar, and show you how to download resources from the Web.

All told, we think you will be quite impressed with what you can do. As always, the hands-on exercises are essential to our learn-by-doing philosophy.

## MICROSOFT GRAPH

The Microsoft Office suite includes a supplementary application called ***Microsoft Graph,*** which enables you to insert a graph into a presentation in support of numeric data. The program is called from within PowerPoint by choosing an Auto-Layout containing a graph placeholder, then double clicking the placeholder to start Microsoft Graph. You create the graph using commands within Microsoft Graph, then you exit Microsoft Graph and return to your presentation.

Figure 3.1 illustrates the basics of the Microsoft Graph program as it will be used in a hands-on exercise later in the chapter. The program has many of the same commands and capabilities as the charting component of Microsoft Excel. (See Grauer and Barber, *Exploring Microsoft Excel 97,* pages 133–178, Prentice Hall, 1997, for additional information on graphs and charting.)

The ***datasheet*** in Figure 3.1a displays the quarterly sales for each of three salesmen: Tom, Dick, and Harry. The datasheet contains 12 ***data points*** (four quarterly values for each of three salesmen). The data points are grouped into ***data series,*** which appear as rows or columns in the datasheet.

The graph in Figure 3.1b plots the data by row so that you can see the relative performance of each salesman in each quarter. There are three data series (Sales for Tom, Sales for Dick, and Sales for Harry), each with four data points (1st Qtr, 2nd Qtr, 3rd Qtr, and 4th Qtr). The text entries in the first row of the datasheet appear on the X axis as the category names. The text entries in the first column of the datasheet appear as a legend to indicate the name associated with each series.

Figure 3.1c, on the other hand, plots the data by column, making it easy to see the progress of each salesman over the course of the year. This time there are four data series (Sales for 1st Qtr, Sales for 2nd Qtr, Sales for 3rd Qtr, and Sales for 4th Qtr), each with three data points (one each for Tom, Dick, and Harry). The text entries in the first column of the datasheet appear on the X axis as the category names. The text entries in the first row of the datasheet appear in the legend to indicate the name associated with each series.

Figure 3.1d also displays the data series in columns, but uses a different graph type, a stacked column rather than side-by-side columns as in Figure 3.1c. The choice between the two types of graphs depends on your message. If, for example, you want your audience to see each individual's sales in each quarter, the side-by-side graph is more appropriate. If, on the other hand, you want to emphasize the total sales for each salesperson, the stacked column graph is preferable. Note, too, the different scale on the Y axis in the two graphs. The side-by-side graph in Figure 3.1c shows the sales in each quarter and so the Y axis goes only to $90,000. The stacked bars in Figure 3.1d, however, reflect the total sales for each salesperson and thus the scale goes to $250,000.

All three graphs contain the same number of data points (12 in all) but plot them differently to emphasize different information. All three graphs are equally correct, and the choice depends on the message you want to convey.

> **EMPHASIZE YOUR MESSAGE**
>
> A graph is used to deliver a message, and you want that message to be as clear as possible. One way to help put your point across is to choose a title that leads the audience. A neutral title such as *Revenue by Quarter* is vague and requires the audience to reach its own conclusion. A better title might be *Tom Is the Leading Sales Associate* if the objective were to emphasize Tom's contribution. A well-chosen title emphasizes your message.

My Chart - Datasheet

| | | A | B | C | D | E |
|---|---|---|---|---|---|---|
| | | 1st Qtr | 2nd Qtr | 3rd Qtr | 4th Qtr | |
| 1 | Tom | 20.4 | 50 | 90 | 75 | |
| 2 | Dick | 30.6 | 38.6 | 34.6 | 31.6 | |
| 3 | Harry | 45.9 | 46.9 | 45 | 12 | |
| 4 | | | | | | |

(a) The Datasheet (sales in thousands)

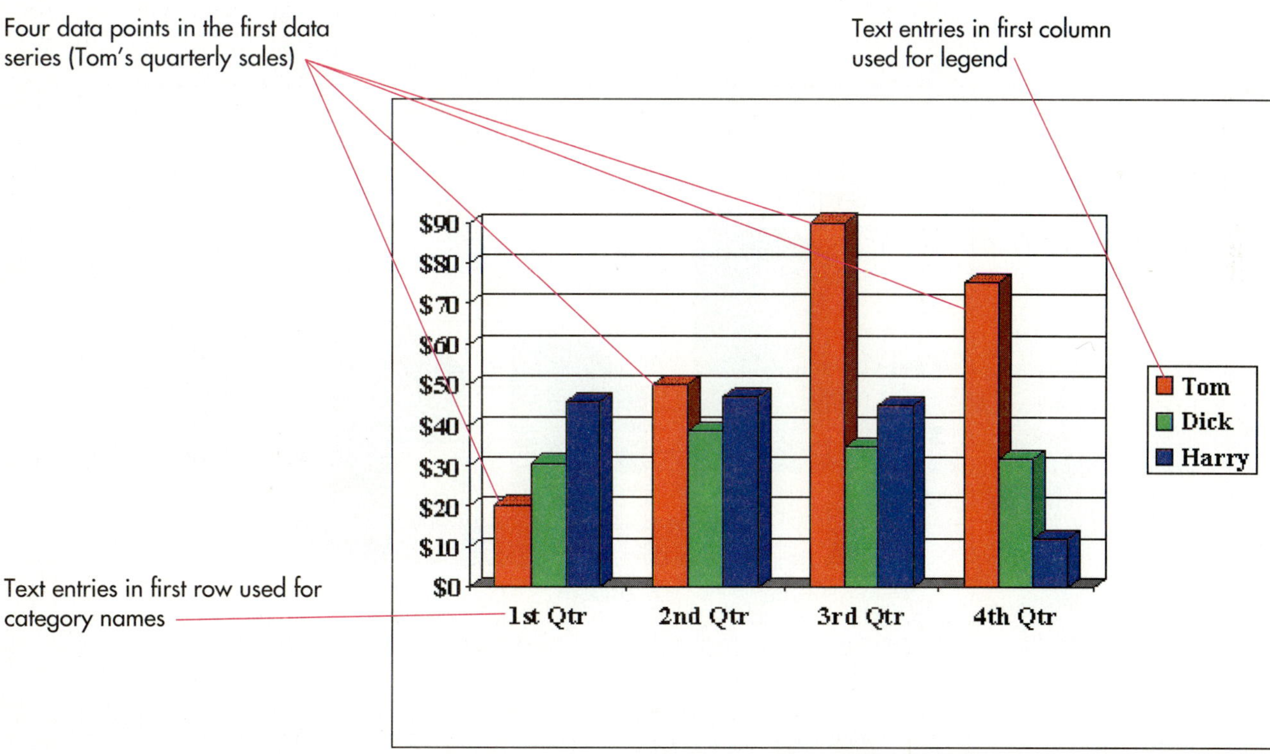


(b) Data Series in Rows (sales in thousands)

**FIGURE 3.1** Microsoft Graph

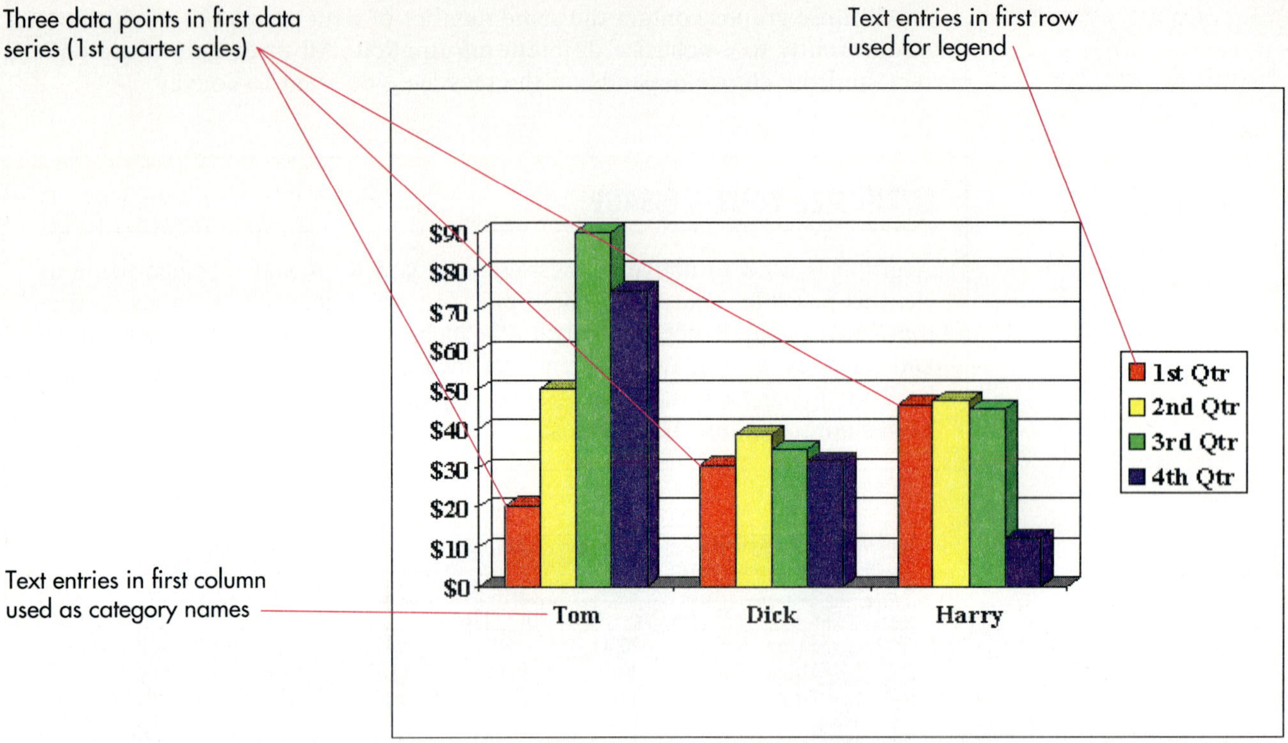


(c) Data Series in Columns (sales in thousands)

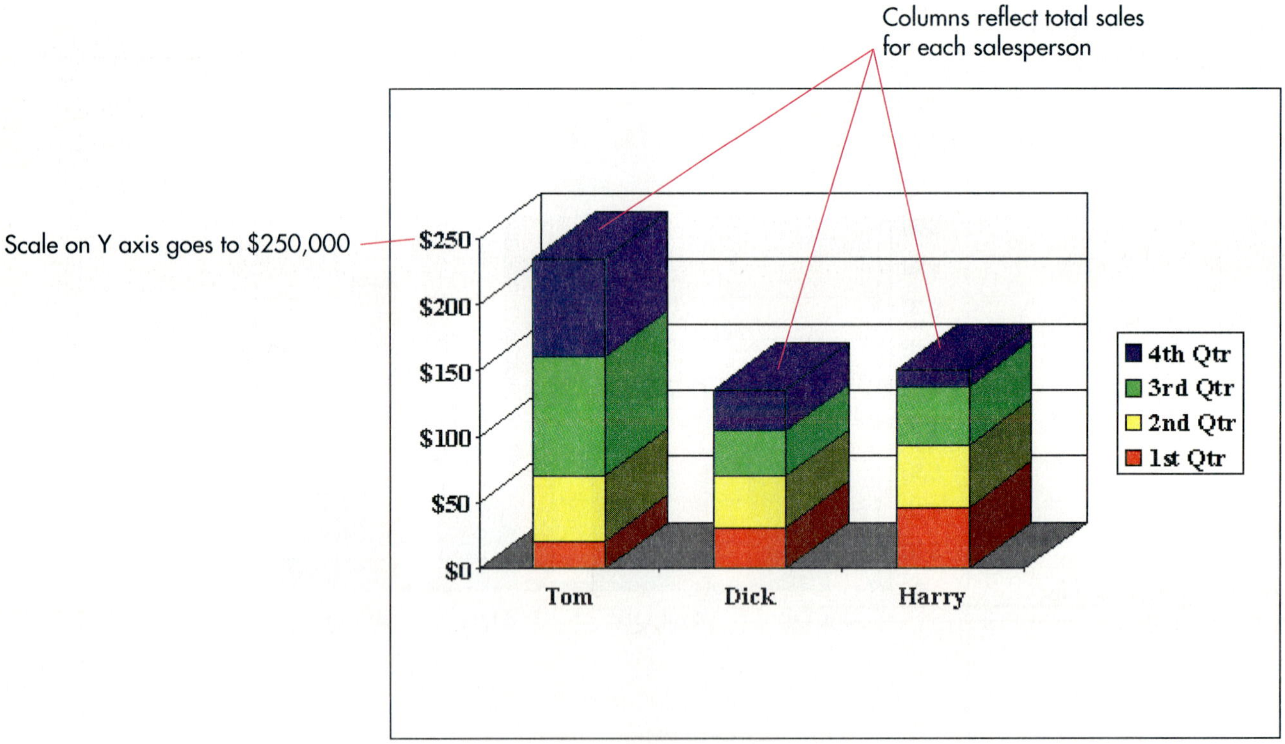


(d) Stacked Column Chart (sales in thousands)

**FIGURE 3.1** Microsoft Graph (continued)

## HANDS-ON EXERCISE 1

*Microsoft Graph*

**Objective:** To use Microsoft Graph to insert a graph into a presentation; to modify the graph to display the data in rows or columns; to change the graph format and underlying data. Use Figure 3.2 as a guide in the exercise.

**STEP 1: Start Microsoft Graph**

- ➤ Start PowerPoint. Click the option button to create a new presentation using a **Blank Presentation.** Click **OK.** You should see the New Slide dialog box.
- ➤ Select (click) the AutoLayout for a chart (it is the AutoLayout at the end of the second row), then click **OK** to add the slide as shown in Figure 3.2a. If necessary, maximize the document window.

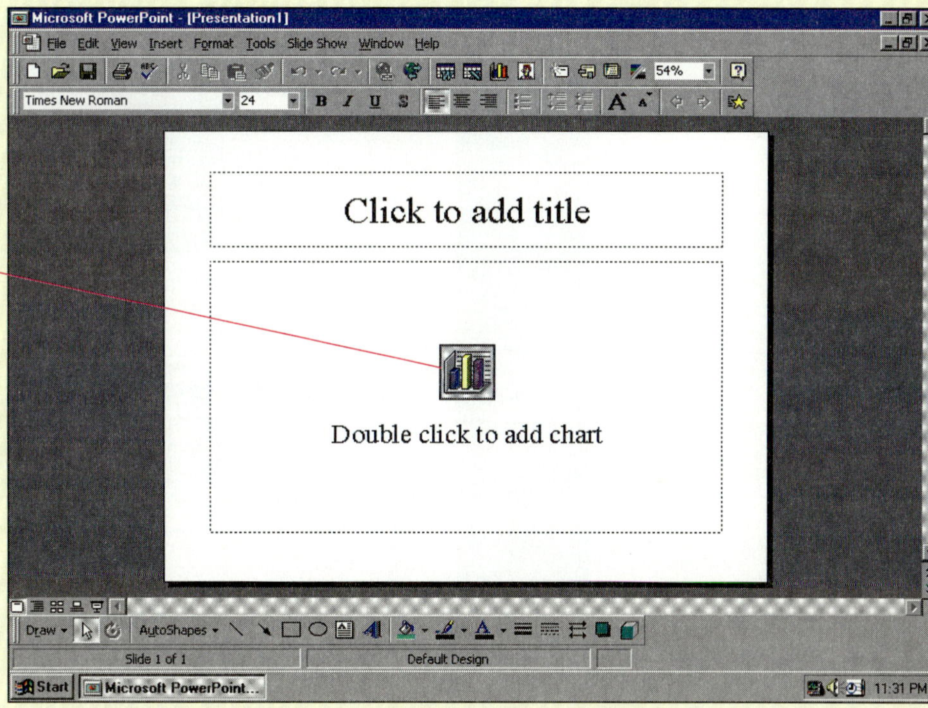


(a) Start Microsoft Graph (step 1)

**FIGURE 3.2** Hands-on Exercise 1

### INSERTING A GRAPH

There are several ways to insert a graph into a presentation. You can choose one of three AutoLayouts containing a placeholder for a graph. You can also pull down the Insert menu and select Chart, or you can click the Insert Chart button on the Standard toolbar. You can also insert a graph created in another application by executing the Insert Object command and selecting the appropriate object, such as a Microsoft Excel chart.

➤ Double click the placeholder to add a chart, which starts the Microsoft Graph application.

**STEP 2: The Default Graph**

➤ The default datasheet and graph should be displayed on your monitor, as shown in Figure 3.2b. The menus and toolbar have changed to reflect the Microsoft Graph application.

➤ Do not be concerned if the numbers in your datasheet are different from those in the figure. (You can create your own graph simply by editing the text and numeric values, as will be described in the next step.)

➤ Click and drag the **title bar** of the datasheet so that you can see more of the graph, as in the figure.

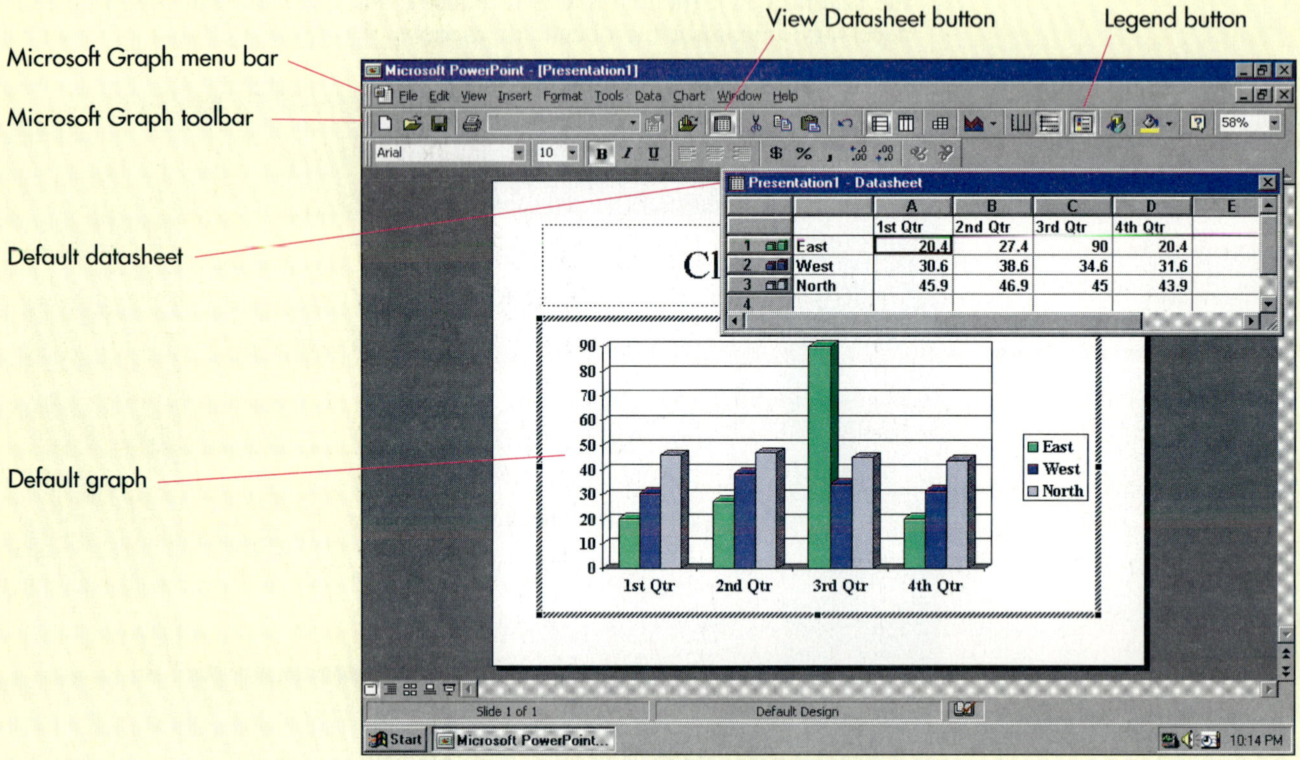


(b) The Default Graph (step 2)

**FIGURE 3.2** Hands-on Exercise 1 (continued)

### IN-PLACE EDITING

Microsoft Graph enables in-place editing as you create and/or modify a graph; that is, you remain in PowerPoint, but the toolbars and pull-down menus are those of Microsoft Graph. The File and Window menus are exceptions, however, and contain PowerPoint commands (so that you can save the presentation and/or view multiple presentations). In-place editing requires that both applications support the Microsoft specification for Object Linking and Embedding 2.0.

- ➤ Click the **View Datasheet button** on the (Microsoft Graph) Standard toolbar to close the datasheet. Click the **View Datasheet button** a second time to open the datasheet.
- ➤ Click the **Legend button** on the Standard toolbar to suppress the legend on the graph. Click the **Legend button** a second time to display the legend.

**STEP 3: Change the Data**

- ➤ Click in **cell B1** of the datasheet (the value for East in the 2nd Quarter). Type **50** and press **enter.** The graph changes automatically to reflect the new data.
- ➤ Change the values of the following cells as follows:
  - Click in **cell D1.** Type **75.**
  - Click in **cell D3.** Type **12.**
  - Click in the cell containing **East.** Type **Tom.**
  - Press the **down arrow key** to move to the cell containing **West.** Type **Dick.**
  - Press the **down arrow key** to move to the cell containing **North.** Type **Harry.**
- ➤ Check that all of the values in your datasheet match those in Figure 3.2c. Click the **Close button** to close the datasheet.

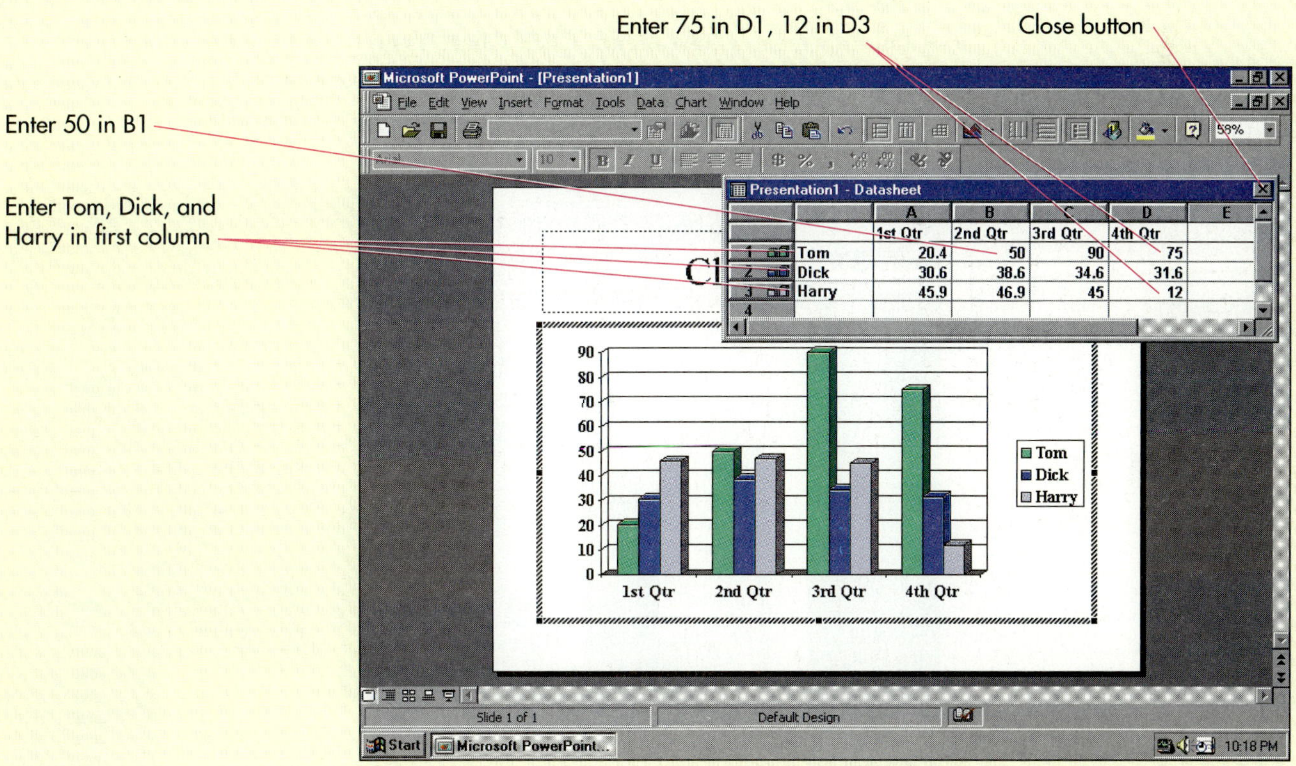


(c) Change the Data (step 3)

**FIGURE 3.2** Hands-on Exercise 1 (continued)

## IMPORT THE DATA

Microsoft Graph enables you to import data from another application (e.g., Microsoft Excel) and use that data as the basis for the graph. Click in the upper-left cell (the cell above row 1 and to the left of column A) to select the entire datasheet. Click the Import File button on the Microsoft Graph toolbar to display an Import File dialog box. Select the appropriate drive and directory containing the file you want to import, select the file, then click the Open command button.

**STEP 4: Change the Orientation and Format**

- Click the **By Column button** on the Standard toolbar to change the data series from rows to columns as shown in Figure 3.2d. The X axis changes to display the names of the salespersons, and the legend indicates the quarter.
- Click the **By Row button** on the Standard toolbar to change the data series back to rows.
- Click the **By Column button** a second time to match the orientation in Figure 3.2d.
- Pull down the **Chart menu.** Click **Chart Type** to display the Chart Type.
- If necessary, click **Column** in the Chart Type list box. Select the stacked column with 3-D visual effect as the Chart subtype. Click **OK.**

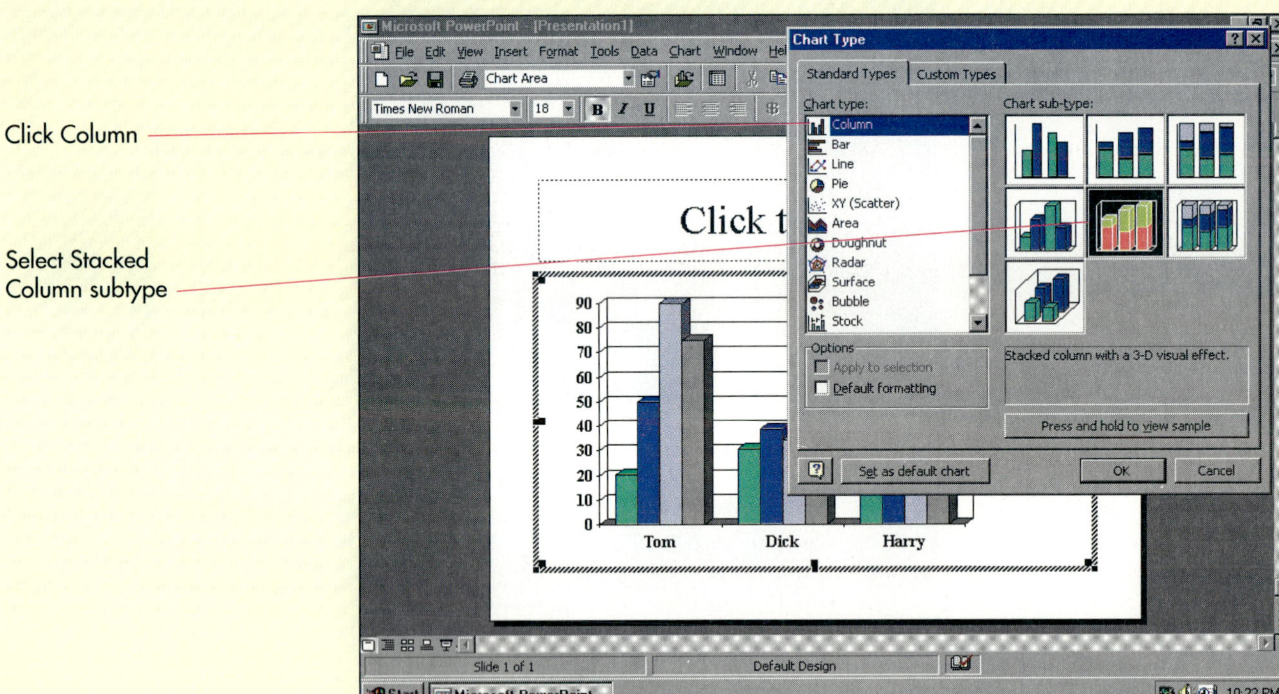


(d) Change the Orientation and Format (step 4)

**FIGURE 3.2** Hands-on Exercise 1 (continued)

## DON'T FORGET HELP

Microsoft Graph includes its own Help system, which functions identically to the Help in any other application. Pull down the Help menu and search on any topic for which you want additional information. Remember, too, that you can print the contents of a Help screen by clicking the Print button in the Help window.

### STEP 5: Return to PowerPoint

- Click outside the chart to exit Microsoft Graph and return to PowerPoint. You should see the stacked column graph in Figure 3.2e.
- Click inside the graph, and the sizing handles appear to indicate the graph is selected. Click and drag a corner sizing handle to increase (decrease) the size of the graph within the slide.
- Click the **title placeholder,** which deselects the graph and positions the insertion point to enter the title. Type **Tom is the Top Sales Associate.**
- Pull down the **File menu** and click **Save** (or click the **Save button** on the Standard toolbar). Save the presentation as **My Chart** in the **Exploring PowerPoint folder.**

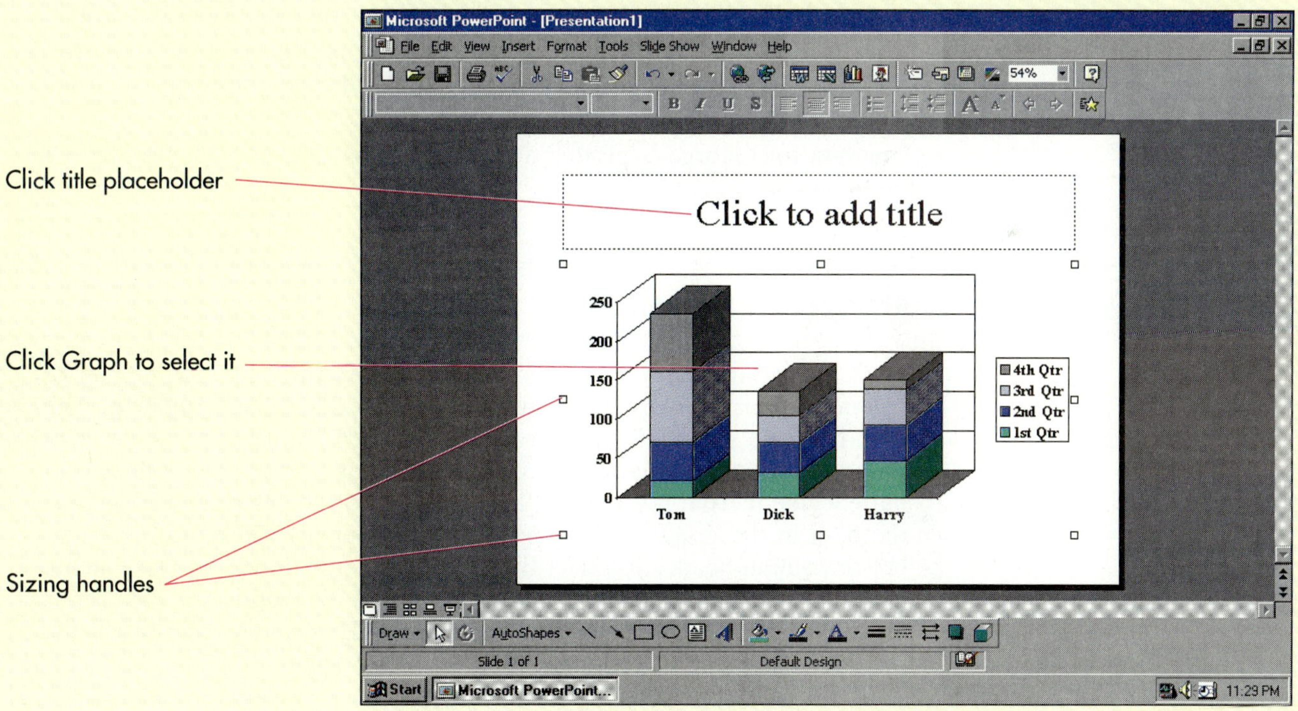


(e) Return to PowerPoint (step 5)

**FIGURE 3.2** Hands-on Exercise 1 (continued)

### TO CLICK OR DOUBLE CLICK

Once you create a graph and return to your presentation, the graph becomes an embedded object, which retains its connection to Microsoft Graph for easy editing. You can click the graph to select it, then move or size the graph just as you would any other Windows object. You can also double click the graph to restart Microsoft Graph (the application that created the graph) and then edit it using the tools of the original application.

**STEP 6: Add a Data Series**

- Point to the graph and click the **right mouse button** to display a shortcut menu, then click **Edit Chart Object.** (You can also double click the graph as described in the previous tip.)
- Once again you are in Microsoft Graph, and the menus and toolbar have changed to reflect this application.
- Click the **View Datasheet button** to reopen the datasheet. If necessary, click and drag the title bar of the datasheet so you can see more of the graph.
- Add an additional data series as follows:
  - Click in the cell under Harry. Type **George,** then press the **right arrow key** to move to cell A4. George appears as a category name on the X axis.
  - Enter **10, 15, 20,** and **25** in cells A4, B4, C4, and D4, respectively. Notice that as you complete each entry, the graph adjusts automatically to reflect the value you just entered.
- The data for George is plotted automatically as shown in Figure 3.2f. Close the datasheet.

### REMOVING A DATA SERIES

To delete a data series, open the datasheet, then click the row number or column header of the data series you want to delete, and press the Del key. The data series will disappear from both the datasheet and the associated graph. Alternatively, you can leave the data series in the datasheet but exclude it from the graph. (This enables you to subsequently include the data in the graph without having to reenter it.) Click the row number or column header to select the data series, pull down the Data menu, and select the Exclude Row/Column command. To restore the data series in the graph, select the series, pull down the Data menu, and select the Include Row/Column command.

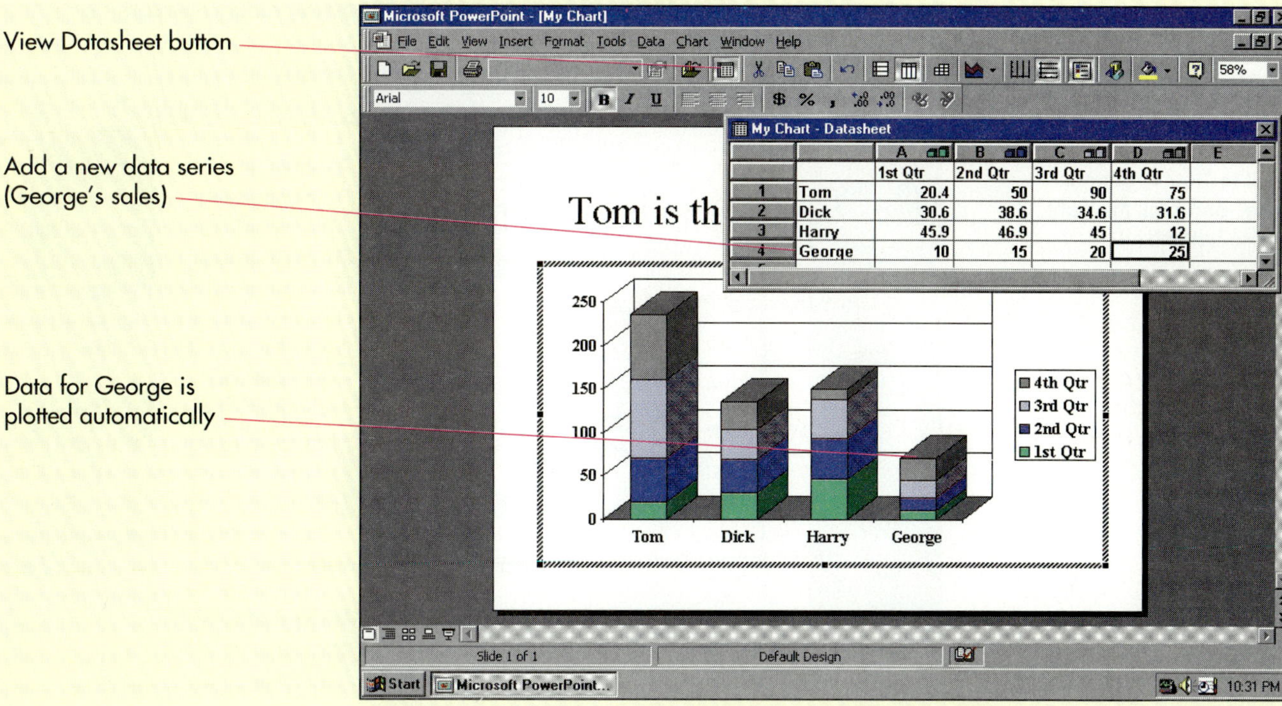


(f) Add a Data Series (step 6)

FIGURE 3.2 Hands-on Exercise 1 (continued)

### STEP 7: The Finishing Touches

➤ You can customize every object within a chart (the legend, axis, plot area, and so on) by pointing to the object and clicking the right mouse button to display a shortcut menu.

➤ Point to the gray section (4th Qtr Sales) of any column and click the **right mouse button** to display a shortcut menu. Click **Format Data Series.**

➤ Click the **Patterns tab** (if necessary) in the Format Data Series dialog box and click **red** as the new color. Click **OK** to close the dialog box. The data series for the fourth quarter has been changed to red as shown in Figure 3.2g.

➤ Point to any value on the vertical axis, then click the **right mouse button** to display the shortcut menu in Figure 3.2g. Click **Format Axis.**

➤ Click the **Number tab** in the Format Number dialog box, then select the **Currency format** within the Category list box. Change the decimal places to 0. Click **OK.** The format of the axis has been changed to include the dollar sign.

### STEP 8: Save the Presentation

➤ Click outside the chart to exit Microsoft Graph and return to PowerPoint. Save the presentation.

➤ Pull down the **File menu** and click **Print** (or click the **Print button**). Click **OK** to print the slide.

➤ Exit PowerPoint if you do not want to continue with the next exercise at this time. Click **Yes** if prompted to save the changes to the presentation.

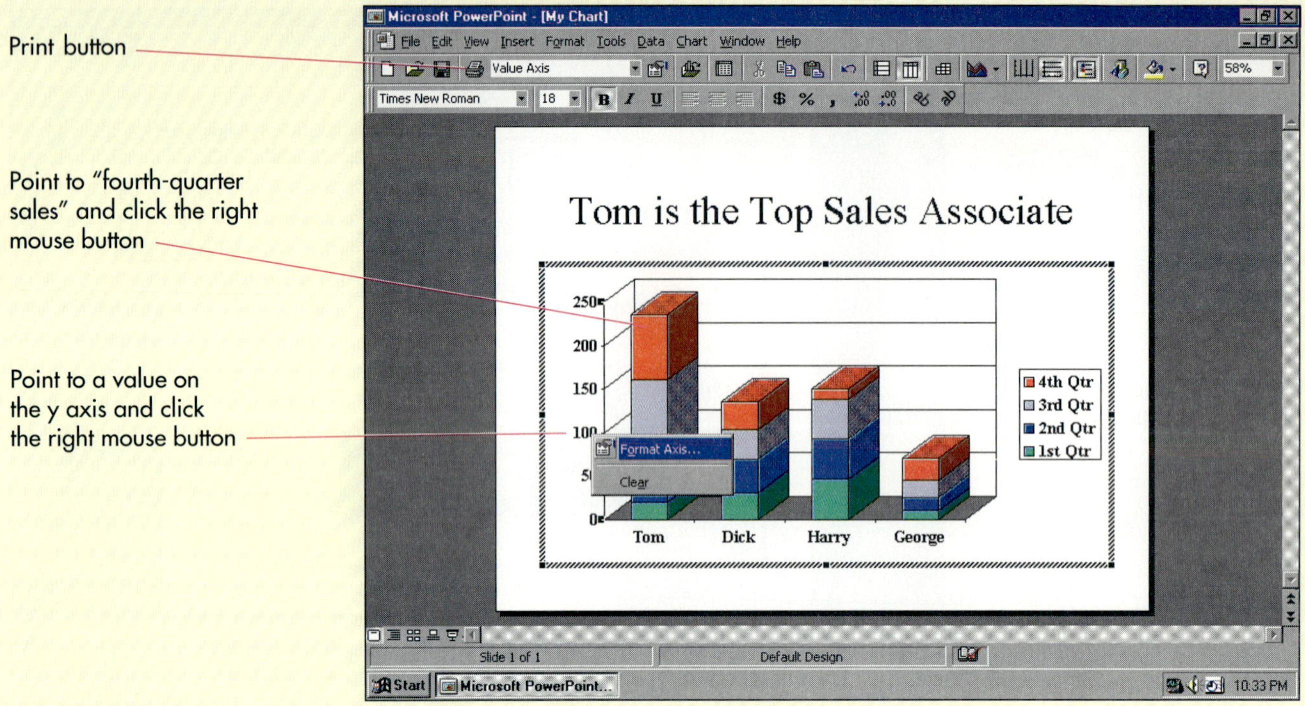


(g) The Finishing Touches (step 7)

**FIGURE 3.2** Hands-on Exercise 1 (continued)

> **THE 3-D VIEW COMMAND**
>
> The 3-D View command enables you to fine-tune the appearance of a graph by controlling the rotation, elevation, and other parameters found within its dialog box. The rotation controls the rotation around the vertical axis and determines how much of the stacked bars you see. The elevation controls the height at which you view the graph. Pull down the Chart menu, select the 3-D View command, then set these parameters as you see fit.

## OFFICE ART

Office 97 contains a powerful set of drawing tools that are collectively known as ***Office Art.*** Even if you are not an artist, you can use these tools to modify existing clip art and thus create new and very different illustrations. Consider, for example, Figure 3.3, which contains an original piece of clip art and five variations. (The clip art was taken from the Cartoons category of the Microsoft Clip Gallery.) We are not artistic by nature and there is no way that we could have created the original duck. We did, however, create all of the variations. All it took was a little imagination and a sense of what can be done.

The tools in Office Art are accessed through the ***Drawing toolbar,*** which is displayed by default in the Slide view and illustrated in Figure 3.4. As with the

**FIGURE 3.3** What You Can Do with Clip Art

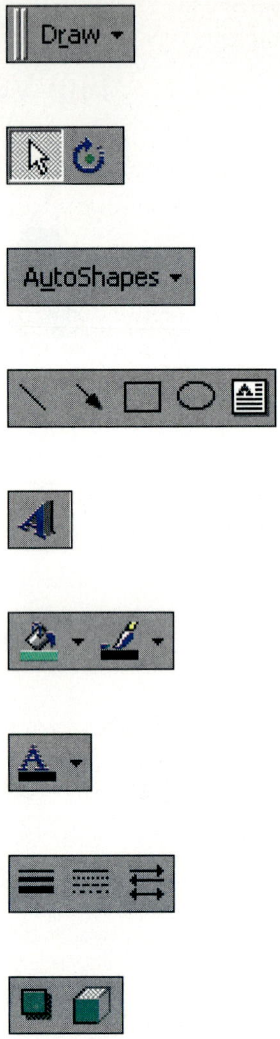


Contains additional commands to modify an existing object

Selects an object; rotates an object

Displays the AutoShapes menu

Creates a line, arrow, rectangle, oval, or text box

Inserts a WordArt object (WordArt is discussed later in the chapter)

Changes the fill color or line color of an object

Changes the font color

Changes the line thickness, line style, or arrow style

Applies a shadow or three-dimensional effect

**FIGURE 3.4** The Drawing Toolbar

other toolbars, there is no need to memorize what the individual buttons do. You can, however, gain a better appreciation of their function by viewing the tools in groups, as is done in Figure 3.4. And, as with all toolbars, you can point to any tool and PowerPoint will display the name of the tool. You can also access the Help menu for detailed information on a specific tool.

The various tools are used to create or modify the objects that appear on a PowerPoint slide. An ***object*** is anything you put on a slide. Select the Line tool, for example, then click and drag to create the line. Once the line is created, you can select it, then change its properties (such as its thickness or style) by using other tools on the Drawing toolbar. Objects (such as lines and arcs) are the building blocks of any drawing. You can create an original drawing of your own, or you can modify an existing drawing (as we did with the ducks) by manipulating its objects to create an entirely different drawing.

The ***Draw menu*** provides access to additional commands that let you modify an object in various ways. The ***Ungroup command*** breaks an object into smaller objects (e.g., it separates the duck and the computer) so you can work with each object on an individual basis. The ***Group command*** does the opposite and combines multiple objects into a single object. The ***Rotate or Flip command*** enables you to change the orientation of an object (e.g., make the duck face left or right or turn him upside down).

The following exercise has you insert a clip art image into a presentation, then modify that image using various tools on the Drawing toolbar. Be flexible and willing to experiment. Try, and try again, and don't be discouraged if you don't succeed initially. Just keep trying, and you will be amazed at what you will be able to do.

## HANDS-ON EXERCISE 2

*You Don't Have to Be an Artist*

**Objective:** To insert clip art into a presentation, then use various tools on the Drawing toolbar to modify the clip art. Use Figure 3.5 as a guide in the exercise.

**STEP 1: Create the Title Slide**

- Create a new presentation:
  - If necessary, start PowerPoint. Click the option button to create a **Blank Presentation** as you have been doing throughout the text. Click **OK.**
  - If PowerPoint is already started, pull down the **File menu** and click **New** (or click the **New button** on the Standard toolbar). If necessary, double click the **Blank Presentation icon** to display the New Slide dialog box.
- You should see the New Slide dialog box with the **AutoLayout** for the title slide already selected. Click **OK** to create the title slide. Click the placeholder for the title. Type **What You Can Do With Clip Art** as shown in Figure 3.5a.
- Click the placeholder for the subtitle. Enter your name.
- Click the **Save button** on the Standard toolbar. Save the presentation as **You Don't Have to Be an Artist** in the **Exploring PowerPoint folder.**

**STEP 2: Add the Clip Art**

- Pull down the **Insert menu** and click **New Slide** (or click the **New Slide button** on the Standard toolbar).
- Select (click) the **Title Only layout.** (This is AutoLayout number 11 and is the third layout in the third row.) Click **OK.**
- Click the **Insert Clip Art button** on the Standard toolbar to display the Microsoft Clip Gallery as shown in Figure 3.5b. Click **OK** if you see a dialog box reminding you that additional clip art is available on a CD-ROM.
- If necessary, click the **Clip Art tab** and select (click) the **Cartoons category.** Select the **Duck and Computer,** then click the **Insert button** to insert the picture into the presentation.
- Close the Picture toolbar if it appears since we do not need to use any of its tools in this exercise.
- Click anywhere on the slide (other than the clip art) to deselect the clip art.
- Click the placeholder for the title. Enter **The Original Clip Art** as the title for the slide. Save the presentation.

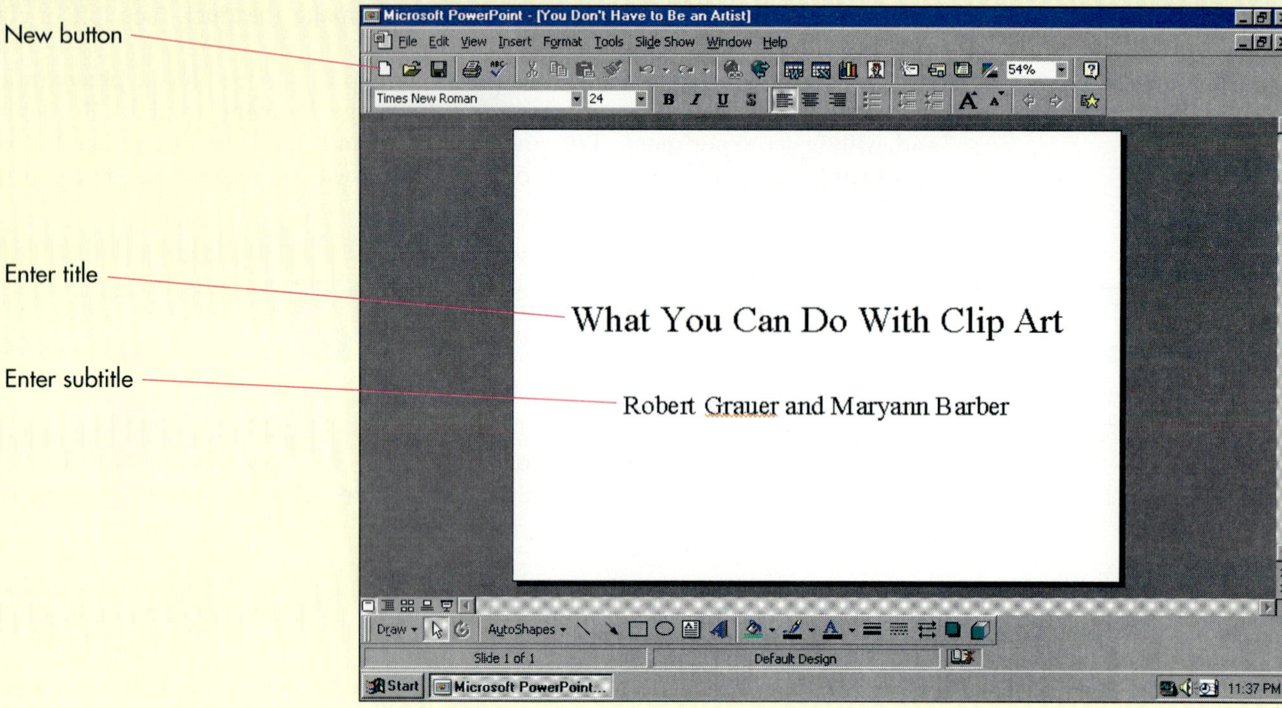


(a) Create the Title Slide (step 1)

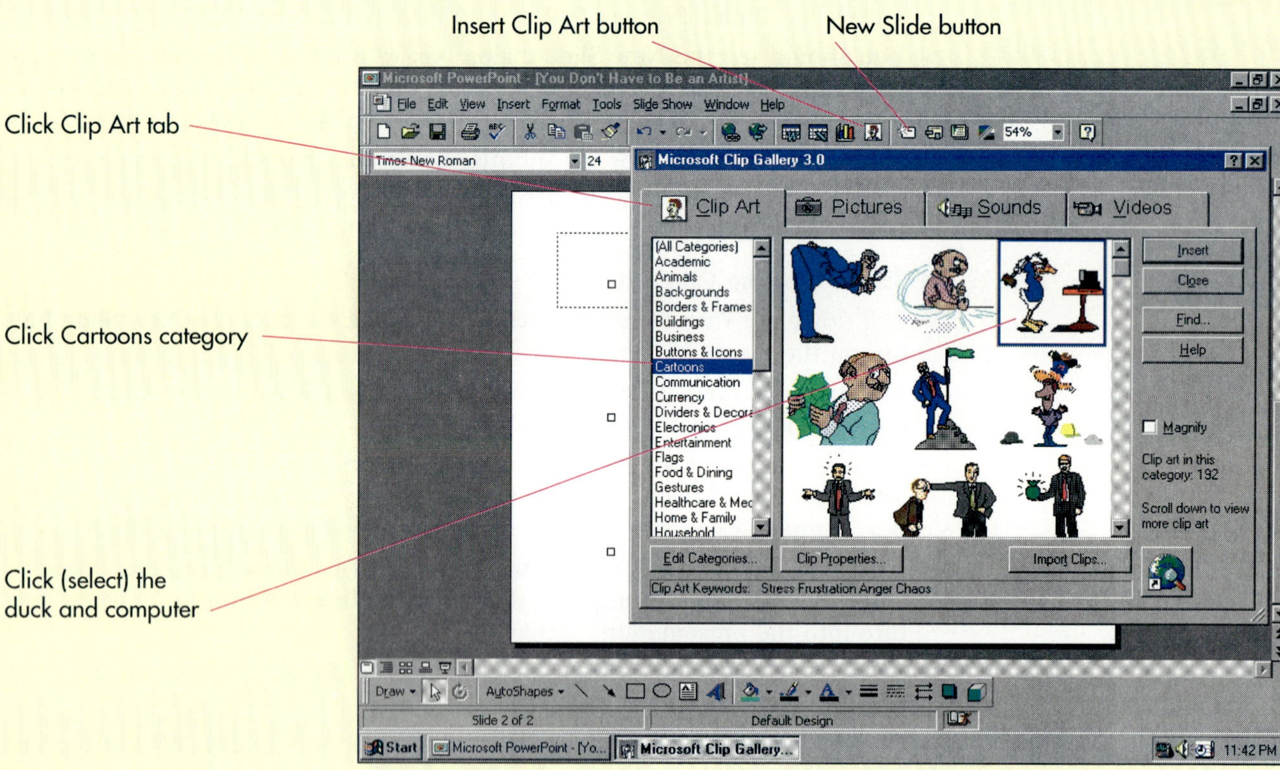


(b) Add the Clip Art (step 2)

FIGURE 3.5 Hands-on Exercise 2

## THE PICTURE TOOLBAR

The Picture toolbar is displayed automatically when a picture (or clip art image) is selected; otherwise it is suppressed. It contains a button to format the picture (which lets you change its size or position, or add a border) as well as a button to crop (erase) part of a picture. As with any toolbar, you can point to a button to display a ScreenTip containing the name of the button, which is indicative of its function.

**STEP 3: Copy the Slide**

- Click the **Slide Sorter View button** on the status bar to change to the view in Figure 3.5c. Slide 2, the slide with the duck, is selected.
- Click the **Copy button** on the Standard toolbar (or press **Ctrl+C**) to copy the slide to the clipboard.
- Click the **Paste button** on the Standard toolbar (or press **Ctrl+V**) to paste the contents of the clipboard into the presentation. This creates a new slide (slide 3), which is identical to slide 2.
- Click the **Paste button** four additional times so that you wind up with seven slides in all, as shown in Figure 3.5c. There are now six identical slides of the duck smashing the computer.
- Save the presentation.

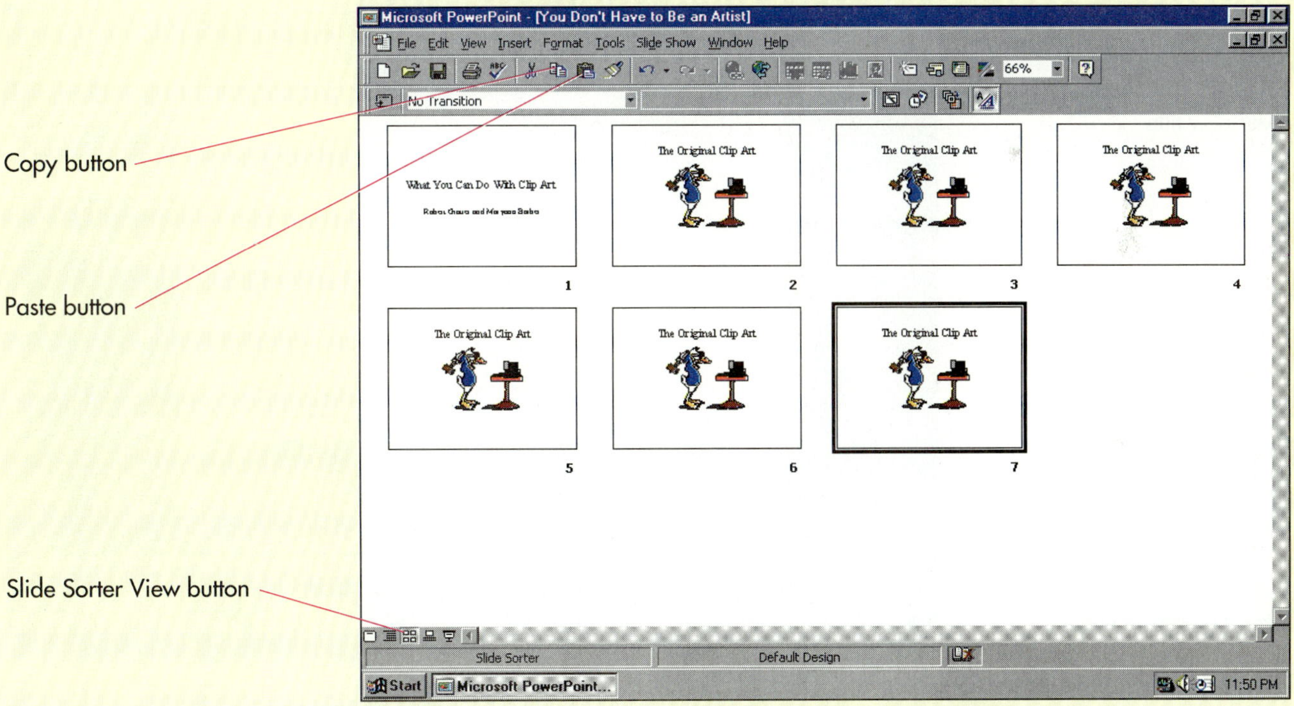


(c) Copy the Slide (step 3)

**FIGURE 3.5** Hands-on Exercise 2 (continued)

### CUT, COPY, AND PASTE

Ctrl+X (the X is supposed to remind you of a pair of scissors), Ctrl+C, and Ctrl+V are keyboard equivalents to cut, copy, and paste, respectively, and apply to each application in Microsoft Office, as well as Windows applications in general. (The keystrokes are easier to remember when you realize that the operative letters—X, C, and V—are next to each other at the bottom left side of the keyboard.) Alternatively, you can use the Cut, Copy, and Paste buttons on the Standard toolbar.

**STEP 4: The Ungroup Command**

- Double click **slide 3** to simultaneously select the slide and change to the Slide view, as shown in Figure 3.5d. The status bar should indicate that slide 3 is the current slide.
- Click and drag to select the text of the slide title, then type **Flip Vertically** as the new title.
- Click anywhere on the clip art to select the entire image. You should see eight sizing handles around the image as shown in the figure.
- Click the **Draw menu** on the Drawing toolbar to display additional commands. Click **Ungroup.**

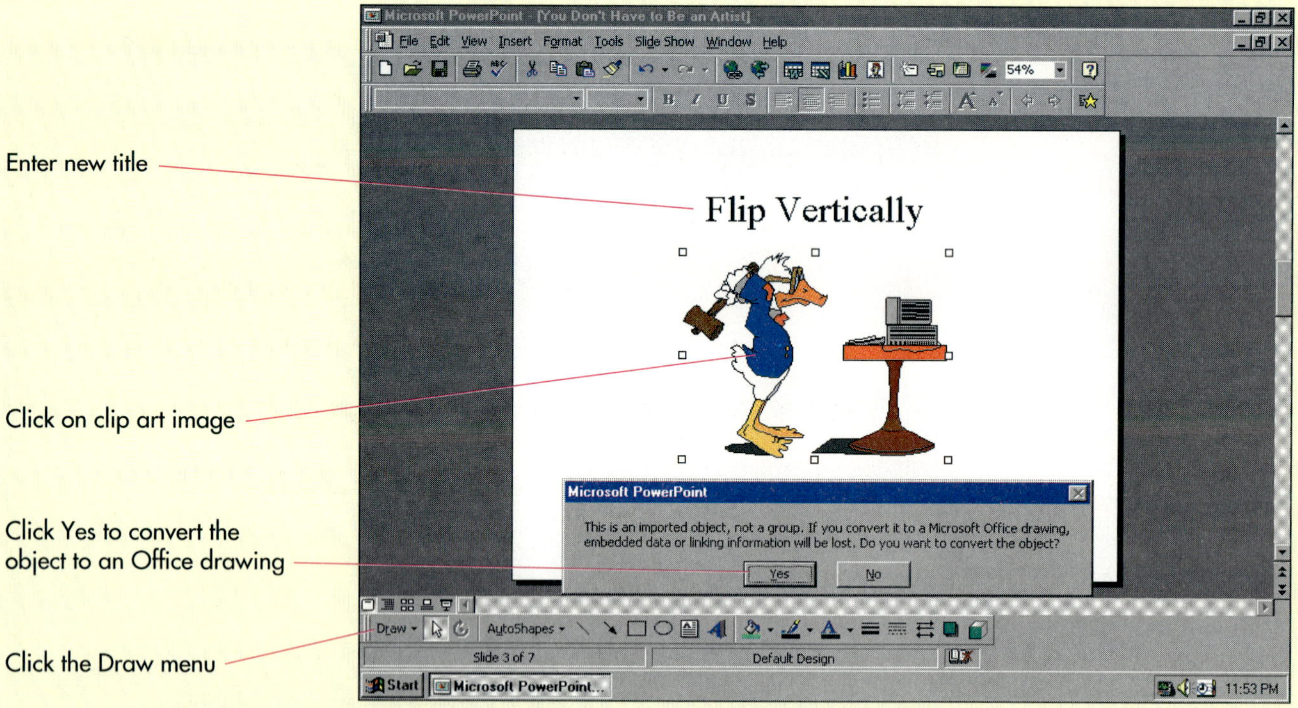


(d) The Ungroup Command (step 4)

FIGURE 3.5 Hands-on Exercise 2 (continued)

- You will see the message in Figure 3.5d. Click **Yes** to convert the object to a Microsoft Office drawing, allowing you to use the PowerPoint tools to edit the image.
- You should see two sets of sizing handles: one set surrounding the duck, and the other set around the computer and the table.
- Click outside the selected area, then click anywhere on the duck to select just the duck.
- Click the **Draw menu** on the Drawing toolbar. Click **Rotate or Flip,** then click the **Flip Vertical command.** The duck is now upside down.
- Save the presentation.

### DISPLAY THE ROTATE OR FLIP TOOLBAR

The exercise makes frequent use of the Flip Horizontal and Flip Vertical commands that can be accessed more easily from a toolbar. Click the Draw menu on the Drawing toolbar, then click the Rotate or Flip command to display the Rotate or Flip menu. Point to the top of the menu (which is actually a title bar), then click and drag to display the Rotate or Flip toolbar. You can leave the toolbar floating on the desktop or you can anchor it along an edge. (Double click the gray background of the toolbar to toggle between a docked or floating toolbar.)

**STEP 5: Copy and Flip Horizontally**

- Press the **PgDn key** (or click the **Next Slide button** at the bottom of the scroll bar) to move to slide 4. (You can also drag the scroll box (slide elevator) on the vertical scroll bar to move to slide 4.)
- Click and drag to select the slide title, then type **Copy and Flip Horizontally** as the new title as shown in Figure 3.5e.
- Click the clip art to select it, then drag the clip art to the left edge of the slide. Ungroup the duck and the computer as in the previous step.
- Click outside the selected objects. Select just the duck. Click the **Copy button** on the Standard toolbar (which copies the duck to the clipboard).
- Click the **Paste button** on the Standard toolbar. You should see a second duck on top of the first duck.
- Click and drag the second duck past the computer all the way to the right of the slide as shown in Figure 3.5e.
- Click the **Draw menu** on the Drawing toolbar, click **Rotate or Flip,** then click **Flip Horizontal.** Move the table and/or the ducks to adjust the spacing as desired.
- Save the presentation.

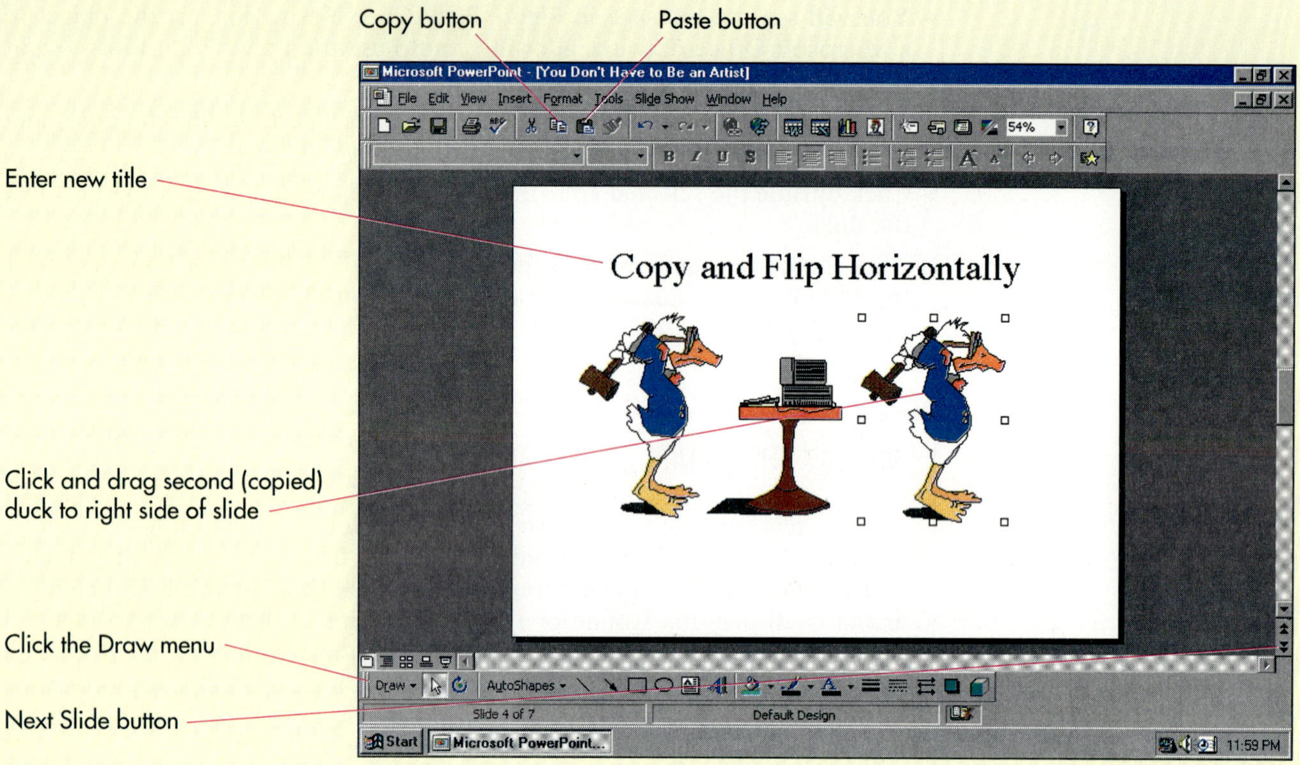


(e) Copy and Flip Horizontally (step 5)

**FIGURE 3.5** Hands-on Exercise 2 (continued)

> **ALIGNING OBJECTS**
>
> You can improve the appearance of any slide by precisely aligning the objects it contains. Press and hold the Shift key to select the objects you want to align. Click the Draw menu on the Drawing toolbar, click Align or Distribute, then choose the alignment you want (left, center, right, top, middle, or bottom) from the cascade menu.

**STEP 6: Change Colors**

- Press the **PgDn key** to move to slide 5. Click and drag to select the text of the slide title, then type **Change Colors** as the new title as shown in Figure 3.5f.
- Repeat the actions from the previous step to copy the duck and flip him horizontally:
  - Click and drag the clip art to the left side of the slide, then **ungroup** the duck and the computer.

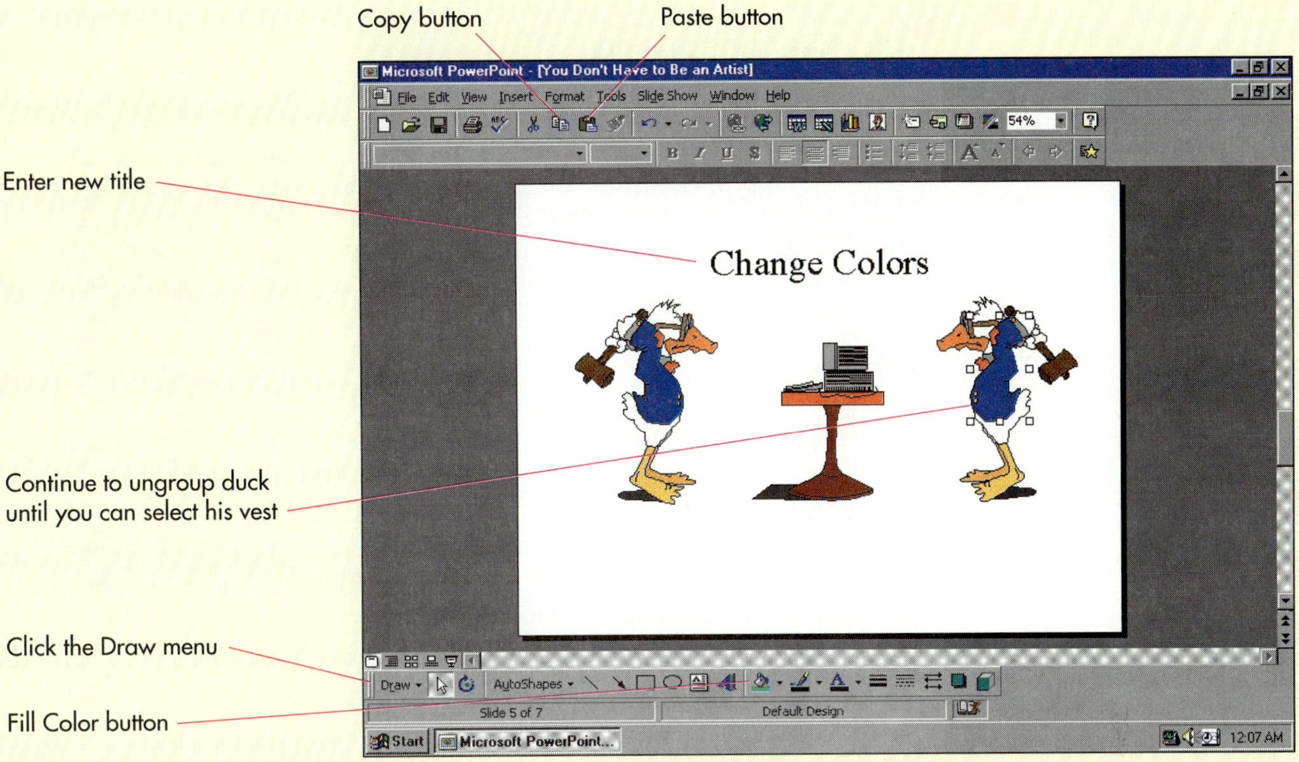


(f) Change Colors (step 6)

**FIGURE 3.5** Hands-on Exercise 2 (continued)

- Click outside the selected area to deselect both objects. Select the duck, click the **Copy button,** click the **Paste button,** then drag the second duck to the right of the computer.
- Click the **Draw button** on the Drawing toolbar, click **Rotate or Flip,** and click **Flip Horizontal.**

➤ Check that the duck on the right is still selected, then execute the **Ungroup Command** to ungroup the objects that make up this duck and his hammer. The duck is now a separate object; the hammer and shadow are a second object.

➤ Click outside the selected objects, then click the duck. Execute the **Ungroup Command** to ungroup the objects that make up the duck.

➤ Continue to ungroup the duck until you have separated his vest from his tie. Click outside the selected objects, then click the **duck's vest** to select just the vest as shown in Figure 3.5f.

➤ Click the **down arrow** on the **Fill Color button** on the Drawing toolbar, then click **More Fill Colors.** Choose a shade of green to change the vest to green.

➤ Repeat these steps to change the costume of the other duck to a black vest with a blue tie.

➤ Save the presentation.

## FILL, LINE, AND SHADOW

All drawn objects have attributes (characteristics) that determine the appearance of the object. To change an attribute, select the object, then click the appropriate tool on the Drawing toolbar. You can apply a shadow. You can change the style of the exterior line and/or the color of the line. You can also change the interior (fill) color of the object and/or the fill pattern.

**STEP 7: Ungroup and Resize**

- Press the **PgDn key** to move to slide 6. Click and drag to select the text of the slide title, then type **Ungroup and Resize** as the new title.
- Check that the title is still selected. Pull down the **Format menu.** Click **Alignment.** Click **Right** to move the slide title to the right as shown in Figure 3.5g.
- Ungroup the duck and computer. Click outside the selected areas, then select the duck. Click and drag the duck to the upper left part of the slide.
- Click the computer and table, and upgroup these objects.
- Click outside the selected items, then click and drag the table under the duck.
- Click the computer. Drag a **corner handle** to increase the size of the computer, then click and drag to position the computer closer to the duck.

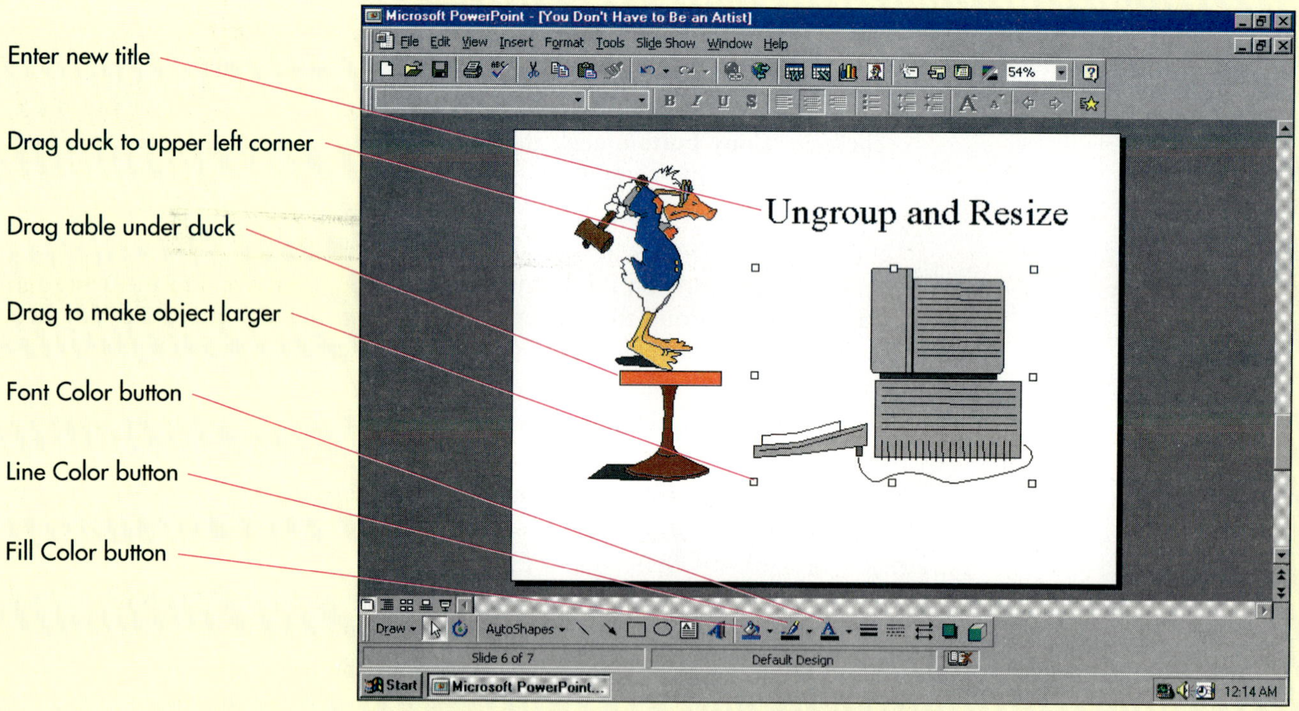


(g) Ungroup and Resize (step 7)

**FIGURE 3.5** Hands-on Exercise 2 (continued)

## PICK UP THE MOUSE

You always seem to run out of room on your real desk just when you need to move the mouse a little further. The solution is to pick up the mouse and move it closer to you—the pointer will stay in its present position on the screen, but when you put the mouse down you will have more room on your desk in which to work.

**STEP 8: The Duplicate Command**

- Press the **PgDn key** to move to slide 7. Click and drag to select the slide title, then type **Get Your Ducks in a Row** as the new title as shown in Figure 3.5h.
- Click and drag the clip art to the left side of the slide, then **ungroup** the duck and the computer. Click outside the selection to deselect both items, then click and drag the computer and table to the right of the slide.
- Select the duck. Pull down the **Edit menu** and click **Duplicate** (a combination of the Copy and Paste commands). You will see a second duck to the right of the first. Drag the second duck to the right until the ducks are separated as shown in Figure 3.5h.

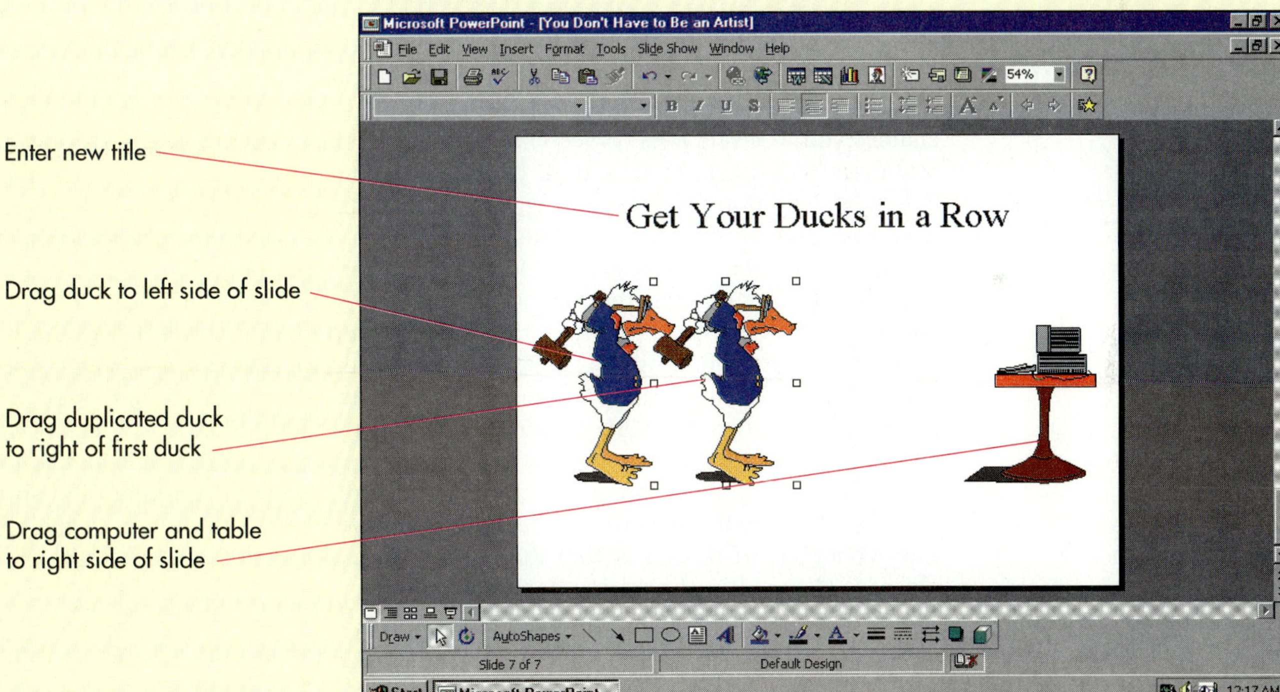


(h) The Duplicate Command (step 8)

**FIGURE 3.5** Hands-on Exercise 2 (continued)

- ➤ Pull down the **Edit menu** a second time and click the **Duplicate command** a second time. A third duck will appear. (The distance between the second and third ducks is equal to the distance between the first and second ducks.)
- ➤ Execute the **Duplicate command** a third time to create the fourth and final duck. Change the vest colors as you see fit.
- ➤ Save the presentation.

**STEP 10: Print the Audience Handouts**

- ➤ Pull down the **File menu.** Click **Page Setup.** If necessary, click the **Portrait option button** to change the orientation for the Notes, Handouts, and Outline. Click **OK.**
- ➤ Pull down the **File menu.** Click **Print** to produce the Print dialog box. Click the **drop-down arrow** in the Print What list box. Click **Handouts (2 slides per page).**
- ➤ Check that the **All option button** is selected. Check the box to **Frame Slides.** Click **OK** to print the handouts.
- ➤ Save the presentation. Exit PowerPoint if you do not want to continue with the next exercise at this time.

## OBJECT LINKING AND EMBEDDING

One of the primary advantages of the Windows environment is the ability to create a document containing data from multiple applications. This is accomplished through ***Object Linking and Embedding*** (OLE, pronounced "oh-lay") and it enables you to insert data (objects) from other applications into a PowerPoint presentation. You have, in fact, used OLE every time you inserted a clip art object into a presentation. You used it again at the beginning of this chapter to insert a chart created with the Microsoft Graph application. The next several pages describe other types of objects you can use to enhance a presentation.

In actuality, linking and embedding are two different techniques. The essential difference between the two is that embedding places the object into the presentation, whereas linking does not. In other words, an ***embedded object*** is stored within the presentation, and the presentation, in turn, becomes the only user (container) of that object. A ***linked object,*** on the other hand, is stored in its own file, and the presentation is one of many potential containers of that object. The presentation does not contain the object per se, but only a representation of the object as well as a pointer (link) to the file containing the object (the source document). The advantage of linking is that the presentation is updated automatically if the object is changed in the source document.

The choice between linking and embedding depends on how the object will be used. Linking is preferable if the object is likely to change and your presentation requires the latest version. Linking should also be used when the same object is placed in many documents, so that any change to the object has to be made in only one place (the source document). Embedding should be used if you need to take the presentation with you—for example, if you intend to show the presentation on a different computer.

The easiest way to link or embed an object is through the appropriate AutoLayout as shown in Figure 3.6. Choose the AutoLayout for an Object slide as shown in Figure 3.6a, then double click the object placeholder to display the Insert Object dialog box in Figure 3.6b. The object types displayed within the dialog box depend on the applications that are installed on your system.

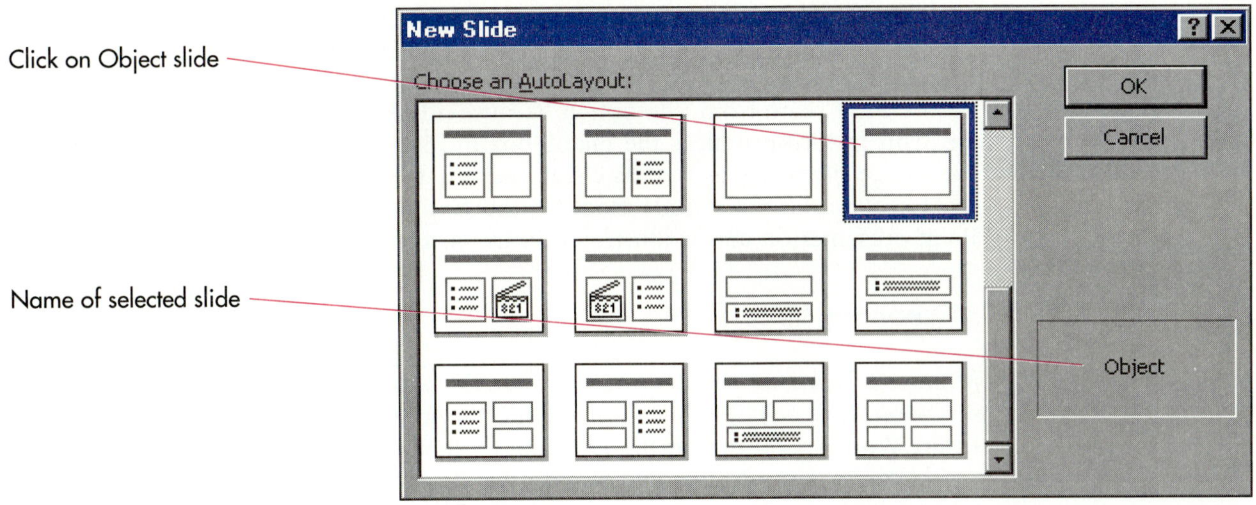


(a) The AutoLayout

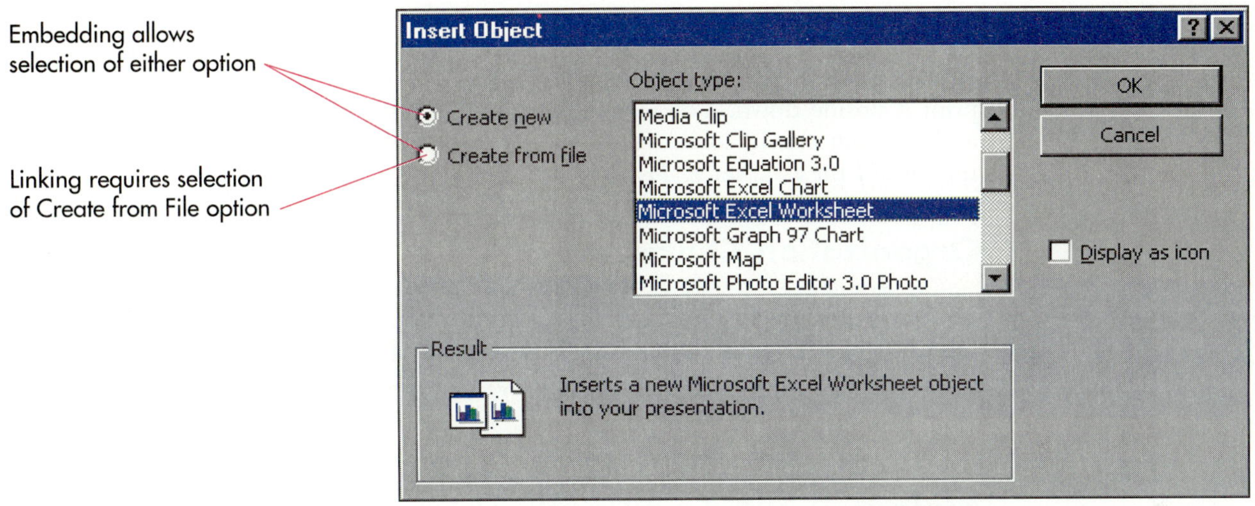


(b) Insert Object Dialog Box

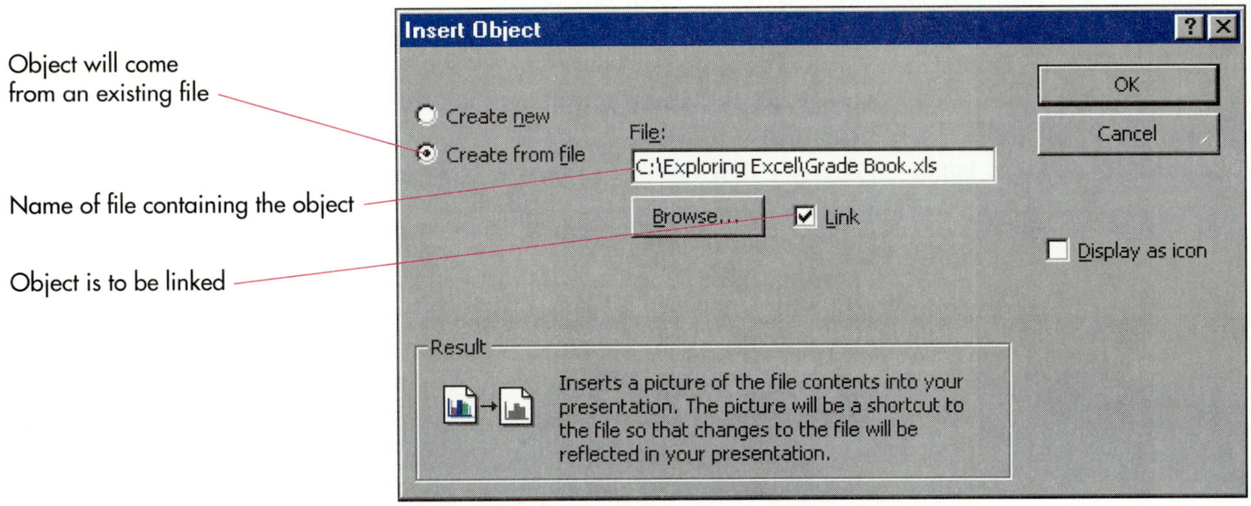


(c) Create the Link

**FIGURE 3.6** Object Linking and Embedding

The option buttons to create a new object or to create the object from an existing file are mutually exclusive, in that you choose one or the other. If you embed an object, you can choose either option. If you link, however, you must choose the Create from File option because a linked object has to exist in its own file. This in turn produces the dialog box in Figure 3.6c, in which you must enter the source file name as well as check the box to create a link. The example links the Excel workbook, Grade Book in the Exploring Excel folder, to the PowerPoint presentation and is illustrated in the next hands-on exercise.

## Microsoft WordArt

***Microsoft WordArt*** enables you to create decorative text to add interest to a presentation. It is available from every Office application and is called by clicking the Insert WordArt button on the Drawing toolbar.

WordArt is intuitive and easy to use. In essence, you choose a style for the text from among the selections in the dialog box of Figure 3.7a, then you enter the specific text as shown in Figure 3.7b. Figure 3.7c shows the completed WordArt object, which can be moved and sized just like any other Windows object.

WordArt even has its own toolbar, which enables you to modify a WordArt object in subtle ways. You can rotate text in any direction, add three-dimensional effects, display the text vertically down the page, shade it, slant it, arch it, or even print it upside down. You're limited only by your imagination. It's fun, it's easy, and you can create some truly dynamite documents. (See practice exercise 1 at the end of the chapter.)

## Organization Charts

***Microsoft Organization Chart*** is yet another application included with Microsoft Office; it enables you to create an organization chart and embed it into a presentation. You start the application by choosing the AutoLayout containing an organization chart or by creating an object slide and choosing Microsoft Organization Chart as the object.

A partially completed organization chart is shown in Figure 3.8. To add additional boxes, you just click the appropriate command button at the top of the window. The coworker buttons create a box on the same level to the left or right of the current box. The subordinate command button creates a box under the current box, while the manager button creates a box above the current box. To delete a box, select the box, then press the Del key.

You can change the design of the connecting lines and/or the boxes in the chart, as well as their color. You can also change the font and/or alignment of the text within the individual boxes. Microsoft Organization Chart is illustrated in the hands-on exercise that follows shortly.

## Sound

Sound can be linked or embedded into a presentation just like any other object. Realize, however, that sound requires additional hardware, namely a sound card and speakers, and we urge you to include these options on any machine you buy. (Sound may not be available in a laboratory setting for obvious reasons.)

Sounds exist as separate files that are inserted into a presentation through the Insert Object command as illustrated in the following hands-on exercise. Additional information about the different types of sound files is found in Appendix B, Introduction to Multimedia.

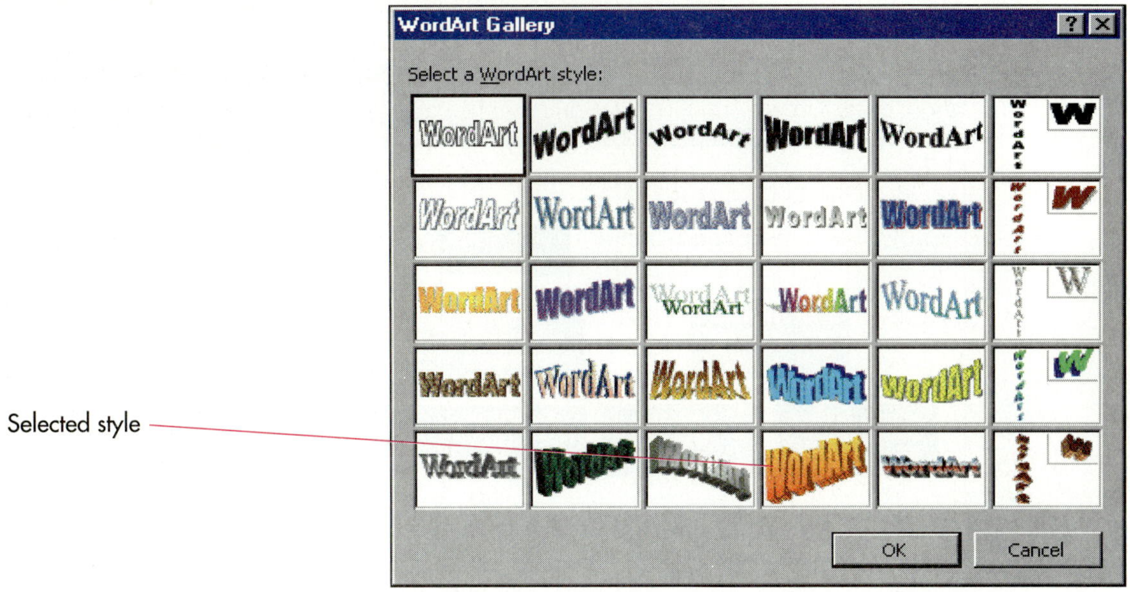


(a) WordArt Gallery

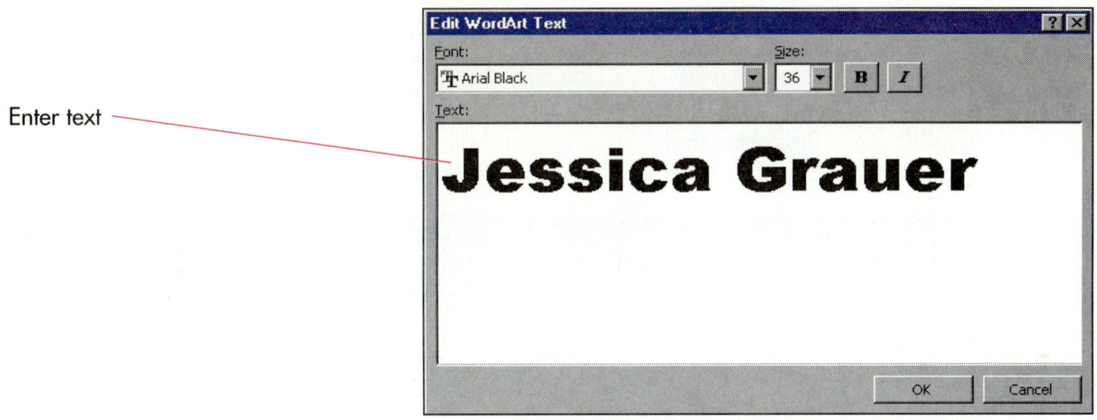


(b) Enter the Text

(c) The Completed WordArt Object

FIGURE 3.7 WordArt

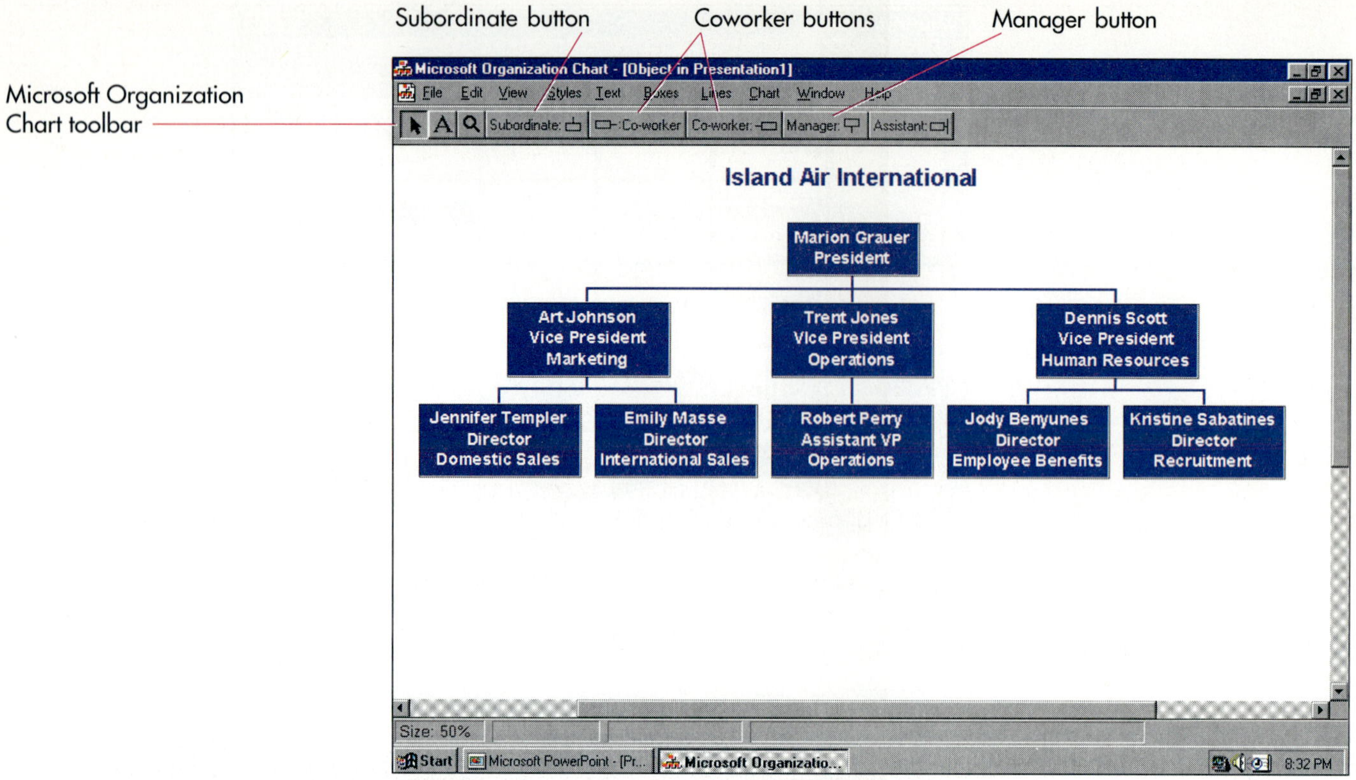


**FIGURE 3.8** Organization Chart

# HANDS-ON EXERCISE 3

## *Object Linking and Embedding*

**Objective:** To link an Excel worksheet to a PowerPoint presentation; to embed an organization chart, a WordArt object, and a sound file into a PowerPoint presentation. Use Figure 3.9 as a guide in doing the exercise. Completion of the exercise requires that Microsoft Excel be installed on your system.

**STEP 1: Create the Title Slide**

➤ Create a new presentation:

- If necessary, start PowerPoint. Click the option button to create a **Blank Presentation,** then click **OK.**
- If PowerPoint is already started, pull down the **File menu** and click **New** (or click the **New button** on the Standard toolbar). If necessary, double click the **Blank Presentation icon** to display the New Slide dialog box.

➤ You should see the New Slide dialog box with the AutoLayout for the title slide already selected. Click **OK** to create the title slide.

➤ Click the placeholder for the title and enter **Object Linking and Embedding** as the title of the presentation. Click the placeholder for the subtitle. Enter your name as indicated.

**STEP 2: Add an Object Slide**

- Click the **Save button** on the Standard toolbar. Save the presentation as **Object Linking and Embedding** in the **Exploring PowerPoint folder.**
- Click the **New Slide button** on the Standard toolbar to add a second slide. You should see the New Slide dialog box.
- Click the **down arrow** and scroll through the available slide layouts until you can select the **Object slide** (AutoLayout number 16). Click **OK.**
- You should see the slide in Figure 3.9a.

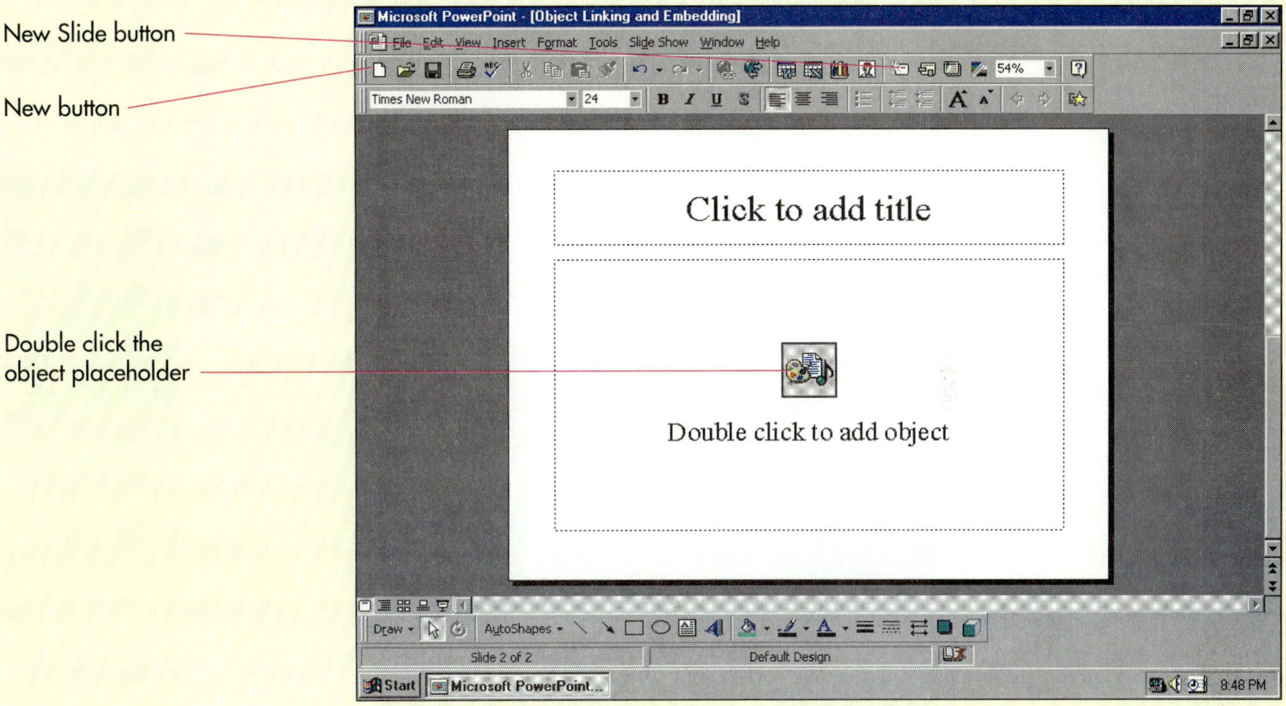


(a) Add an Object Slide (step 2)

FIGURE 3.9 Hands-on Exercise 3

### THE AUTOLAYOUTS ARE NUMBERED

Each of the 24 AutoLayouts has an assigned number, corresponding to its position within the New Slide dialog box. (The layouts are numbered consecutively from left to right and top to bottom.) The number can be used as a shortcut to select the AutoLayout in lieu of clicking; type 2, for example, to select a bulleted list (the second slide in row 1). Other frequently used AutoLayouts include a title slide (number 1), a graph and title (number 8), an organization chart and title (number 7), an object and title (number 16), and a blank slide (number 12).

**STEP 3: Insert the Excel Worksheet**

- Double click the **placeholder** to add an object, which displays the Insert Object dialog box. Scroll through the **Object Type** list box until you can select **Microsoft Excel Worksheet.**
- Click the option button for **Create from File** to display the dialog box in Figure 3.9b.
- Click the **Browse button** to display the Browse dialog box. Click the **down arrow** on the Look In list box and select the **Exploring PowerPoint folder.**
- Select the **Grade Book workbook** from within the Exploring PowerPoint folder. Click **OK** to close the Browse dialog box.
- If necessary, clear the Link check box as we want to embed (rather than link) the worksheet into the presentation. Click **OK** to insert the worksheet into the presentation.

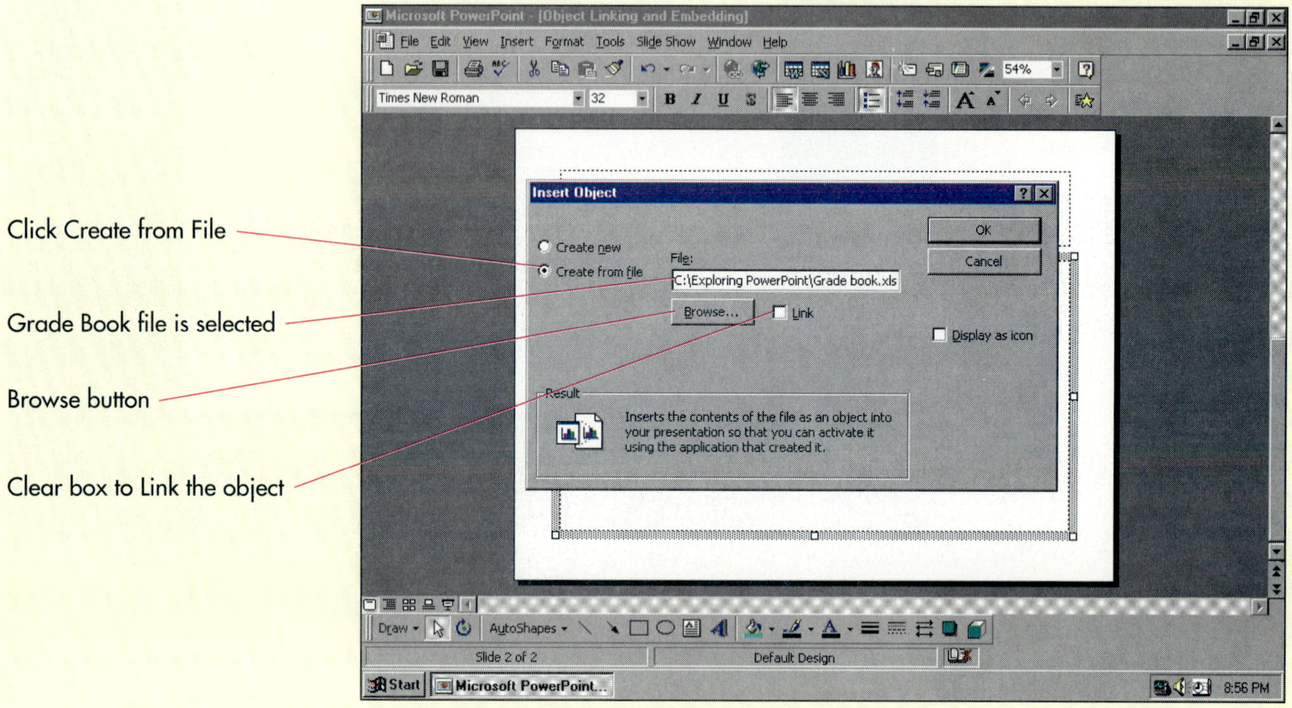


(b) Insert the Excel Worksheet (step 3)

**FIGURE 3.9** Hands-on Exercise 3 (continued)

> **IN-PLACE EDITING**
>
> In-place editing enables you to double click an Excel worksheet in order to edit the object. You remain in PowerPoint, but the toolbars and pull-down menus are those of Excel. The File and Window menus are exceptions, however, and contain PowerPoint commands to save the presentation and/or view multiple presentations.

**STEP 4: Complete the Slide**

- You should see the worksheet in Figure 3.9c. The sizing handles indicate that the worksheet is currently selected and can be moved and sized like any other Windows object.
- Click anywhere outside the worksheet to deselect it. The sizing handles disappear.
- Click the **title placeholder** and type **CIS120 Grade Book** as the title of the slide.
- Save the presentation.

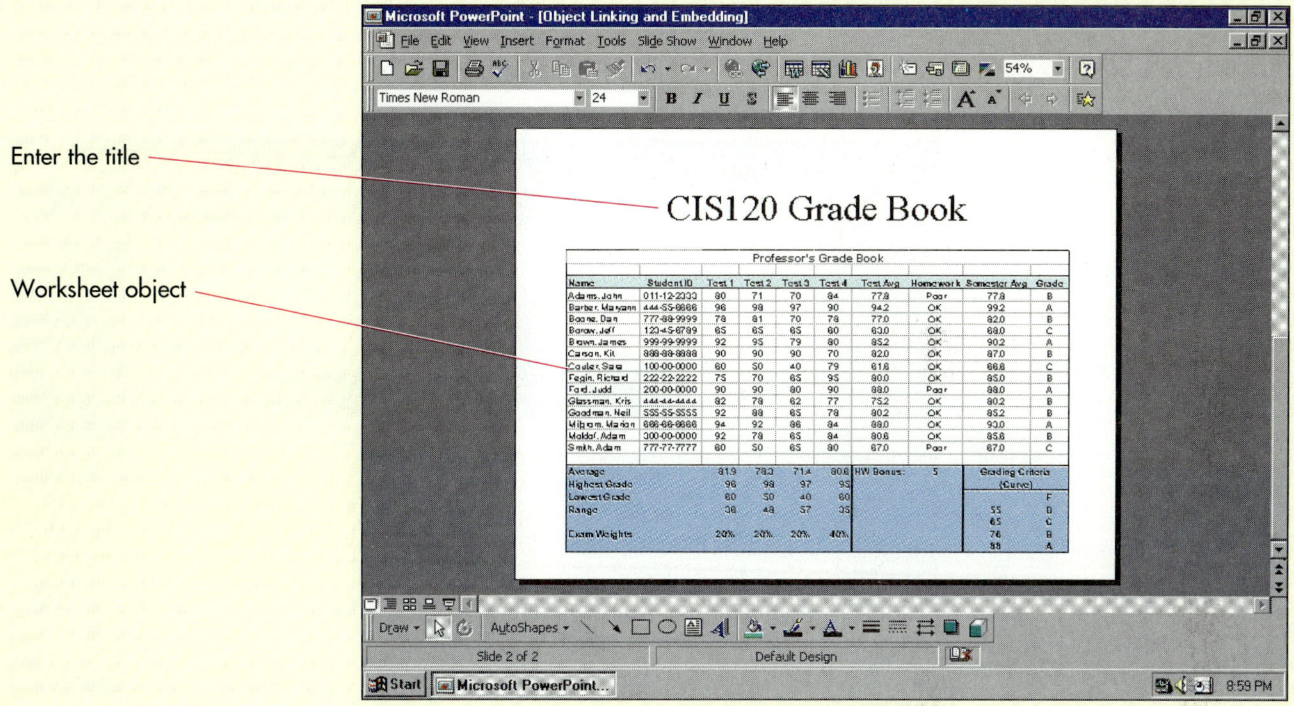


(c) Complete the Slide (step 4)

**FIGURE 3.9** Hands-on Exercise 3 (continued)

## LINKING VERSUS EMBEDDING

Linking is very different from embedding as it provides a dynamic connection between the source and destination documents. A linked object (e.g., an Excel worksheet) is tied to the destination document (e.g., a PowerPoint presentation) in such a way that any changes to the source file are automatically reflected in the destination document. Linking is especially useful when the same object is inserted in multiple documents, as changes to the object are made in only one place (in the source file). A linked object must be saved as a separate file. An embedded object, on the other hand, is inserted directly into a document and need not exist in its own file.

**STEP 5: Create the Organization Chart**

- Click the **New Slide button** on the Standard toolbar. Click the AutoLayout for an **Organization chart.**
- Click **OK** to add the slide, then double click the placeholder to add the organization chart.
- You should see a window titled **Microsoft Organization Chart** open within the PowerPoint window, as shown in Figure 3.9d. Click the **Maximize button** of the Microsoft Organization Chart window.
- The text in the first box is already selected. Type your name and press **enter** to move to the second line. Type **President** for your title.
- Click in the first box in the second row. Enter the name of a friend as Vice President of Marketing. (Press **enter** to move to a second line.) Add two additional friends as Vice Presidents of Operations and Human Resources.

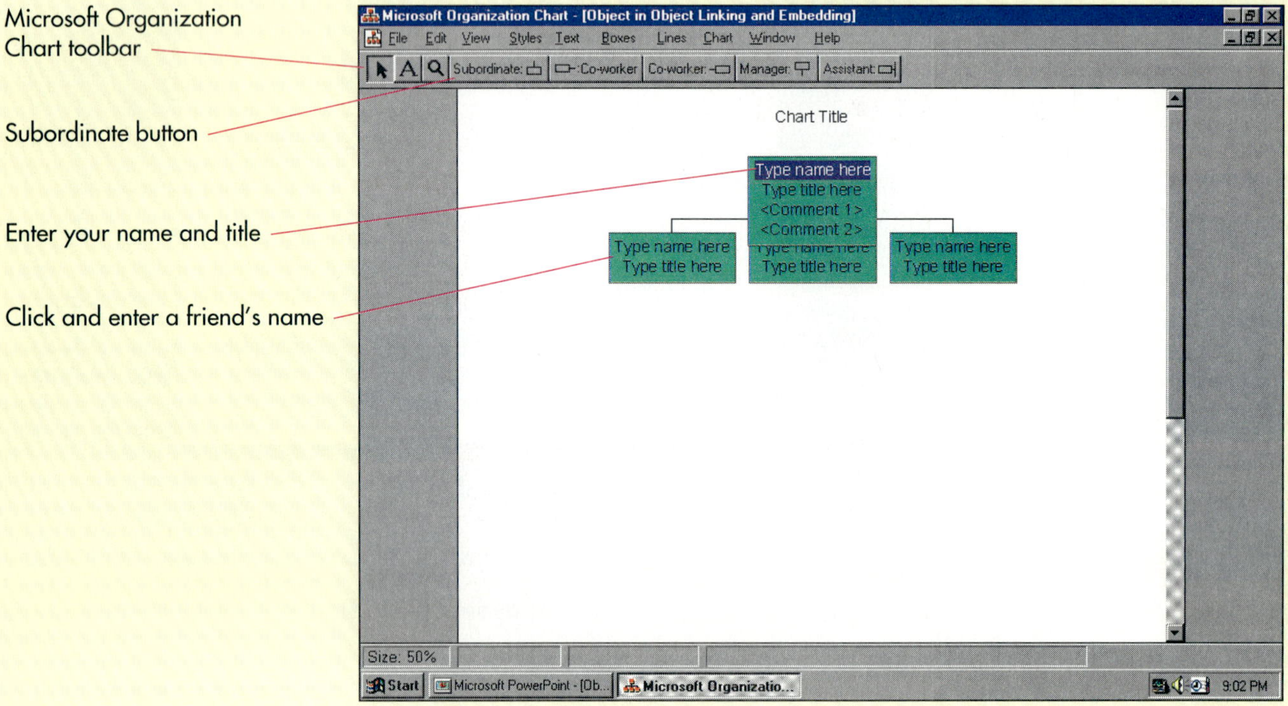


(d) Create the Organization Chart (step 5)

**FIGURE 3.9** Hands-on Exercise 3 (continued)

**STEP 6: Complete the Organization Chart**

- You can add detail to the chart by entering additional boxes for subordinates or coworkers. Enter the subordinates as shown in Figure 3.9e:
    - To add a subordinate, click the subordinate button on the Organization Chart toolbar, then click the box under which the subordinate is to appear.
    - To add a coworker, manager, or assistant, follow the same procedure as for a subordinate.
    - To enter a person's name and title in an existing box, click in the box, then enter the text. Press the **enter key** to go from line to line.
    - To delete a box, click in the box to select it, then press the **Del key.**

New Slide button

Enter new title

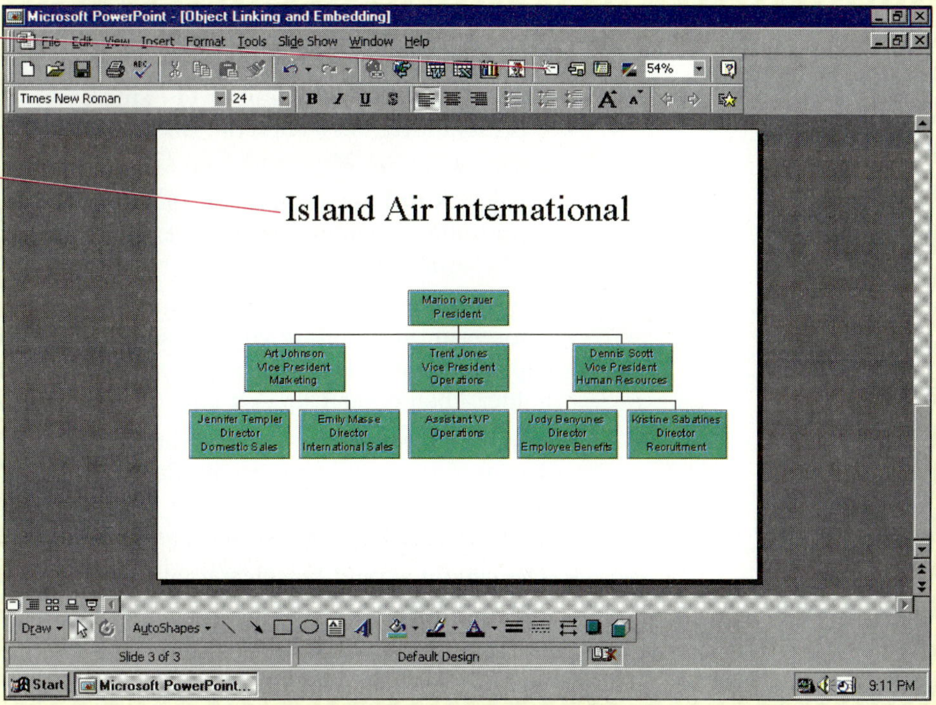


(e) Complete the Organization Chart (step 6)

FIGURE 3.9 Hands-on Exercise 3 (continued)

- Pull down the **File menu.** Click **Exit and Return to Object Linking and Embedding** (the name of the presentation).
- Click **Yes** when asked whether to update the object. You should see an organization chart similar to the one in Figure 3.9e.
- Click the placeholder for the slide title. Enter the name of your organization.
- Save the presentation

## CUSTOMIZE THE ORGANIZATION CHART

You can change the appearance of an organization chart by selecting a box or line, then executing the appropriate formatting command. It's generally best, however, to retain a uniform appearance by formatting the entire chart at one time. Press Ctrl+A to select the chart, pull down the Boxes menu, then select the command to change the box color, border style, border color, or border line style. To change the line color, style, or thickness, select all of the lines (pull down the Edit menu, click Select, and click Connecting lines), then choose the desired commands from the Lines menu.

**STEP 7: Clip Art and AutoShapes**

➤ Click the **New Slide button,** then do one of the following:

- Click **AutoLayout Number 11** (Title only), click **OK** to add the slide to the presentation, then click the **Insert Clip Art button** on the Standard toolbar to display the Microsoft Clip Gallery dialog box, *or*
- Click **AutoLayout Number 16** (Object), click **OK** to add the slide to the presentation, then double click the placeholder to add the object. Choose **Microsoft Clip Gallery** from the list of available objects and click **OK** to display the Clip Gallery dialog box.

➤ Choose an appropriate clip art image. Click **Insert,** then move and size the clip art so that it is positioned as shown in Figure 3.9f. Click in the title placeholder, then enter **Clip Art and AutoShapes** as the title for this slide.

➤ Click the **down arrow** on the **AutoShapes button** on the Drawing toolbar to display the AutoShapes menu. Select (click) **Callouts,** then select the **Cloud callout** at the end of the first row. Click and drag on the slide where you want the callout to go. Release the mouse.

➤ The callout should be selected automatically:

- Type **I can do this!** as the caption. (You must enter the text when the callout is selected.)
- If necessary, click and drag the callout to adjust its size or position.
- To change the Fill color or Line color, click the appropriate tool on the Drawing toolbar, then select one of the displayed colors.

➤ Click outside the callout to deselect it.

➤ Save the presentation.

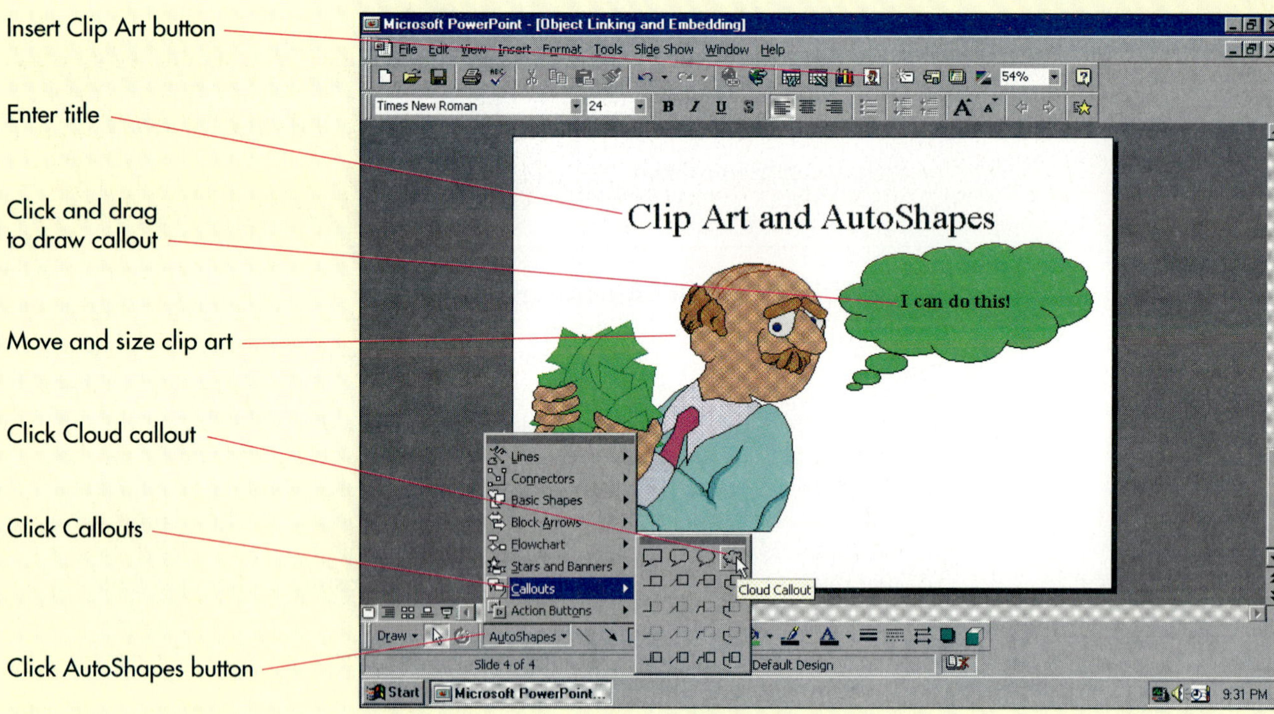


(f) Clip Art and AutoShapes (step 7)

FIGURE 3.9 Hands-on Exercise 3 (continued)

## AUTOSHAPES

An AutoShape is a predefined shape that is drawn automatically when you select its icon from the AutoShapes menu, then click and drag in the slide. (To display the AutoShapes menu, click the AutoShape tool on the Drawing toolbar.) To place text inside an AutoShape, select the shape and start typing. You can also change the fill color or line thickness by selecting the shape, then clicking the appropriate button on the Drawing toolbar. See practice exercise 3 at the end of the chapter.

**STEP 8: The Slide Finder**

- You can insert slides from other presentations into the current presentation. Pull down the **Insert menu.** Click **Slides from Files** to display the Slide Finder dialog box in Figure 3.9g. (The My Chart presentation is not yet visible.)
- Click the **Browse button,** then select the **Exploring PowerPoint folder** where you have been saving your work. Select (click) the **My Chart presentation** that you created in the first hands-on exercise.
- Click the **Open button,** then click the **Display button** to view the slides in this presentation (there is only one slide).
- Select the slide, then click the **Insert button** to insert the slide containing the chart into this presentation. (The new slide is inserted after the current slide.) Close the Slide Finder dialog box.
- Save the presentation.

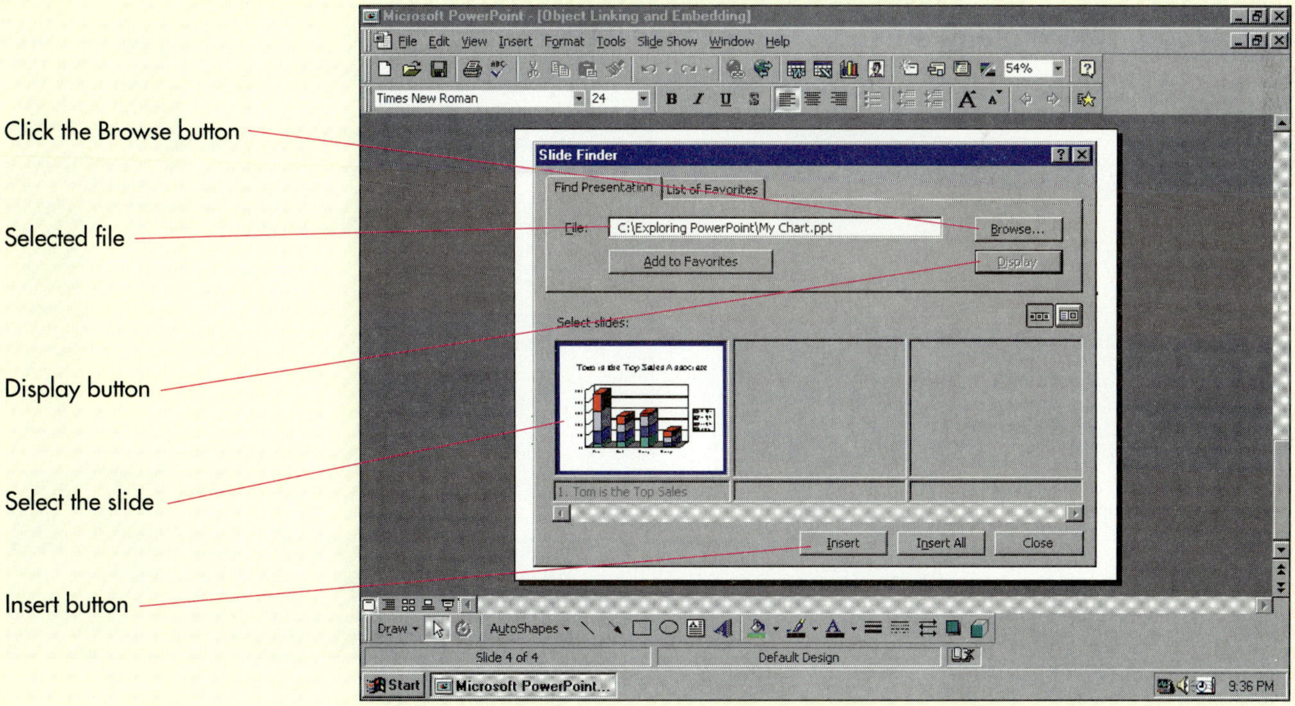


(g) The Slide Finder (step 8)

FIGURE 3.9 Hands-on Exercise 3 (continued)

## THE SLIDE FINDER

You work hard to develop individual slides and thus you may find it useful to reuse a slide from one presentation to the next. Pull down the Insert menu, click the Slides from Files command to display the Slide Finder dialog box, then browse until you locate the presentation containing the slide or slides you want to use. Open the presentation, then click the Display button to view the slides it contains. Select the slides individually, or press and hold the Shift key to select multiple slides, click Insert, then close the Slide Finder dialog box.

**STEP 9: WordArt**

- You should be on the fifth (of five) slides. Click the **New Slide button** on the status bar, click the AutoLayout for a **blank slide** (or type **12** as the number of the desired layout), then click **OK** to add the slide.
- Click the **Insert WordArt button** on the Drawing toolbar to display the WordArt Gallery dialog box. Choose any style you like (we took the fourth style from the left in the first row). Click **OK.**
- You should see the Edit WordArt text box as shown in Figure 3.9h. Enter **The End** as the text for your WordArt object.
- Click **OK** to close the Edit WordArt text box and insert the WordArt into your presentation. Save the presentation.

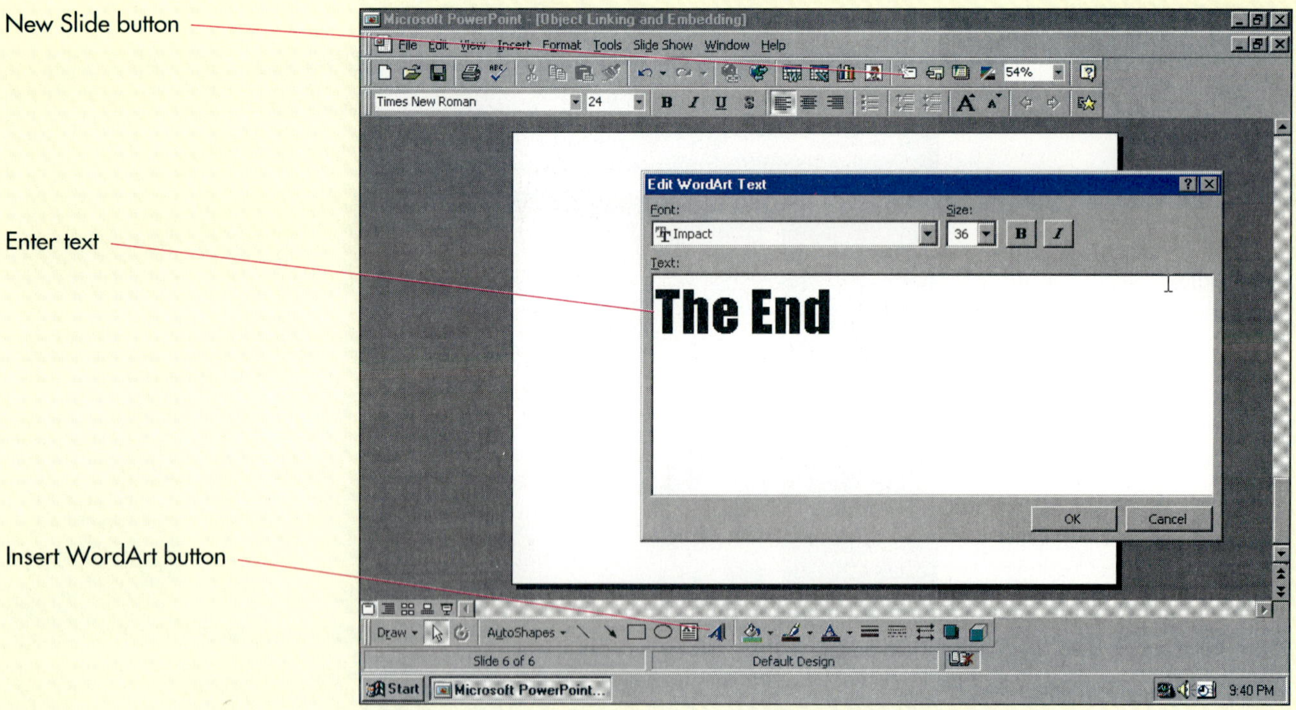


(h) WordArt (step 9)

**FIGURE 3.9** Hands-on Exercise 3 (continued)

## THE WORDART TOOLBAR

The WordArt toolbar is the easiest way to change an existing WordArt object. It is displayed automatically when a WordArt object is selected; otherwise it is suppressed. As with any toolbar, you can point to a button to display a ScreenTip containing the name of the button, which is indicative of its function. You will find buttons to display the text vertically, change the style or shape, and/or edit the text.

**STEP 10: WordArt Continued**

- Move and size the WordArt object just as you would any other Windows object:
  - Click and drag a corner sizing handle to increase the size of the WordArt until it takes the entire slide.
  - Point to the middle of the WordArt object (the mouse pointer changes to a double cross), then click and drag to position the WordArt in the middle of the slide.
- Click the **drop-down arrow** for the **Fill Color tool** on the Drawing toolbar to display the available fill colors as shown in Figure 3.9i. Select (click) **blue** to change the color of the WordArt object.
- Experiment with other tools, on either or both the Drawing and WordArt toolbars, to enhance the WordArt image.
- Save the presentation.

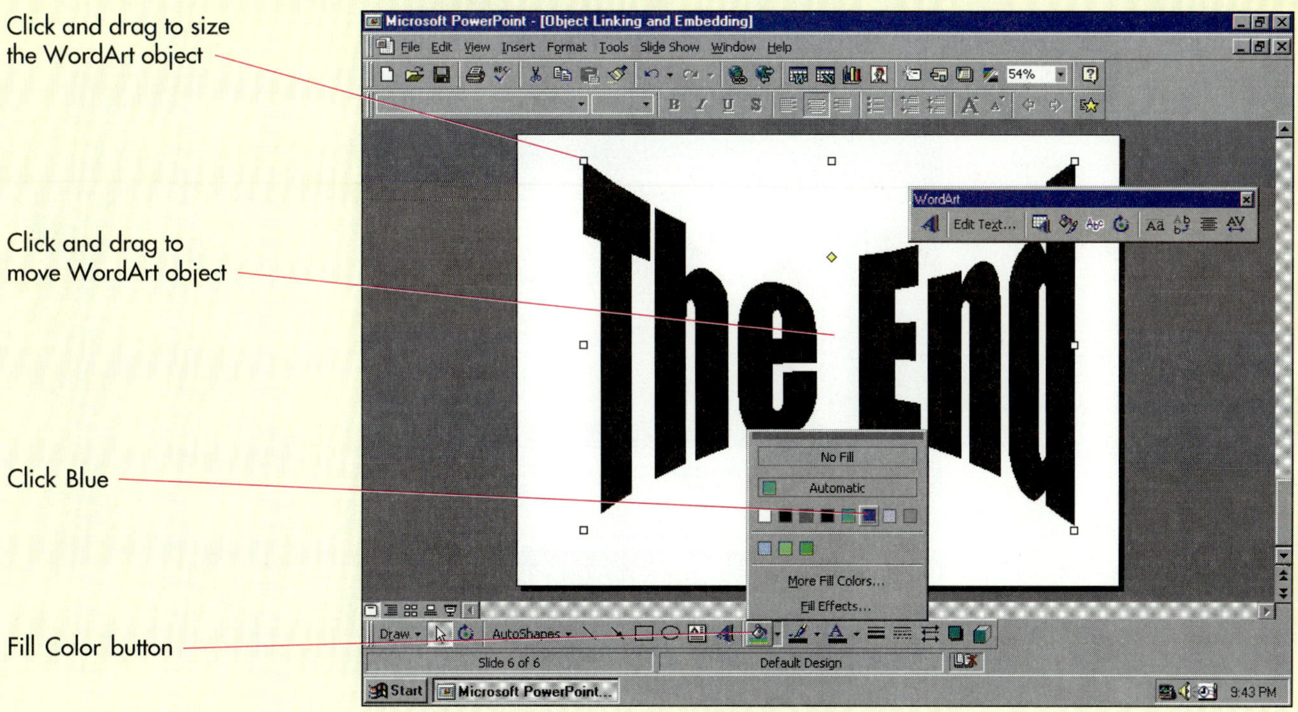


(i) WordArt continued (step 10)

**FIGURE 3.9** Hands-on Exercise 3 (continued)

### THE THIRD DIMENSION

You can make your WordArt images even more dramatic by adding 3-D effects. You can tilt the text up or down, right or left, increase or decrease the depth, and change the shading. Pull down the View menu, click Toolbars, click Customize to display the complete list of toolbars, then check the box to display the 3-D Settings toolbar. Select the WordArt object, then experiment with various tools and special effects. The results are even better if you have a color printer.

**STEP 11: Insert a Sound**

- Pull down the Insert menu. Click **Movies and Sound,** then click **Sound from File** to display the Insert Sound dialog box in Figure 3.9j.
- Change to the Exploring PowerPoint folder if you cannot locate the Office97 folder, which comes up by default.
- Select (click) the **Applause sound,** then click **OK** to insert the file into the presentation.
- A tiny microphone should appear in the middle of the slide to indicate that the sound file has been embedded on the slide. Double click the microphone to play the sound and hear the applause. (Your machine has to have a sound card if you are to actually hear the applause.)
- Save the presentation.

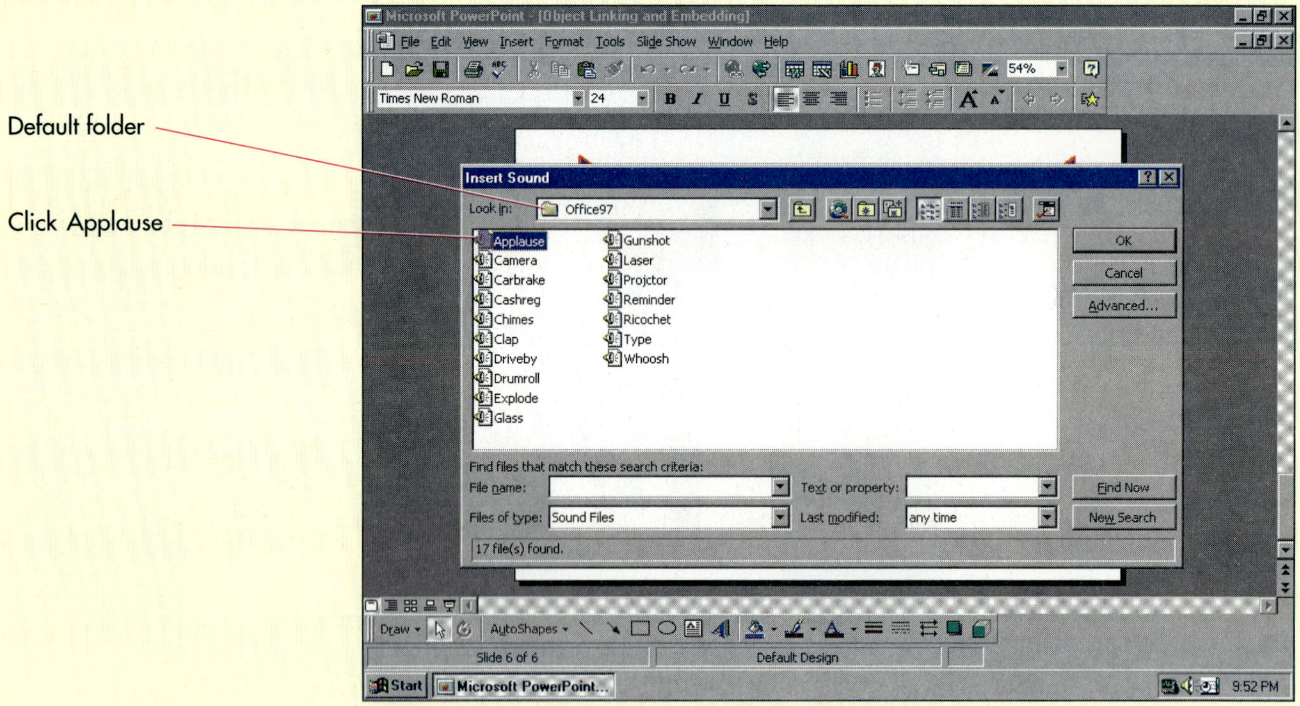


(j) Insert a Sound (step 11)

FIGURE 3.9 Hands-on Exercise 3 (continued)

### THE WINDOWS 95 FIND COMMAND

We supplied the sound of applause, but you are likely to have many other sound files on your system, any one of which can be embedded into a presentation. The easiest way to locate these files is through the Windows 95 Find command. Click the Start button, click (or point to) the Find command, then click Files or Folders to display the Find dialog box. Enter *.wav (the "wav" indicates a sound file) in the Named text box and My Computer in the Look In box. Click Find Now. Use the right mouse button to click and drag a file from the Find Files window onto your presentation. Release the mouse, then click the Copy Here command to embed the sound onto the slide.

**STEP 12: Custom Animation**

- Click and drag the sound icon to the upper right portion of the slide. Point to the icon, click the **right mouse button** to display a shortcut menu, then click **Custom Animation** to display the Custom Animation dialog box in Figure 3.9k.
- Click the **Timing tab.** Select the **Media 2 object,** click the **Animate option button,** then click the **Automatically option button.** Enter **1** second in the associated list box to play the applause automatically one second after the slide appears. Click **OK** to accept the settings and close the dialog box.
- Save the presentation.

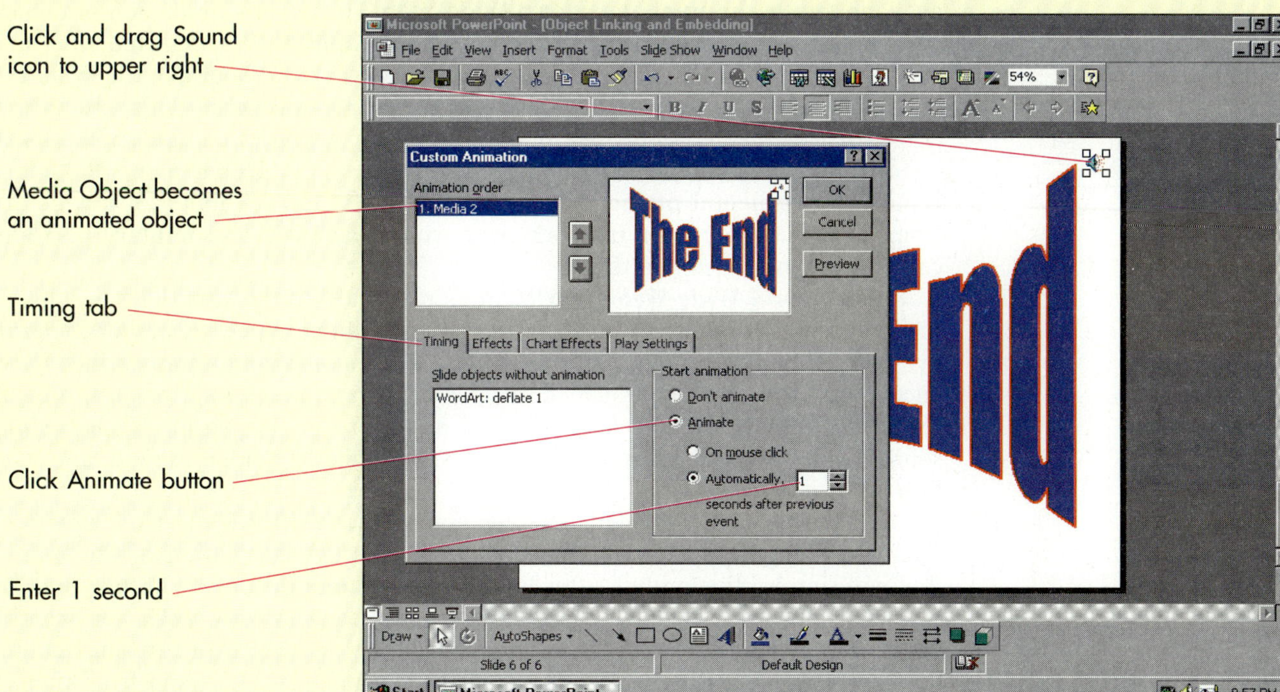


(k) Custom Animation (step 12)

**FIGURE 3.9** Hands-on Exercise 3 (continued)

### THE SLIDE ELEVATOR

PowerPoint uses the scroll box (common to all Windows applications) in the vertical scroll bar as an elevator to move up and down within the presentation. Click and drag the elevator to go to a specific slide; as you drag you will see a Scroll Tip indicating the slide you are about to display. Release the mouse when you see the number (title) of the slide you want.

**STEP 13: Applause, Applause**

- Press **Ctrl+Home** to move to the first slide in the presentation, then click the **Slide Show button** to view the presentation.
- Click the **left mouse button** (or press the **PgDn key**) to move from slide to slide until you come to the end of the presentation. The applause you hear on the last slide is for your efforts in this exercise.
- Click the mouse a final time to return to the Slide view. Exit PowerPoint if you do not want to continue with the next exercise at this time.

## RESOURCES FROM THE INTERNET AND WORLD WIDE WEB

The resources in the Microsoft Clip Gallery in Office 97 are impressive when compared to previous versions of Microsoft Office, but pale in comparison to what is available on the Internet and World Wide Web. Hence, any discussion of enhancing a presentation through clip art and/or photographs must also include the Internet. We begin with a brief description of the Internet and World Wide Web, then we describe how to incorporate these resources into a PowerPoint presentation.

The ***Internet*** is a network of networks that connects computers across the country and around the world. It grew out of a U.S. Department of Defense (DOD) experimental project begun in 1969 to test the feasibility of a wide area (long distance) computer network over which scientists and military personnel could share messages and data.

The ***World Wide Web*** (WWW, or simply, the Web) is a very large subset of the Internet, consisting of those computers containing hypertext and/or hypermedia documents. A ***hypertext document*** is a document that contains a link (reference) to another document, which may be on the same computer or even on a different computer, with the latter located anywhere in the world. ***Hypermedia*** is similar in concept, except that it also provides links to graphic, sound, and video files.

Either type of document enables you to move effortlessly from one document (or computer) to another. And therein lies the fascination of the Web, in that you simply click on link after link to go from one document to the next. You can start your journey at your professor's home page in New York, for example, which may contain a link to the Library of Congress, which in turn may contain links to other documents. So, off you go to Washington D.C., and from there to a different document on a different computer across the country or perhaps around the world.

Figure 3.10 depicts how the Internet can be used in conjunction with a PowerPoint presentation. The first task is to locate the resource, which in this example is a photograph from the Dinosaur Hall at the National Museum of

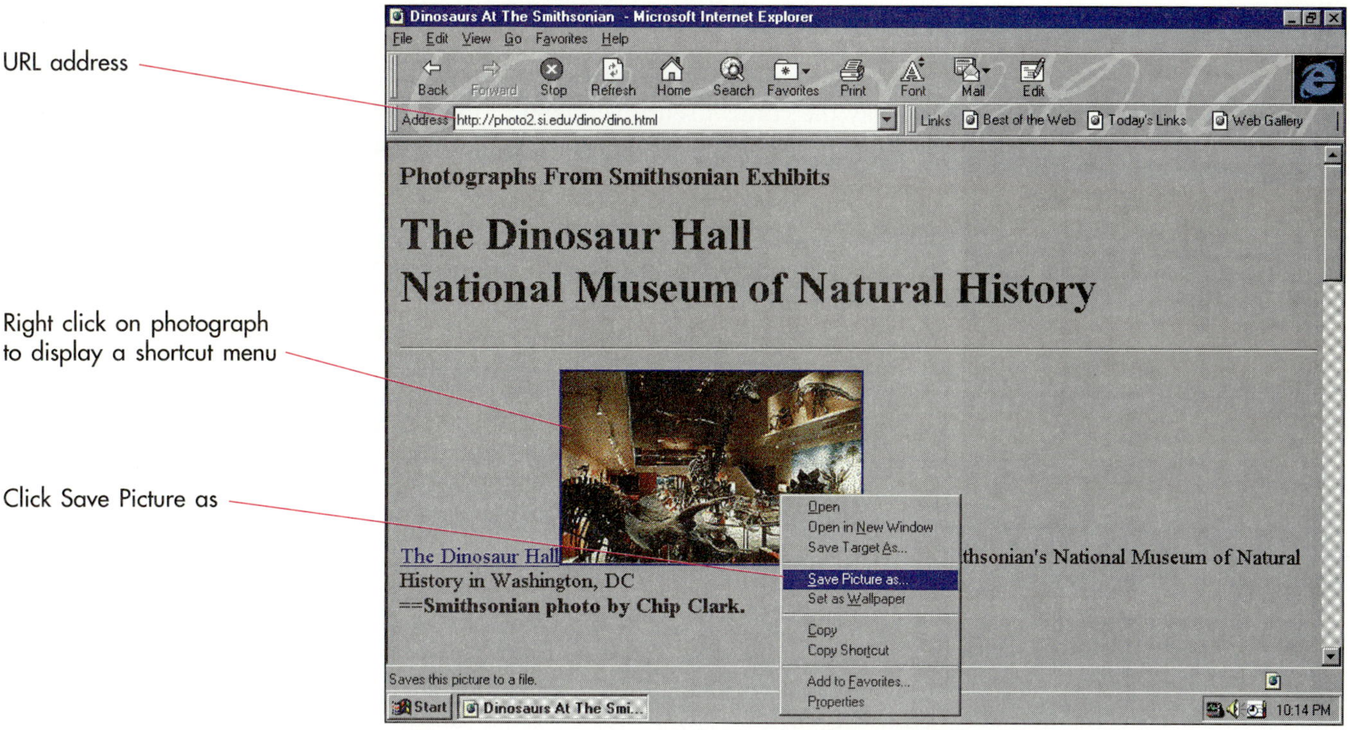


(a) Identify the Resources

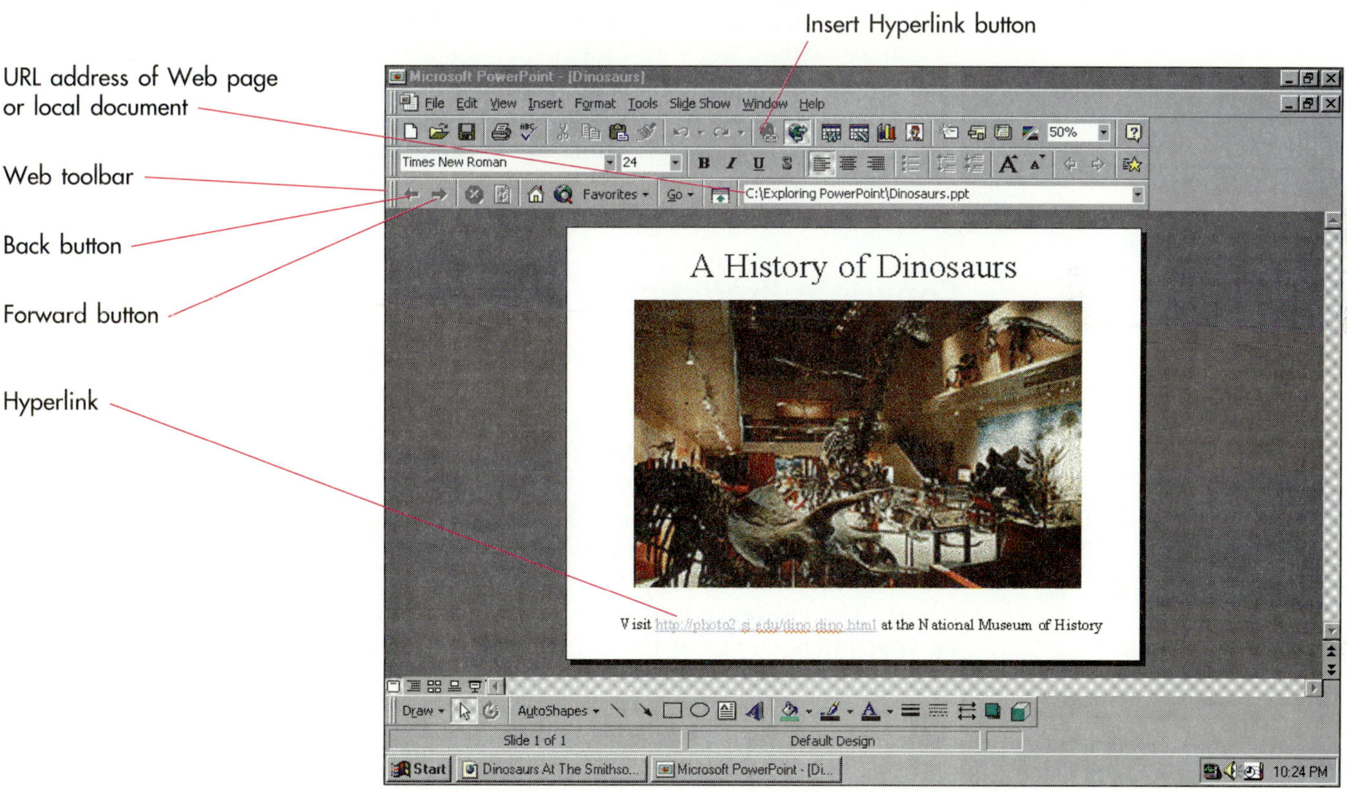


(b) The PowerPoint Slide

**FIGURE 3.10** The Internet as a Resource

Natural History. To do this you start your Web browser (e.g., Internet Explorer), then you use your favorite search engine to locate the required information (perhaps a photograph of a dinosaur). Once this is done, right click on the photograph to display the context-sensitive menu in the figure, then click the Save Picture as command to download the file to your hard drive.

Next, you start PowerPoint, using the ***Insert Picture command*** to insert the picture that was just downloaded into a presentation. You can also use the ***Insert Hyperlink command*** to insert a hyperlink onto a slide, which you can click during the slide show, and provided you have an Internet connection, your Web browser will display the associated page.

Look carefully at the screen in Figure 3.10b, which displays the ***Web toolbar*** immediately under the Formatting toolbar. (The Web toolbar is displayed by executing the Toolbars command from the View menu.) The Web toolbar contains buttons similar to those on the toolbar in Internet Explorer. You can, for example, enter the address (URL) of a Web page (or a local document) to activate your browser and access the page. You can use the Favorites button to add a page to your list of favorites, and/or open a previously added page. You can click the Back and Forward buttons to move between previously displayed pages. And, as with any toolbar, ScreenTips are displayed when you point to a button to display the name of the button, which is indicative of its function.

**MULTITASKING**

Multitasking, the ability to run multiple applications at the same time, is one of the primary advantages of the Windows environment. Entering a Web address within the Web toolbar automatically opens Internet Explorer so that both applications (PowerPoint and Internet Explorer) are open on your desktop. You can maximize both windows, then switch back and forth between the open applications by clicking the appropriate button on the Windows taskbar.

## Copyright Protection

A ***copyright*** provides legal protection to a written or artistic work, giving the author exclusive rights to its use and reproduction, except as governed under the fair use exclusion as explained below. Anything on the Internet or World Wide Web should be considered copyrighted unless the document specifically says it is in the ***public domain,*** in which case the author is giving everyone the right to freely reproduce and distribute the material.

Does this mean you cannot use statistics and other facts that you find while browsing the Web? Does it mean you cannot download an image to include in a report? The answer to both questions depends on the amount of the material and on your intended use of the information. It is considered ***fair use,*** and thus not an infringement of copyright, to use a portion of the work for educational, nonprofit purposes, or for the purpose of critical review or commentary. In other words, you can use a quote, downloaded image, or other information from the Web, provided you cite the original work in your footnotes and/or bibliography. Facts themselves are not covered by copyright, so you can use statistical and other data without fear of infringement. Be sure, however, to cite the original source in your document.

The following exercise takes you to the home page of the ***National Aeronautics and Space Administration (NASA),*** where you will download an image for inclusion into a PowerPoint presentation.

# HANDS-ON EXERCISE 4

## *The Internet as a Resource*

**Objective:** To download a picture from the Internet and use it in a PowerPoint presentation. Use Figure 3.11 as a guide in the exercise. The exercise requires that you have an Internet connection.

### STEP 1: The Web Toolbar

- Start PowerPoint. Click the option button to create a **Blank Presentation,** then enter the title slide for your presentation as shown in Figure 3.11a. Drag the title placeholder to the top of the slide.
- Save the presentation as **The Web as a Resource** in the **Exploring PowerPoint folder** that you have used throughout the text.
- Point to any toolbar, then click the **right mouse button** to display a context-sensitive menu, which lists the available toolbars. Click **Web** to display the Web toolbar. Do not be concerned if the position of your toolbars is different from ours.
- Click the **Address box.** Enter **www.nasa.gov** (the http:// is assumed), then press the **enter key** to connect to this site. Your Web browser (e.g., Internet Explorer) will open automatically after which you should be connected to NASA's home page. If necessary, maximize the Internet Explorer window.

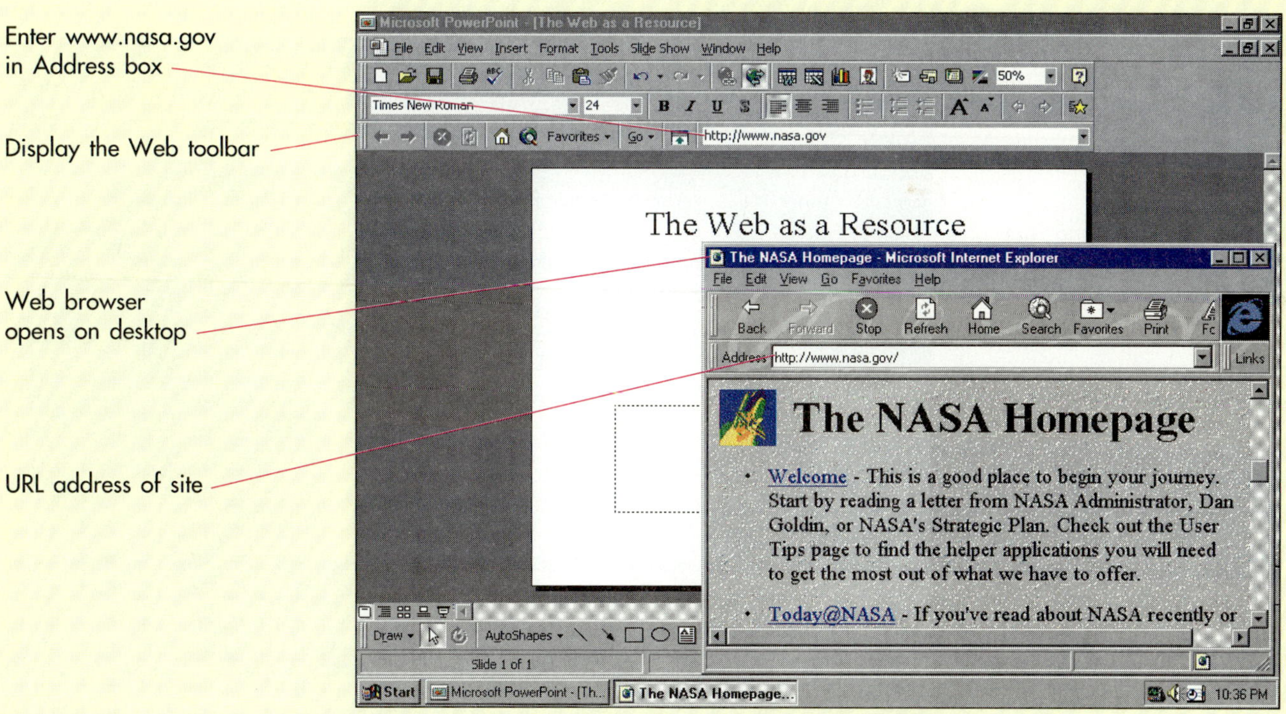


(a) The Web Toolbar (step 1)

**FIGURE 3.11** Hands-on Exercise 4

**STEP 2: Download the Picture**

- Scroll down NASA's home page to see the descriptions of the various links, then click the link to **Today@NASA** to view current information. Scroll down the page of today's stories until you find a link that interests you. It does not matter which link you choose.
- We chose the link to **Updated Photo and Video Galleries Online,** which led eventually to pictures from the various Apollo missions as shown in Figure 3.11b. (The site is changing continually, however, and you may not be able to locate our exact picture. It doesn't matter.)
- Select any picture on the NASA site, click the **right mouse button** to display a shortcut menu, then click the **Save Picture as command** to display the Save As dialog box.
  - Click the **drop-down arrow** in the Save in list box to specify the drive and folder in which you want to save the graphic (e.g., the Exploring PowerPoint folder on drive C).
  - The file name and file type are entered automatically by Internet Explorer. (You may change the name, but don't change the file type.) Click the **Save button** to download the image. Remember the file name and location as you will need to access the file in the next step.
- The Save As dialog box closes automatically as soon as the picture has been downloaded to your PC.
- Click the link that says **Select here if you wish to read the caption.** You will need the descriptive information later in the exercise.

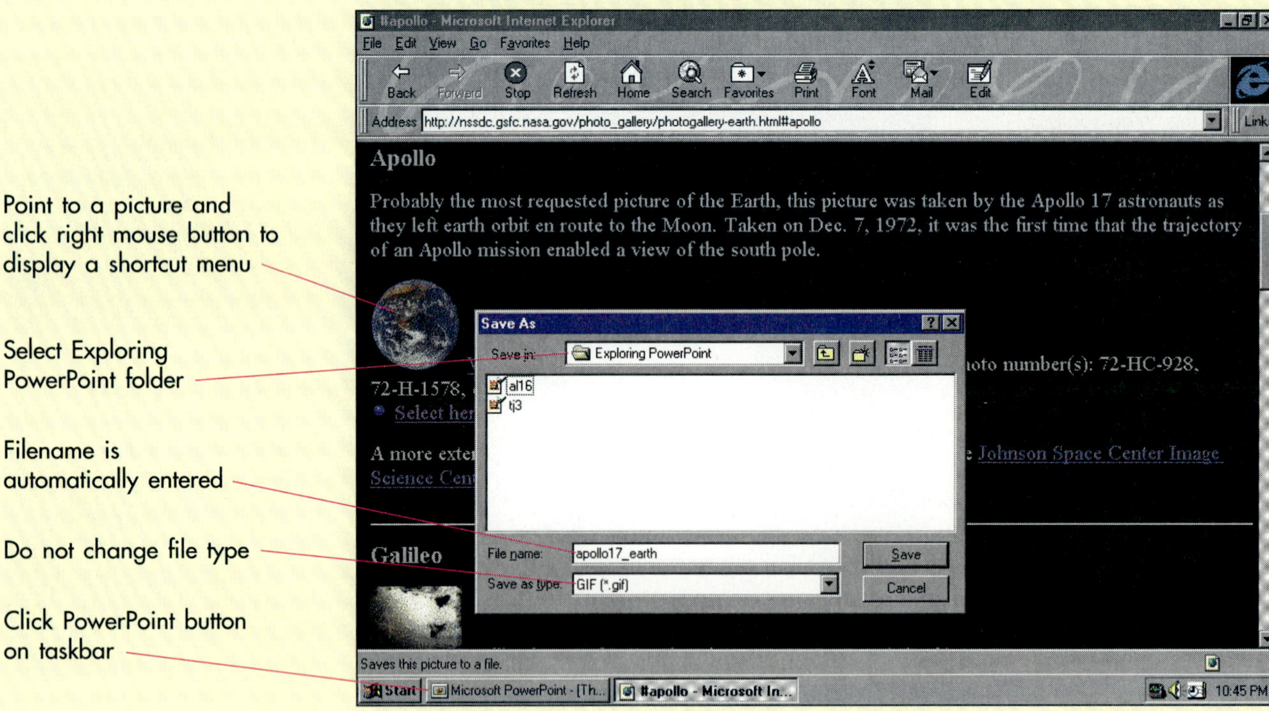


(b) Download the Picture (step 2)

**FIGURE 3.11** Hands-on Exercise 4 (continued)

## THE THUMBNAIL SKETCH

Graphics add to the visual appeal of a Web page, but they also add significantly to the time required to display the page. Hence, many Web designers include a thumbnail sketch (a small version of the larger image) to preview the picture without having to wait the extra time to display the entire image. The user can click the thumbnail sketch to see the complete image if he or she desires to do so.

**STEP 3: Insert the Picture**

- Click the **PowerPoint button** on the Windows taskbar to return to PowerPoint. Click the **New Slide button** on the Standard toolbar to display the New Slide dialog box, then choose a blank slide and click **OK.**
- Pull down the **Insert menu,** point to (or click) **Picture,** then click **From File** to display the Insert Picture dialog box shown in Figure 3.11c.
- Click the **drop-down arrow** on the Look in text box to select the drive and folder where you previously saved the picture (e.g., the Exploring Word folder on drive C).
- Select (click) **APOLLO17_EARTH,** which is the file containing the picture of the earth as seen from Apollo 17. Click **Insert** and the picture will appear in your presentation.
- Save the presentation.

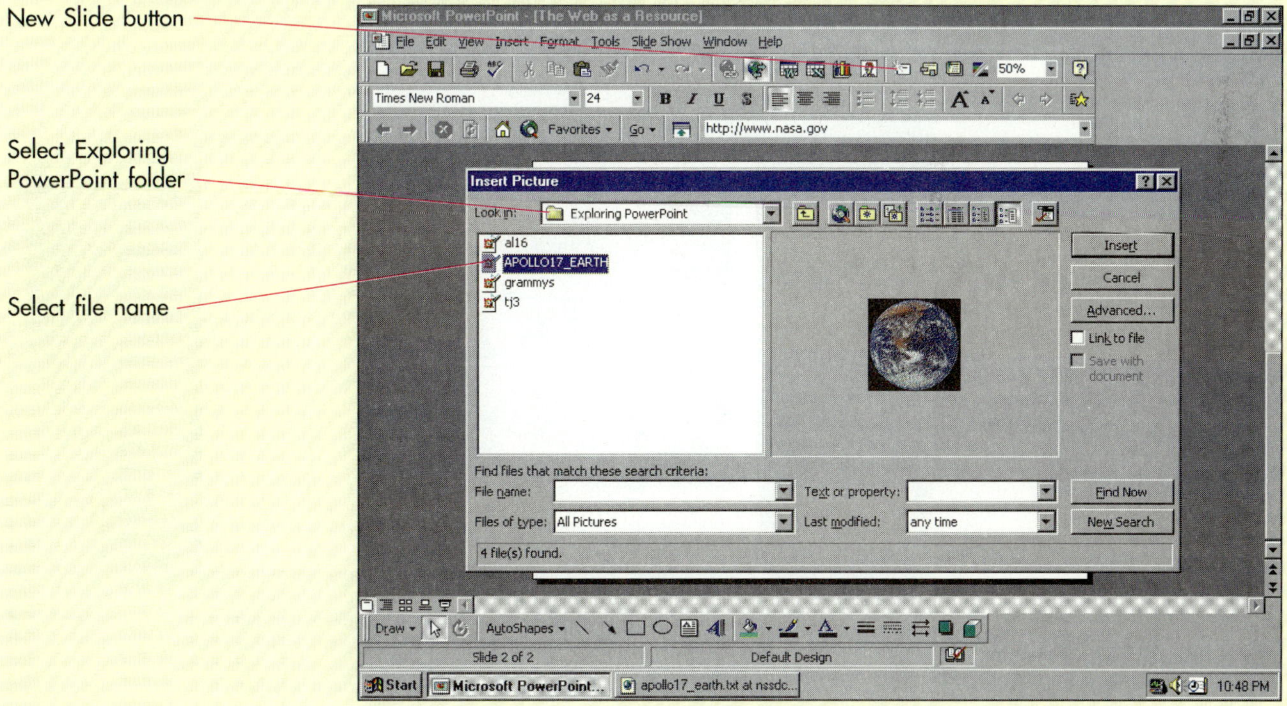


(c) Insert the Picture (step 3)

**FIGURE 3.11** Hands-on Exercise 4 (continued)

> **THE CLIPBOARD**
>
> Use the Windows clipboard (an area of memory available to every application) to copy text from one application to another. Go to the Web page containing the text you want to copy (e.g., the descriptive information about the photograph), click and drag within Internet Explorer to select the text, then press Ctrl+C to copy the selected text to the Windows clipboard. Switch to PowerPoint, click on the slide where you want the text to go, then press Ctrl+V to paste the text into the presentation. Be sure to credit your sources.

### STEP 4: Add Text to the Slide

- Move and/or size the picture so that your slide is similar to Figure 3.11d. Click the **Textbox tool** on the Drawing toolbar, then click and drag on the right side of the slide to create a text box.
- Enter the text as shown in Figure 3.11d. If necessary, change to an appropriate font and point size such as **24 point Times New Roman.**
- Click the **Textbox tool** a second time, then click and drag below the picture to create a second text box. Enter the text as shown in the figure. We used the same font as in the previous text box (Times New Roman), but chose a smaller size **(18 point).**
- Save the presentation.

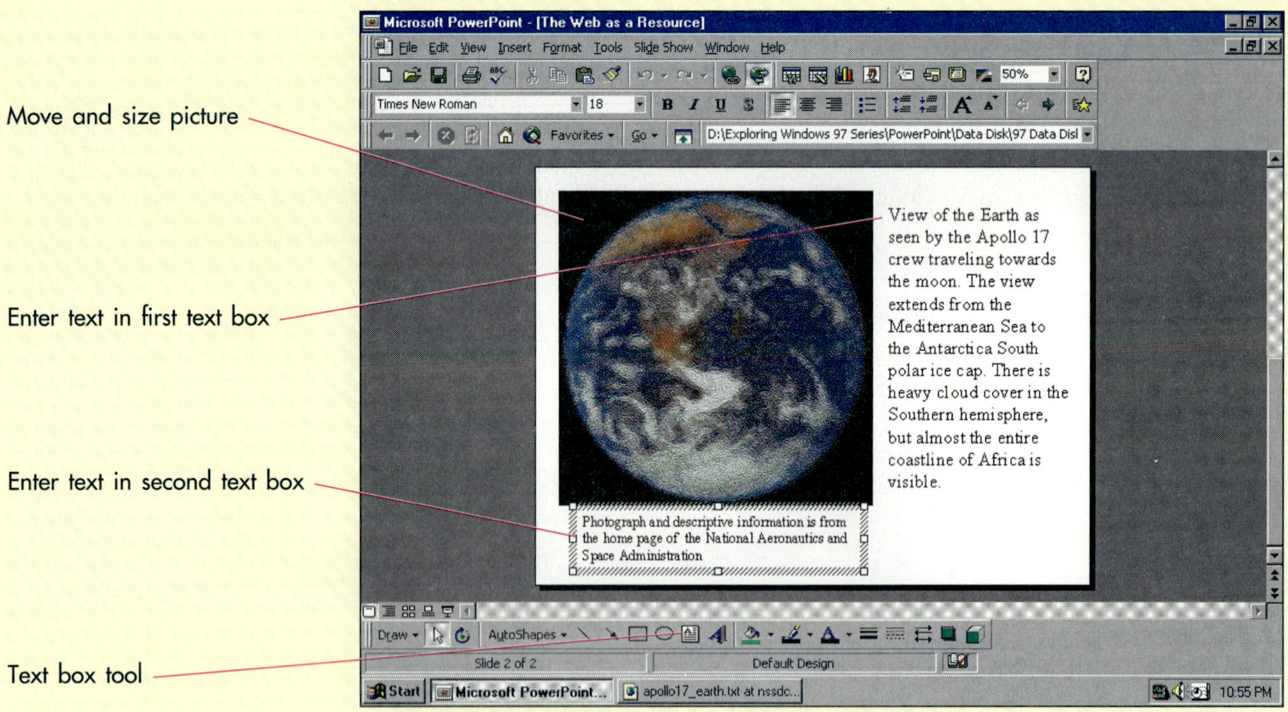


(d) Add Text to the Slide (step 4)

**FIGURE 3.11** Hands-on Exercise 4 (continued)

## CROPPING A PICTURE

The picture of the earth is perfect for this exercise. Other times, however, you may want to crop (erase) part of a picture. To do so, select the picture to display the Picture toolbar and the sizing handles. Click the Cropping tool (the ScreenTip will display the name of the tool), then click and drag a sizing handle to crop the part of the picture you want to erase. Click elsewhere in the document to deselect the picture.

**STEP 5: Insert a Hyperlink**

- Click and drag to select the text, **National Aeronautics and Space Administration,** as shown in Figure 3.11e.
- Pull down the **Insert menu** and click **Hyperlink** (or click the **Insert Hyperlink button** on the Standard toolbar) to display the Insert Hyperlink dialog box. Type **www.nasa.gov** (the http:// is assumed). Click **OK** to close the Insert Hyperlink dialog box.
- Click elsewhere in the slide to deselect the text, which now appears as a hyperlink (i.e., it will be underlined in a different color).
- Save the presentation.

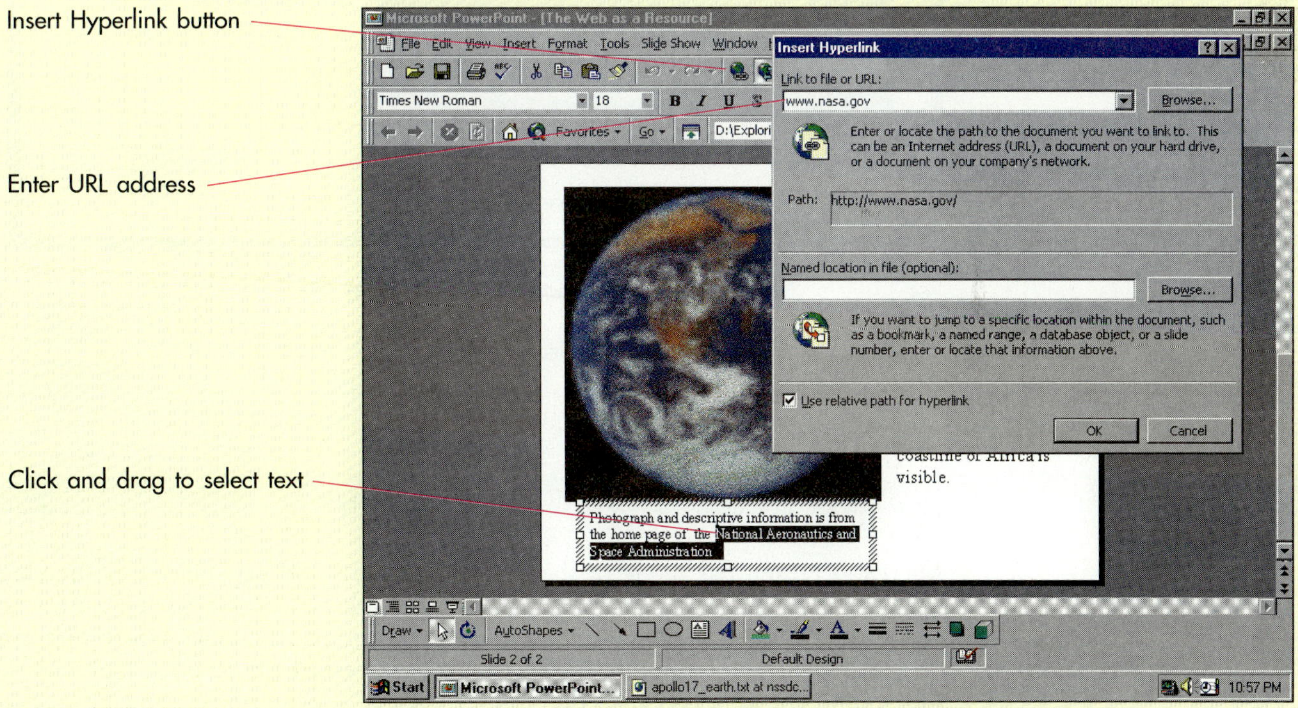


(e) Insert a Hyperlink (step 5)

FIGURE 3.11 Hands-on Exercise 4 (continued)

**STEP 6: Test the Hyperlink**

- Change to the **Slide Show view.** Point to the hyperlink. The mouse pointer changes to a hand and you see a ScreenTip indicating the associated Web address as shown in Figure 3.11f.
- Click the hyperlink to open (reactivate) Internet Explorer and branch to the indicated Web page. Take a few minutes to explore NASA's home page, then close Internet Explorer.
- Exit PowerPoint. Click **Yes** if asked to save the presentation.

Point to the hyperlink; click to open Web browser and go to specified Web page

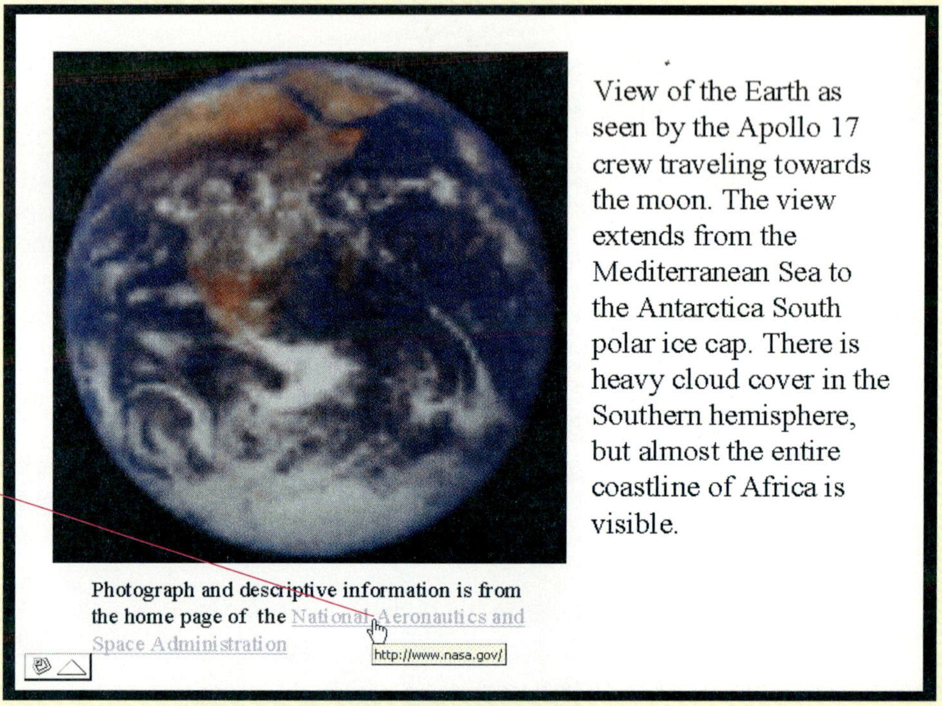


(f) Test the Hyperlink (step 6)

**FIGURE 3.11** Hands-on Exercise 4 (continued)

## SUMMARY

Microsoft Graph has many of the same commands and capabilities as the charting component of Microsoft Excel. After a graph has been inserted into a presentation, it becomes an embedded object that retains its connection to Microsoft Graph. Thus, you can double click the graph to restart Microsoft Graph and edit the graph. You can also click the graph to select it as an object on a PowerPoint slide, then move or size the graph just as you would any other Windows object.

Office 97 contains a powerful set of drawing tools that are collectively known as Office Art. Even if you are not an artist, you can use these tools to modify existing clip art and thus create new and very different illustrations.

Object Linking and Embedding (OLE) enables you to link or embed information (objects) created in other applications. The choice between linking and embedding depends on how the object will be used. Linking is preferable if the object is likely to change and your presentation requires the latest version, or when the same object is shared among many destination documents. Embedding should be used if you plan to show the presentation on a different computer from the one used to create the presentation.

Microsoft WordArt enables you to add special effects to text, then embed the text object into a presentation. WordArt is called from within PowerPoint by clicking the Insert WordArt tool on the Drawing toolbar.

Microsoft Organization Chart enables you to create an organization chart and embed it into a presentation. The application is called from within PowerPoint by choosing the AutoLayout containing an organization chart or by creating an object slide and choosing Microsoft Organization Chart as the object type.

PowerPoint enables you to embed a sound file or a video clip (a movie) into a presentation. Movies do not require additional hardware. Sound requires a sound board and speakers.

Resources from the Internet and World Wide Web can be downloaded for inclusion in a PowerPoint presentation. Hyperlinks can be added to any slide, which when clicked during a slide show will open a Web browser to display the associated page. The Web toolbar contains buttons similar to those on the toolbar in Internet Explorer.

## KEY WORDS AND CONCEPTS

AutoShape
Category names
Copyright
Data points
Data series
Datasheet
Destination document
Drawing toolbar
Embedded object
Group command
Hypermedia document
Hypertext document
In-place editing
Insert Hyperlink command
Insert Picture command
Internet
Linked object
Microsoft Clip Gallery
Microsoft Graph
Microsoft Organization Chart
Microsoft WordArt
Object
Object Linking and Embedding
Office Art
Public domain
Sound
Source document
Ungroup command
Web toolbar
World Wide Web

## MULTIPLE CHOICE

**1.** What happens if you click the Datasheet button on the Microsoft Graph toolbar twice in a row?
   (a) The datasheet is closed (hidden)
   (b) The datasheet is opened (displayed)
   (c) The datasheet is in the same status (either opened or closed) as it was before it was clicked
   (d) Impossible to determine

**2.** Which of the following is true of data series that are plotted in rows?
   (a) The first row in the datasheet contains the category names for the X axis
   (b) The first column in the datasheet contains the legend
   (c) Both (a) and (b)
   (d) Neither (a) nor (b)

3. Which of the following is true of data series that are plotted in columns?
   (a) The first column in the datasheet contains the category names for the X axis
   (b) The first row in the datasheet contains the legend
   (c) Both (a) and (b)
   (d) Neither (a) nor (b)

4. What happens if you select a slide in the Slide Sorter view, click the Copy button, then click the Paste button twice in a row?
   (a) You have made one additional copy of the slide
   (b) You have made two additional copies of the slide
   (c) You have made three additional copies of the slide
   (d) The situation is impossible because you cannot execute the Paste command twice in a row

5. How do you size an object so that it maintains the original proportion between height and width?
   (a) Drag a sizing handle on the left or right side of the object to change its width, then drag a sizing handle on the top or bottom edge to change the height
   (b) Drag a sizing handle on any of the corners
   (c) Both (a) and (b)
   (d) Neither (a) nor (b)

6. What happens if you select an object, then execute the Flip Vertical command twice in a row?
   (a) The object has been rotated 90 degrees
   (b) The object has been rotated 180 degrees (turned upside down)
   (c) The object has been rotated 270 degrees
   (d) The object has been rotated 360 degrees and is in the same position as when you started

7. What is the difference between clicking and double clicking an embedded object?
   (a) Clicking selects the object; double clicking starts the application that created the object
   (b) Double clicking selects the object; clicking starts the application that create the object
   (c) Clicking changes to the Slide Sorter view; double clicking changes to the Outline view
   (d) Double clicking changes to the Slide Sorter view; clicking changes to the Outline view

8. Under which circumstances would you choose linking over embedding?
   (a) When the same object is referenced in many different documents
   (b) When an object is constantly changing and you need the latest version
   (c) Both (a) and (b)
   (d) Neither (a) nor (b)

9. Under which circumstances would you choose embedding over linking?
   (a) When you need to show a presentation on a different computer
   (b) When the same object is referenced in many different documents
   (c) Both (a) and (b)
   (d) Neither (a) nor (b)

10. Which of the following can be created as an embedded object?
    (a) A graph created by Microsoft Graph
    (b) Text created by Microsoft WordArt
    (c) Clip art
    (d) All of the above

11. Which of the following is true regarding the Web toolbar?
    (a) It enables you to enter the address of a Web page from within a PowerPoint presentation
    (b) It enables you to add a Web page to a list of favorite pages
    (c) It contains a button to return to previous Web pages
    (d) All of the above

12. How do you insert clip art onto an existing slide?
    (a) Pull down the Insert menu, click Object, then choose Microsoft Clip Gallery from the list of available objects
    (b) Click the Insert Clip Art button on the Standard toolbar
    (c) Pull down the Insert menu, click Picture, and click the Clip Art command
    (d) All of the above

13. How do you create a new slide containing a graph?
    (a) Create a blank slide, then pull down the Insert menu and click the Chart command
    (b) Create a blank slide, then click the Insert Chart button on the Standard toolbar
    (c) Click the New Slide button, select an AutoLayout containing a chart, then double click the placeholder for the chart in the Slide view
    (d) All of the above

14. What happens if you select an object, click the Copy command, move to a new slide, and click the Paste command?
    (a) Nothing because you cannot copy and paste an object on two different slides
    (b) The selected object has been moved from the first slide to the second slide
    (c) The selected object has been copied from the first slide to the second slide
    (d) The selected object has been copied from the first slide to the second slide, and in addition, remains on the clipboard from where it can be pasted onto another slide

15. What happens if you select an object, click the Cut command, move to a new slide, and click the Paste command?
    (a) Nothing because you cannot copy and paste an object on two different slides
    (b) The selected object has been moved from the first slide to the second slide
    (c) The selected object has been copied from the first slide to the second slide
    (d) The selected object has been copied from the first slide to the second slide, and in addition, remains on the clipboard from where it can be pasted onto another slide

### ANSWERS

| | | |
|---|---|---|
| **1.** c | **6.** d | **11.** d |
| **2.** c | **7.** a | **12.** d |
| **3.** c | **8.** c | **13.** d |
| **4.** b | **9.** a | **14.** d |
| **5.** b | **10.** d | **15.** b |

# PRACTICE WITH POWERPOINT 97

1. Microsoft WordArt is an ideal tool to create the title slide of a presentation, as can be seen from Figure 3.12. Open the Object Linking and Embedding presentation created in the third hands-on exercise and do the following:
   a. Switch to the Slide Sorter view. Select the Title Slide, then press the Del key to delete the slide.
   b. Click the New Slide button on the Standard toolbar to insert a new slide. Choose AutoLayout 12 for a blank slide. Click OK.
   c. Double click the new slide to change to the slide view. Click the Insert WordArt button on the Drawing toolbar to start WordArt.
   d. You're on your own. Duplicate our slide or, better yet, create your own. Let's see how creative you can be and how much impact you can add.

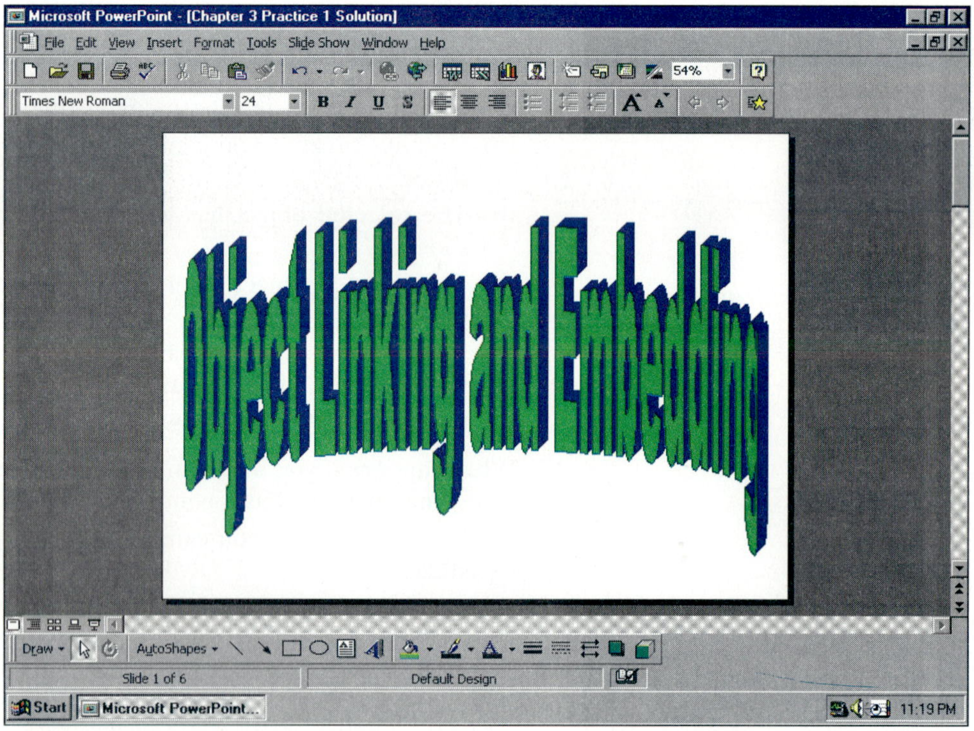


FIGURE 3.12 Screen for Practice Exercise 1

2. Microsoft Organization Chart offers considerable flexibility in the appearance of an organization chart as shown by the chart in Figure 3.13. You can change the line thickness, style, or color for the boxes or connecting lines. You can change the shape of a border and/or add a shadow effect. You can change the font and/or color of text within a box.

   All of these changes are done within the context of *select-then-do;* that is, you select the box (or boxes) for which the change is to apply, then you execute the appropriate command. (To select multiple boxes, press and hold the Shift key as you click additional boxes. You can also use the Select commands in the Edit menu.) Open the Object Linking and Embedding presentation created in the third hands-on exercise and do the following:

   a. Switch to the Slide Sorter view. Select the slide with the organization chart.
   b. Double click the slide to change to the Slide view. Double click the Organization Chart to edit the chart so that it matches Figure 3.13.
   c. Change the box and/or line style as you see fit.
   d. Print a full-page version of the revised slide and submit it to your instructor as proof you did the exercise.

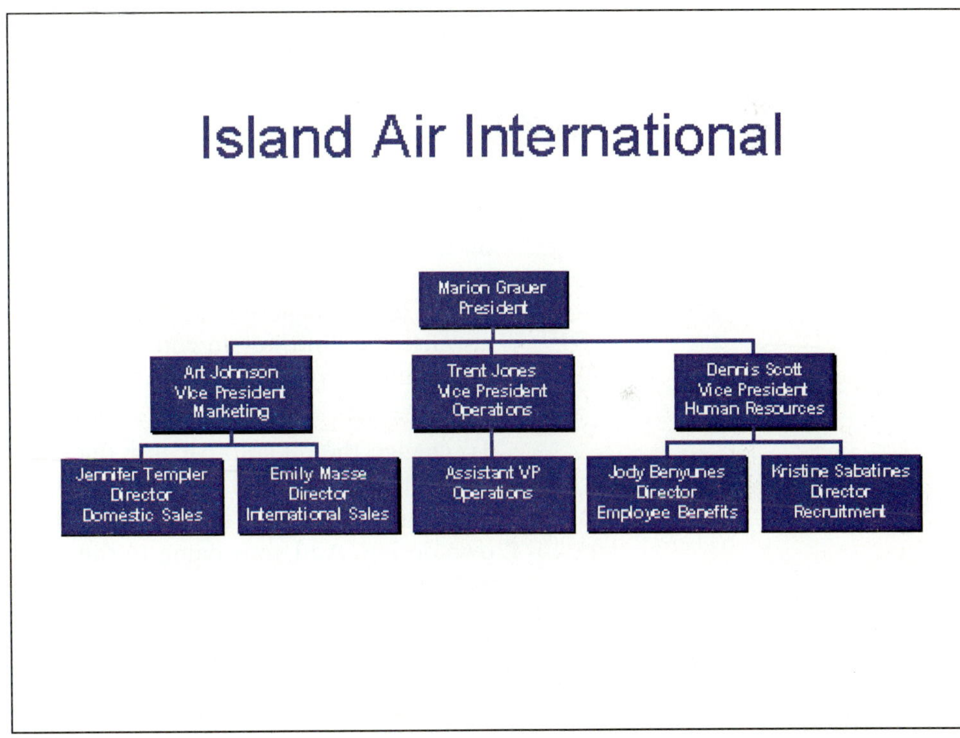


**FIGURE 3.13** Screen for Practice Exercise 2

3. Exploring AutoShapes: Figure 3.14 displays a single slide containing a variety of AutoShapes. Open the presentation created in the third hands-on exercise and do the following:

   a. Add a blank slide immediately before the last slide.
   b. Click the AutoShapes tool on the Drawing toolbar to display the AutoShapes menu. Click and drag the top of the menu to make it a floating toolbar.

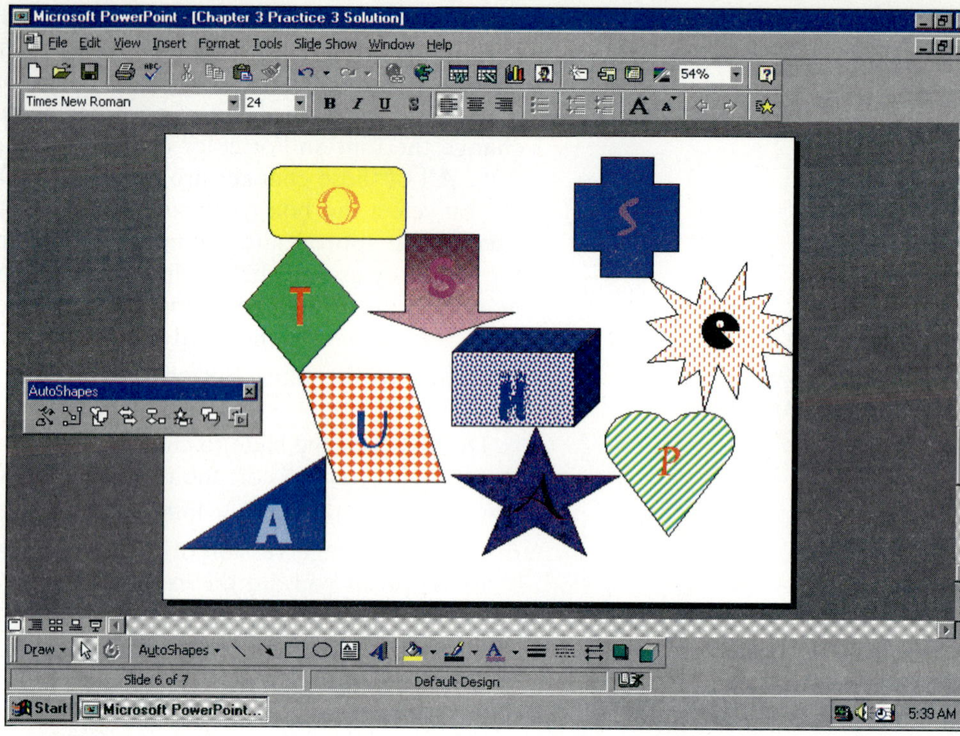


**FIGURE 3.14** Screen for Practice Exercise 3

c. Point to an AutoShape, then click and drag in the slide to create the shape on the slide. (You can press and hold the Shift key as you drag for special effects; for example, press and hold the Shift key as you drag the ellipse or rectangle tool to draw a circle or square, respectively. You can also use the Shift key in conjunction with the Line tool to draw a perfect horizontal or vertical line, or a line at a 45-degree angle.)

d. To place text inside a shape, select the shape and start typing.

e. To change the fill color or line thickness, select the shape, then click the appropriate button on the Drawing toolbar.

f. Use these techniques to duplicate Figure 3.14, or better yet, create your own design. Add your name to the completed slide and submit it to your instructor.

**4.** Figure 3.15 shows two additional examples of what you can do with clip art. The smaller slide on the edge of the page contains the original clip art image. The full-size slide shows the modified slide and is the objective of the exercise. To create Figure 3.15a:

a. Create a blank slide in any presentation. Click the Insert Clip Art button on the Standard toolbar to open the Microsoft Clip Gallery. Add the image from the Cartoons category.

b. Select the clip art image and move it to the right side of the slide. Click the Copy and Paste buttons on the Standard toolbar to copy the image, then drag the copied image to the left side of the slide.

c. Select the image on the right, then ungroup the clip art to convert it to a Microsoft Office drawing. Click the Draw button on the Drawing toolbar, click Rotate or Flip, and click Flip Horizontal.

d. Continue to ungroup the image, changing various colors as appropriate.

e. Click and drag the Rectangle tool to draw a rectangle under our demanding friends. Do not be concerned if the rectangle is on top of the men and you cannot see their elbows. Check that the rectangle is still selected, then click the Fill Color button on the Drawing toolbar to change the color of the rectangle to brown. You can also change the texture (fill color).

f. Click the rectangle to select it. Click the Draw button on the Drawing toolbar, click Order, and click Send to back.

g. Add the AutoShape with the indicated text. Add your name to the slide.

(a) Clip Art 1

(b) Clip Art 2

FIGURE 3.15 Screens for Practice Exercise 4

To create Figure 3.15b:

h. Create a blank slide in any presentation. Click the Insert Clip Art button on the Standard toolbar to open the Microsoft Clip Gallery. Add the image from the Cartoons category.

i. Click and drag the image to size and position it as shown in Figure 3.15b.

j. Copy the clip art image, then click and drag the copied image so that the figures are separated from one another.

k. Ungroup all of the elements in the copied image. Select just the smile, then flip and resize the smile to change it to a frown. (This takes a little practice.)

l. Use the Fill Color tool on the Drawing toolbar to recolor the clothing.

m. Click and drag the Text tool on the Drawing toolbar to create the first text box, then type *There's Good News* in the text box. Be sure the text is still selected, then change the font, size, and color as you see fit.

n. Repeat step (m) to create the second text box. Print both slides and submit them to your instructor.

EXPLORING WWW

5. Every sport, and indeed every team, has its own home page. Basketball and football fans, for example, can visit www.nba.com and www.nfl.com, respectively, from where you can click links to your local teams. Similar pages exist for other leagues as well. And if you don't know where to start, consider the ESPN home page in Figure 3.16.

Choose your favorite sport, team, or player, then create a presentation of six to ten slides. You can create a presentation to announce your own All Star team, with pictures and statistics for each player. Alternatively, you could focus on the career of a specific player. The possibilities are endless.

FIGURE 3.16 Screen for Practice Exercise 5

# Case Studies

## Before and After

As you already know, PowerPoint provides a set of drawing tools to develop virtually any type of illustration. Even if you are not artistic, you can use these tools to modify existing clip art and thus create new and very different illustrations. All it takes is a little imagination and a sense of what can be done. Choose any clip art image(s), then modify that image(s) to create an entirely different effect. Present your results in a three-slide presentation consisting of a title slide, a "before slide" showing the original image(s), and an "after slide" showing the modifications. Print the audience handouts for your presentation, three slides per page, and be sure to check the box to frame the slides. Ask your instructor to hold a class contest in which the class votes to determine the most creative application.

## Photographs versus Clip Art

The right clip art can enhance a presentation, but there are times when clip art just won't do. It may be too juvenile or simply inappropriate. Photographs offer an alternative and are inserted into a presentation through the Insert Picture command. Once inserted into a presentation, photographs can be moved or sized just like any other Windows object. The CD-ROM version of the Clip Gallery contains a series of photographs. We invite you to explore these photographs, then report back to the class on their quality and cost.

## The National Debt

The national debt is staggering—more than $5 trillion, or approximately $20,000 for every man, woman, and child in the United States. The annual budget is approximately $1.5 trillion, and Congress has yet to eliminate the deficit, which exceeds $100 billion annually.

Use the Internet to obtain exact figures for the current year, then use this information to create a presentation pleading for fiscal sanity. Do some additional research and obtain data on the budget, the deficit, and the national debt for the years 1945, 1967, and 1980. The numbers may surprise you. For example, how does the interest expense for the current year compare to the total budget in 1967 (at the height of the Viet Nam War)? To the total budget in 1945 (at the end of World War II)?

## File Compression

Photographs add significantly to the appearance of a presentation, but they also add to its size. Accordingly, you might want to consider acquiring a file compression program to facilitate copying large files to a floppy disk in order to transport your presentations to and from school, home, or work. You can download an evaluation copy of the popular WinZip program at www.winzip.com. Investigate the subject of file compression, then submit a summary of your findings to your instructor.

## Copyright Infringement

It's fun to download images from the Web for inclusion in a presentation, but is it legal? Copyright protection (infringement) is one of the most pressing legal issues on the Web. Search the Web for sites that provide information on current copyright law. One excellent site is the copyright page at the Institute for Learning Technologies at www.ilt.columbia.edu/projects/copyright. Another excellent reference is the page at www.benedict.com. Research these and other sites, then summarize your findings in a short note to your instructor.

## Our Last Case

Once again we refer you to the Valupack on the CD-ROM version of Microsoft Office to view a 45-slide presentation that introduces (and reviews) the major features in PowerPoint. The presentation is called "QuikStrt" and is found in the Tutorial folder within the Valupack folder on the CD-ROM. It is a multimedia presentation that incorporates music, video, as well as the various other features discussed in this chapter. Sit back, relax, and enjoy the show.

A

# APPENDIX A: TOOLBARS

## OVERVIEW

Microsoft PowerPoint has fourteen predefined toolbars that provide access to commonly used commands. The toolbars are displayed in Figure A.1 and are listed here for convenience. They are: the Standard, Formatting, Animation Effects, Common Tasks, Control Toolbox, Drawing, Picture, Reviewing, Shadow Settings, Stop Recording, Visual Basic, Web, WordArt, and 3-D Settings toolbars. The Standard and Formatting toolbars are displayed by default and appear immediately below the menu bar. The other predefined toolbars are displayed (hidden) at the discretion of the user.

The buttons on the toolbars indicate their functions. Clicking the Printer button, for example (the fourth button from the left on the Standard toolbar), executes the Print command. If you are unsure of the purpose of any toolbar button, point to it, and a ScreenTip will appear that displays its name.

You can display multiple toolbars at one time, move them to a new location, customize their appearance, or suppress their display.

- To display or hide a toolbar, pull down the View menu and click the Toolbars command. Select (deselect) the toolbar(s) that you want to display (hide). The selected toolbar(s) will be displayed in the same position as when last displayed. You may also point to any toolbar and click with the right mouse button to bring up a shortcut menu that lets you select the toolbar to be displayed (hidden). In either case, if you do not see the desired toolbar listed, click the Customize command to display the list of all available toolbars. Click the check box for the desired toolbar(s) and then click Close.
- To change the size of the buttons, suppress the display of the ScreenTips, or display the associated shortcut key (if available) with the ScreenTips, pull down the View menu, click Toolbars, and click Customize to display the Customize dialog box. If necessary, click the Options tab, then select (deselect) the appropriate check box.

- Toolbars are either docked (along the edge of the window) or floating (in their own window). A toolbar moved to the edge of the window will dock along that edge. A toolbar moved anywhere else in the window will float in its own window. Docked toolbars are one tool wide (high), whereas floating toolbars can be resized by clicking and dragging a border or corner as you would with any window.
    - To move a docked toolbar, click anywhere in the gray background area and drag the toolbar to its new location. You can also click and drag the move handle (the pair of parallel lines) at the left of the toolbar.
    - To move a floating toolbar, drag its title bar to its new location.
- To customize one or more toolbars, display the toolbar(s) on the screen. Then pull down the View menu, click Toolbars, click Customize to display the Customize dialog box, and select the Toolbars tab. Alternatively, you can click on any toolbar with the right mouse button, select Customize from the shortcut menu, and then click the Toolbars tab.
    - To move a button, drag the button to its new location on that toolbar or any other displayed toolbar.
    - To copy a button, press the Ctrl key as you drag the button to its new location on that toolbar or any other displayed toolbar.
    - To delete a button, drag the button off the toolbar and release the mouse button.
    - To add a button, click the Commands tab in the Customize dialog box, select the category from the Categories list box that contains the button you want to add, then drag the button to the desired location on the toolbar. (To see a description of a tool's function before adding it to a toolbar, select the tool, then click the Description command button.)
    - To restore a predefined toolbar to its default appearance, pull down the View menu, click Toolbars, click Customize, click the Toolbars tab, select (highlight) the desired toolbar, and click the Reset command button.
- Buttons can also be moved, copied, or deleted without displaying the Customize dialog box.
    - To move a button, press the Alt key as you drag the button to the new location.
    - To copy a button, press the Alt and Ctrl keys as you drag the button to the new location.
    - To delete a button, press the Alt key as you drag the button off the toolbar.
- To create your own toolbar, pull down the View menu, click Toolbars, click Customize, click the Toolbars tab, then click the New command button. Alternatively, you can click on any toolbar with the right mouse button, select Customize from the shortcut menu, click the Toolbars tab, and then click the New command button.
    - Enter a name for the toolbar in the dialog box that follows. The name can be any length and can contain spaces.
    - The new toolbar will appear on the screen. Initially it will be big enough to hold only one button. Add, move, and delete buttons following the same procedures as outlined above. The toolbar will automatically size itself as new buttons are added and deleted.
    - To delete a custom toolbar, pull down the View menu, click Toolbars, click Customize, and click the Toolbars tab. *Verify that the custom toolbar to be deleted is the only one selected (highlighted).* Click the Delete command button. Click Yes to confirm the deletion. (Note that a predefined toolbar cannot be deleted.)

**Standard Toolbar**

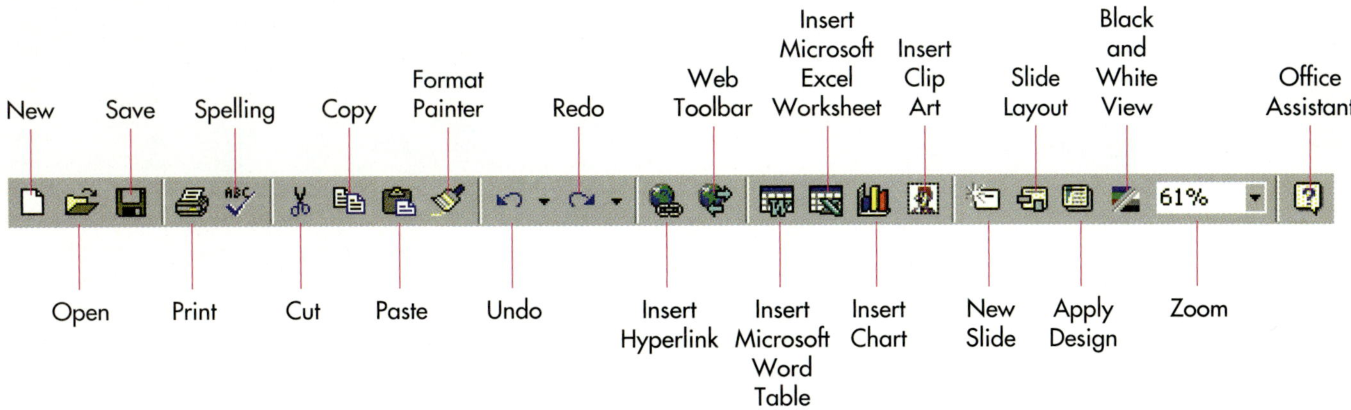


**Formatting Toolbar**

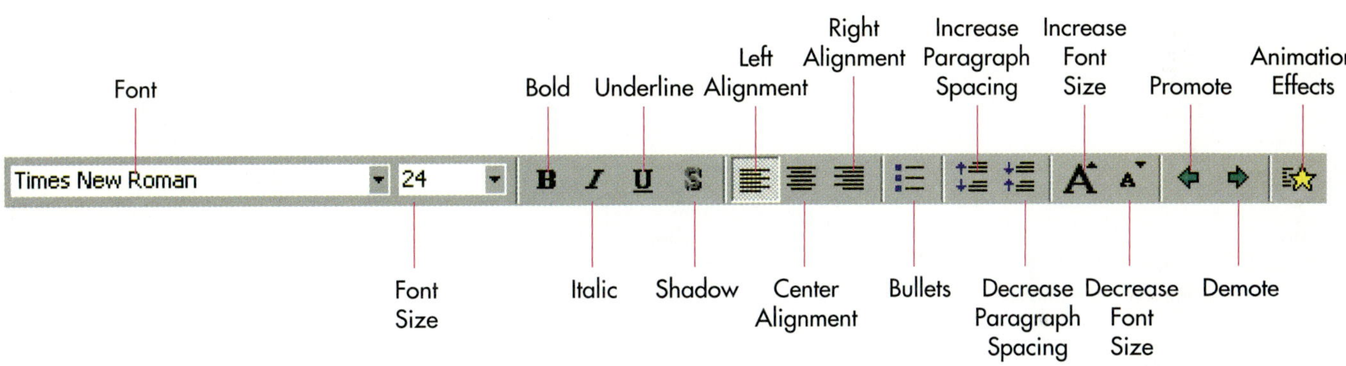


**Animation Effects Toolbar**

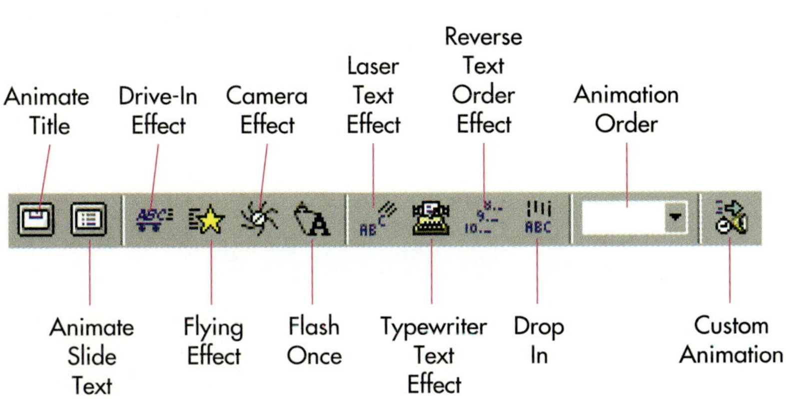


FIGURE A.1 Toolbars

**Common Tasks Toolbar**

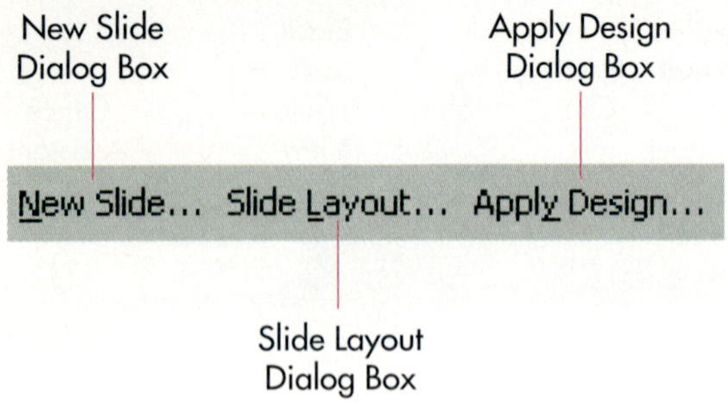


**Control Toolbox Toolbar**

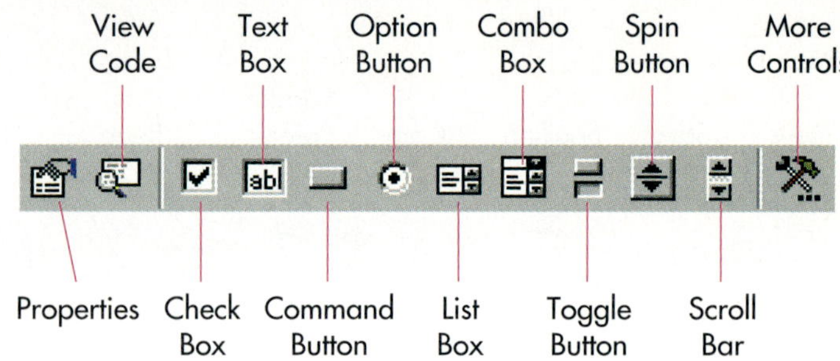


**Drawing Toolbar**

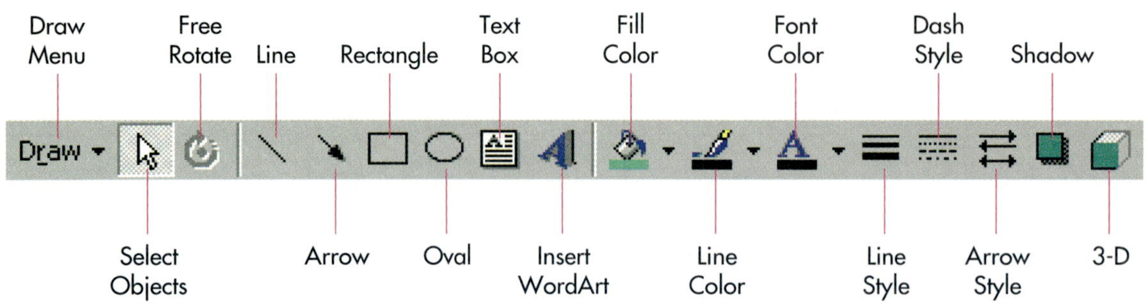


**Picture Toolbar**

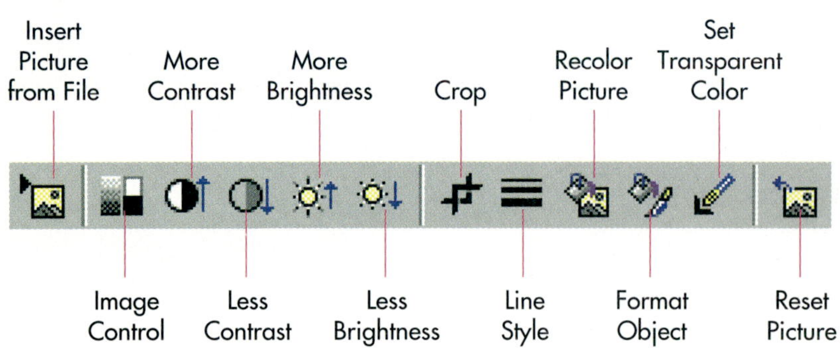


**Reviewing Toolbar**

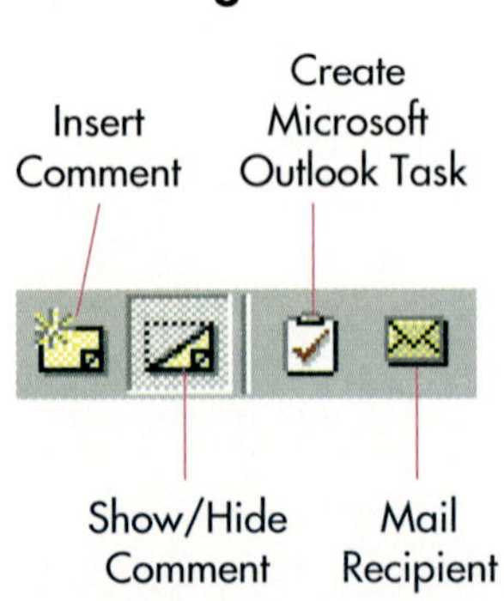


**Shadow Settings Toolbar**

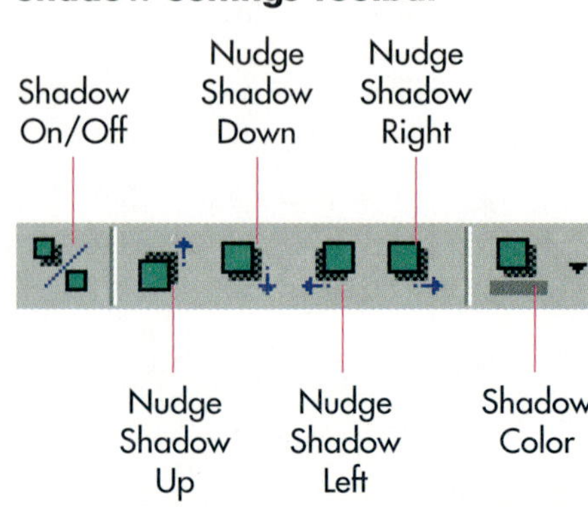


FIGURE A.1 Toolbars (continued)

**Stop Recording Toolbar**

**Visual Basic Toolbar**

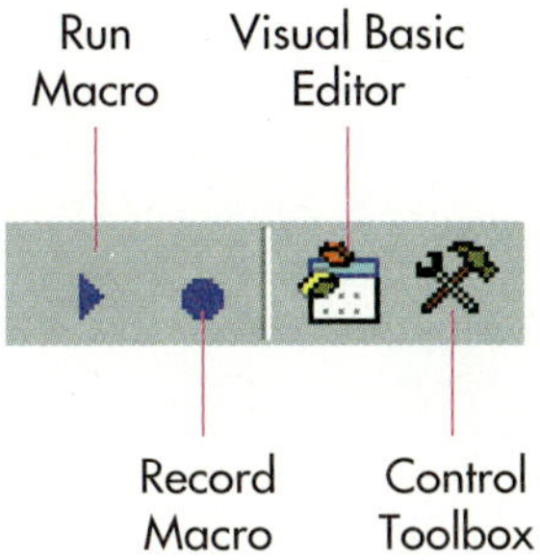


**Web Toolbar**

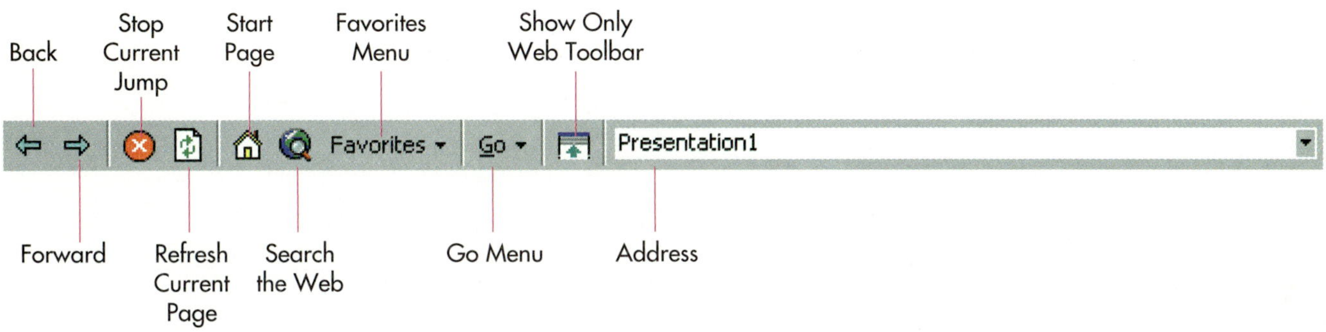


**WordArt Toolbar**

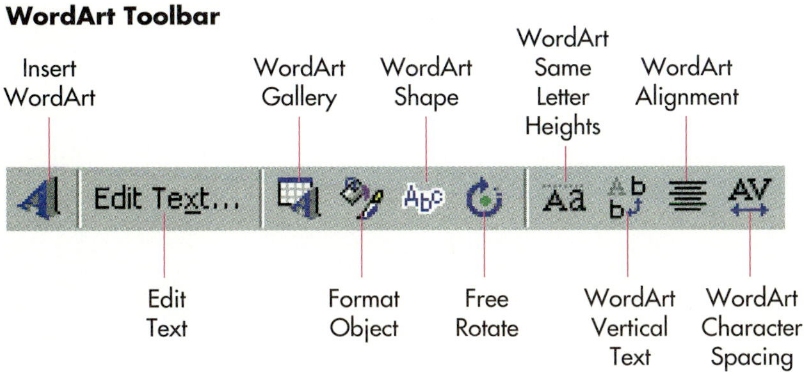


**3-D Settings Toolbar**

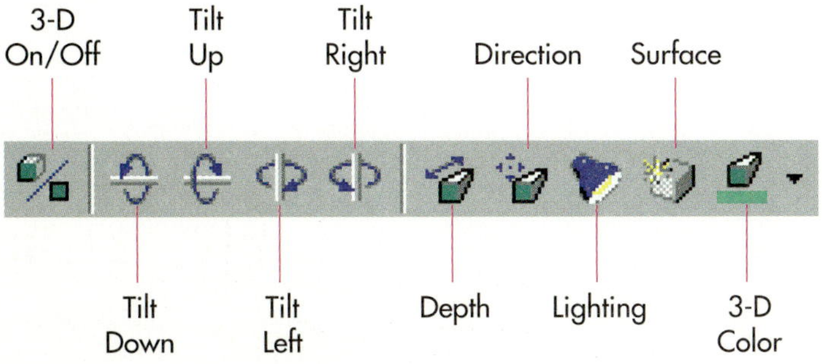


FIGURE A.1 Toolbars (continued)

B

# APPENDIX B: INTRODUCTION TO MULTIMEDIA

## OVERVIEW

Multimedia combines the text and graphics capability of the PC with high-quality sound and video. The combination of different media, under the control of the PC, has opened up a new world of education and entertainment. This appendix introduces you to the basics of multimedia and shows you how to incorporate sound and video into a PowerPoint presentation.

We begin with a brief discussion of the hardware requirements needed to run multimedia applications. We explain the various file types that are associated with multimedia and discuss the support that is built into Windows 95. The appendix also contains two hands-on exercises that let you apply the conceptual material. The first exercise is independent of PowerPoint and has you experiment with various sound and video files to better acquaint you with the capabilities of multimedia. The second exercise shows you how to create your own multimedia presentation.

## THE MULTIMEDIA COMPUTER

Multimedia is possible only because of recent advances in technology that include faster microprocessors, CD-ROM, and sophisticated sound and video boards. But how fast a microprocessor do you really need? What type of CD-ROM and sound card should you consider? The answer is critical to both the consumer and the developer. The consumer wants a system that is capable of running "typical" multimedia applications. The developer, on the other hand, wants to appeal to the widest possible audience and must write an application so that it runs on the "typical" configuration.

To guide developers, and to let the public know about the specific hardware needed, the Multimedia PC Working Group of the Software Publishers Association was established to determine the suggested minimum specification for a multimedia computer. Three standards have been published to date—MPC-1, MPC-2, and MPC-3, in 1991, 1993, and 1995, respectively, as shown in Figure B.1. Implicit in each standard is the requirement that the system retail for less than $2,000. Technology has advanced so quickly, however, that the current standard (MPC-3) is well below today's entry-level computer. MPC-4 was not available at the time we went to press (June 1997) but you can check the Web site (www.spa.org/mpc) for additional information. Realize also that in addition to the equipment listed in the table, you will need speakers to amplify the sound, a microphone if you want to record your own sounds, and a joystick for games.

| | MPC-1 (1991) | MPC-2 (1993) | MPC-3 (1995) |
|---|---|---|---|
| **CPU** | 80386 16MHz | 80486SX 25MHz | 75MHz Pentium |
| **RAM** | 2MB | 4MB | 8MB |
| **Disk capacity** | 30MB | 160MB | 540MB |
| **Sound card** | 8 bit | 8 bit | 16 bit with multivoice internal synthesizer |
| **CD-ROM** | Single speed | Double speed | Quadruple speed |
| **Video system** | VGA (640 × 480) | SVGA (800 × 600) | 30 frames/second at 320 × 240 pixels |

FIGURE B.1 The Multimedia PC

### WHAT IS MMX TECHNOLOGY?

Intel has enhanced its Pentium processor through an additional set of 57 instructions that are collectively known as MMX technology. The instructions are designed to process video, audio, and graphical data more efficiently and increase the speed of a Pentium processor by approximately 20 percent. You do not need an MMX processor to run multimedia applications; it helps significantly, however, and you should not purchase a computer without it.

## THE BASICS OF MULTIMEDIA

A few years ago, multimedia was an extra. Today, it is a virtual standard and everyone has a favorite multimedia application. But did you ever stop to think of how the application was created? Or of the large number of individual files that are needed for the sound and visual effects that are at the heart of the application? In this section we look at the individual components—the sound and video files—that comprise a multimedia application.

### Sound

The sound you hear from your PC is the result of a sound file (stored on disk or a CD-ROM) being played through the sound card in your system. There are, however, two very different types of sound files—a WAV file and a MIDI file. Each is discussed in turn.

A ***WAV file*** is a digitized recording of an actual sound (a voice, music, or special effects). It is created by a chip in the sound card that converts a recorded sound (e.g., your voice by way of a microphone) into a file on disk. The sound card divides the sound wave into tiny segments (known as samples) and stores each sample as a binary number. The quality of the sound is determined by two factors—the sampling rate and the resolution of each sample. The higher each of these values, the better the quality, and the larger the corresponding file.

The ***sampling rate*** (or frequency) is the number of samples per second and is expressed in KHz (thousands of samples per second). The higher the sampling rate, the more accurately the sound will be represented in the wave file. Common sampling rates are 11KHz, 22KHz, and 44KHz. The ***resolution*** is the number of bits (binary digits) used to store each sample. The more bits the better. The first sound cards provided for only eight bits and are obsolete. Sixteen bits are standard in today's environment.

WAV files, even those that last only a few seconds, grow large very quickly. Eight-bit sound, for example, at a sampling rate of 11KHz (11,000 samples a second) requires approximately 11KB of disk space per second. Thirty seconds of sound at this sampling rate will take some 330KB. If you improve the quality by using a 16-bit sound card, and by doubling the sampling rate to 22KHz, the same 30 seconds of sound will consume 1.3MB, or almost an entire high-density floppy disk!

A ***MIDI file*** (Musical Instrument Digital Interface) is very different from a WAV file and is used only to create music. It does not store an actual sound (as does a WAV file), but rather the instructions to create that sound. In other words, a MIDI file is the electronic equivalent of sheet music. The advantage of a MIDI file is that it is much more compact than a WAV file because it stores instructions to create the sound rather than the sound itself.

## Video

An ***AVI*** (Audi-Video Interleaved) ***file*** is the Microsoft standard for a digital video (i.e., a multimedia) file. It takes approximately 4.5MB to store one second of *uncompressed* color video in the AVI format. That may sound unbelievable, but you can verify the number with a little arithmetic.

A single VGA screen contains approximately 300,000 (640 × 480) pixels, each of which requires (at least) one byte of storage to store the color associated with that pixel. Allocating one byte (or 8 bits) per pixel yields only 256 (or $2^8$) different colors. It is more common, therefore, to define color palettes based on two or even three bytes per pixel, which yield 65,536 ($2^{16}$) and 16,777,216 ($2^{24}$) colors, respectively. The more colors you have, the better the picture, but the larger the file.

In addition, to fool the eye and create the effect of motion, the screen must display at least 15 screens (frames) a second. If we multiply 300,000 bytes per frame times 15 frames per second, we arrive at the earlier number of 4.5MB of data for each second of video. Storage requirements of this magnitude are clearly prohibitive, in that an entire 640MB CD would hold less than three minutes of video. And even if storage capacity were not a problem, it's simply not possible for a CD-ROM to deliver almost 5MB of data per second to the PC. Clearly something had to be done to deliver video to the PC market.

Full-motion video is made possible in two ways, by reducing the size of the window in which the movie clip is displayed, and through file compression. Think, for a moment, of the movie clips you have seen (or consider the Basket.AVI file in Figure B.2) and realize that it is displayed in a window that is only 240 × 180 as opposed to a full (640 × 480) VGA screen. The smaller window immediately reduces the storage requirements.

Even more significant than a reduced window is the availability of sophisticated compression-decompression algorithms that dramatically reduce the storage requirements. In essence, these algorithms do not store every pixel in every frame, but only information about how pixels change from frame to frame. The details of file compression are not important at this time. What is important is that you appreciate the amount of data that is required for multimedia applications.

Realize, too, that even with the smaller window and file compression, AVI files are still inordinately large. The 3½-second movie clip in Figure B.2, for example, requires 670KB. Nevertheless, compare this requirement to our earlier calculations, which showed that an uncompressed video running on a VGA screen would take approximately 4.5MB per second!

### THE AVI (AUDIO VIDEO INTERLEAVED) STANDARD

The AVI format was introduced in 1992 and specified a standard video clip of 160 × 120 pixels, or one-sixteenth of a VGA screen. The tiny screen was not overly impressive to the public at large, but it represented a significant technical achievement. Improved technology such as the local bus, multi-speed CDs, better compression algorithms, and faster microprocessors have resulted in today's superior video clips.

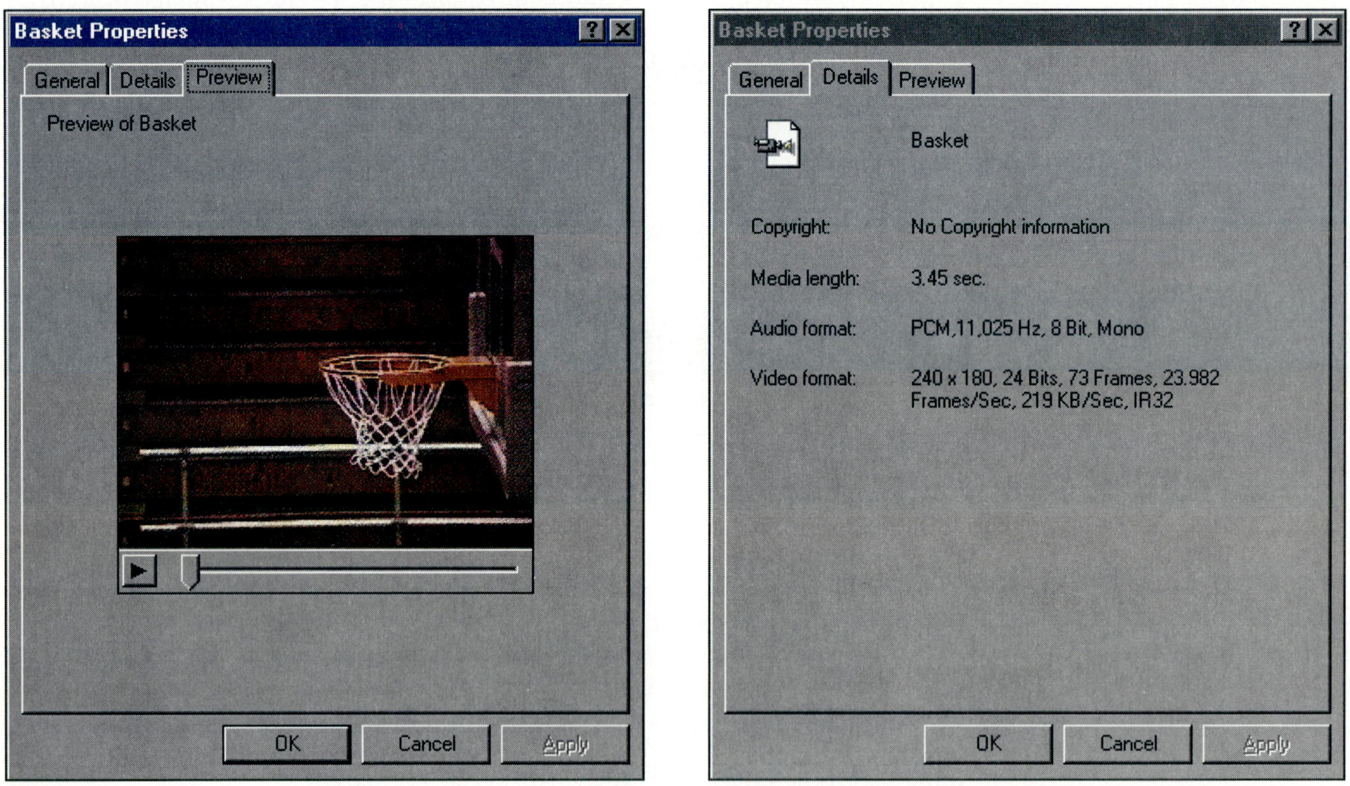


(a) Preview

(b) Details

FIGURE B.2 Movie Clip

## Windows 95 Support

Windows 95 includes the necessary software (in the form of accessories) to play the various types of multimedia files. The appropriate accessory is opened automatically when you double click a media file type from within Windows Explorer or My Computer. The software can also be accessed from the Start button by clicking Programs, then Accessories, then Multimedia. Each accessory is described briefly below, then illustrated in a hands-on exercise.

The ***Sound Recorder*** is used to record and/or play a WAV file. Options within the Sound Recorder let you record at different qualities (such as CD or radio), add special effects such as an echo, or change the speed. You can even play the sound backwards.

The ***Media Player*** lets you play audio (MIDI), video, or animation files. ***Volume Control*** enables you to control the volume and/or balance of your sound card. The ***CD Player*** enables you to play audio CDs in a CD-ROM drive while you work on your PC. The controls on the Windows CD player look just like those on a regular CD player. It also has many of the same features, such as random play, and a programmable playback order.

The following exercise lets you experiment with the various types of multimedia files we have described.

### ORDINARY FILES

A multimedia file is just like any other file with respect to ordinary file operations. Thus, you can point to the file in My Computer or Windows Explorer, then click the right mouse button to display a menu to cut or copy the file, rename or delete the file, or display its properties. You can also use the right mouse button to click and drag the file to a different drive or folder or to create a shortcut on the desktop.

## HANDS-ON EXERCISE 1

*Introduction to Multimedia*

**Objective:** To locate and play WAV, MIDI and AVI files. The exercise requires a sound card but can be done without a CD-ROM. Use Figure B.3 as a guide in the exercise.

**STEP 1: A WAV File**

- Click the **Start button** on the Windows 95 taskbar. Click (or point to) **Programs,** then click **Windows Explorer.** Click the **maximize button** so that Windows Explorer takes the entire desktop as shown in Figure B.3a.
- Select the **Exploring PowerPoint folder** that you have been using throughout the text. If necessary, pull down the **View menu** and click **Details.**
- Pull down the **View menu** a second time. Click **Options,** then click the **View tab** in the Options dialog box. Clear the box (if necessary) to **Hide MS-DOS file extensions.** Click **OK.**

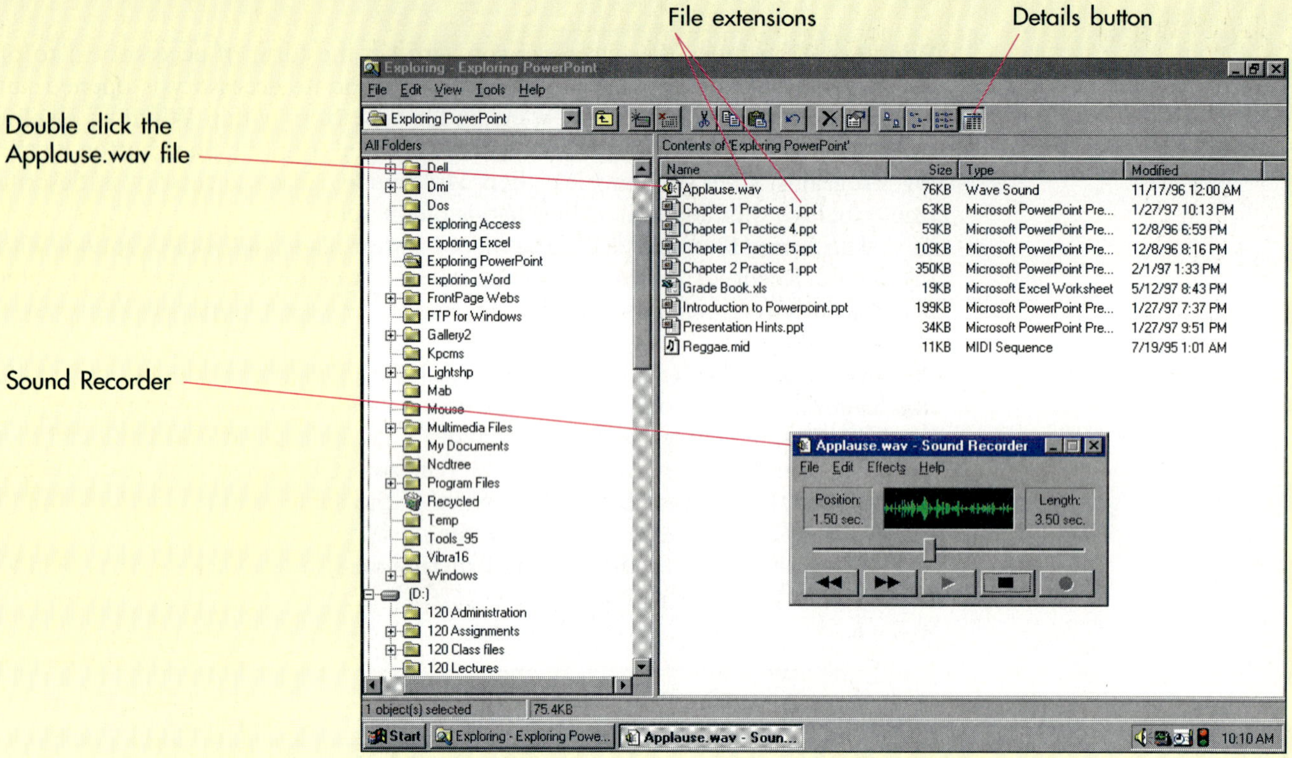


(a) A WAV File (step 1)

**FIGURE B.3** Hands-on Exercise 1

- Double click the **Applause.wav file** to play the file. The Sound Recorder opens automatically as you hear the applause, then closes after the sound is complete.
- Point to the **Applause.wav file,** then click the **right mouse button** to display a context-sensitive menu. Click **Properties** to display the Properties dialog box, then click the **Details tab** to see additional information about this file.
- Close the Properties dialog box.

## RECORD YOUR OWN WAV FILES

You can record your own WAV files, provided you have a microphone; then you can link or embed those files in a PowerPoint presentation. To create a new sound (WAV) file, right click in the folder that is to contain the file, click New, then click Wave Sound to specify the type of object you want to create. Change the default file name, then double click the file to open the Sound Recorder. Click the Record button to start recording and the Stop button when you have finished. Click the Play button to hear the recorded sound. Close the Sound Recorder, then use the Insert Sound command in PowerPoint to insert the sound file into a presentation.

### STEP 2: A MIDI File

- Double click the **Reggae file** to listen to the sound of Reggae music. The Media Player opens automatically as shown in Figure B.3b. Unlike the Wav files, which typically last only a few seconds, the MIDI files are musical compositions that play for longer periods.
- Experiment with the controls on the Media Player:
  - Click the **Pause button** to suspend playing.
  - Click the **Play button** (which appears after you click the Pause button) to resume playing.
  - Click the **Stop button** to stop playing.
  - Click the **Rewind button** to return to the beginning of the recording.
- Close the Media Player when you are finished listening.

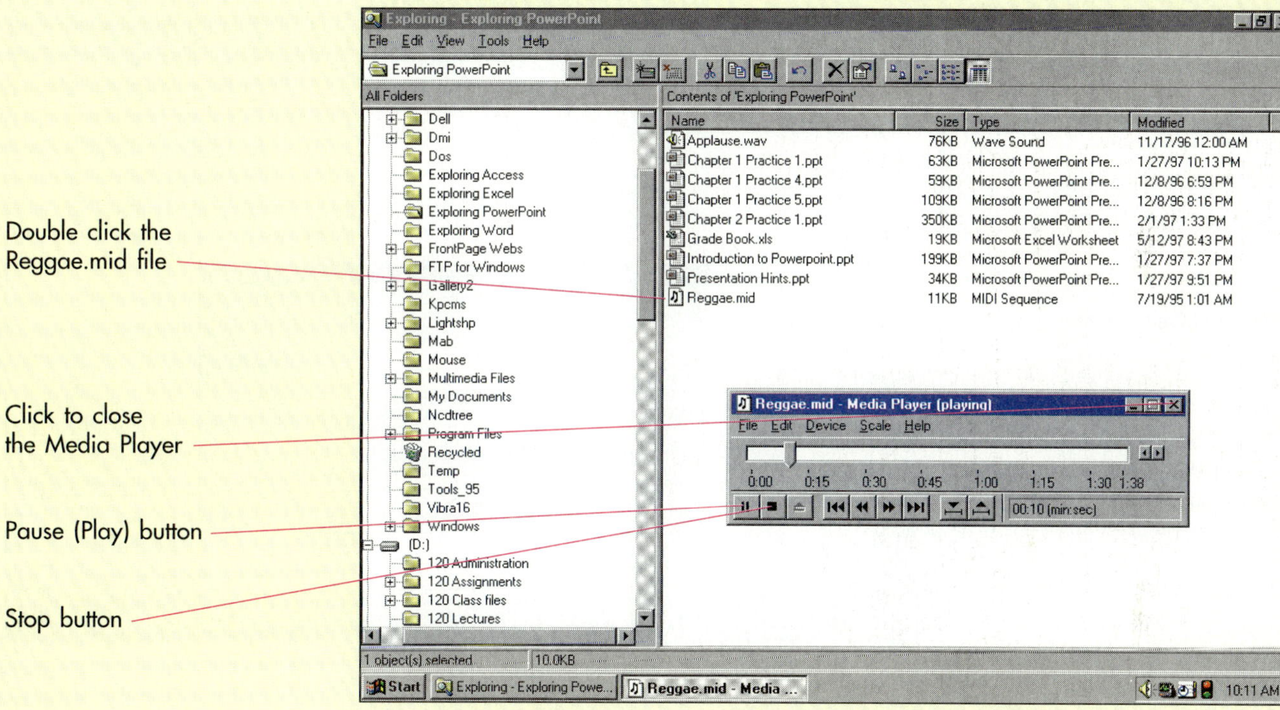


(b) A MIDI File (step 2)

**FIGURE B.3** Hands-on Exercise 1 (continued)

> **WAV FILES VERSUS MIDI FILES**
>
> A WAV file stores an actual sound whereas a MIDI file stores the instructions to create the sound. Because a WAV file stores a recorded sound, it can represent any type of sound—a voice, music, or special effects. A MIDI file can store only music. WAV files, even those that last only a few seconds, are very large because the sound is sampled thousands of times a second to create the file. MIDI files, however, are much more compact because they store the instructions to create the sound rather than the sound itself.

### STEP 3: The Find Command

- Movie clips (AVI files) are quite large, and hence we did not include any of these files in the Exploring PowerPoint folder. Thus, you need to search for an AVI file in order to play it.
- Click the **Start button** on the Windows 95 taskbar. Click (or point to) the **Find command,** then click **Files or Folders** to display the dialog box in Figure B.3c. The size and/or position of the dialog box may be different from the one in the figure.
  - Enter ***.AVI** (the type of file you are searching for) in the Named text box.
  - Click the **drop-down arrow** in the **Look in** list box and select drive C.
  - Be sure the **Include subfolders** box is checked.

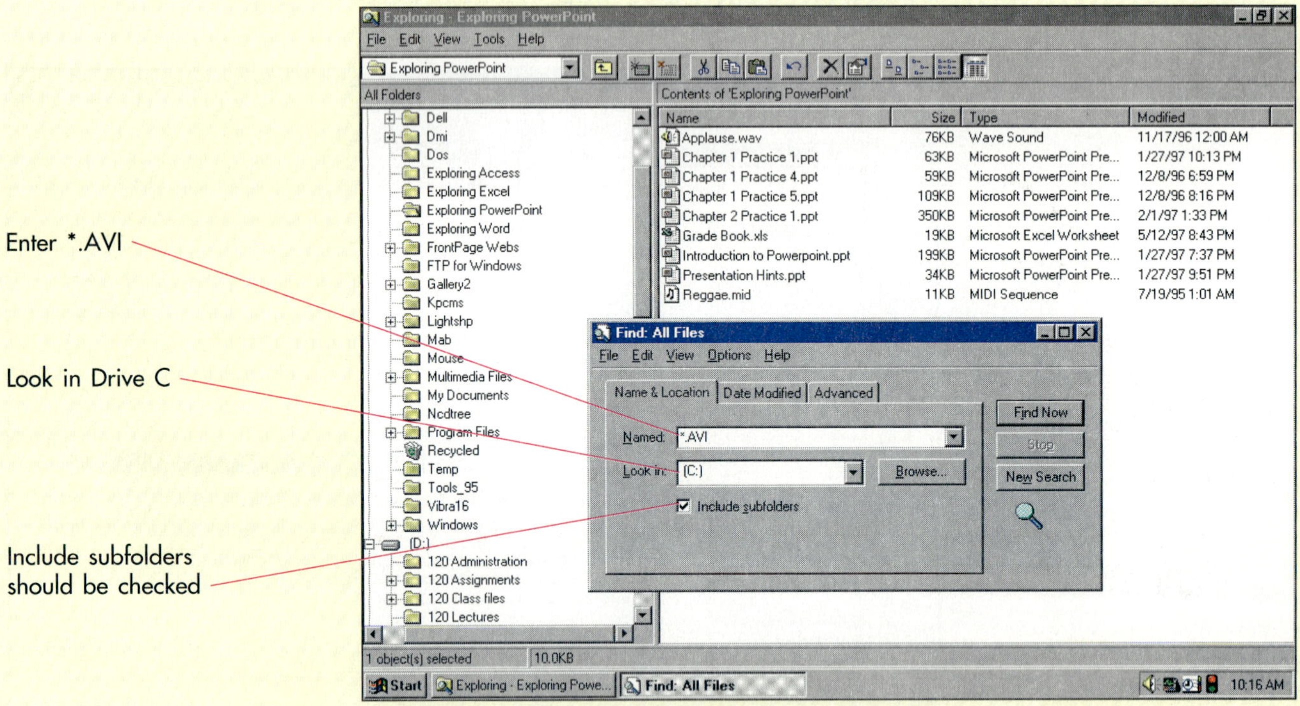


(c) The Find Command (step 3)

**FIGURE B.3** Hands-on Exercise 1 (continued)

> **FILE EXTENSIONS**
>
> Long-time DOS users will recognize the three-character extension at the end of a file name, which indicates the file type. The extensions are displayed or hidden according to an option in the View menu in My Computer or the Windows Explorer. Windows 95 maintains the file extension for compatibility, and in addition, displays an icon next to the file name to indicate the file type. The icons are more easily recognized in the Large Icons view as opposed to the Details view. Extensions of WAV and MID denote a wave form and MIDI file, respectively. An AVI (Audio-Video Interleaved) file is the Microsoft standard for a multimedia file with video and sound.

- Click the **Find Now button** to begin the search, then watch the status bar as Windows searches for the specified files and folders.

➤ The results of the search are displayed within the Find Files dialog box and should contain multiple AVI files. If you do not see any files at all, check the search parameters, then repeat the search.

**STEP 4: Play an AVI File**

➤ Maximize the Find Files dialog box as shown in Figure B.3d. The results of your search may be different from ours, but at the very least you should see various AVI files from the Windows Help folder.

➤ Double click the **Taskswch.avi** file to play this movie as shown in Figure B.3d.

Double click the Taskswch.avi file

Media Player opens to play the Taskswch.avi file

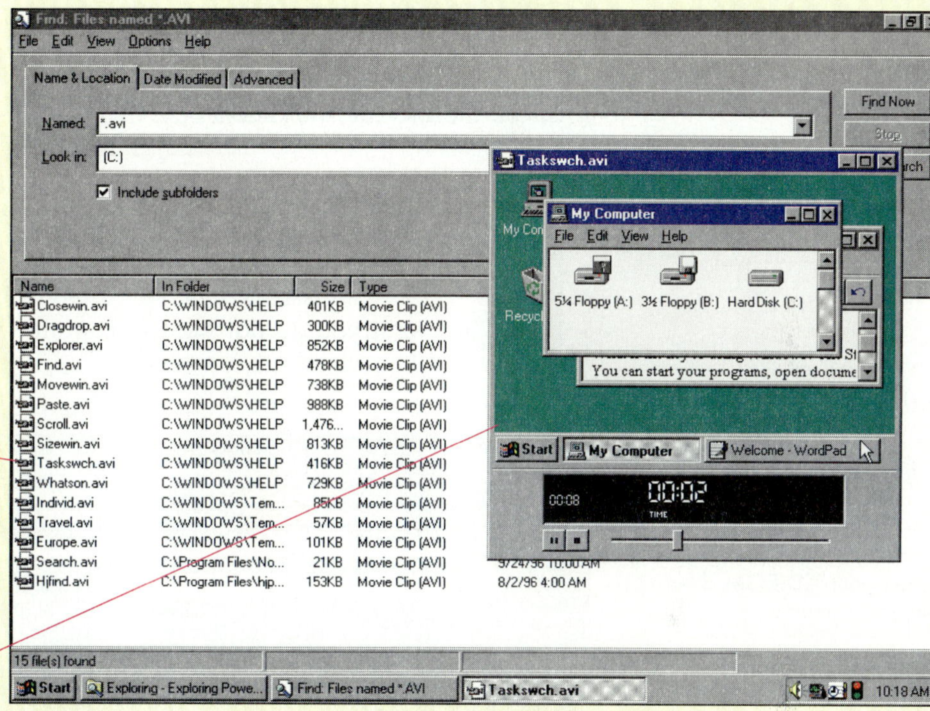


(d) Play an AVI File (step 4)

**FIGURE B.3** Hands-on Exercise 1 (continued)

## THE WINDOWS 95 HELP COMMAND

The answer to almost anything you need to know about Windows is available through the Help command if only you take the trouble to look. Click the Start button, then click Help to display the Help topics dialog box. Click the Index tab, type *ta* (the first two letters in *task switching*), double click *task switching* when it appears in the open list box, then double click *The Basics* in the Topics Found dialog box to display a help screen for the Windows desktop. Click any of the indicated topics and follow the on-screen instructions to play the AVI files in the Windows Help folder.

- The movie is relatively unimpressive—it takes only a few seconds and illustrates the use of the taskbar to switch between open applications. Nevertheless, it is more than 400KB in size and illustrates the complexity of creating a movie clip.
- View as many movie clips as you like, then close the Find Files dialog box when you are finished.

**STEP 5: A More Interesting AVI File**

- This step requires the Office 97 CD as the best AVI files, for purposes of demonstration, are found on this CD.
- Click the **Start button** on the Windows 95 taskbar. Click the **Find command,** then click **Files or Folders** to display the Find Files dialog box.
- Enter ***.avi** (the type of file you are searching for) in the Named text box. Click the **drop-down arrow** in the **Look in** list box and select the drive for your CD (drive F on our system).
- Check the **Include subfolders** box, then click the **Find Now button** to begin the search.
- The results of the search should reference multiple files in the Books folder from the Office 97 CD as shown in Figure B.3e. Double click one or more files to view a movie clip.
- Close the Find Files dialog box. Close the Windows Explorer.
- Exit Windows if you do not want to continue with the next exercise at this time.

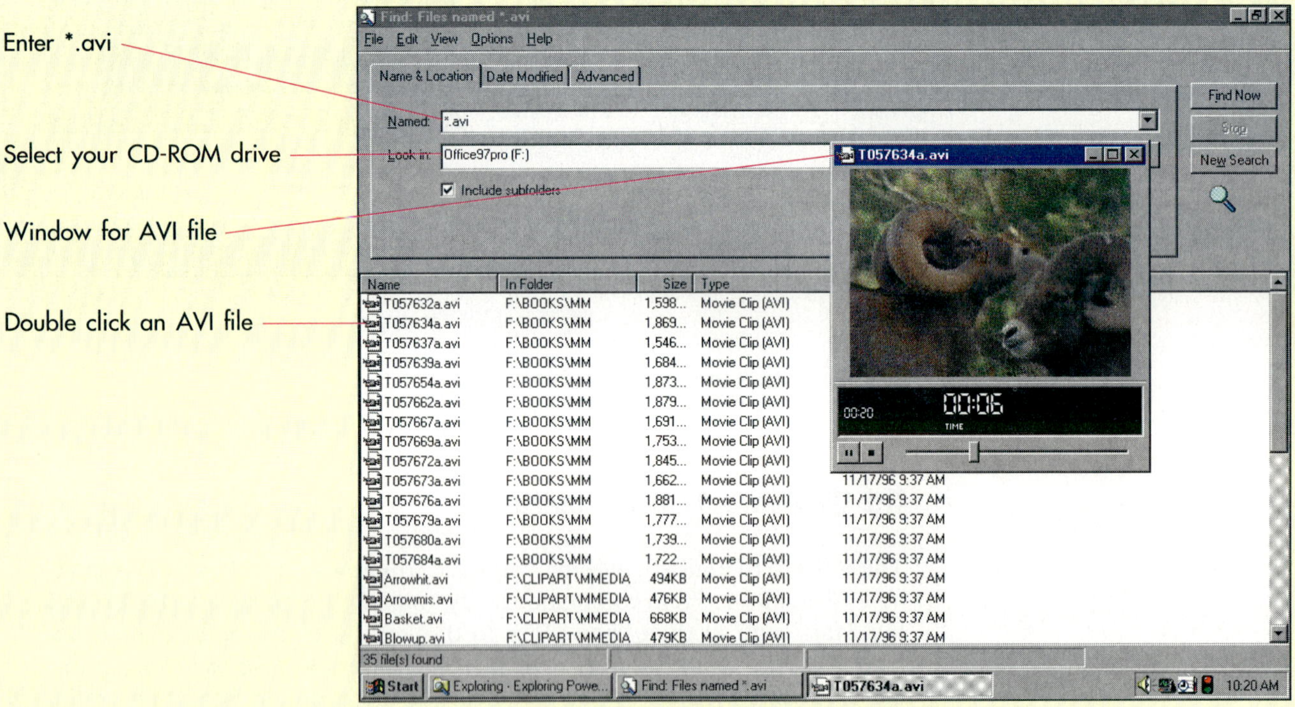


(e) A More Interesting AVI File (step 5)

FIGURE B.3 Hands-on Exercise 1 (continued)

The exercise just completed had you explore the elements of multimedia and experiment with individual files. You learned about the different types of sound files and saw the impact of a movie clip. The effectiveness of multimedia, however, depends on integrating the various elements into a cohesive unit.

A multimedia presentation is a show, and like any show it requires careful planning if it is to be successful. The actors in a show, or the objects on a PowerPoint slide, must be thoroughly scripted so that the performance is as effective as possible. Consider now Figure B.4, which contains one of the slides in the presentation you will create.

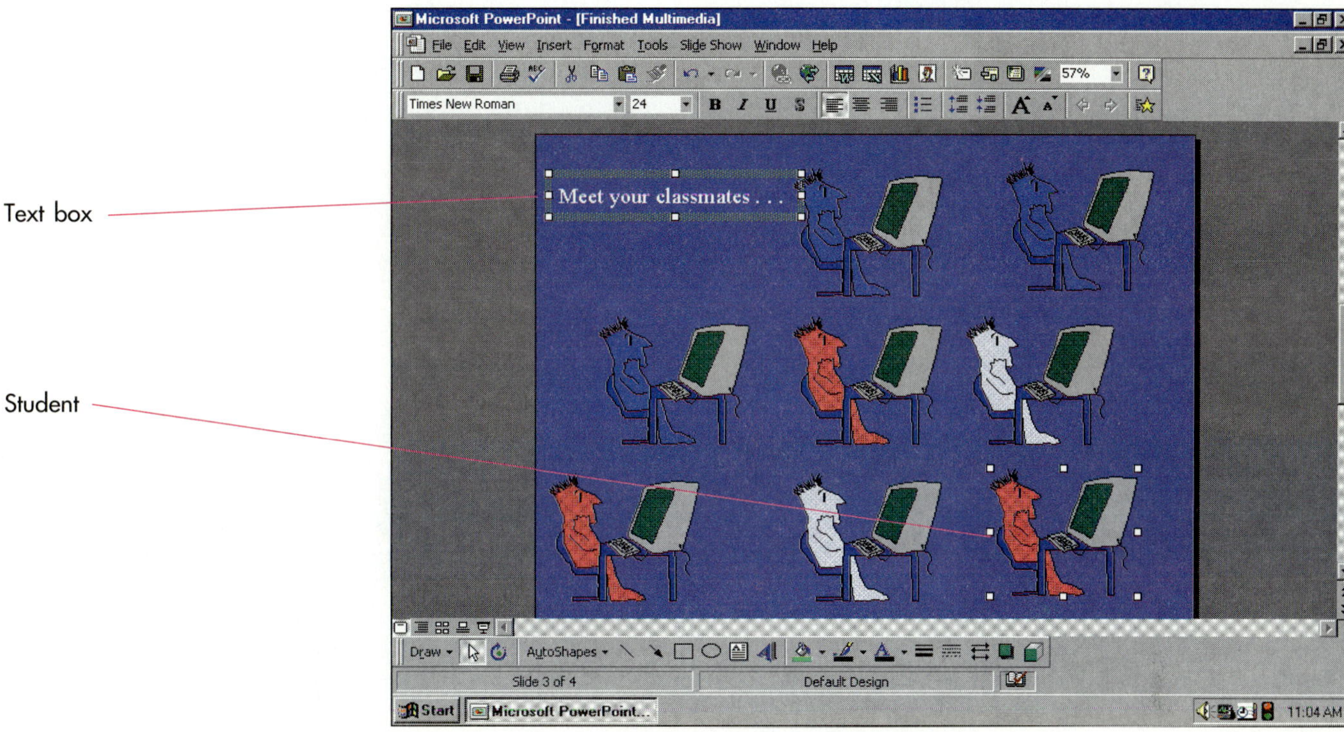


(a) The Slide

**FIGURE B.4** Animation Settings

### THE MICROSOFT CLIP GALLERY

The Microsoft Clip Gallery contains over 100MB including 3,000 clip art images, 100 photographs, 28 sounds, and 20 movie clips. To insert a movie clip into a PowerPoint presentation, click the Insert Clip Art button on the Standard toolbar to display the Clip Gallery dialog box, click the Video tab, select the desired file (such as the basket clip shown earlier in the chapter), and click the Insert button. To play the clip, change to the Slide Show view, then click the object.

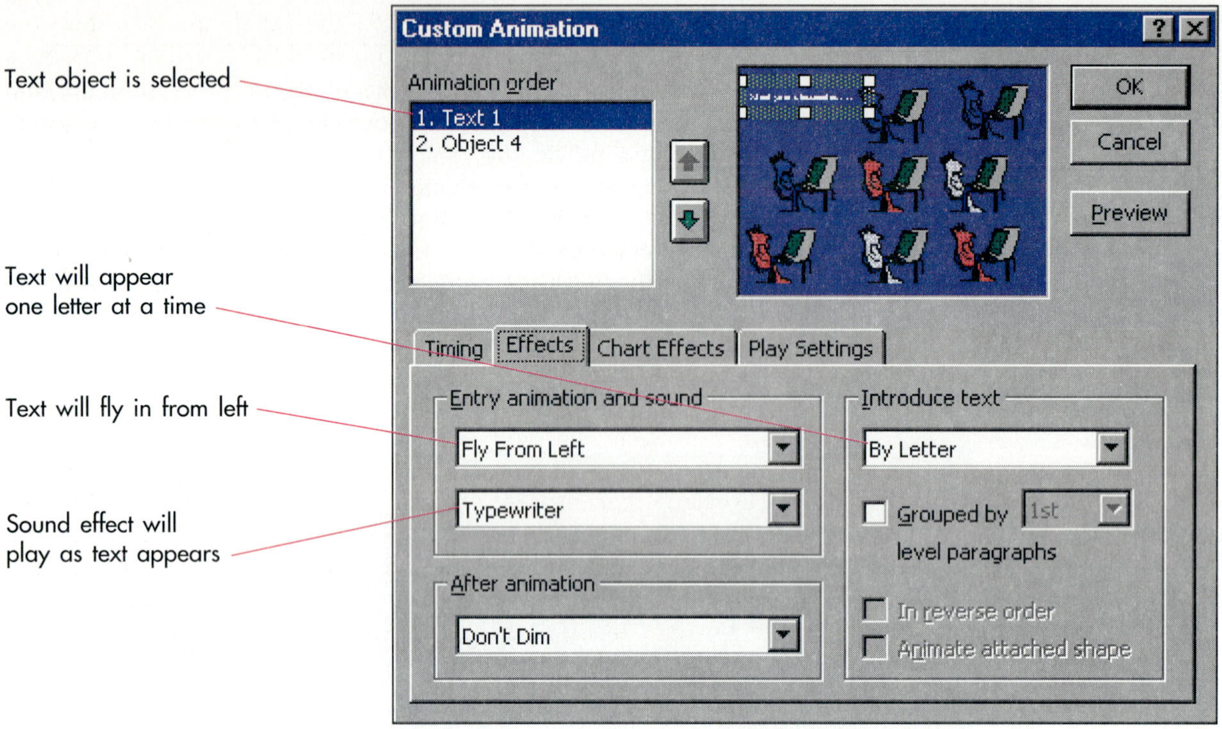


(b) Text Object

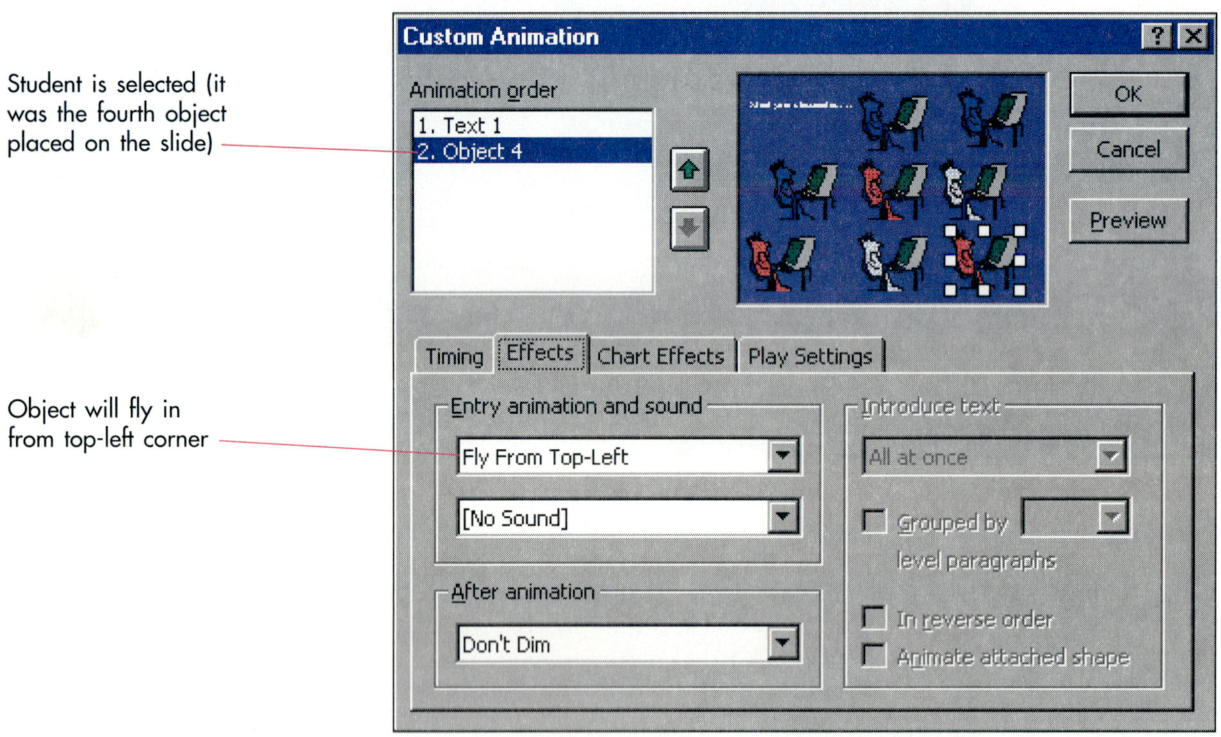


(c) Student

FIGURE B.4 Animation Settings (continued)

Figure B.4a contains the actual slide, whereas Figure B.4b and B.4c show the dialog boxes associated with two of the objects on the slide. The slide contains a total of nine objects (a single text box and eight students). Each of these objects is an "actor" in the presentation and requires instructions as to when to appear on stage and how to make that entrance.

You, as director, have decided that seven of the students will be in place on the slide when it is shown initially. The text will then enter from the left, after which the last student will appear from the top left. The ***Custom Animation command*** (in the Slide Show menu) is the means by which you convey your directions. Figure B.4b displays the Custom Animation dialog box for the text that is to fly in from the left, letter by letter, accompanied by the sound of a typewriter. The text is shown first in the animation order list box since it is to appear before the student.

Figure B.4c shows the dialog box for the student in the lower right corner (which is designated as object 4 because it was the fourth student placed on the slide when it was created). The Student is to fly in silently from the top left. No other objects (students) appear in the animation order list box, since there are no animation effects for the other students (they are in place when the slide is first shown). These instructions may sound complicated, but they work beautifully, as you will see in the next hands-on exercise.

## HANDS-ON EXERCISE 2

*Creating a Multimedia Presentation*

**Objective:** To add music (a MIDI file) to the first slide of a presentation so that it plays continually throughout the presentation; to use the Custom Animation command to control the appearance of objects on a slide. Use Figure B.5 as a guide in the exercise.

**STEP 1: Add the Music**

- Open the **Multimedia** presentation in the **Exploring PowerPoint folder** as shown in Figure B.5a. Save the presentation as **Finished Multimedia.**
- Pull down the **Insert menu.** Click **Movies and Sounds,** then click **Sound from File** to display the Insert Sound dialog box in Figure B.5a.
- Click the **down arrow** in the Look in text box to select the **Exploring PowerPoint folder.** Select **Reggae,** then click **OK** to insert the sound file.

### LOOK FOR OTHER MUSIC

Click the Start button on the Windows 95 taskbar, click (or point to) the Find command, then click Files or Folders to display the Find All Files dialog box. Click the Name & Location tab, click in the Named text box, and enter *.MID (the file type you are searching for). Click the drop-down arrow in the Look in list box and select My Computer to search all of the drives on your system. Be sure the Include subfolders box is checked, then click the Find Now button to begin the search. Once a MIDI file is found, you can right click and drag the file from the Find All Files dialog box to the PowerPoint slide.

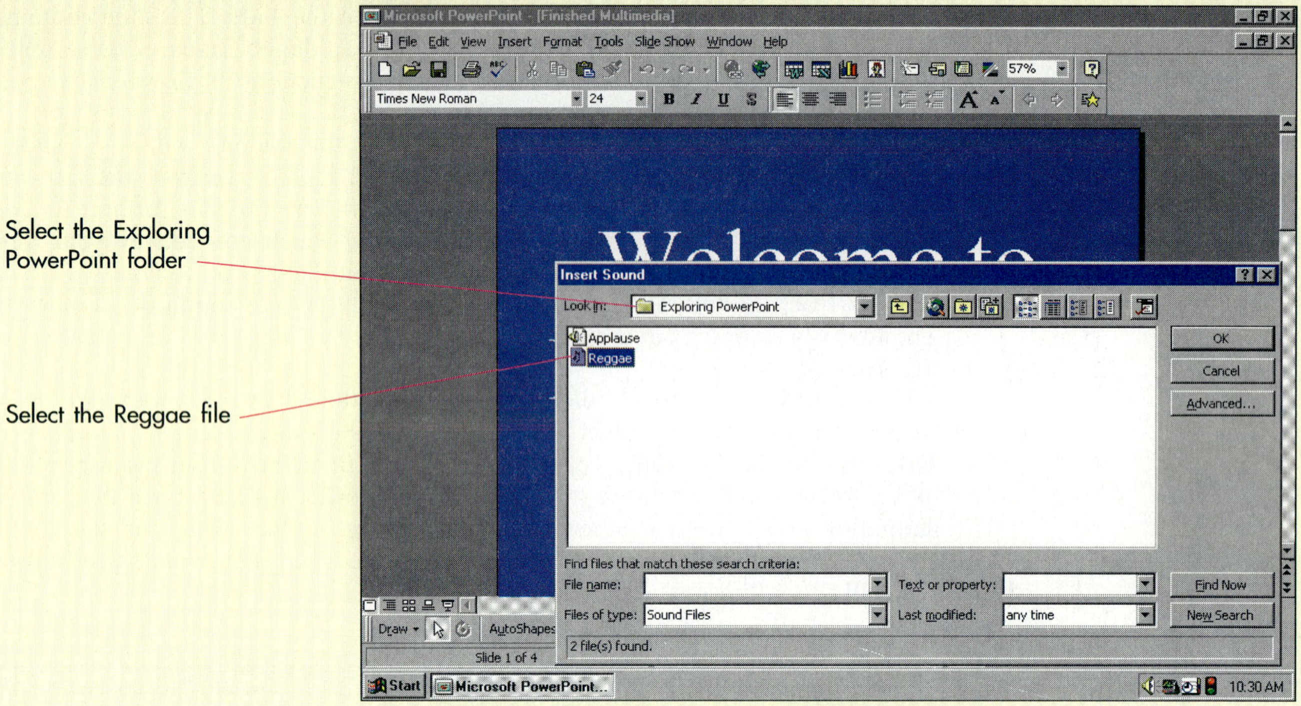


(a) Add the Music (step 1)

**FIGURE B.5** Hands-on Exercise 2

**STEP 2: Set the Music Options**

- You should see a small microphone in the middle of the title slide indicating that a sound file has been embedded on this slide.
- Click and drag the **sound icon** (the microphone corresponding to the Reggae sound file) to the bottom left of the slide. Pull down the **Slide Show menu** and click **Custom Animation** to display the Custom Animation dialog box.
- Select the options shown in Figure B.5b. Thus, click the check box to **Play using animation order,** click the option button to **Continue slide show,** click the option button to stop playing after the specified number of slides, then enter **4 slides** in the associated text box.
- Click the **More options command button** to display the Play Options dialog box. Check the box to **loop until stopped.** Verify that your settings match those in Figure B.5b. Click **OK** to close the Play Options dialog box.
- Click the **Timing tab,** then click the option button to animate automatically after zero seconds. Click **OK** to close the Custom Animation dialog box.
- Click the **Slide Show button** above the status bar to begin the show. The music should begin to play automatically because of the previous command.
- Click the mouse to move to the next slide (with a clip art image of an instructor). The music continues to play as you move from one slide to the next.
- Press the **Esc key** to stop the music. Press the **Esc key** a second time to cancel the slide show and return to the Slide view.
- Save the presentation.

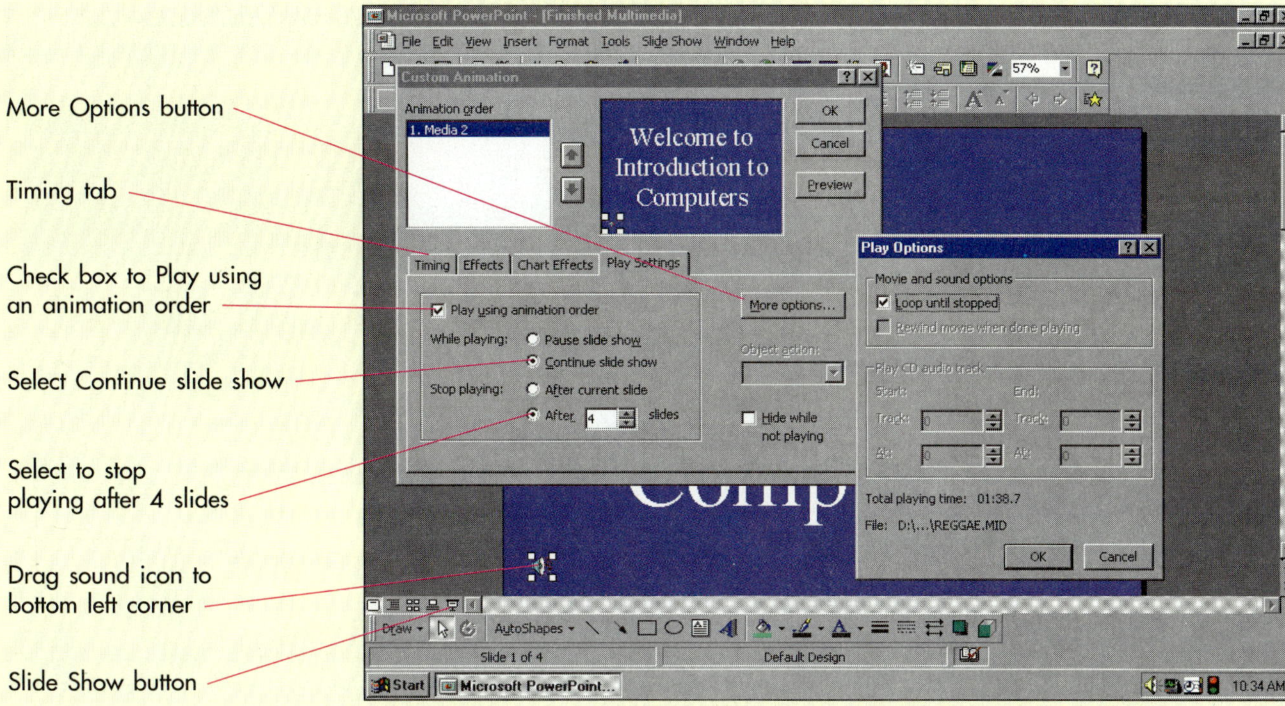


(b) Set the Music Options (step 2)

**FIGURE B.5** Hands-on Exercise 2 (continued)

### THE VOICE OVER

Use the Sound Recorder to create a voice-over narration that you can play during a self-running presentation. Music and/or narration are especially effective in standalone presentations such as those found in a kiosk or demonstration booth. The only disadvantage is the large file size. The Sound Recorder creates a WAV file, which requires a minimum of 11KB/second. Thus a 30-second sound byte results in a 330KB file.

**STEP 3: Animate the Title Slide**

- Press **Ctrl+Home** to move to the first slide, then click anywhere within the title to select the title as shown in Figure B.5c. Pull down the **Slide Show menu** and click **Custom Animation** to display the Custom Animation dialog box.
- Click the **Timing tab.** Text 1 (corresponding to the title) is selected automatically and appears initially as an object without animation. Click the **Animate option button,** which moves the text under Media 2 in the animation order. In other words, the music will play before the animation effect for the text.

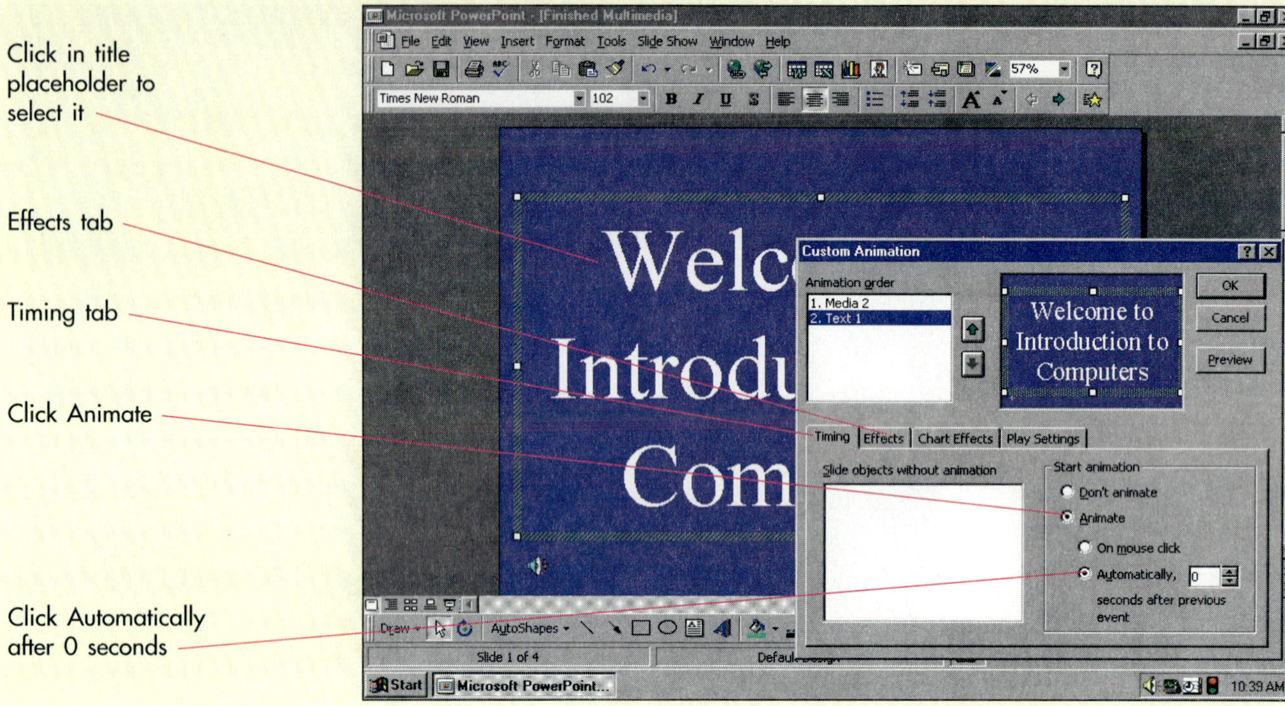


(c) Animate the Title Slide (step 3)

**FIGURE B.5** Hands-on Exercise 2 (continued)

- Click the option button to animate **Automatically** after zero seconds. This will display the title without your having to click the mouse.
- Click the **Effects tab.** Click the **down arrow** in the first Entry animation and sound list box. Select **Fly from Left** as the desired effect. Click the **down arrow** on the Introduce Text list box and select **By Letter.** Click **OK.**
- Click the **Slide Show button** above the status bar. This time you will not only hear the music, but you will also see the letters fly in from the left.
- Press the **Esc key** after you see the title to stop the music, then press the **Esc key** a second time to return to the Slide view and continue working.
- Save the presentation.

### YOU'RE THE DIRECTOR

No one ever said that multimedia was quick or easy. Creating an effective presentation takes time, much more time than you might expect initially, as each slide has to be choreographed in detail. Think of yourself as the director who must tell the actors (the objects on a slide) when to come on stage and how to make their entrance. It takes a lot of patience and practice.

**STEP 4: Animate the Student Slide**

- Use the Slide Elevator (or press the **PgDn key** twice) to select the third slide as shown in Figure B.5d.
- Click the **Slide Show button** to view this slide as it will appear in the slide show. There are no animation effects and all of the students appear at the same time. Press **Esc** to return to the slide view.
- Pull down the **Edit menu** and click **Select All** (or press **Ctrl+A**) to select all of the objects (the text and the eight students) on this slide. Pull down the **Slide Show menu** and click **Custom Animation** to display the Custom Animation dialog box.
- Click the **Timing tab.** Click the **Animate** option button, which moves the objects to the Animation order list at the top of the dialog box. Click the option button to animate **Automatically** after zero seconds.
- Click the **Effects tab.** Click the **down arrow** in the first Entry animation and sound list box. Select **Fly from Right** as the desired effect.
- Click the up or down arrow on the scroll bar in the Animation order list box, then click **Text 1,** which deselects all of the other objects. Select **Fly from Left** as the effect for the text. Select **By Letter.**
- Click **OK** to accept these settings and close the dialog box.
- Click the **Slide Show button** to view this slide with the animation effects you added. The text should appear first, followed by the students in the order they were added to the slide when the slide was created initially. Press **Esc** to return to the slide view.

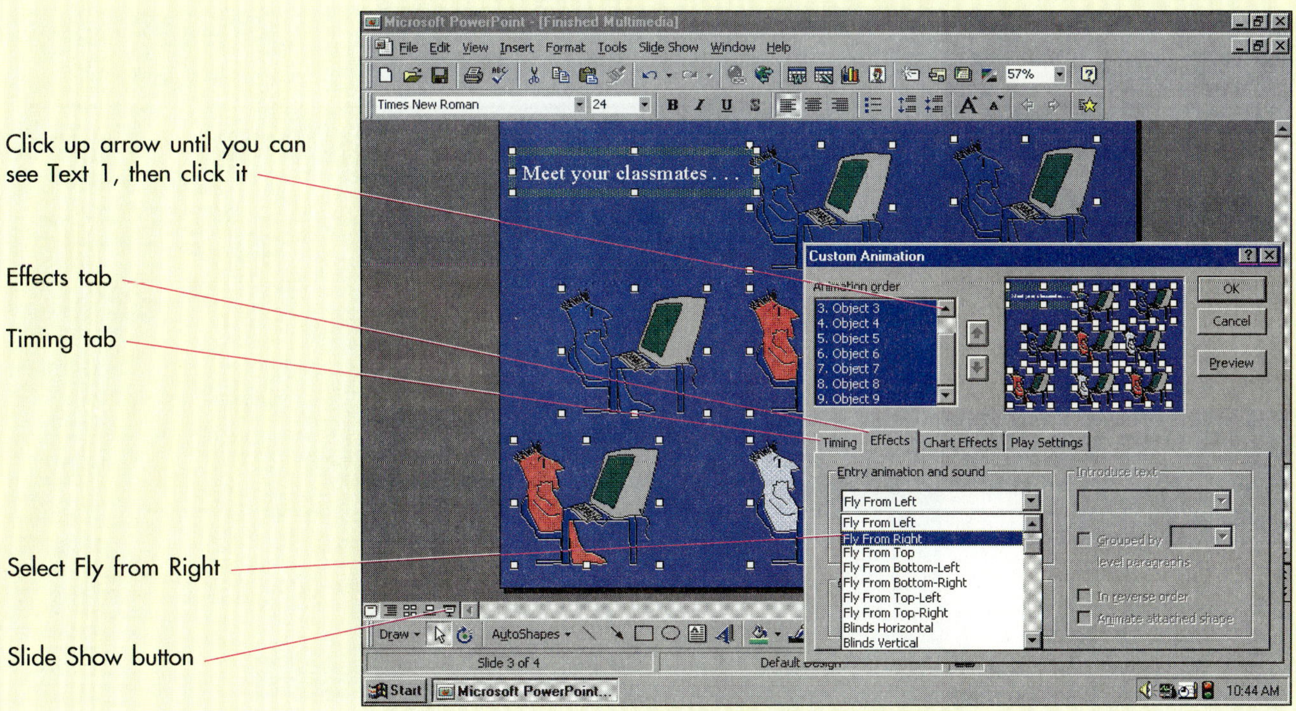


(d) Animate the Student Slide (step 4)

**FIGURE B.5** Hands-on Exercise 2 (continued)

## THE ANIMATION EFFECTS TOOLBAR

The Animation Effects toolbar is the easiest way to change the order in which objects appear on a slide. Point to any visible toolbar, click the right mouse button, then click Animation Effects to display (hide) the toolbar. Select the object on the slide, click the drop-down arrow on the Animation Order list box, then choose the appropriate number (e.g., 1, if the object is to appear first).

**STEP 5: Rehearse the Timings**

➤ Press **Ctrl+Home** to return to the first slide. Pull down the **Slide Show menu.** Click the **Rehearse Timings command.**

➤ The first slide appears in the Slide Show view, and the Rehearsal dialog box is displayed in the lower right corner of the screen. Click the mouse to register the elapsed time and move to the next slide.

➤ The second slide in the presentation should appear as shown in Figure B.5e with the animation effects built in. The cumulative time appears on the left (00:01:06 seconds). The time for this specific slide (00:00:16 seconds) is shown at the right.

- Click the **Repeat button** to redo the timing for the slide. (You won't see the new timing until the slide concludes.)

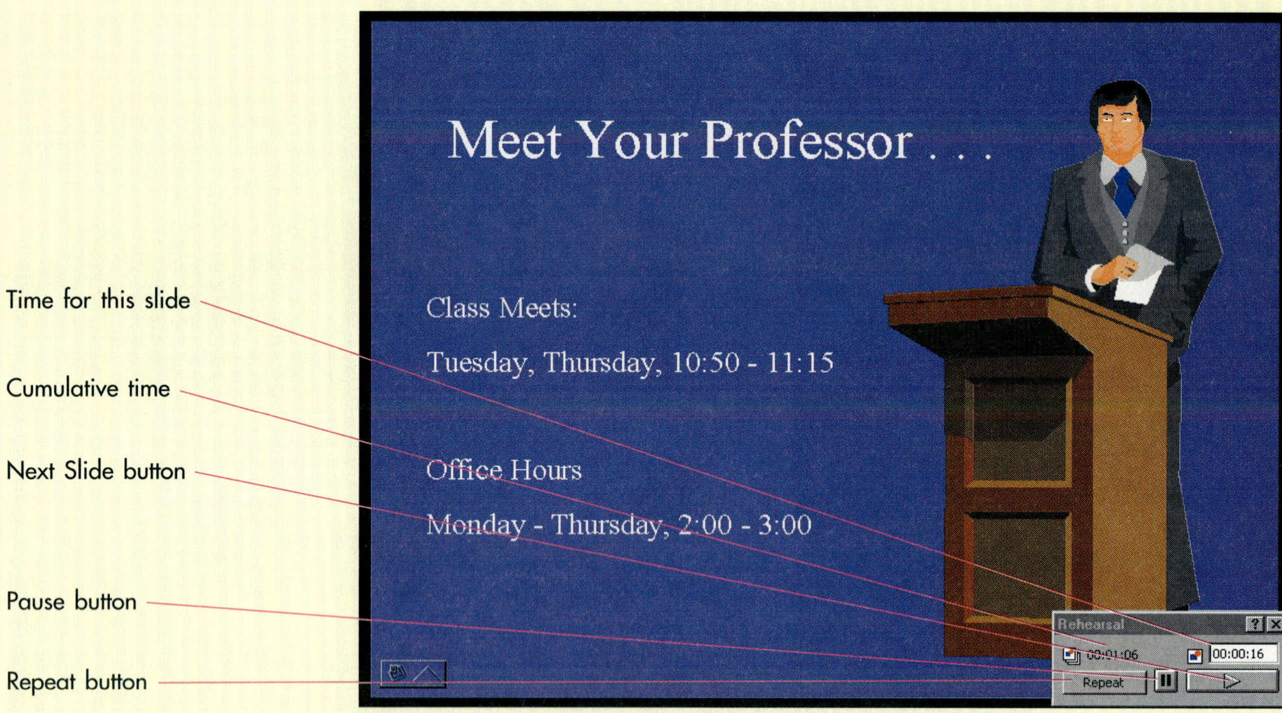


(e) Rehearse the Timings (step 5)

**FIGURE B.5** Hands-on Exercise 2 (continued)

- Click the **Pause button** to (temporarily) stop the clock. Click the Pause button a second time to resume the clock. (The music continues to play.)
- Click the **Next slide button** to record the timing and move to the next slide.
- Continue rehearsing the show until you reach the last slide (containing the PC and other equipment), then click on this last slide to end the presentation. Be sure to click the mouse so it will record the timing for the last slide.

➤ You should see a dialog box at the end of the presentation that indicates the total time of the slide show. Click **Yes** when asked whether you want to record the new timings. Click **Yes** when asked if you want to review the timings in the Slide Sorter view.

➤ Save the presentation.

**STEP 6: Set Up the Show**

➤ You should be back in the Slide Sorter view, with the timings recorded under each slide. Pull down the **Slide Show menu** and click **Set Up show** to display the Set Up show dialog box as shown in Figure B.5f.

➤ Check the box to **Loop continuously until Esc.**

➤ Click the **All option button** under Slides, click the **Using timings if present** option button under Advance slides. Click **OK** to accept the settings and close the Set Up show dialog box.

➤ Press **Ctrl+Home** to move to the first slide. Click the **Slide Show button** to view the show one last time. End the show by clicking at the appropriate place in the last slide or by pressing the **Esc key.**

➤ Save the presentation. Exit PowerPoint. Welcome to Multimedia!!

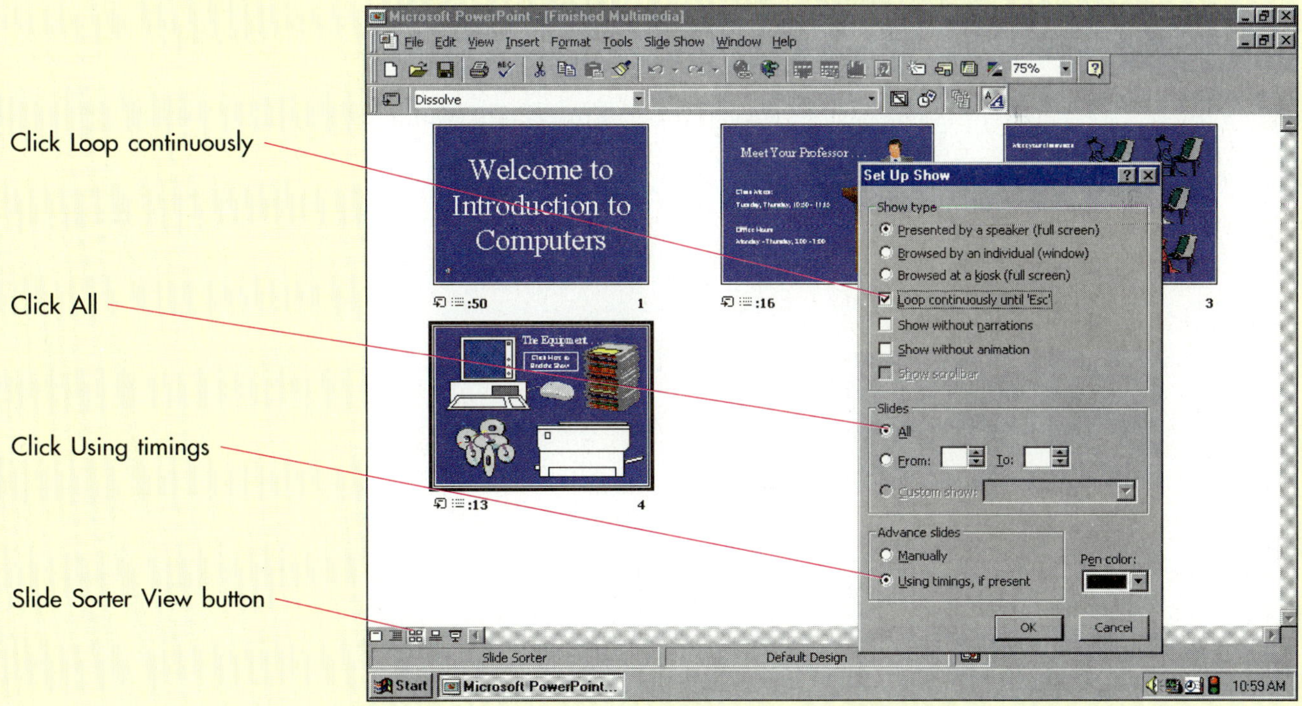


(f) Set Up the Show (step 6)

**FIGURE B.5** Hands-on Exercise 2 (continued)

## SUMMARY

The Multimedia PC Marketing Council has established a minimum specification for a multimedia computer that is intended to guide both the consumer and the developer. Three standards—MPC-1, MPC-2, and MPC-3—have been published to date.

There are two types of sound files, WAV files and MIDI files. A WAV file records an actual sound and requires large amounts of disk space because the sound is sampled several times a second to create the file. A MIDI file is much more compact than a WAV file because it stores the instructions to create the sound rather than the actual sound. A WAV file can represent any type of sound (a voice, music, or special effects) because it is a recorded sound. A MIDI file is the electronic equivalent of sheet music and can store only music. An AVI (Audi-Video Interleaved) file is the Microsoft standard for a digital video (multimedia) file.

Windows 95 provides the software tools necessary to play the various types of multimedia files. The accessories can be accessed through the Start button or through shortcuts in the Multimedia folder.

The slides in a multimedia production must be carefully scripted with respect to when and how each object is to appear. The Custom Animation command is the means by which the information is specified.

## KEY WORDS AND CONCEPTS

Animation settings
AVI file
CD Player
Custom Animation command
File compression
File extensions
Media player
MIDI file
MPC-1
MPC-2
MPC-3
Multimedia
PowerPoint Multimedia CD
Resolution
Sampling rate
Sound recorder
Volume Control
WAV file

# PREREQUISITES: ESSENTIALS OF WINDOWS 95

## OBJECTIVES

**After reading this appendix you will be able to:**

1. Describe the objects on the Windows desktop; describe the programs available through the Start button.
2. Explain the function of the minimize, maximize, restore, and close buttons; move and size a window.
3. Discuss the function of a dialog box; describe the elements in a dialog box and the various ways in which information is supplied.
4. Use the Help menu to learn about features in Windows 95; format a floppy disk and implement a screen saver by following instructions from the Help menu.
5. Use the Internet Explorer to access the Internet and download the practice files for the *Exploring Windows* series.
6. Use Windows Explorer to locate a specific file or folder; describe the views available for Windows Explorer.
7. Describe how folders are used to organize a disk; create a new folder; copy and/or move a file from one folder to another.
8. Delete a file, then recover the deleted file from the Recycle Bin.

## OVERVIEW

***Windows 95*** is a computer program (actually many programs) that controls the operation of your computer and its peripherals. ***Windows 97*** improves on Windows 95 to bring elements of the Internet to the desktop. Windows 97 was not available when we went to press, but we expect it to follow the same conventions as Windows 95. Thus, our introduction applies to both, as it emphasizes the common features of file management in support of Microsoft Office 97. (Microsoft Office runs equally well under Windows 95, Windows 97, or Windows NT.)

One of the most significant benefits of the Windows environment is the common user interface and consistent command structure that is imposed on every Windows application. Once you learn the basic concepts and techniques, you can apply that knowledge to every Windows application. This appendix teaches you those concepts so that you will be able to work productively in the Windows environment. It is written for you, the computer novice, and assumes no previous knowledge about a computer or about Windows. Our goal is to get you "up and running" as quickly as possible so that you can do the work you want to do.

We begin with an introduction to the Windows desktop, the graphical user interface that lets you work in intuitive fashion by pointing at icons and clicking the mouse. We identify the basic components of a window and describe how to execute commands and supply information through various elements in a dialog box. We introduce you to My Computer, an icon that is present on every Windows desktop, then show you how to use My Computer to access the various components of your system.

The appendix also shows you how to manage the hundreds (indeed, thousands) of files that are stored on the typical system. We show you how to create a new folder (the electronic equivalent of a manila folder in a filing cabinet) and how to move or copy a file from one folder to another. We show you how to rename a file, how to delete a file, and how to recover a deleted file from the Recycle Bin.

The appendix also contains four hands-on exercises, which enable you to apply the conceptual discussion in the text at the computer. The exercises are essential to the learn-by-doing philosophy we follow throughout the *Exploring Windows* series.

## THE DESKTOP

Windows creates a working environment for your computer that parallels the working environment at home or in an office. You work at a desk. Windows operations take place on the ***desktop.***

There are physical objects on a desk such as folders, a dictionary, a calculator, or a phone. The computer equivalents of those objects appear as ***icons*** (pictorial symbols) on the desktop. Each object on a real desk has attributes (properties) such as size, weight, and color. In similar fashion, Windows assigns properties to every object on its desktop. And just as you can move the objects on a real desk, you can rearrange the objects on the Windows desktop.

Figure 1a displays the desktop when Windows is first installed on a new computer. This desktop has only a few objects and is similar to the desk in a new office, just after you move in. Figure 1b displays a different desktop, one with several open windows, and is similar to a desk during the middle of a working day. Do not be concerned if your Windows desktop is different from ours. Your real desk is arranged differently from those of your friends, and so your Windows desktop will also be different.

The simplicity of the desktop in Figure 1a helps you to focus on what is important. The ***Start button,*** as its name suggests, is where you begin. Click the Start button (mouse operations are described on page 9) and you see a menu that lets you start any program (e.g., Microsoft Word or Microsoft Excel) on your computer. The Start button also contains a ***Help command*** through which you can obtain information about every aspect of Windows.

Each icon on the desktop in Figure 1a provides access to an important function within Windows. ***My Computer*** enables you to browse the disk drives and optional CD-ROM drive that are attached to your computer. ***Network Neighborhood*** extends your view of the computer to include the accessible drives on the network to which your machine is attached, if indeed it is part of a network. (You

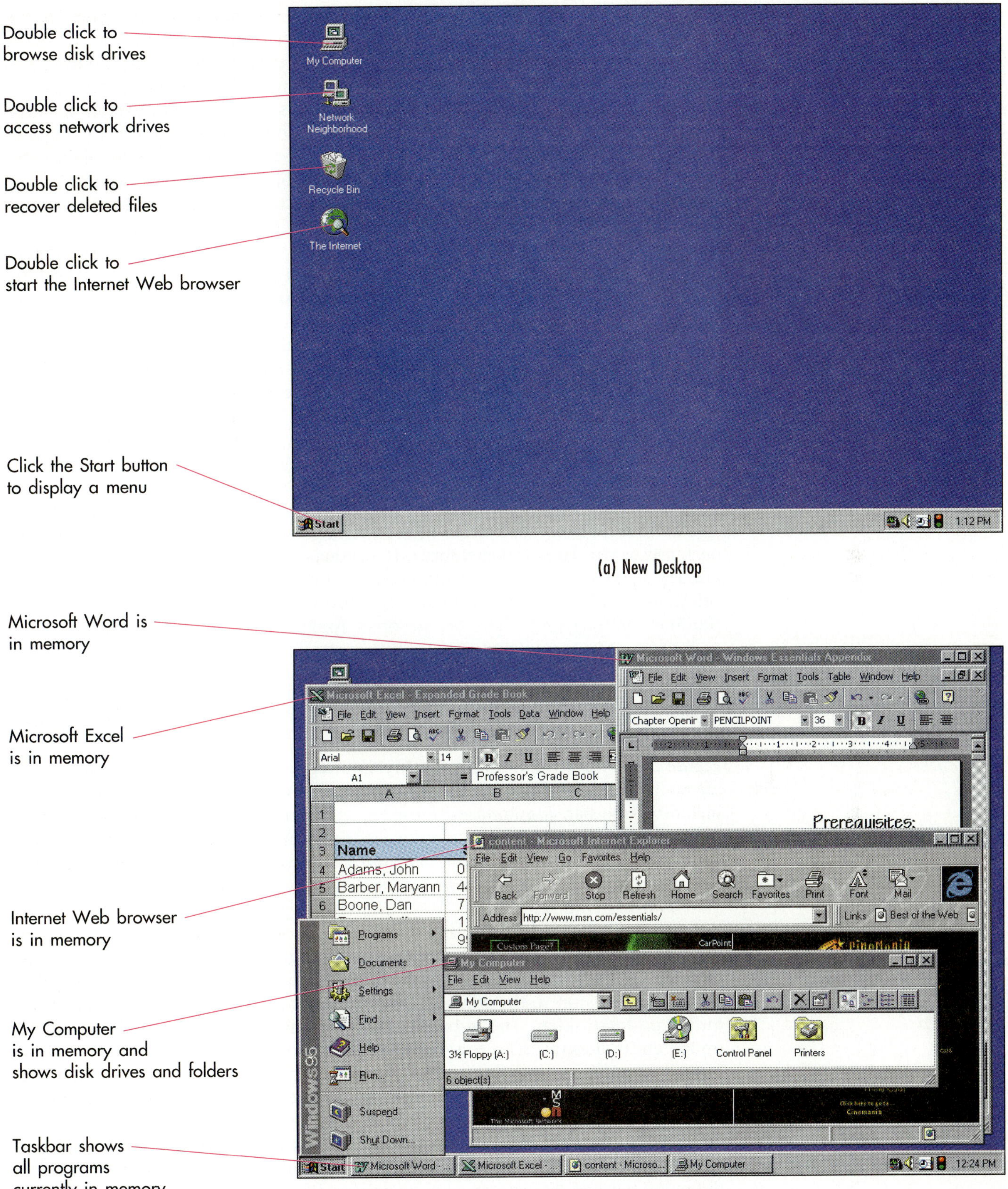


(a) New Desktop

(b) A Working Desktop

**FIGURE 1** The Windows Desktop

will not see this icon if you are not connected to a network.) The ***Recycle Bin,*** described later in the appendix, allows you to recover a file that was previously deleted. Double clicking the ***Internet icon*** starts the Web browser and initiates a connection to the Internet (assuming you have the necessary hardware).

Each icon on the desktop in Figure 1a opens into a window containing additional objects when you open (double click) the icon. Double click My Computer in Figure 1a, for example, and you see the objects contained in the My Computer window of Figure 2. The contents of the My Computer window depend on the hardware of the specific computer system. Our system, for example, has one floppy drive, two hard (fixed) disks, and a CD-ROM. The My Computer window also contains the Control Panel and Printer folders, which allow access to functions that control other elements in the environment on your computer. (A ***folder,*** called a directory under MS-DOS, may in turn contain other folders and/or individual files.)

The desktop in Figure 1b contains additional windows that display programs that are currently in use. Each window has a title bar that displays the name of the program and the associated document. You can work in any window as long as you want, then switch to a different window. ***Multitasking,*** the ability to run several programs at the same time, is one of the major benefits of the Windows environment. It lets you run a word processor in one window, a spreadsheet in a second window, surf the Internet in a third window, play a game in a fourth window, and so on.

The ***taskbar*** at the bottom of the desktop shows all of the programs that are currently active (open in memory). It contains a button for each open program and lets you switch back and forth between those programs by clicking the appropriate button. The taskbar in Figure 1a does not contain any buttons (other than the Start button) since there are no open applications. The taskbar in Figure 1b, however, contains four additional buttons, one for each open window.

## ANATOMY OF A WINDOW

Figure 2 displays two views of the My Computer window and labels its essential elements. Every window has the same components as every other window, which include a title bar, a minimize button, a maximize or restore button, and a close button. Other elements that may be visible include a horizontal and/or vertical scroll bar, a menu bar, a status bar, and a toolbar. Every window also contains additional objects (icons) that pertain specifically to the programs or data associated with that window.

The ***title bar*** appears at the top of the window and displays the name of the window—for example, My Computer in both Figures 2a and 2b. The icon at the extreme left of the title bar provides access to a control menu that lets you select operations relevant to the window. The ***minimize button*** shrinks the window to a button on the taskbar. The ***maximize button*** enlarges the window so that it takes up the entire desktop. The ***restore button*** (not shown in Figure 2) appears instead of the maximize button after a window has been maximized, and restores the window to its previous size. The ***close button*** closes the window and removes it from the desktop.

The ***menu bar*** appears immediately below the title bar and provides access to pull-down menus (as discussed later in the appendix). A ***toolbar*** appears below the menu bar and lets you execute a command by clicking a button as opposed to pulling down a menu. The ***status bar*** at the bottom of the window displays information about the window as a whole or about a selected object within a window.

A ***vertical*** (or ***horizontal***) ***scroll bar*** appears at the right (or bottom) border of a window when its contents are not completely visible and provides access

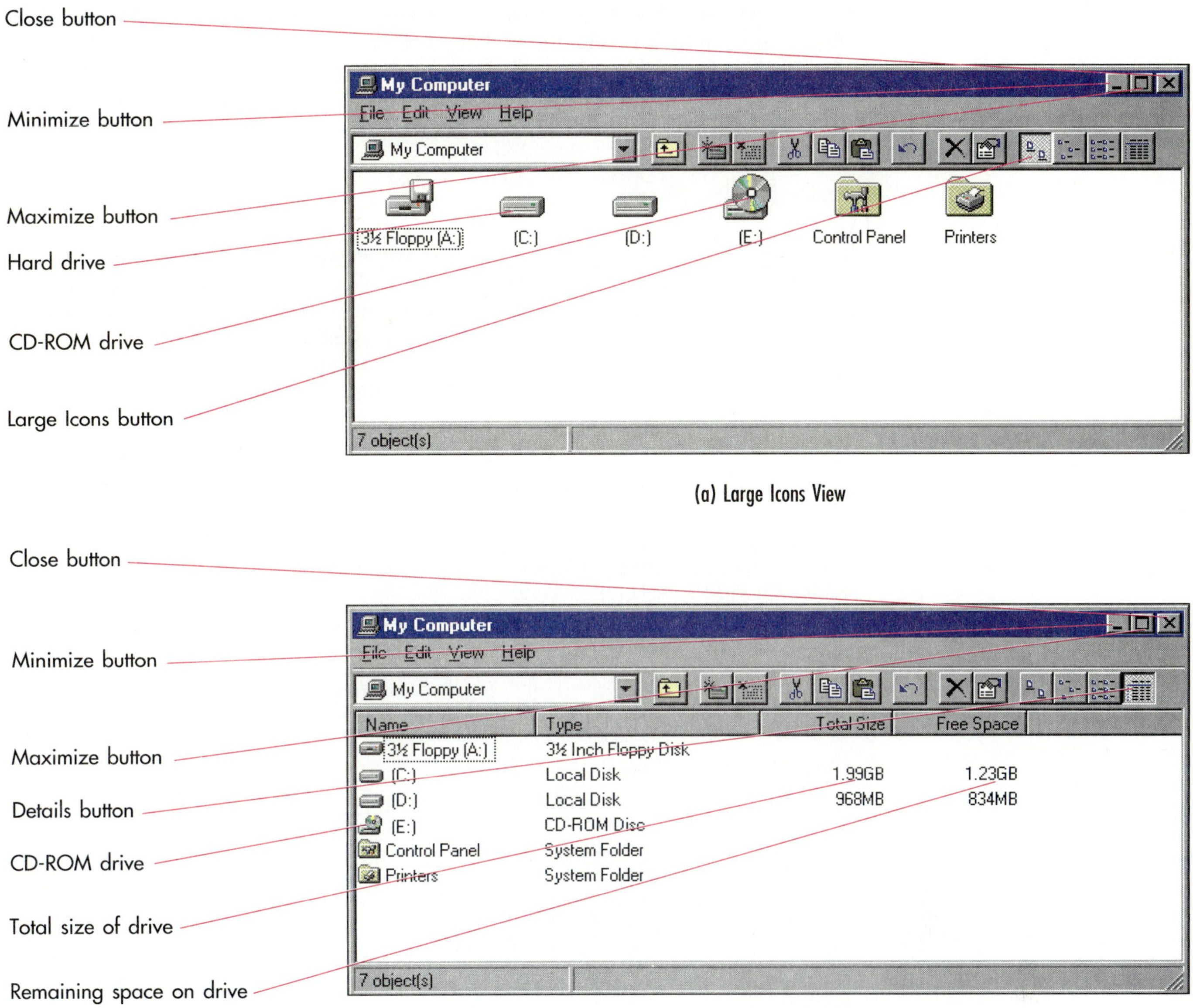


(b) Details View

**FIGURE 2** Anatomy of a Window

to the unseen areas. Scroll bars do not appear in Figure 2 since all six objects in the window are visible.

The objects in any window can be displayed in four different views according to your preference or need. The choice between the views depends on your personal preference. You might, for example, choose the ***Large Icons view*** in Figure 2a if there are only a few objects in the window. The ***Details view*** in Figure 2b displays additional information about each object including the type of object, the total size of the disk, and the remaining space on the disk. You switch from one view to the next by choosing the appropriate command from the View menu or by clicking the corresponding button on the toolbar.

## Moving and Sizing a Window

A window can be sized or moved on the desktop through appropriate actions with the mouse. To ***size a window,*** point to any border (the mouse pointer changes to a double arrow), then drag the border in the direction you want to go—inward to shrink the window or outward to enlarge it. You can also drag a corner (instead of a border) to change both dimensions at the same time. To ***move a window*** while retaining its current size, click and drag the title bar to a new position on the desktop.

## Pull-down Menus

The menu bar provides access to ***pull-down menus*** that enable you to execute commands within an application (program). A pull-down menu is accessed by clicking the menu name or by pressing the Alt key plus the underlined letter in the menu name; for example, press Alt+V to pull down the View menu. Three pull-down menus associated with My Computer are shown in Figure 3.

The commands within a menu are executed by clicking the command or by typing the underlined letter (for example, C to execute the Close command in the File menu) once the menu has been pulled down. Alternatively, you can bypass the menu entirely if you know the equivalent keystrokes shown to the right of the command in the menu (e.g., Ctrl+X, Ctrl+C, or Ctrl+V to cut, copy, or paste as shown within the Edit menu).

A ***dimmed command*** (e.g., the Paste command in the Edit menu) means the command is not currently executable, and that some additional action has to be taken for the command to become available.

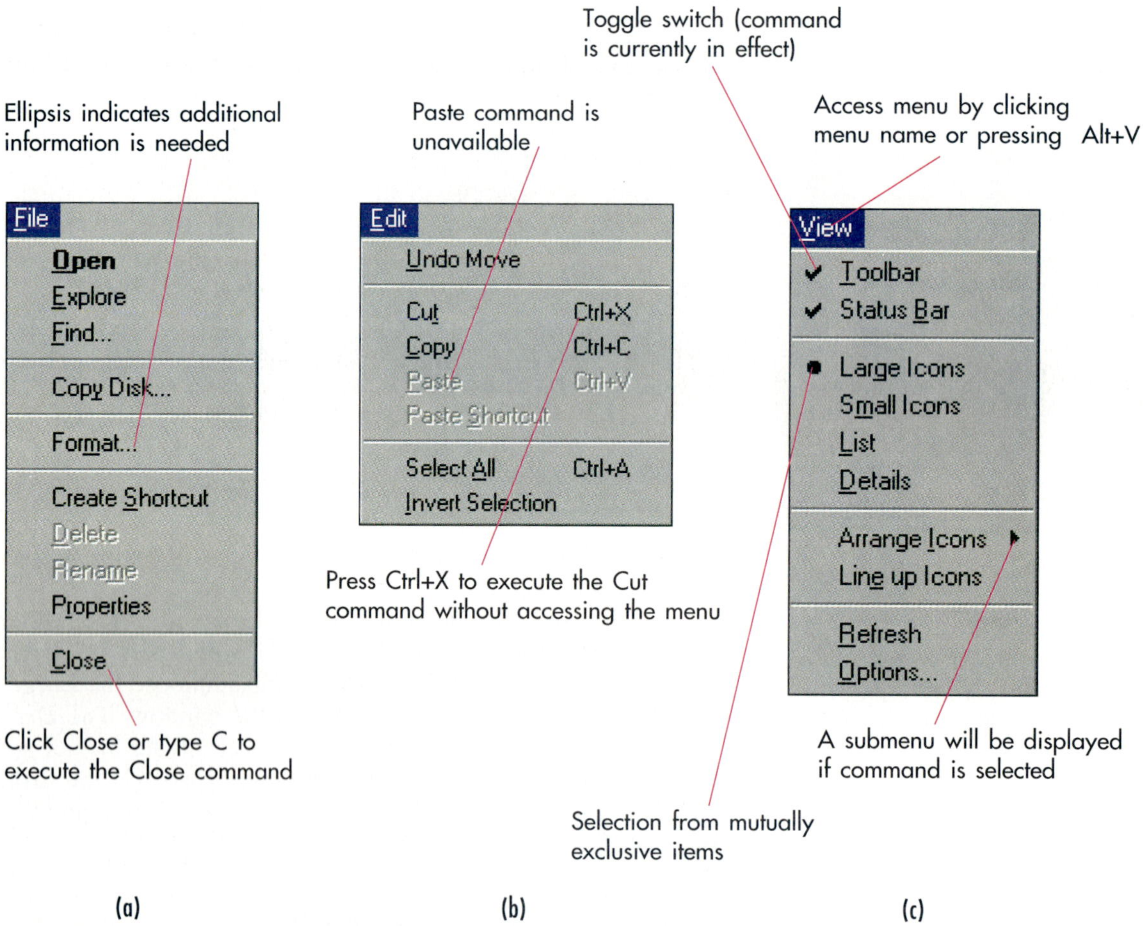


**FIGURE 3** Pull-down Menus

An ***ellipsis*** (. . .) following a command indicates that additional information is required to execute the command; for example, selection of the Format command in the File menu requires the user to specify additional information about the formatting process. This information is entered into a dialog box (discussed in the next section), which appears immediately after the command has been selected.

A ***check*** next to a command indicates a toggle switch, whereby the command is either on or off. There is a check next to the Toolbar command in the View menu of Figure 3, which means the command is in effect (and thus the toolbar will be displayed). Click the Toolbar command and the check disappears, which suppresses the display of the toolbar. Click the command a second time and the check reappears, as does the toolbar in the associated window.

A ***bullet*** next to an item (e.g., Large Icons in Figure 3c) indicates a selection from a set of mutually exclusive choices. Click another option within the group (e.g., Small Icons) and the bullet will disappear from the previous selection (Large Icons) and appear next to the new selection (Small Icons).

An ***arrowhead*** after a command (e.g., the Arrange icons command in the View menu) indicates that a ***submenu*** (also known as a cascaded menu) will be displayed with additional menu options.

## Dialog Boxes

A ***dialog box*** appears when additional information is needed to execute a command. The Format command, for example, requires information about which drive to format and the type of formatting desired.

***Option (radio) buttons*** indicate mutually exclusive choices, one of which must be chosen—for example, one of three Format Type options in Figure 4a. Click a button to select an option, which automatically deselects the previously selected option.

***Check boxes*** are used instead of option buttons if the choices are not mutually exclusive or if an option is not required. Multiple boxes can be checked as in Figure 4a, or no boxes may be checked as in Figure 4b. Individual options are selected (cleared) by clicking the appropriate check box.

A ***text box*** is used to enter descriptive information—for example, Bob's Disk in Figure 4a. A flashing vertical bar (an I-beam) appears within the text box when the text box is active, to mark the ***insertion point*** for the text you will enter.

A ***list box*** displays some or all of the available choices, any one of which is selected by clicking the desired item. A ***drop-down list box,*** such as the Capacity list box in Figure 4a, conserves space by showing only the current selection. Click the arrow of a drop-down list box to display the list of available options. An ***open list box,*** such as those in Figure 4b, displays multiple choices at one time. (A scroll bar appears within an open list box if some of the choices are not visible and provides access to the hidden choices.)

A ***tabbed dialog box*** provides multiple sets of options. The dialog box in Figure 4c, for example, has two tabs, each with its own set of options. Click either tab (the General tab is currently selected) to display the associated options.

The ***What's This button*** (a question mark at the right end of the title bar) provides help for any item in the dialog box. Click the button, then click the item in the dialog box for which you want additional information. The ***Close button*** (the X at the extreme right of the title bar) closes the dialog box.

All dialog boxes also contain one or more ***command buttons,*** the functions of which are generally apparent from the specific button's name. The Start button, in Figure 4a, for example, initiates the formatting process. The OK command button in Figure 4b accepts the settings and closes the dialog box. The Cancel button does just the opposite—it ignores (cancels) any changes made to the settings, then closes the dialog box without further action.

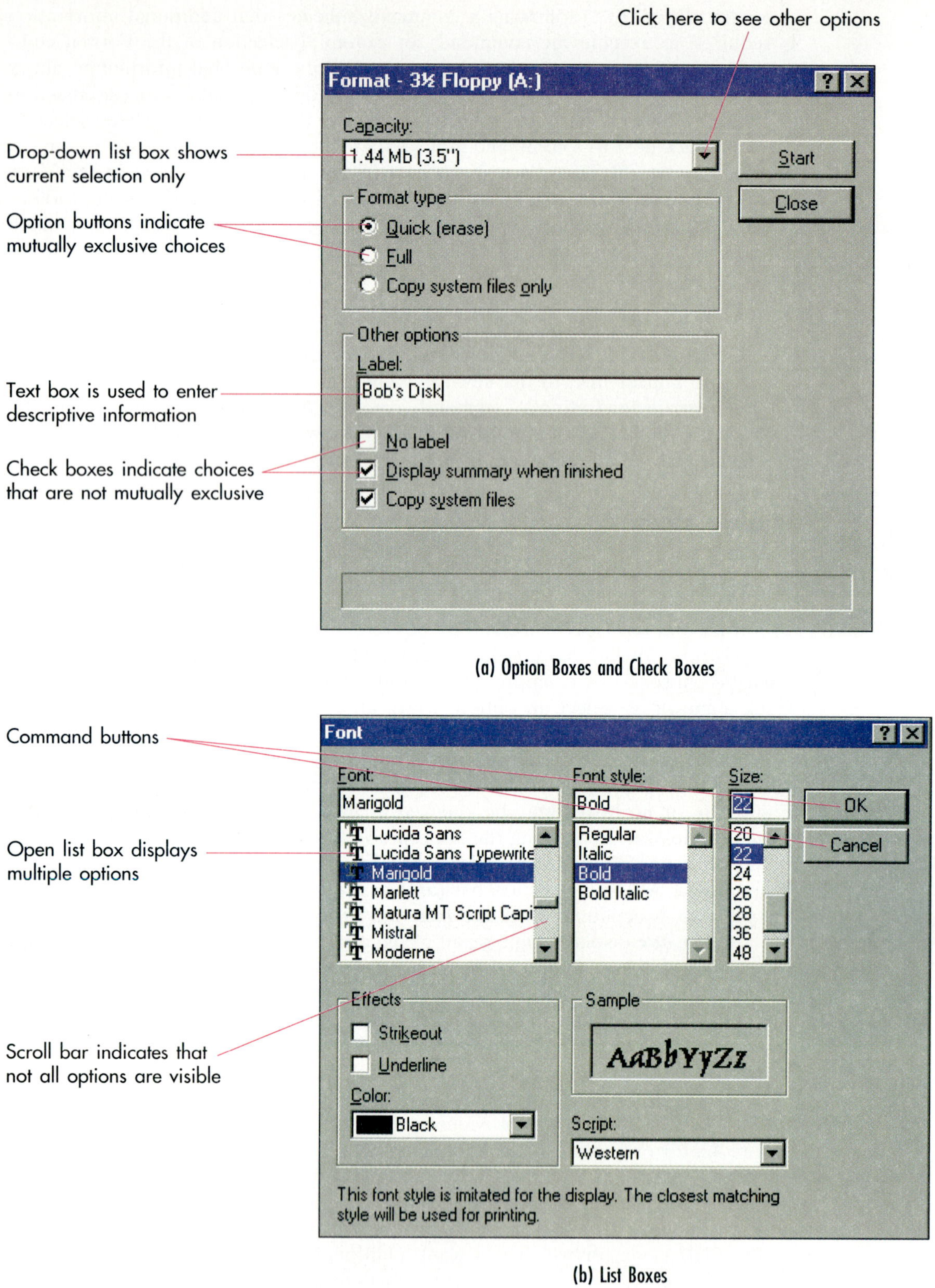


FIGURE 4 Dialog Boxes

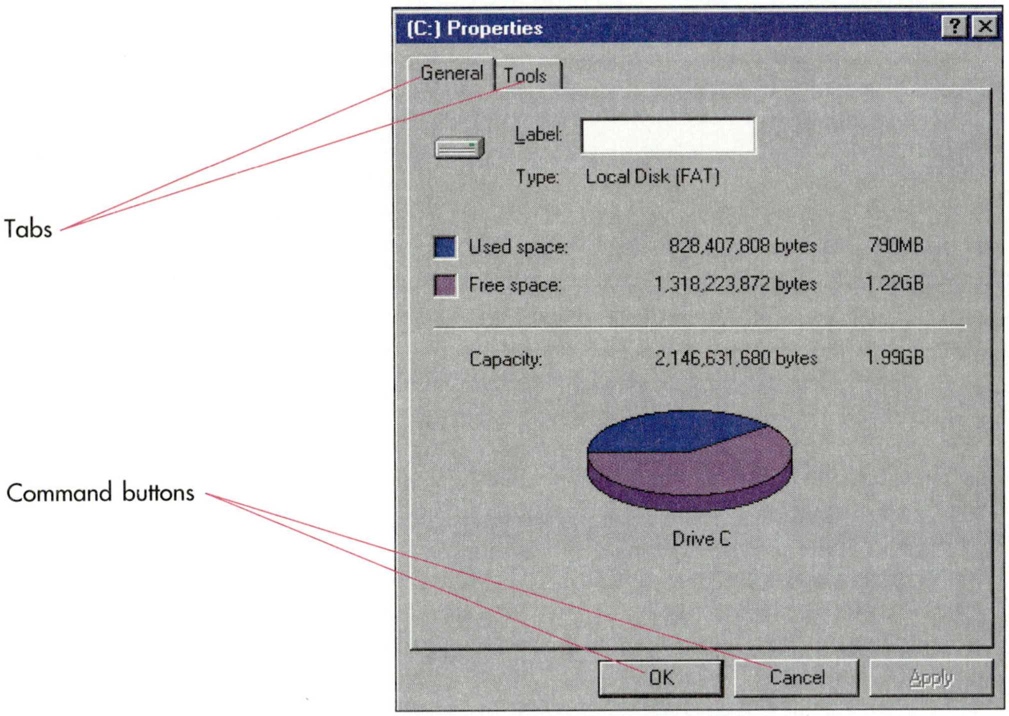


(c) Tabbed Dialog Box

FIGURE 4 Dialog Boxes (continued)

## THE MOUSE

The mouse is indispensable to Windows and is referenced continually in the hands-on exercises throughout the text. There are four basic operations with which you must become familiar:

- To ***point*** to an object, move the mouse pointer over the object.
- To ***click*** an object, point to it, then press and release the left mouse button; to ***right click*** an object, point to the object, then press and release the right mouse button.
- To ***double click*** an object, point to it, then quickly click the left button twice in succession.
- To ***drag*** an object, move the pointer to the object, then press and hold the left button while you move the mouse to a new position.

The mouse is a pointing device—move the mouse on your desk and the ***mouse pointer,*** typically a small arrowhead, moves on the monitor. The mouse pointer assumes different shapes according to the location of the pointer or the nature of the current action. You will see a double arrow when you change the size of a window, an I-beam as you insert text, a hand to jump from one help topic to the next, or a circle with a line through it to indicate that an attempted action is invalid.

The mouse pointer will also change to an hourglass to indicate that Windows is processing your command, and that no further commands may be issued until the action is completed. The more powerful your computer, the less frequently the hourglass will appear, and conversely, the less powerful your system, the more you see the hourglass.

### THE MICROSOFT INTELLIMOUSE

Microsoft has created a new mouse for Office 97. The mouse contains a wheel between the left and right buttons, allowing you to scroll through a document by rotating the wheel forward or back. You can also increase (or decrease) the magnification by holding the Ctrl key as you rotate the wheel on the mouse. Additional information is available from the IntelliPoint Online User's Guide. (Click the Start button, point to Programs, point to Microsoft Input Devices, and then point to Mouse.)

### The Mouse Versus the Keyboard

Almost every command in Windows can be executed by using either the mouse or the keyboard. Most people start with the mouse but add keyboard shortcuts as they become more proficient. There is no right or wrong technique, just different techniques, and the one you choose depends entirely on personal preference in a specific situation. If, for example, your hands are already on the keyboard, it is faster to use the keyboard equivalent. Other times, your hand will be on the mouse and that will be the fastest way.

In the beginning, you may wonder why there are so many different ways to do the same thing, but you will eventually recognize the many options as part of Windows' charm. It is not necessary to memorize anything, nor should you even try; just be flexible and willing to experiment. The more you practice, the sooner all of this will become second nature to you.

## THE HELP MENU

Windows has an extensive ***Help menu*** that contains information about virtually every topic in Windows. We believe that the best time to learn about Help is when you begin your study of Windows. Help is available at any time, and is accessed most easily by clicking the ***Help command*** on the Start menu, which displays the Help Topics dialog box in Figure 5.

The ***Contents tab*** in Figure 5a is similar to the table of contents in an ordinary book. The major topics are represented by books, each of which can be opened to display additional topics. These topics may be viewed and/or printed to access the indicated information.

The ***Index tab*** in Figure 5b is analogous to the index of an ordinary book. Type the first several letters of the topic you want to look up, click the topic when it appears in the window, then click the Display button to view the information. The Help screens are task-specific and provide easy-to-follow instructions.

The ***Find tab*** (not shown in Figure 5) contains a more extensive listing of entries than does the Index tab. It lets you enter a specific word (or Windows term), then it returns every Help screen that contains that word.

EXPLORING WWW

### MICROSOFT ON THE WEB

The Microsoft Web site provides information beyond that found in the Help menu. Go to the Microsoft home page (www.microsoft.com), then click the Support tab where you choose the application. You will find articles about new features in the application, answers to frequently asked questions, as well as the knowledge base used by Microsoft support engineers.

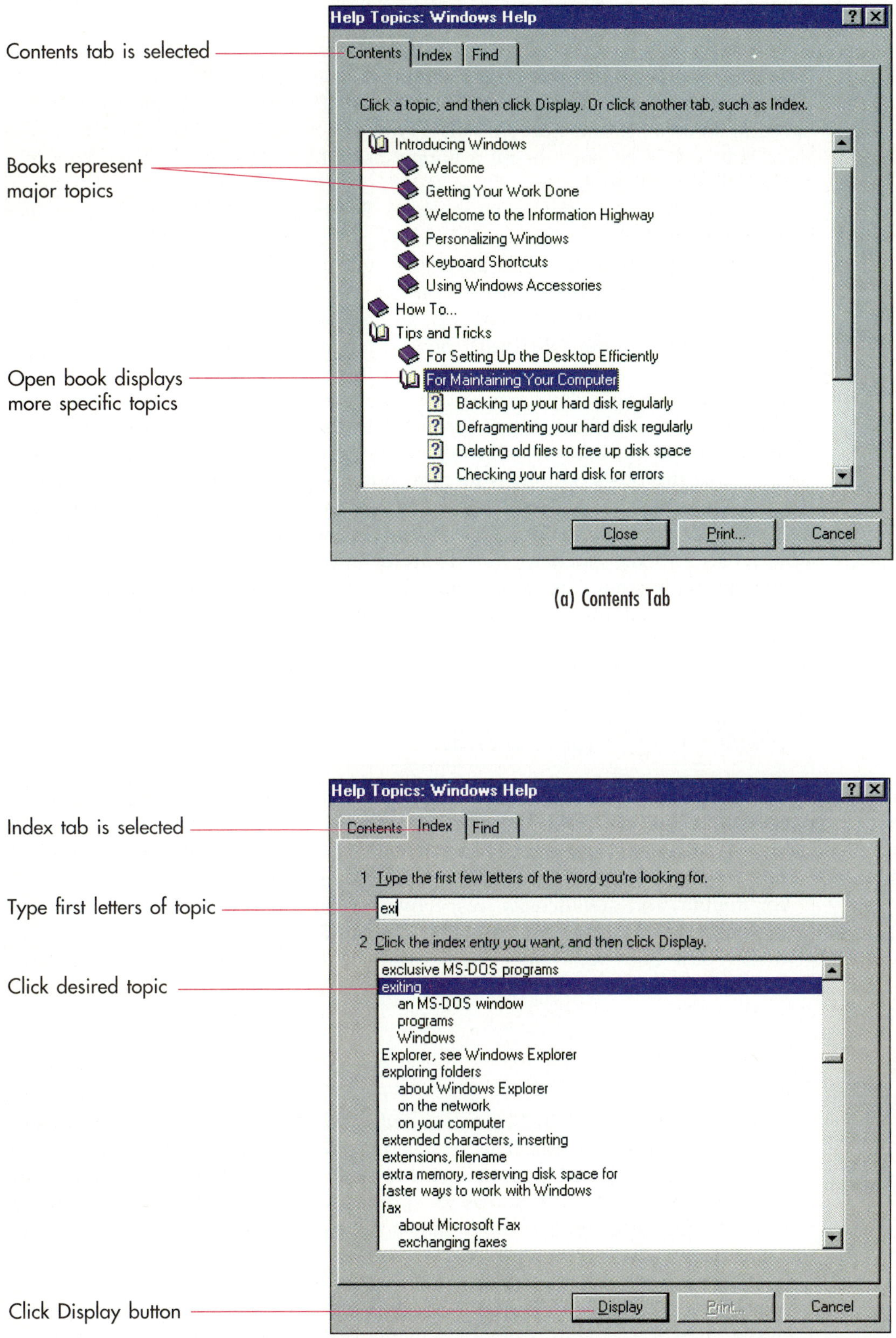


(a) Contents Tab

(b) Index Tab

**FIGURE 5** The Help Command

## FORMATTING A FLOPPY DISK

You will soon begin to work on the computer, which means that you will be using various applications to create different types of documents. Each document is saved in its own file and stored on disk, either on a hard disk (e.g., drive C) if you have your own computer, or on a floppy disk (drive A) if you are working in a computer lab at school.

Even if you have your own machine, however, you will want to copy files from the hard disk to a floppy disk for backup. Thus, you need to purchase a floppy disk(s), and further, you need to format the floppy disk so that it will be able to store the files you create. (You can purchase preformatted floppy disks, but it is very easy to format your own, and we provide instructions in the hands-on exercise that follows.) Be aware, however, that formatting erases any data that was previously on a disk, so be careful not to format a disk with important data (e.g., one containing today's homework assignment).

Formatting is accomplished through the ***Format command.*** The process is straightforward and has you enter all of the necessary information into a dialog box. One of the box's options is to copy system files onto the disk while formatting it. These files are necessary to start (boot) your computer, and if your hard disk were to fail, you would need a floppy disk with the system (and other) files in order to start the machine. (See Help for information on creating a ***boot disk*** containing the system files.) For ordinary purposes, however, you do not put the system files on a floppy disk because they take up space you could use to store data.

### FORMAT AT THE PROPER CAPACITY

A floppy disk should be formatted at its rated capacity or else you may be unable to read the disk. There are two types of 3½-inch disks, double-density (720KB) and high-density (1.44MB). The easiest way to determine the type of disk you have is to look at the disk itself for the label DD or HD, for double- and high-density, respectively. You can also check the number of square holes in the disk; a double-density disk has one, whereas a high-density disk has two.

## LEARNING BY DOING

Learning is best accomplished by doing, and so we come to the first of four hands-on exercises in this appendix. The exercises enable you to apply the concepts you have learned, then extend those concepts to further exploration on your own. The exercise welcomes you to Windows 95, shows you how to open, move, and size a window on the desktop, how to format a floppy disk, and how to use Help to install a screen saver.

A ***screen saver*** is a special program that protects your monitor by producing a constantly changing pattern after a designated period of inactivity. It is a delightful way to personalize your computer and an excellent illustration of how the Help menu can aid you in accomplishing a specific task. The answer to almost everything you need to know is found in one type of help or another. Start with the Help menu, then go to the Microsoft web site (www.microsoft.com) if you need additional information.

# HANDS-ON EXERCISE 1

## *Welcome to Windows*

**Objective:** To turn on the computer and start Windows; to use the Help facility; to open, move, and size a window; and to format a floppy disk. Use Figure 6 as a guide in the exercise.

**STEP 1: Start the Computer**

- The floppy drive should be empty prior to starting your machine. This ensures that the system starts by reading files from the hard disk (which contains the Windows files) as opposed to a floppy disk (which does not).
- The number and location of the on/off switches depend on the nature and manufacturer of the devices connected to the computer. The easiest possible setup is when all components of the system are plugged into a surge protector, in which case only a single switch has to be turned on. In any event, turn on the monitor, printer, and system unit.
- Your system will take a minute or so to get started after which you should see the desktop in Figure 6a. Do not be concerned if the appearance of your desktop is different from ours.
- You may see additional objects on the desktop in Windows 95 and/or the active desktop content in Windows 97.

Click the Start button to see a menu

(a) Start the Computer (step 1)

**FIGURE 6** Hands-on Exercise 1

**STEP 2: Open My Computer**

- Point to the **My Computer icon,** click the **right mouse button,** then click the **Open command** from the shortcut menu. (Alternatively, you can double click the icon to open it directly.)
- My Computer will open into a window as shown in Figure 6b. Do not be concerned if the contents of your window or its size and position on the desktop are different from ours.
- Pull down the **View menu** (point to the menu and click). Make or verify the following selections (you have to pull down the menu each time you choose a different command):
  - The **Toolbar command** should be checked. The Toolbar command functions as a toggle switch. Click the command and the toolbar is displayed; click the command a second time and the toolbar disappears.
  - The **Status bar command** should be checked. The status bar command also functions as a toggle switch.
  - **Large Icons** should be selected as the current view.
- Click the **Details button** on the toolbar to change to this view. Click the **Large Icons button** to return to this view.
- Pull down the **View menu** a final time. Click the **Arrange Icons command** and (if necessary) click the **AutoArrange command** so that a check appears.
- Click outside the menu (or press the **Esc key**) if the command is already checked.

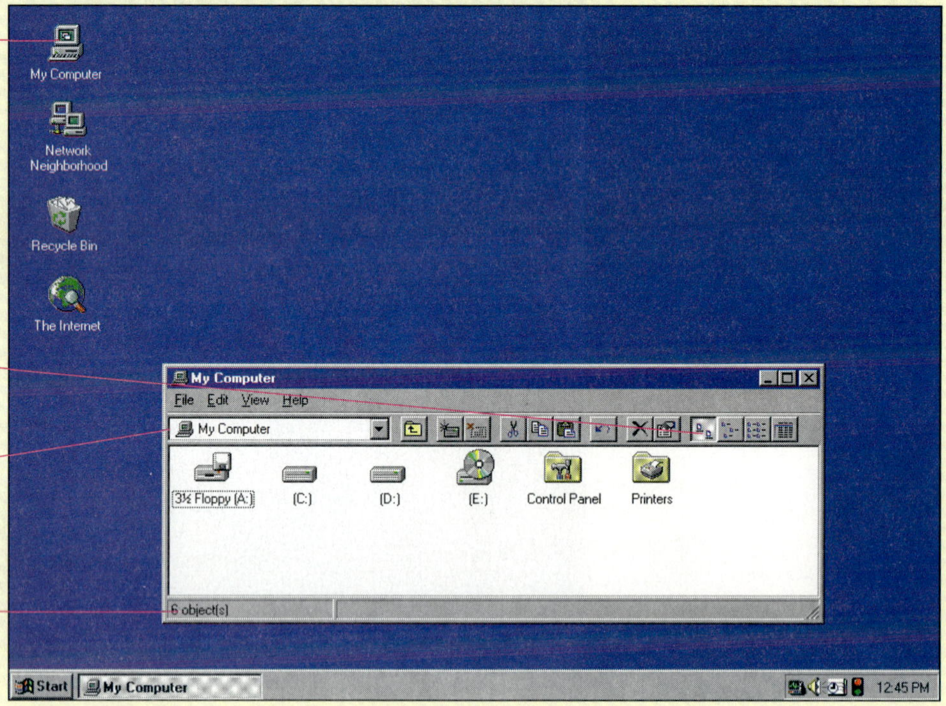


(b) My Computer (step 2)

**FIGURE 6** Hands-on Exercise 1 (continued)

## DESIGNATING THE DEVICES ON A SYSTEM

The first (usually only) floppy drive is always designated as drive A. (A second floppy drive, if it were present, would be drive B.) The first (often only) hard disk on a system is always drive C, whether or not there are one or two floppy drives. A system with one floppy drive and one hard disk (today's most common configuration) will contain icons for drive A and drive C. Additional hard drives (if any) and/or the CD-ROM are labeled from D on.

**STEP 3: Move and Size a Window**

- Click the **maximize button** so that the My Computer window expands to fill the entire screen.
- Click the **restore button** (which replaces the maximize button and is not shown in Figure 6c) to return the window to its previous size.
- Click the **minimize button** to shrink the My Computer window to a button on the taskbar. Click the My Computer button to reopen the window.
- Move and size the My Computer window on your desk to match the display in Figure 6c:

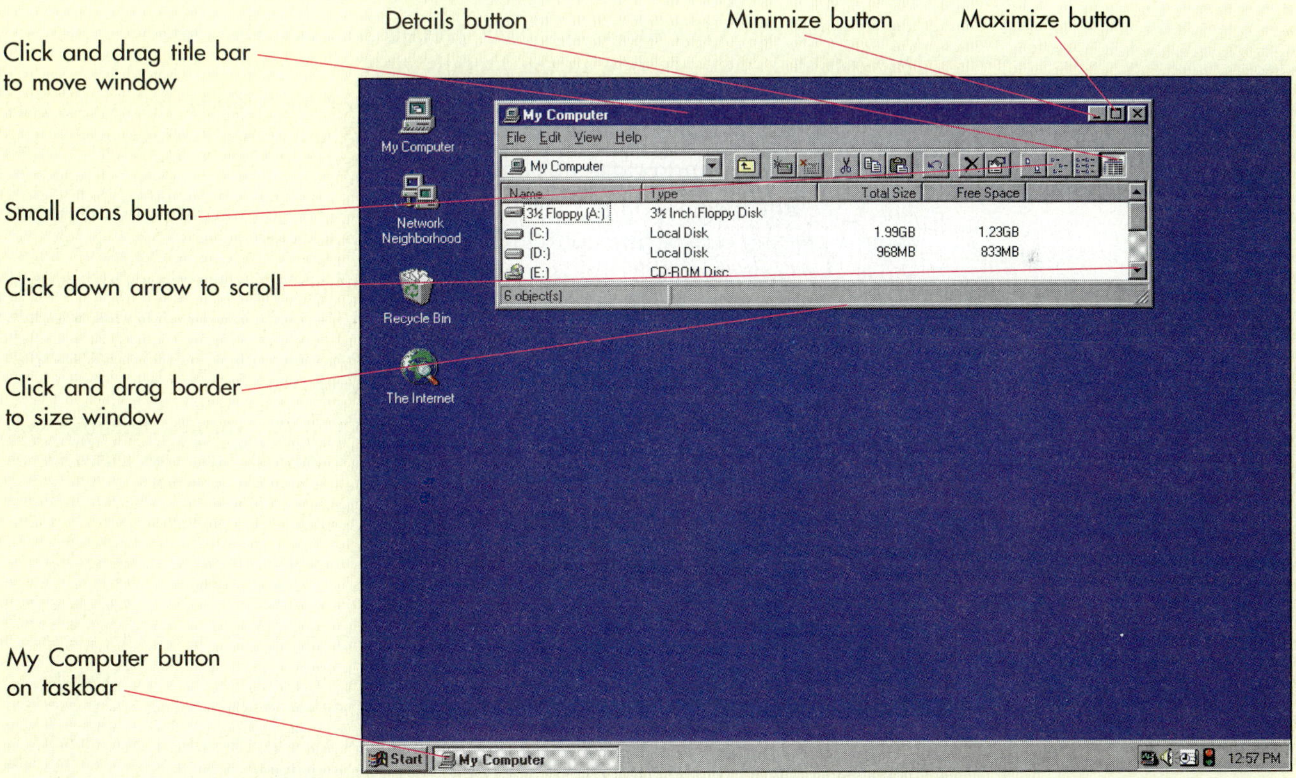


(c) Scrolling (steps 3 and 4)

**FIGURE 6** Hands-on Exercise 1 (continued)

- To change the width or height of the window, click and drag a border (the mouse pointer changes to a double arrow) in the direction you want to go; drag the border inward to shrink the window or outward to enlarge it.
- To change the width and height at the same time, click and drag a corner rather than a border.
- To change the position of the window, click and drag the title bar.

➤ Click the **minimize button** to shrink the My Computer window to a button on the taskbar. My Computer is still open and remains active in memory.

➤ Click the **My Computer button** on the taskbar to reopen the window.

### THE CONTROL PANEL

The Control Panel contains the utility programs (tools) used to change the hardware and/or software settings for the devices on your system (e.g., modem, monitor, mouse, and so on). Double click the Control Panel icon within My Computer to open the Control Panel window, then double click the icon of the device whose settings you want to modify. Additional information can be obtained through the Help facility.

**STEP 4: Scrolling**

➤ Pull down the **View menu** and click **Details** (or click the Details button on the toolbar). You are now in the Details view as shown in Figure 6c.

➤ If necessary, click and drag the bottom border of the window inward so that you see the vertical scroll bar in Figure 6c. The scroll bar indicates that the contents of the window are not completely visible.

➤ Click the **down arrow** on the scroll bar. The top line (for drive A) disappears from view and a new line containing the Control Panel comes into view.

➤ Click the **down arrow** a second time, which brings the Printers folder into view at the bottom of the window as the icon for drive C scrolls off the screen.

➤ Click the **Small icons** button on the toolbar. The scroll bar disappears because the contents of the window become completely visible.

➤ Click the **Details button** on the toolbar. The scroll bar returns because you can no longer see the complete contents. Move and/or size the window to your personal preference.

### SCREENTIPS

Point to any button on the toolbar and Windows displays a ScreenTip containing the name of the button, which is indicative of its function. You can also point to other objects on the desktop to see similar ScreenTips. Point to the clock at the right end of the taskbar, for example, and you will see a ScreenTip with today's date. Point to the Start button and you will see a ScreenTip telling you to click here to begin.

**STEP 5: Online Help**

- Click the **Start button** on the taskbar, then click the **Help command** to display the Help Topics dialog box in Figure 6d.
- Click the **Index tab** as shown in Figure 6d. Type **For** (the first letters in formatting, the topic you are searching for). The Help system automatically displays the topics beginning with the letters you enter.
- Click **Disks** (under formatting) from the list of displayed topics, then click the **Display command button** (or double click the topic to avoid having to click the command button).
- The Help Topics dialog box is replaced by a Windows Help window with instructions on how to format a floppy disk.

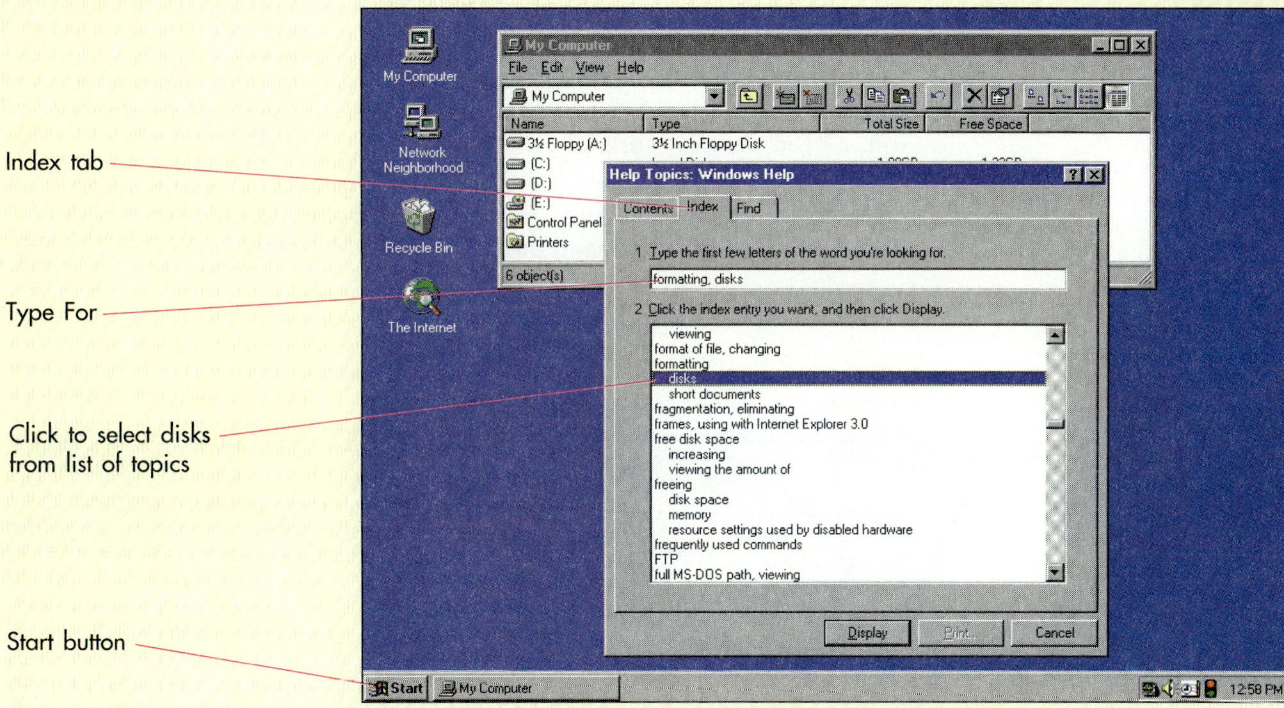


(d) The Help Command (step 5)

**FIGURE 6** Hands-on Exercise 1 (continued)

> **PRINT THE HELP TOPIC**
>
> You can print the contents of any Help window by pointing anywhere within the window and clicking the right mouse button to display a shortcut menu. Click Print Topic, then click the OK command button in the resulting dialog box to print the topic.

**STEP 6: Format a Floppy Disk**

- Place a floppy disk in drive A. Remember, formatting erases everything on the disk, so be sure that you do not need anything on the disk you are about to format. Read the instructions in the Help window in Figure 6.3e, then follow our instructions, which provide more detail.
- Click the icon for **drive A.** Pull down the **File menu** and click **Format.** You will see the dialog box in Figure 6e.
  - Set the **Capacity** to match the floppy disk you purchased (1.44MB for a high-density disk and 720KB for a double-density disk).
  - Click the **Full option button** to choose a full format. This option is well worth the extra time as it ensures the integrity of your disk.
  - Click the **Label text box** if it's empty or click and drag over the existing label if there is an entry. Enter a new label (containing up to 11 characters) such as **Bob's Disk** as shown in Figure 6e.
  - Click the **Start command button** to begin the formatting operation. This will take about a minute and you can see the progress of the formatting process at the bottom of the dialog box.
- After the formatting process is complete, you will see an informational dialog box with the results of the formatting operation. Read the information, then click the **Close command button** to close the informational dialog box.
- Close the Format dialog box. Close the Help window.

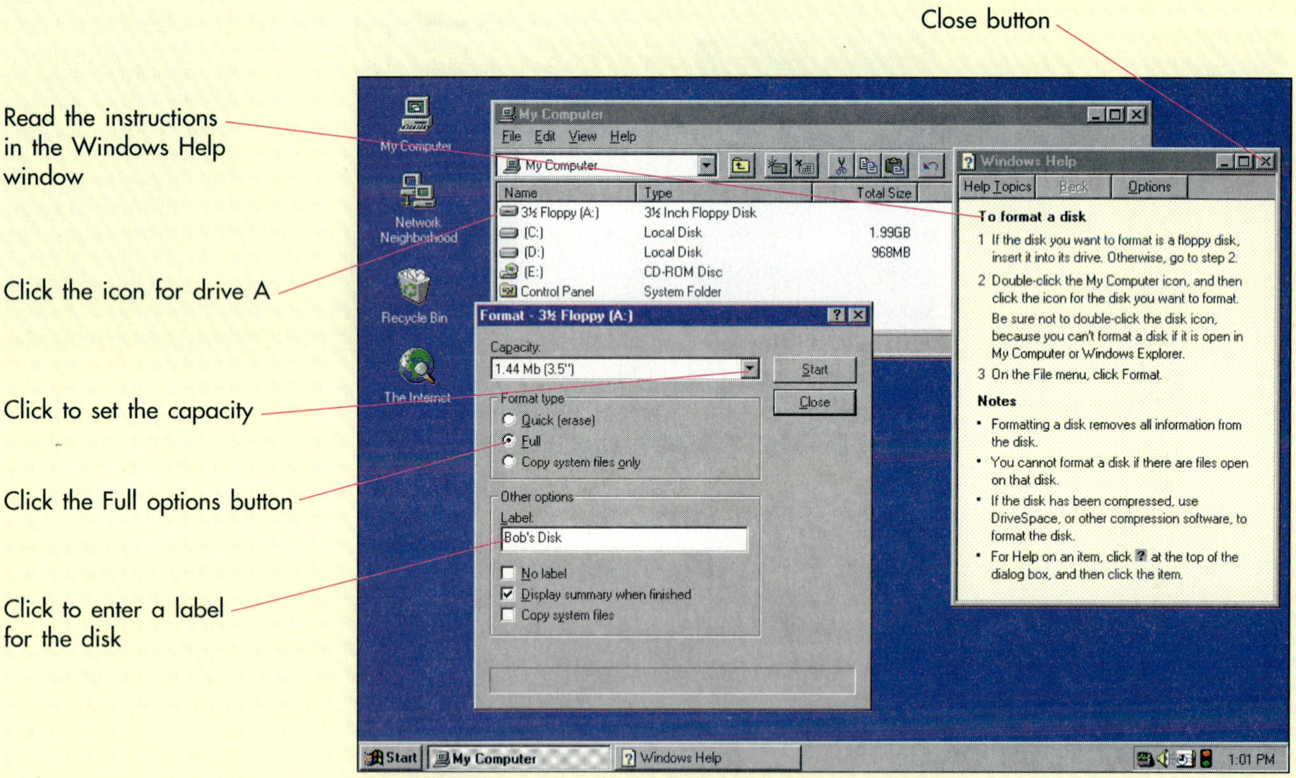


(e) Format a Floppy Disk (step 6)

**FIGURE 6** Hands-on Exercise 1 (continued)

## WHAT'S THIS?

The What's This button (a question mark) appears in the title bar of almost every dialog box. Click the question mark, then click the item you want information about (which then appears in a pop-up window). To print the contents of the pop-up window, click the right mouse button inside the window, and click Print Topic. Click outside the pop-up window to close the window and continue working.

**STEP 7: Implement a Screen Saver**

- If you are working in a lab environment, it is possible that your network administrator has disabled the ability to implement a screen saver, and that you will be unable to complete this step. If this is true at your site, skip the instructions below and go to step 8.
- Click the **Start button,** click the **Help command** to display the Help Topics dialog box, then click the **Index tab.** Type **Scr** (the first letters in *screen,* the topic you are searching for).
- Click **Screen Savers** from the list of displayed topics, then click the **Display button.** (You can also double click the topic to avoid having to click the command button.)
- You will see a second dialog box listing the available topics under Screen Savers. **Double click** the topic that begins **Protecting your screen.** You should see the Help window in Figure 6f. Click the **shortcut jump button** to display the Display Properties dialog box.
- Click the **drop-down arrow** in the Screen Saver box to display the available screen savers. Click one or more of the available screen savers until you come to one you like.
- Click the **OK command button** to accept the screen saver and exit the dialog box. Click the **Close button** to close the Windows Help window.

## PROPERTIES EVERYWHERE

The fastest way to implement a screen saver (or to change the color or other properties of the desktop) is to display the Properties dialog box for the desktop. Point to the desktop, click the right mouse button to display a context-sensitive menu, then click Properties to open the Display Properties dialog box. Click the Screen Saver tab, make the appropriate selections, then click OK to accept the settings and close the dialog box.

**STEP 8: Exit Windows**

- Click the **Start button,** then click the **Shut Down command.** You will see a dialog box asking whether you're sure that you want to shut down the computer. (The option button to shut down the computer is already selected.)
- Click the **Yes command button,** then wait as Windows gets ready to shut down your system. Wait until you see another screen indicating that it is OK to turn off the computer.

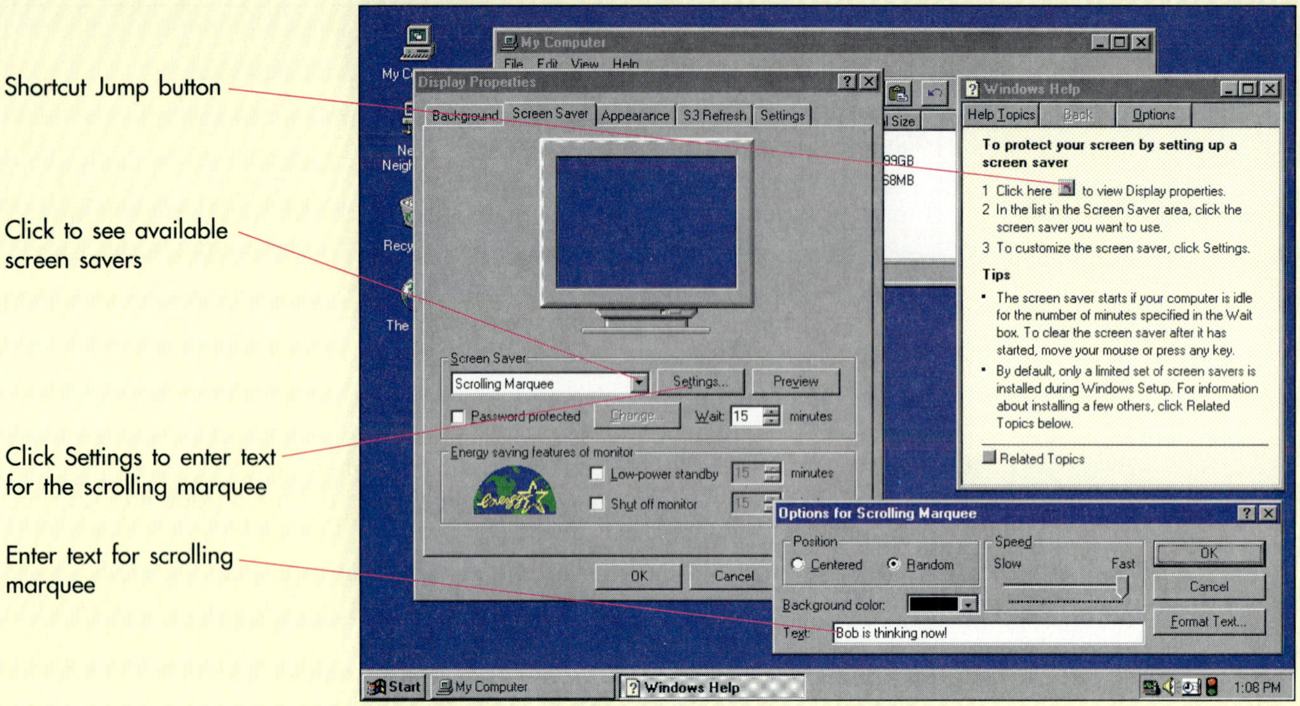


(f) Implement a Screen Saver (step 7)

**FIGURE 6** Hands-on Exercise 1 (continued)

### SUBSCRIBE TO WINNEWS

Consider a subscription to the Microsoft WinNews letter to stay abreast of what is happening in the Windows world. The subscription is free and the newsletter is delivered automatically to your e-mail address. To subscribe to the newsletter, send an e-mail message to enews99@microsoft.nwnet.com. The message should contain a single line with the text **Subscribe WinNews.**

## FILES AND FOLDERS

The ultimate purpose of any computer system is to do useful work. This, in turn, requires the acquisition of various application software, such as Microsoft Office. Each document, spreadsheet, presentation, or database that you create is stored in a file on a disk, be it a hard disk or a floppy disk. It is important, therefore, that you understand the basics of file management so that you will be able to retrieve these files at a later time.

A ***file*** is data that has been given a name and stored on disk. There are, in general, two types of files, ***program files*** and ***data files.*** Microsoft Word and Microsoft Excel are program files. The documents and spreadsheets created by these programs are data files. A ***program file*** is executable because it contains instructions that tell the computer what to do. A ***data file*** is not executable and can be used only in conjunction with a specific program.

A file must have a name so that it can be identified. The file name can contain up to 255 characters and may include spaces and other punctuation. (This is very different from the rules that existed under MS-DOS, which limited file names to eight characters followed by an optional three-character extension.) Long file names permit descriptive entries such as *Term Paper for Western Civilization* (as opposed to a more cryptic *TPWCIV* that would be required under MS-DOS).

Files are stored in ***folders*** to better organize the hundreds (often thousands) of files on a hard disk. A Windows folder is similar in concept to a manila folder in a filing cabinet and contains one or more documents (files) that are somehow related to each other. An office worker stores his or her documents in manila folders. In Windows, you store your data files (documents) in electronic folders on disk.

Folders are the key to the Windows storage system. You can create any number of folders to hold your work just as you can place any number of manila folders into a filing cabinet. You can create one folder for your word processing documents and a different folder for your spreadsheets. Alternatively, you can create a folder to hold all of your work for a specific class, which may contain a combination of word processing documents and spreadsheets. The choice is entirely up to you and you can use any system that makes sense to you. Anything at all can go into a folder—program files, data files, even other folders.

Figure 7 displays two views of a folder containing six documents. The name of the folder (Homework) appears in the title bar next to the icon of an open folder. The minimize, maximize, and close buttons appear at the right of the title bar. A toolbar appears below the menu bar in each view.

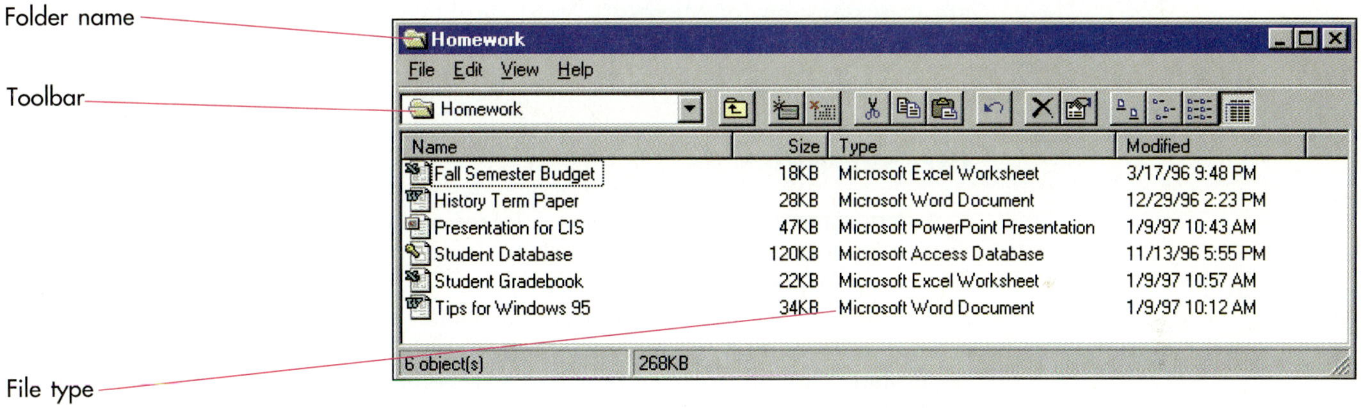


(a) Details View

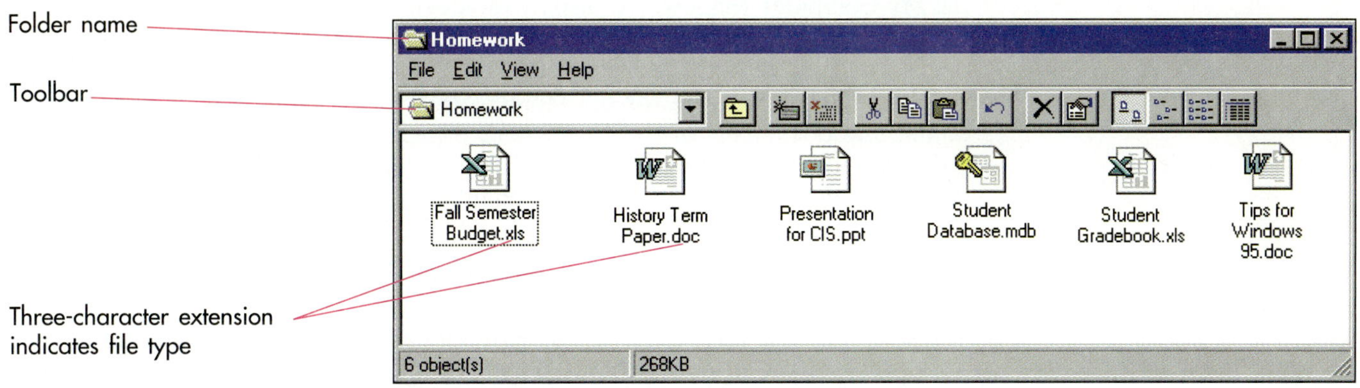


(b) Large Icons View

**FIGURE 7** The Homework Folder

The Details view in Figure 7a displays a small icon representing the application that created the file. It also shows the name of each file in the folder (note the descriptive file name), the file size, the type of file, and the date and time the file was last modified. Figure 7b illustrates the Large Icons view, which displays only the file name and an icon representing the application that created the file. The choice between views depends on your personal preference. (A Small Icons view and List view are also available.)

## File Type

Every data file has a specific ***file type*** that is determined by the application used to create the file. One way to recognize the file type is to examine the Type column in the Details view as shown in Figure 7a. The History Term Paper, for example, is a Microsoft Word document. The Student Gradebook is a Microsoft Excel worksheet.

You can also determine the file type (or associated application) from any view by examining the application icon displayed next to the file name. Look carefully at the icon next to the History Term Paper in Figure 7a, for example, and you will recognize the icon for Microsoft Word. The application icon is recognized more easily in the Large Icons view in Figure 7b.

Still another way to determine the file type is through a three-character extension, which is appended to the file name. (A period separates the filename from the extension.) Each application has a unique extension that is automatically assigned to the file name when the file is created. DOC and XLS, for example, are the extensions for Microsoft Word and Excel, respectively. The extension may be suppressed or displayed according to an option in the View menu of My Computer (or the Windows Explorer), but is best left suppressed in Windows 95/97.

## My Computer

It is important to be able to locate a folder and/or its documents so that you can retrieve a document and go to work. Assume, for example, that you are looking for a term paper in American History that you began yesterday and saved in a folder called Homework. You know the folder is somewhere on drive C, but you are not quite sure where. You need to locate the folder in order to open the term paper and continue working. One way to accomplish this is through My Computer as shown in Figure 8.

You begin by double clicking the My Computer icon on the desktop to open the My Computer window and display the devices on your system. Next, you double click the icon for drive C since it contains the folder you are looking for. This opens a second window, which displays all of the folders on drive C. And finally, you double click the icon for the Homework folder to open a third window containing the documents in the Homework folder. Once in the Homework folder, you can double click the icon of an existing document, which starts the associated application and opens the document, enabling you to begin work.

## The Exploring Windows Practice Files

There is only one way to master Windows 95 and that is to practice at the computer. One of the most important skills you need to acquire is that of file management; that is, you must be proficient in moving and copying files from one drive (or folder) to another. To do so requires that you have a series of files with which to work. Accordingly, we have created a set of practice files that we reference in the next several hands-on exercises. Your instructor will make these files available to you in a variety of ways:

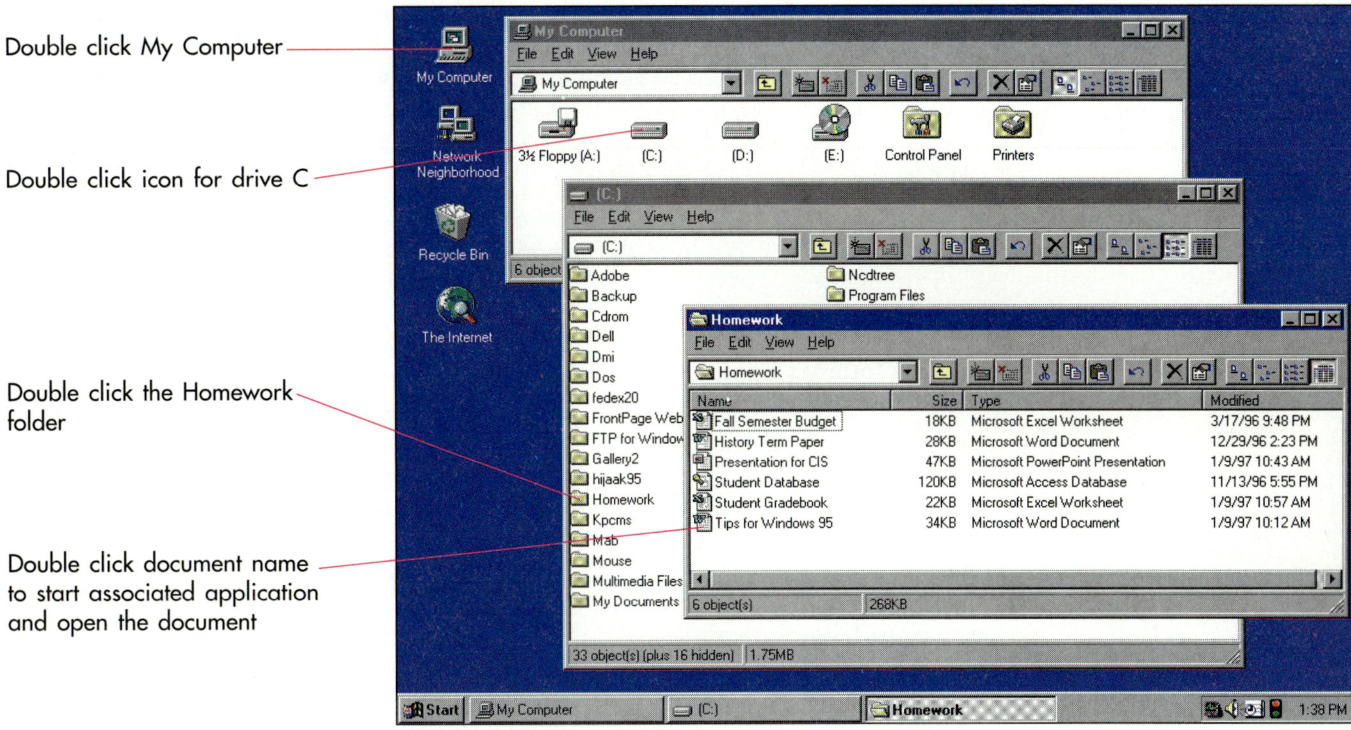


**FIGURE 8** Browsing My Computer

- The files can be downloaded from our Web site, as described in the next hands-on exercise. This assumes you have access to the Internet, and further, that you have a basic proficiency with a browser such as the ***Internet Explorer.***
- The files might be on a network drive, in which case you can use My Computer (or the Windows Explorer, which is discussed later in the chapter) to copy the files from the network drive to a floppy disk. The procedure to do this is described in hands-on exercise 3 later in the chapter.
- There may be an actual data disk in the computer lab. Go to the lab with a floppy disk, then use the Copy Disk command to duplicate the data disk to create a copy for yourself.

It doesn't matter how you obtain the practice files, only that you are able to do so. Indeed, you may try different techniques in order to gain additional practice with the Windows environment. All three methods will place the practice files on a floppy disk; hence you need the formatted floppy disk that was created in the first hands-on exercise. Note, too, the techniques described in the hands-on exercises apply to the practice files for any book in the *Exploring Windows* series.

EXPLORING WWW

### THE EXPLORING WINDOWS SERIES

The text you are reading is one of several books in the *Exploring Windows* series, many of which reference a series of practice files for use with the hands-on exercises. One way to access these files is from the Prentice Hall Web site at www.prenhall.com/grauer. You can also go to Bob Grauer's home page (www.bus.miami.edu/~rgrauer) and click the *Exploring Windows* link. Bob's home page also provides links to the classes he is teaching at the University of Miami.

# HANDS-ON EXERCISE 2

## *The Practice Files (via the World Wide Web)*

**Objective:** To download the practice files from the *Exploring Windows* Web site. The exercise requires a formatted floppy disk and access to the Internet. Use Figure 9 as a guide in the exercise.

### STEP 1: The *Exploring Windows* Series

- Start Internet Explorer. If you are working in class, your instructor will provide additional instructions. At home, however, it is incumbent on you to be able to know how to access the Internet.
- If necessary, click the **maximize button** so that the Internet Explorer takes the entire desktop. Enter the address of the site you want to visit as shown in Figure 9a.
  - Pull down the **File menu,** click the **Open command** to display the Open dialog box, and enter **www.prenhall.com/grauer** (the http:// is assumed). Click **OK.**
  - *Or,* click in the **Address box** below the toolbar, which automatically selects the current address (so that whatever you type replaces the current address). Enter the address of the site you want to visit, **www.prenhall.com/grauer** (the http:// is assumed). Press the **enter key.**
- You should see the *Exploring Windows* home page as shown in Figure 9a. Click the book **Exploring Office 97** to display the page for this series. Click the link to **Office 97.**

Enter the address of the site you want to visit

Click the link to Office 97

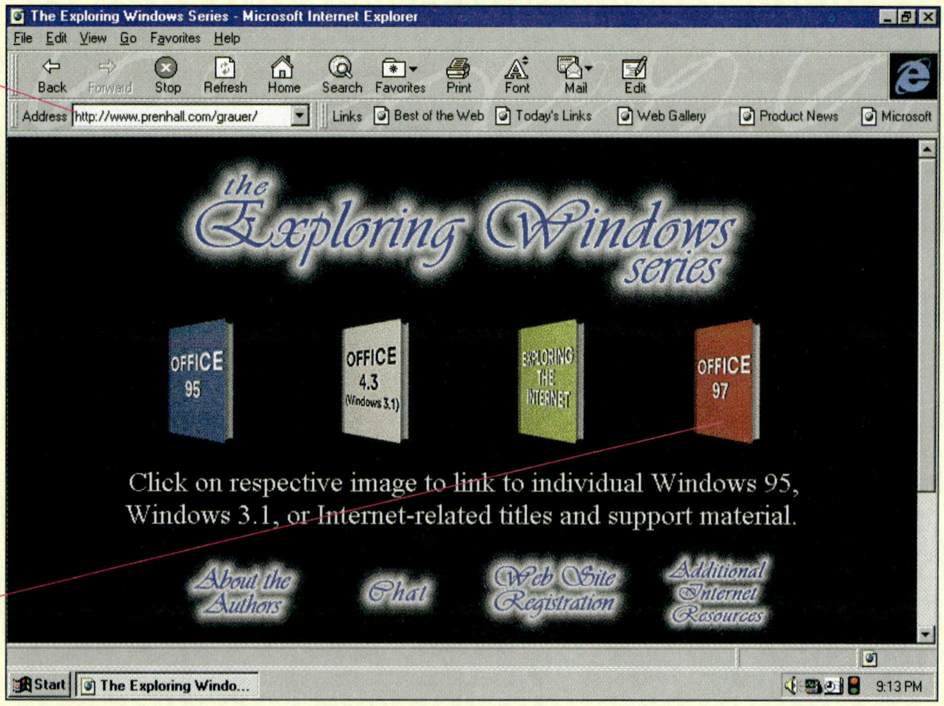


(a) The *Exploring Windows* series (step 1)

**FIGURE 9** Hands-on Exercise 2

## UNABLE TO LOCATE SERVER OR SERVER NOT RESPONDING

Two things must occur in order for Internet Explorer to display the requested document—it must locate the server on which the document is stored, and it must be able to connect to that computer. The error message "Unable to Locate Server" will appear if you enter the Web address incorrectly. Click the Address bar and re-enter the Web address, being sure to enter it correctly. You may also see the message "Server Down or Not Responding," which implies that Internet Explorer located the server but was unable to connect because the site is busy. This means that too many visitors are already there and you need to try again later in the day.

**STEP 2: Download the Practice Files**

- You should see a screen listing the various books for Office 97. Click the link to **Windows Prerequisites** to display the screen in Figure 9b. (The Save As dialog box is not yet visible.)
- Click **prerequisites.exe** (the file you will download to your PC). The File Download window opens, and after a few seconds, an Internet Explorer dialog box opens as well. The option button to **Save it to disk** is selected. Click **OK** to display the Save As dialog box in Figure 9b:
  - The **desktop** is selected as the destination in the Save in box. If this is not the case, click the **drop-down arrow** on the Save in box and select the desktop. Click **Save** to download the file.

(b) Download the Practice Files (step 2)

**FIGURE 9** Hands-on Exercise 2 (continued)

- If you are unable to save to the desktop because your network administrator has disabled this capability at your site, select drive A in the Save in box instead of the desktop (place a formatted floppy disk in drive A).

➤ The File Download window will reappear on your screen and show you the process of the downloading operation. Be patient, as this may take a few minutes. (The Exploring Prerequisites file is 52KB in size.) The File Download window will close automatically when downloading is complete.

➤ Minimize (do not close) Internet Explorer. The Internet Explorer window shrinks to a button on the taskbar, but the application remains open in memory. (We return to Internet Explorer in step 5.)

## ABOUT INTERNET EXPLORER

Pull down the Help menu and click About Internet Explorer to see which version of the Internet Explorer you are using. Our exercises were done with Version 3.00, but you may have a later version if you installed the software after publication of our text. The command structure may vary slightly from one version to the next, but you should be able to complete the exercise without a problem, as long as you are running Version 3.00 or higher.

**STEP 3: Install the Practice Files**

➤ Double click the **Prerequisites icon** from the desktop or drive A, depending on where you downloaded the file.

- If you downloaded the file to the desktop, the Prerequisites icon should be visible on the desktop and you can simply double click the icon.
- If you downloaded the file to a floppy disk, double click the **My Computer icon** on the desktop to open the My Computer window, double click the icon for **drive A,** then double click the **Prerequisites icon.**

➤ You will see a dialog box thanking you for selecting the *Exploring Windows* series. Click **OK** when you have finished reading the dialog box to begin (or cancel) the installation.

## FILE COMPRESSION

Software and other files are typically compressed to reduce the amount of storage space a file requires on disk and/or the time it takes to download the file. In essence, you download a compressed file from a Web site, then you uncompress the file on a local drive. Ideally a compressed file is created as a self-extracting (executable) file as opposed to a zip file, which requires a utility program outside Windows 95. Our files are executable. Thus, all you have to do is double click the executable file after it has been downloaded, and it will automatically install (uncompress) the practice files for you.

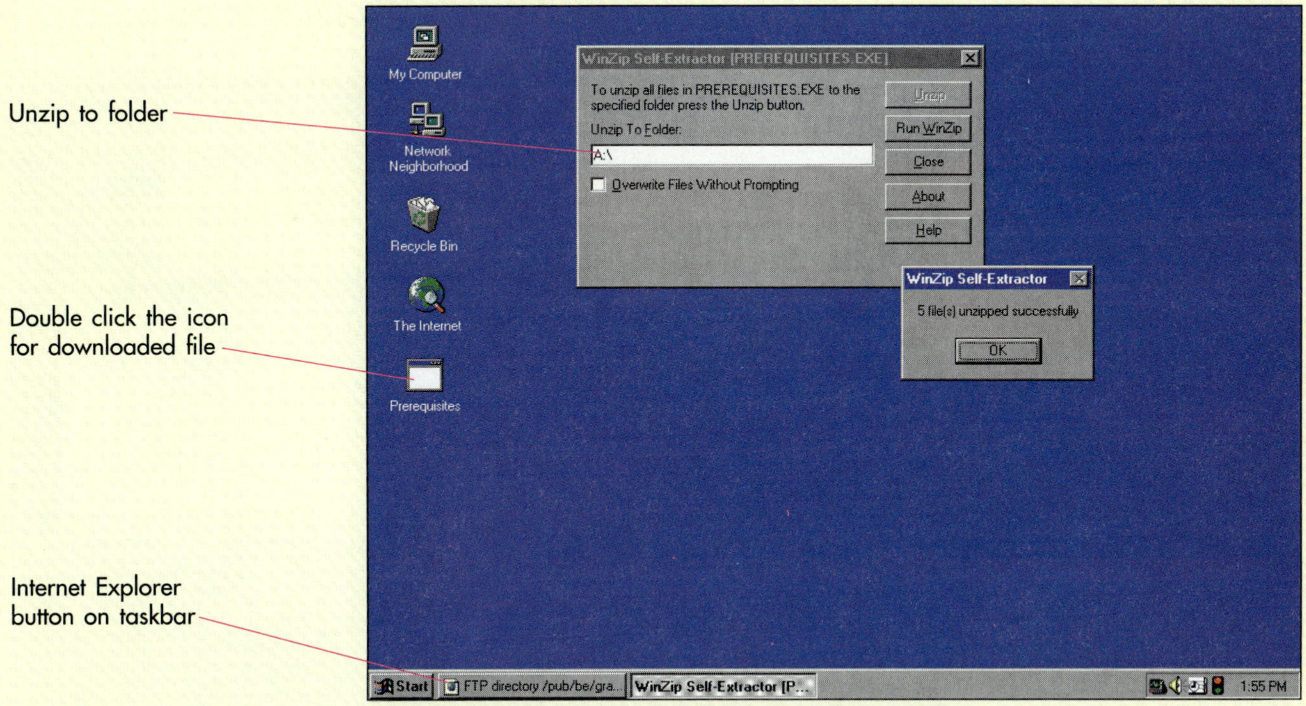


(c) Install the Practice Files (step 3)

**FIGURE 9** Hands-on Exercise 2 (continued)

- If necessary, place a floppy disk in drive A, then verify that the Unzip to Folder text box is specified as A:\ (the floppy disk). If it is not, enter **A:** in the text box as shown in Figure 9c.
- Click the **Unzip button** to extract the practice files and copy them into the designated folder.
- Click **OK** after you see the message indicating that the files have been unzipped successfully. Close the WinZip dialog box.
- The practice files have been extracted and copied to drive A.

**STEP 4: Open My Computer**

- Double click **My Computer** to open the My Computer window in Figure 9d. If necessary, pull down the **View menu** to display the toolbar. Click the **Large Icons view.**
- Double click the icon for **drive A** to open a second window, which displays the contents of drive A. Use the **View menu** to display the toolbar, then change to the **Details view.**
- You should see five files, which are the practice files on the data disk. (There are three Word files, one Excel file, and one PowerPoint file.) These are the files that will be used in a hands-on exercise later in the chapter.
- Select (click) the **Prerequisites icon** on the desktop. Press the **Del key** to erase this file as it is no longer needed. Click **Yes** when asked whether to remove this file.
- Close the windows for drive A and My Computer as they are no longer needed in this exercise.

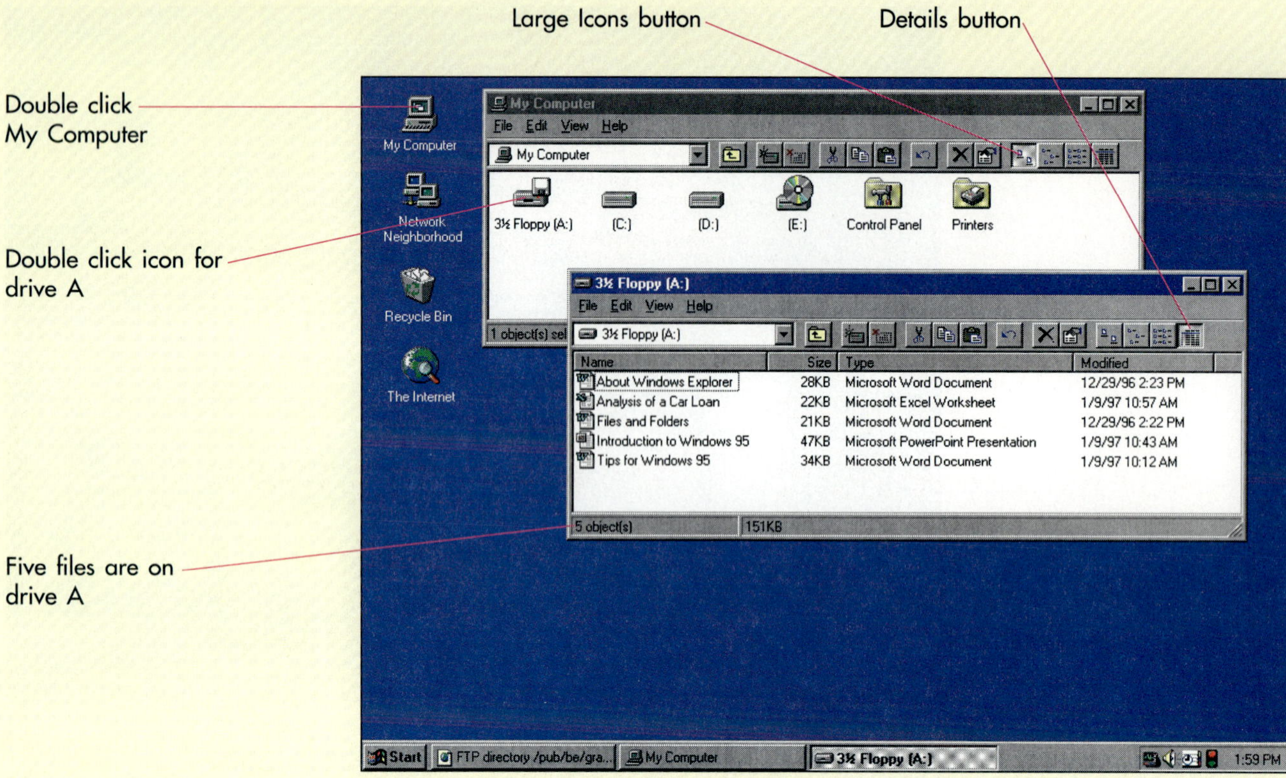


(d) Open My Computer (step 4)

**FIGURE 9** Hands-on Exercise 2 (continued)

### ONE WINDOW OR MANY

By default, My Computer opens a new window every time you open a new drive or folder. The multiple windows can clutter a desktop rather quickly, and hence you may prefer to change the display in the current window to the new drive or folder rather than open a new window. Pull down the View menu, click Options, click the Folder tab, then click the option button to browse folders using a single window.

**STEP 5: Microsoft on the Web**

- Click the **Internet Explorer button** on the taskbar to return to Internet Explorer. Click in the **Address box** below the toolbar. Enter **www.microsoft.com** Press the **enter key.**
- You should see Microsoft's home page. Click the link to **Products,** then scroll until you can click the link to **Windows 95** to display the page in Figure 9e.
- Your screen will be different from ours, as Microsoft is continually updating its information. Click any links that appeal to you to view additional information that is available from Microsoft via the Web.

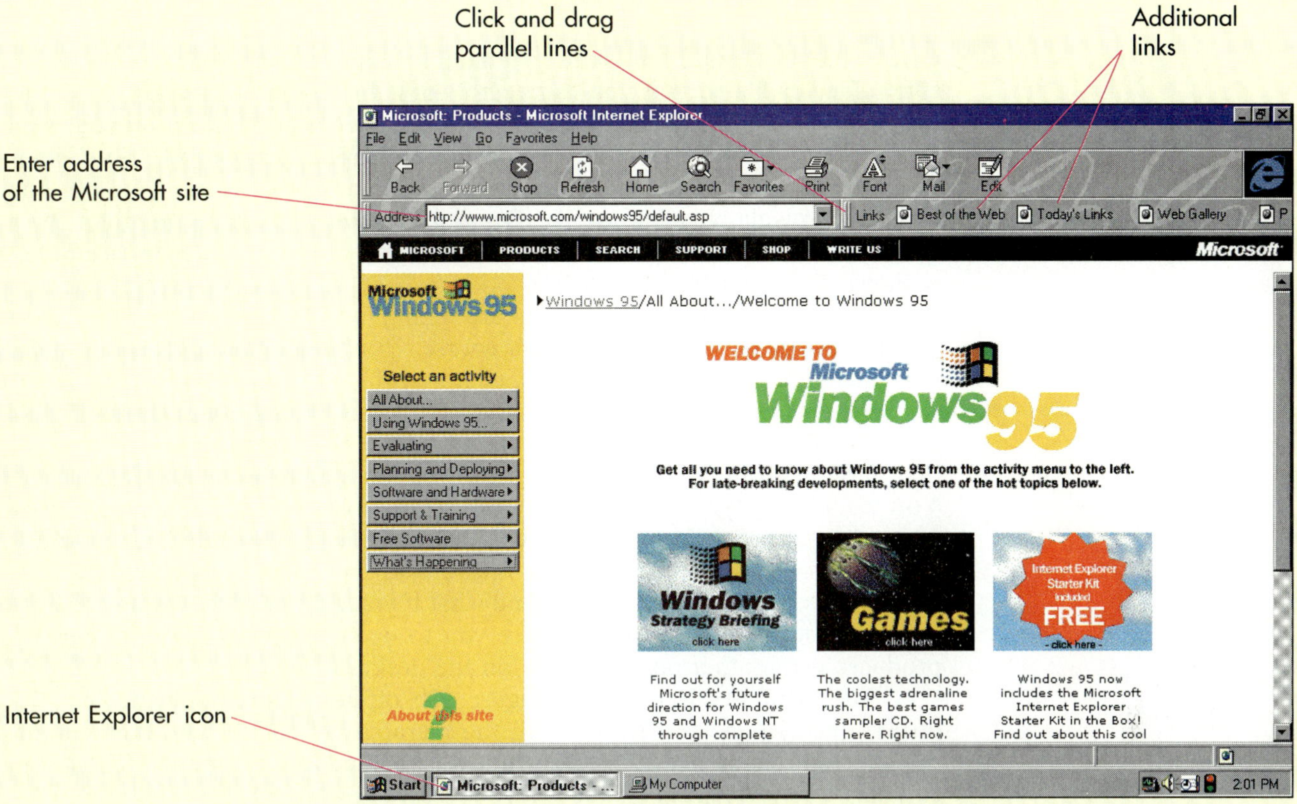


(e) Windows 95 Home Page (step 5)

**FIGURE 9** Hands-on Exercise 2 (continued)

- You may also want to view additional sites suggested by Internet Explorer. If necessary, click and drag the parallel lines that appear to the right of the address box (the mouse pointer changes to a two-headed arrow) to display additional links.
- Click the **Best of the Web** or the **Today's Links button** to explore the current cool sites suggested by Internet Explorer.
- We don't know what you will find, but you can expect something interesting every day.
- Click the hyperlinks that interest you and off you go. Happy surfing!

## SET A TIME LIMIT

We warn you that the Web is addictive, and that once you start surfing, it is difficult to stop. We suggest, therefore, that you set a time limit before you begin, and that you stick to it. Tomorrow is another day, with new places to explore.

One of the most important skills you need to acquire is the ability to locate a specific folder or file so that you can go to work. In essence you need to be able to copy, move, rename, and even delete the various files and folders on your system. There are two basic ways to accomplish these tasks. You can use My Computer to open successive windows until you come to the file or folder you are looking for. Alternatively, you can use the ***Windows Explorer*** to locate the object by navigating the hierarchical structure of your system. The difference between the two is shown in Figure 10.

Assume, for example, that you are taking five classes this semester, and that you are using the computer in each course. You've created a separate folder to hold the work for each class and have stored the contents of all five folders on a single floppy disk. Assume further that you need to retrieve your third English assignment so that you can modify it and submit the revised version.

You can use My Computer to browse the system as shown in Figure 10a. You would start by opening My Computer, double clicking the icon for drive A to open a second window, then double clicking the icon for the English folder to display its documents. The process is intuitive, but it can quickly lead to a desktop cluttered with open windows. And what if you next needed to work on a paper for Art History? That would require you to open the Art History folder, which produces yet another open window on the desktop.

The Windows Explorer in Figure 10b offers a more sophisticated way to browse the system, as it shows both the hierarchy of folders and the contents of the selected folder. The Explorer window is divided into two panes. The left pane contains a ***tree diagram*** of the entire system showing all drives and, optionally, the folders in each drive. One (and only one) object is always selected in the left pane, and its contents are displayed automatically in the right pane.

Look carefully at the tree diagram in Figure 10b and note that the English folder is currently selected. The icon for the selected folder is an open folder to differentiate it from the other folders, which are closed and are not currently selected. The right pane displays the contents of the selected folder (English in Figure 10b) and is seen to contain three documents, Assignments 1, 2, and 3. The right pane is displayed in the Details view, but could just as easily have been displayed in another view (e.g., Large or Small Icons) by clicking the appropriate button on the toolbar.

As indicated, only one folder can be selected (open) at a time in the left pane, and its contents are displayed in the right pane. To see the contents of a different folder (e.g., Accounting), you would click the Accounting folder, which automatically closes the English folder and opens the Accounting folder.

The tree diagram in the left pane displays the drives and their folders in hierarchical fashion. The desktop is always at the top of the hierarchy and contains My Computer, which in turn contains various drives, each of which contains folders, which in turn contain documents and/or additional folders. Each object may be expanded or collapsed by clicking the plus or minus sign, respectively.

Look again at the icon next to My Computer in Figure 10b and you see a minus sign, indicating that My Computer has been expanded to show the various drives on the system. There is also a minus sign next to the icon for drive A to indicate that it too has been expanded to show the folders on the disk. Note, however, the plus sign next to drives C and D, indicating that these parts of the tree are currently collapsed and thus their subordinates are not visible.

A folder may contain additional folders and thus individual folders may also be expanded or collapsed. The minus sign next to the Finance folder in Figure 10b, for example, shows that the folder has been expanded and contains two

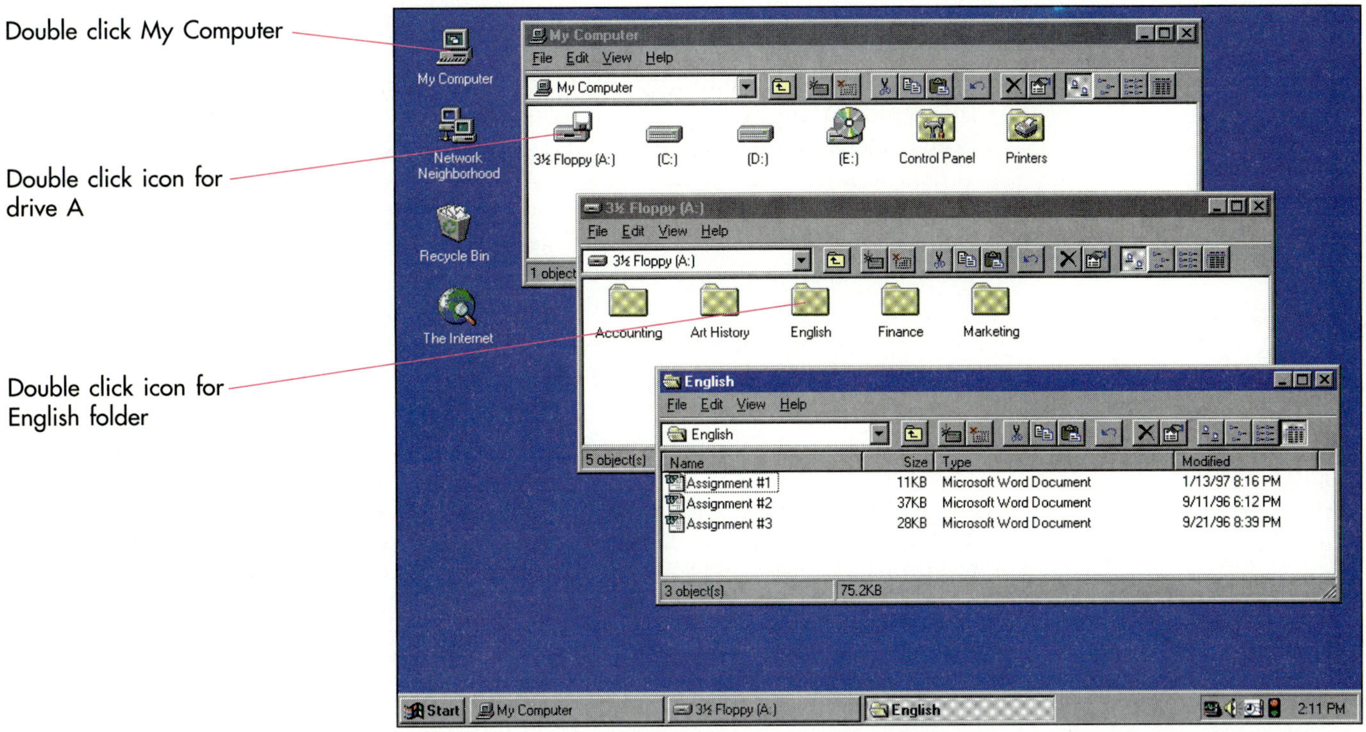


(a) My Computer

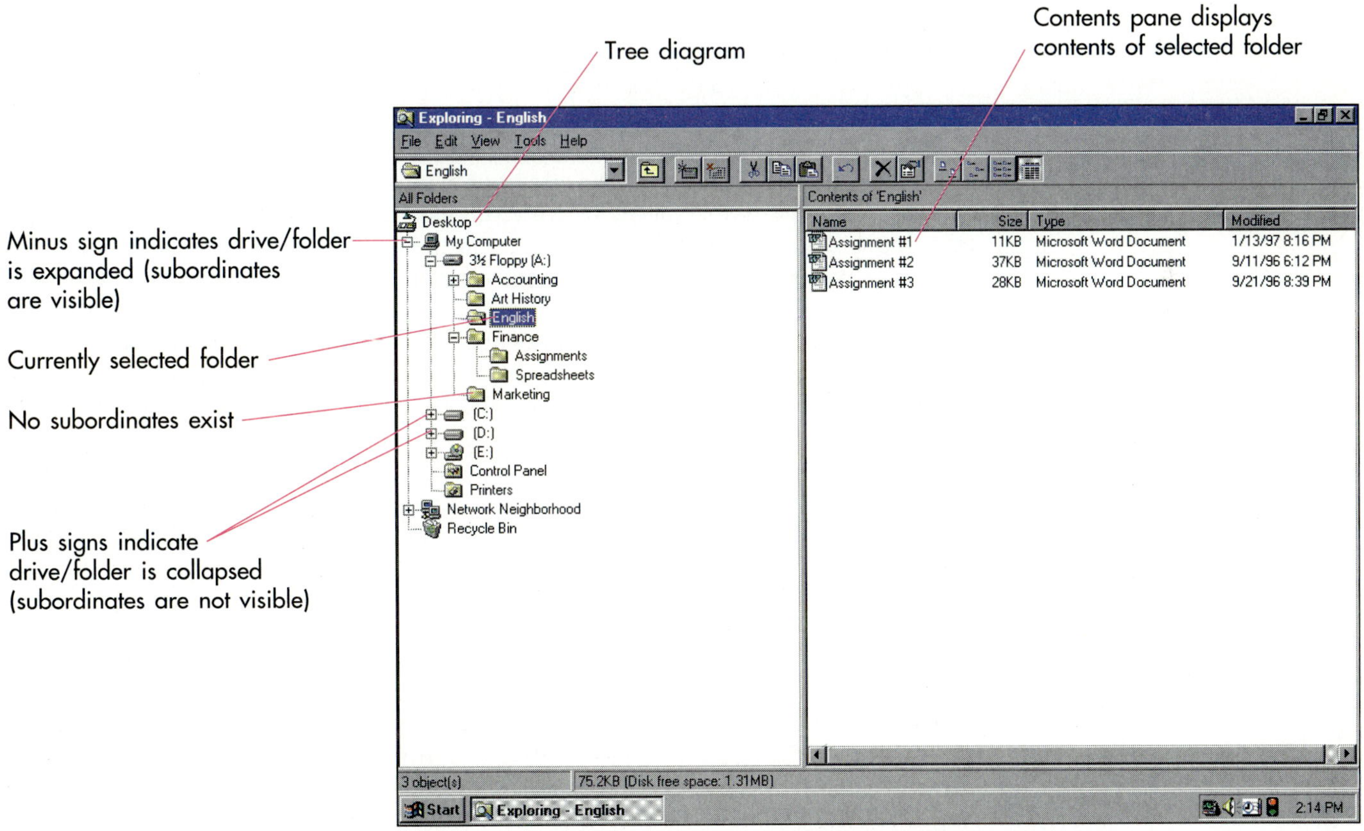


(b) Windows Explorer

**FIGURE 10** Working with Files and Folders

additional folders, for Assignments and Spreadsheets, respectively. The plus sign next to the Accounting folder, however, indicates the opposite; that is, the folder is collapsed and its subordinate folders are not currently visible. A folder with neither a plus or minus sign, such as Art History or Marketing, does not contain additional folders and cannot be expanded or collapsed.

The advantage of the Windows Explorer over My Computer is the uncluttered screen and ease with which you switch from one folder to the next. If, for example, you wanted to see the contents of the Art History folder, all you would do would be to click its icon in the left pane, which automatically changes the display in the right pane to show the documents in Art History. The Explorer also makes it easy to move or copy a file from one folder or drive to another, as you will see in the hands-on exercise, which follows shortly.

### ORGANIZE YOUR WORK

Organize your folders in ways that make sense to you, such as a separate folder for every class you are taking. You can also create folders within folders; for example, a correspondence folder may contain two folders of its own, one for business correspondence and one for personal letters. Use descriptive names for your folders so that you will remember their contents. (A name may contain up to 255 characters, including spaces.)

## The Practice Files

As indicated, there are several ways to obtain the practice files associated with the various books in the *Exploring Windows* series. You can download the files from our Web site as described in the previous hands-on exercise. Alternatively, you can use the Windows Explorer to copy the files from a network drive (at school) to a floppy disk, as will be demonstrated in the following hands-on exercise.

The Windows Explorer is especially useful for moving or copying files from one folder or drive to another. You simply select (open) the folder that contains the file, use the scroll bar in the left pane (if necessary) so that the destination folder is visible, then click and drag the file(s) from the right pane to the destination folder. The Explorer is a powerful tool, but it takes practice to master.

### EXPLORE THE PRACTICE FILES

The practice files are intended to teach you the basics of file management, but they are also interesting in and of themselves. The *Tips for Windows 95* document, for example, contains several tips that appeared throughout this appendix. The *Introduction to Windows 95* presentation summarizes much of the material in this appendix. *Analysis of a Car Loan* is an Excel workbook that computes a monthly car payment based on the cost of a car and the parameters of a loan. Double click any of these files from within the Windows Explorer to start the application and load the document.

# HANDS-ON EXERCISE 3

*The Practice Files (via a local area network)*

**Objective:** To use the Windows Explorer to copy the practice files from a network drive to a floppy disk. The exercise requires a formatted floppy disk and access to a local area network. Use Figure 11 as a guide in the exercise.

**STEP 1: Start the Windows Explorer**

- Click the **Start Button,** click (or point to) the **Programs command,** then click **Windows Explorer** to start this program. Click the **maximize button** so that the Explorer takes the entire desktop as shown in Figure 11a. Do not be concerned if your screen is different from ours.
- Make or verify the following selections using the **View menu.** (You have to pull down the View menu each time you choose a different command.)
  - The **Toolbar command** should be checked.
  - The **Status bar command** should be checked.
  - The **Large Icons view** should be selected.
- Click (select) the **Desktop icon** in the left pane to display the contents of the desktop in the right pane.
- Our desktop contains only the icons for My Computer, Network Neighborhood, the Recycle Bin, and the Internet icon. Your desktop may have different icons, but your screen should otherwise match Figure 11a.

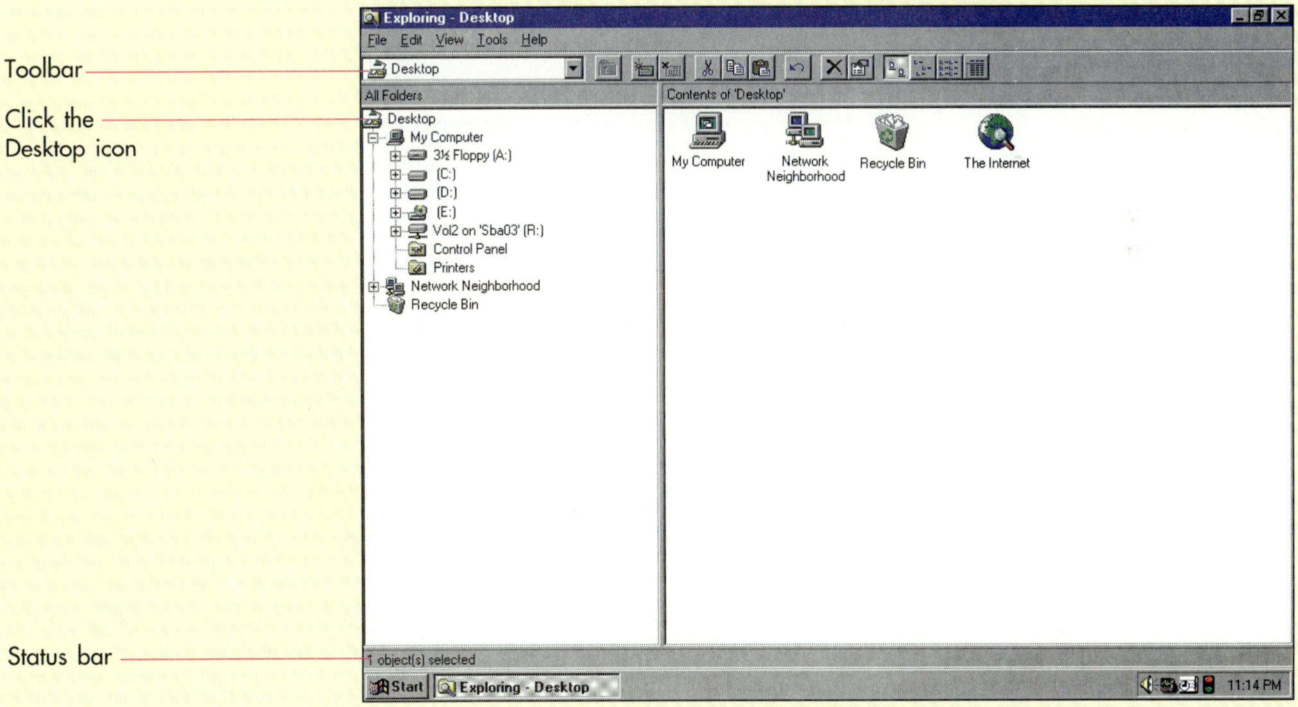


(a) Start the Windows Explorer (step 1)

**FIGURE 11** Hands-on Exercise 3

## FILE EXTENSIONS

Long-time DOS users remember a three-character extension at the end of a file name to indicate the file type—for example, DOC or XLS to indicate a Word document or Excel workbook, respectively. The extensions are displayed or hidden according to the option you establish through the View menu of the Windows Explorer. Pull down the View menu, click the Options command to display the Options dialog box, click the View tab, then check (or clear) the box to hide (or show) MS-DOS file extensions. Click OK to accept the setting and exit the dialog box. We prefer to hide the extensions.

**STEP 2: Additional Practice**

- The objective of this exercise is to obtain the practice files by copying files from a local area network (such as a computer lab at school) using the Windows Explorer. If you already downloaded the practice files from our Web site in the previous hands-on exercise, you can:
  - Use the practice files you already have and go to step 6 to continue with this exercise, *or*
  - Erase all of the files on your floppy disk (just reformat the disk), then proceed with steps 3 through 5 in this exercise.
- We suggest you continue with step 3 in order to practice with the Windows Explorer.

## THE QUICK FORMAT COMMAND

The fastest way to erase the entire contents of a floppy disk is to use the Quick Format command. Start the Windows Explorer and select any drive except the floppy drive. (You cannot format a floppy disk in drive A when drive A is selected). Point to the icon for drive A in the left pane, click the right mouse button to display a shortcut menu, then click the Format command to display the Format dialog box. Click the option button for the Quick (erase) Format, then click the Start button to format the disk and erase its contents.

**STEP 3: Collapse the Individual Drives**

- Click the **minus** (or the plus) **sign** next to My Computer to collapse (or expand) My Computer and hide (display) the objects it contains.
- Toggle the signs back and forth a few times for practice. End with a minus sign next to the My Computer icon as shown in Figure 11b.
- Place a formatted floppy disk in drive A, then click the **plus sign** next to drive A. The plus sign disappears, as drive A does not have any folders.

Click icon to select drive A

Click the plus sign to expand drive

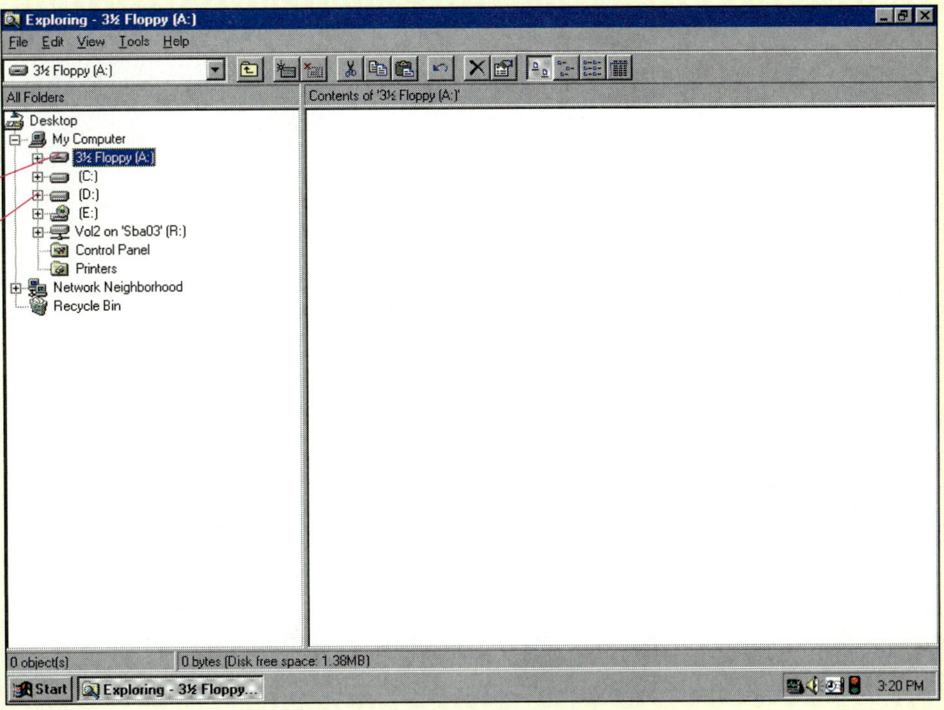


(b) Collapse the Individual Drives (step 3)

FIGURE 11 Hands-on Exercise 3 (continued)

- Click the **plus** (minus) **sign** next to the other drives to toggle back and forth between expanding (collapsing) the individual drives on your system.
- End this step with every drive collapsed; that is, there should be a **plus sign** next to every drive, as shown in Figure 11b.
- Click the drive icon next to drive A to select the drive and display its contents in the right pane. The disk does not contain any files, and hence the right pane is empty.

## THE PLUS AND MINUS SIGN

Any drive, be it local or on the network, may be expanded or collapsed to display or hide its contents. A minus sign indicates that the drive has been expanded and that its folders are visible. A plus sign indicates the reverse; that is, the device is collapsed and its folders are not visible. Click either sign to toggle to the other. Clicking a plus sign, for example, expands the drive, then displays a minus sign next to the drive to indicate that the folders are visible. Clicking a minus sign has the reverse effect—it collapses the drive, hiding its folders.

**STEP 4: Select the Network Drive**

- Click the **plus sign** for the network drive, which contains the files you are to copy (e.g., drive R in Figure 11c). Select (click) the **Exploring Prerequisites**

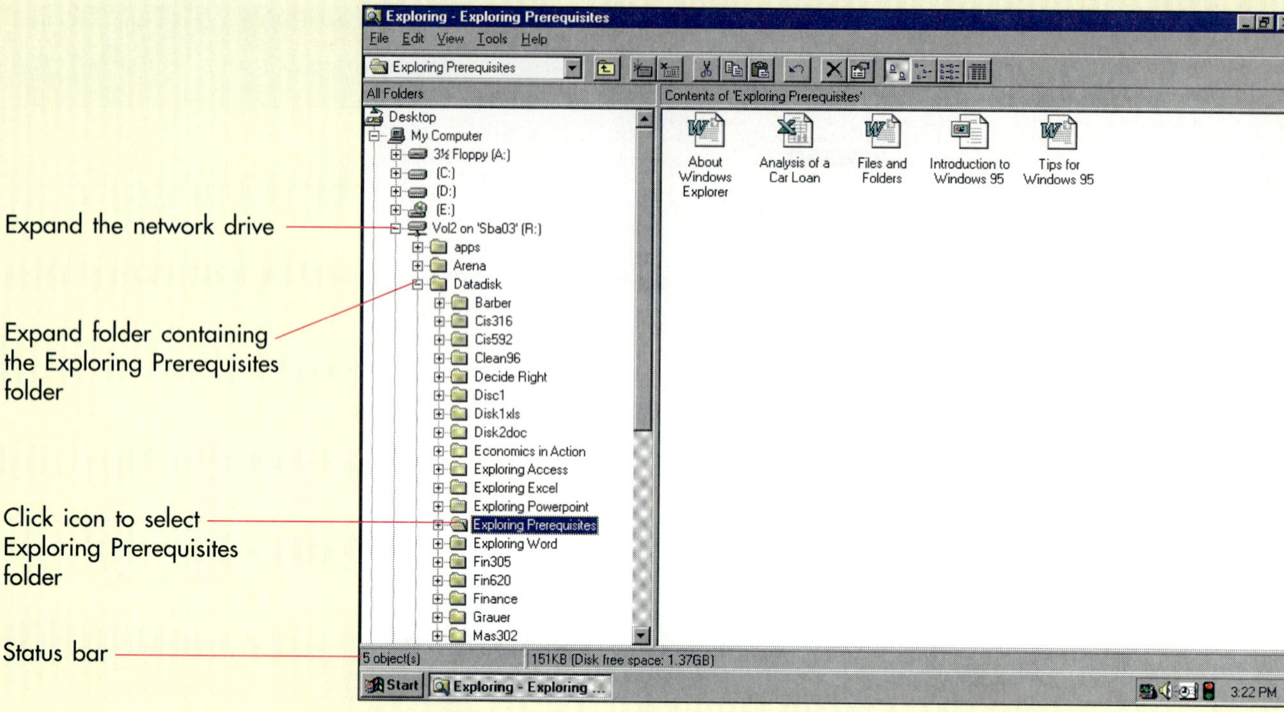


(c) Select the Exploring Prerequisites Folder (step 4)

**FIGURE 11** Hands-on Exercise 3 (continued)

**folder** to select this folder. (You may need to expand other folders on the network drive as per instructions from your professor.) Note the following:

- The Exploring Prerequisites folder is highlighted in the left pane, its icon has changed to an open folder, and its contents are displayed in the right pane.
- The status bar indicates that the folder contains five objects and the total file size is 151KB.

➤ Click the icon next to any other folder to select the folder, which in turn deselects the Exploring Prerequisites folder. (Only one folder in the left pane can be selected at a time.) Reselect (click) the **Exploring Prerequisites folder** and its contents are again visible in the right pane.

➤ Pull down the **View menu** and select **Details** (or click the **Details button** on the toolbar) to change to the Details view. This enables you to see the file sizes of the individual files.

### THE VIEW MENU

The objects in any window can be displayed in four different views—Large Icons, Small Icons, Details, and List—according to your preference or need. The choice of views depends on your personal preference. You can change from one view to another from the View menu, or by clicking the appropriate button on the toolbar. (Windows 97 provides access to a fifth view, the Web view, which displays the addresses of recently visited Web sites.)

### STEP 5: Copy the Individual Files

- ➤ Select (click) the file **About Windows Explorer,** which highlights the file as shown in Figure 11d. The Exploring Prerequisites folder is no longer highlighted because a different object has been selected. The folder is still open, however, and its contents are displayed in the right pane.
- ➤ Click and drag the selected file in the right pane to the **drive A icon** in the left pane:
  - You will see the ⦸ symbol as you drag the file until you reach a suitable destination (e.g., until you point to the icon for drive A). The ⦸ symbol will change to a plus sign when the icon for drive A is highlighted, indicating that the file can be copied successfully.
  - Release the mouse to complete the copy operation. You will see a pop-up window, which indicates the progress of the copy operation. This may take several seconds, depending on the size of the file.
- ➤ Select (click) the file **Tips for Windows 95,** which automatically deselects the previously selected file (About Windows Explorer). Copy the selected file to drive A by dragging its icon from the right pane to the drive A icon in the left pane.
- ➤ Copy the three remaining files to drive A as well. (You can select multiple files at the same time by pressing and holding the **Ctrl key** as you click each file in turn. Point to any of the selected files, then click and drag the files as a group.)
- ➤ Select (click) drive **A** in the left pane, which in turn displays the contents of the floppy disk in the right pane. You should see the five files you have copied to drive A.

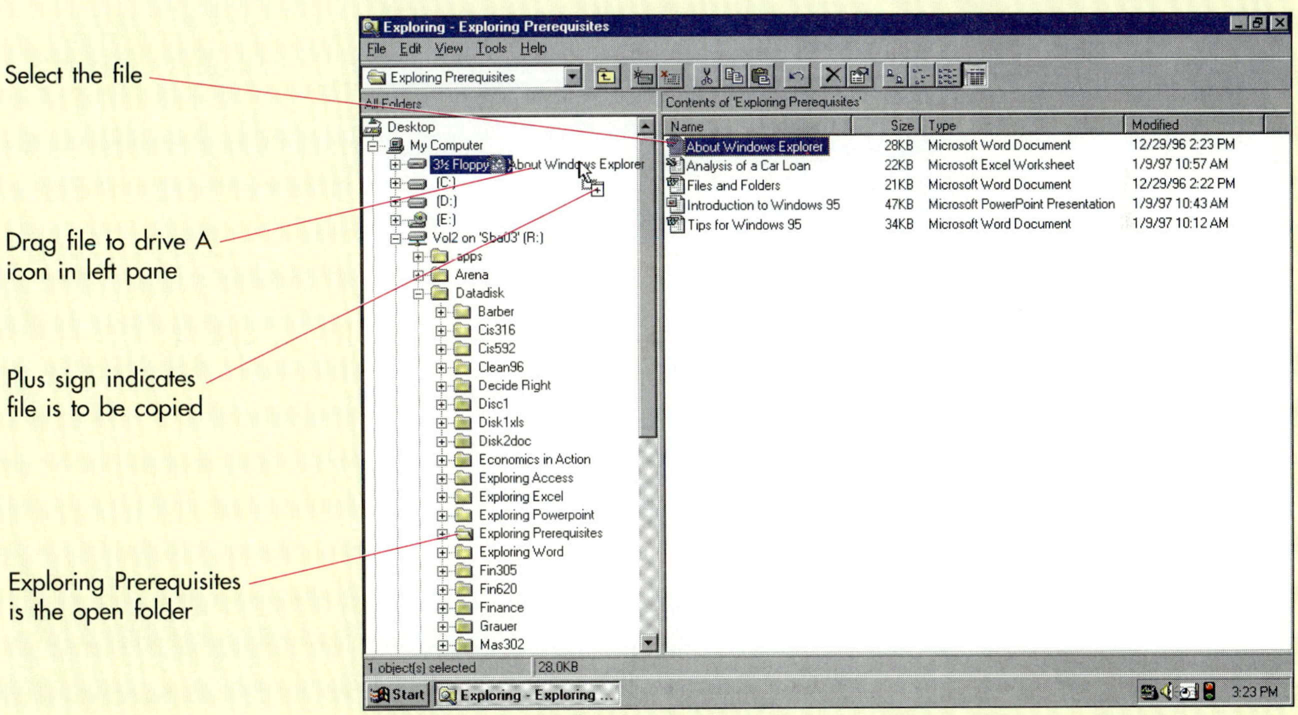


(d) Copy the Practice Files (step 5)

**FIGURE 11** Hands-on Exercise 3 (continued)

## SELECT MULTIPLE FILES

Selecting (clicking) one file automatically deselects the previously selected file. You can, however, select multiple files by pressing and holding the Ctrl key as you click each file in succession. You can also select multiple files that are adjacent to one another by using the Shift key; that is, click the icon of the first file, then press and hold the Shift key as you click the icon of the last file. You can also select every file in a folder through the Select All command in the Edit menu (or by clicking in the right pane and pressing Ctrl+A).

**STEP 6: Check Your Work**

➤ Prove to your instructor that you have done the exercise correctly by capturing the Exploring Windows screen, which appears on your monitor. The easiest way to do this is to use the Paint accessory as shown in Figure 11e. Accordingly:

- Press the **Print Screen key** to copy the current screen display to the clipboard (an area of memory that is available to every Windows application). Nothing appears to have happened, but the screen has in fact been copied to the clipboard.
- Click the **Start button,** click **Programs,** click **Accessories,** then click **Paint** to open the Paint accessory. If necessary, click the **maximize button** so that the Paint window takes the entire desktop.

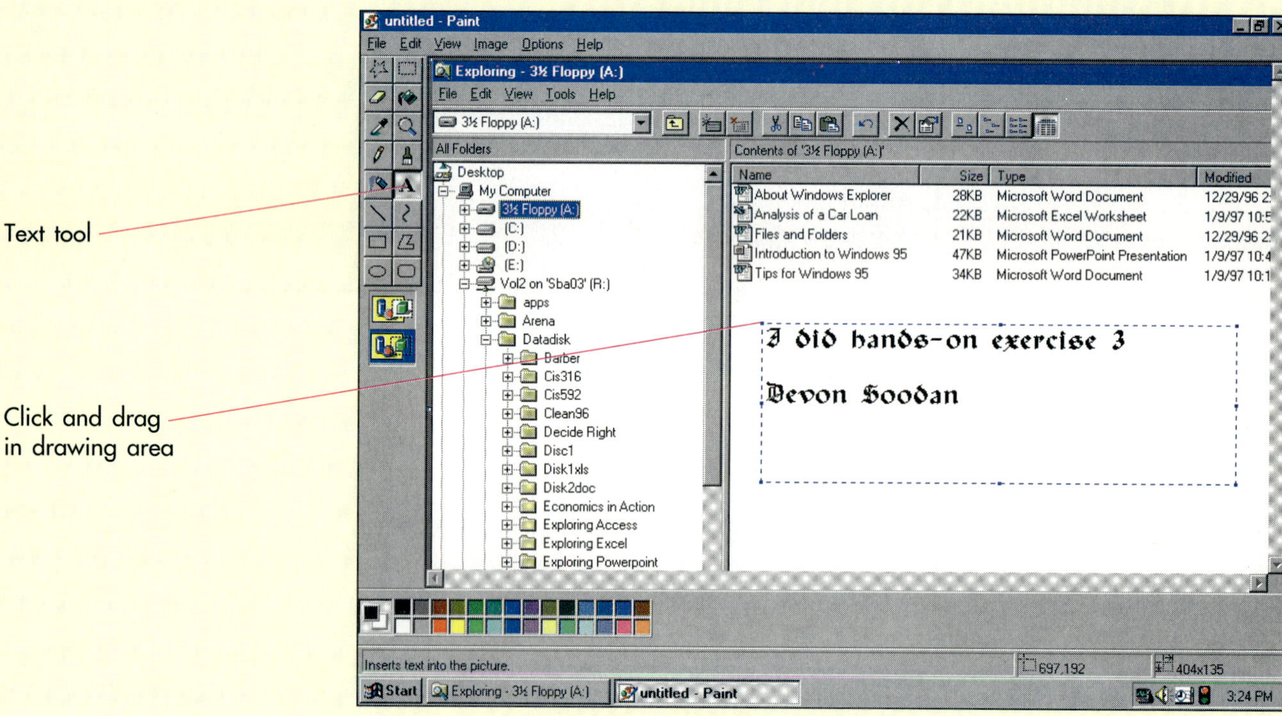


(e) Check Your Work (step 6)

FIGURE 11 Hands-on Exercise 3 (continued)

- Pull down the **Edit menu.** Click **Paste** to copy the screen from the clipboard to the drawing.
- Click the **text tool** (the capital A), then click and drag in the drawing area to create a dotted rectangle that will contain the message to your instructor. Type the text indicating that you did your homework. Click outside the rectangle to deselect it.
- Pull down the **File menu** and click the **Page Setup** command to display the Page Setup dialog box. Click the Landscape option button. Change the margins to one inch all around. Click **OK.**
- Pull down the **File menu** a second time. Click **Print.** Click **OK.** Click the **Close button** to exit Paint. Click **No** if asked to save the file.

➤ Close the Windows Explorer. Exit Windows if you do not want to continue with the next exercise at this time.

### THE PAINT ACCESSORY

The Paint Accessory is included in Windows 95 and is an ideal way to create simple (or, depending on your ability, complex) drawings. There is also a sense of familiarity because the Paint accessory shares the common user interface of every Windows application, which includes a title bar, menu bar, minimize, restore, and close buttons, and vertical and horizontal scroll bars. You may also recognize a familiar command structure. The Print and Paste commands, for example, are found in the File and Edit menus, respectively, in Paint, as they are in every Windows application.

# THE BASICS OF FILE MANAGEMENT

The exercise just completed had you copy the practice files from a drive on a local area network to your own floppy disk. As you grow to depend on the computer, you will create files of your own in various applications (e.g., Word or Excel). Learning how to manage those files is one of the most important skills you can acquire. This section describes the basic operations you will use.

## Moving and Copying a File

Moving and copying a file from one location to another is the essence of file management. It is accomplished most easily by clicking and dragging the file icon from the source drive or folder, to the destination drive or folder, within the Windows Explorer. There is a subtlety, however, in that the result of dragging a file (whether the file is moved or copied) depends on whether the source and destination are on the same or different drives. Dragging a file from one folder to another folder on the same drive moves the file. Dragging a file to a folder on a different drive copies the file. (You can also click and drag a folder, in which case every file in that folder is moved or copied as per the rule for an individual file.)

This process is not as arbitrary as it may seem. Windows assumes that if you drag an object (a file or folder) to a different drive (e.g., from drive C to drive A), you want the object to appear in both places. Hence, the default action when you click and drag an object to a different drive is to copy the object. You can, however, override the default and move the object by pressing and holding the Shift key as you drag.

Windows also assumes that you do not want two copies of an object on the same drive as that would result in wasted disk space. Thus, the default action when you click and drag an object to a different folder on the same drive is to move the object. You can override the default and copy the object by pressing and holding the Ctrl key as you drag. It's not as complicated as it sounds, and you get a chance to practice in the hands-on exercise, which follows shortly.

## Deleting Files

The ***Delete command*** deletes (removes) a file from a disk. The command can be executed in different ways, most easily by selecting a file, then pressing the Del key. Even after a file is deleted, however, you can usually get it back because it is not physically deleted from the hard disk, but moved instead to the Recycle Bin from where it can be recovered.

The ***Recycle Bin*** is a special folder that contains all files that were previously deleted from any hard disk on your system. Think of the Recycle Bin as similar to the wastebasket in your room. You throw out (delete) a report by tossing it into a wastebasket. The report is gone (deleted) from your desk, but you can still get it back by taking it out of the wastebasket as long as the basket wasn't emptied. The Recycle Bin works the same way. Files are not deleted from the hard disk per se, but are moved instead to the Recycle Bin from where they can be restored to their original location.

The Recycle Bin will eventually run out of space, in which case the files that have been in the Recycle Bin the longest are deleted to make room for additional files. Once a file is deleted from the Recycle Bin, however, it can no longer be recovered, as it has been physically deleted from the hard disk. Note, too, that the protection afforded by the Recycle Bin does not extend to files deleted from a floppy disk. Such files can be recovered, but only through utility programs outside of Windows 95.

## Backup

It's not a question of whether it will happen, but when—hard disks die, files are lost, or viruses may infect a system. It has happened to us and it will happen to you, but you can prepare for the inevitable by creating adequate backup *before* the problem occurs. The essence of a backup strategy is to decide which files to back up, how often to do the backup, and where to keep the backup. Once you decide on a strategy, follow it, and follow it faithfully!

Our strategy is very simple—back up what you can't afford to lose, do so on a daily basis, and store the backup away from your computer. You need not copy every file, every day. Instead copy just the files that changed during the current session. Realize, too, that it is much more important to back up your data files than your program files. You can always reinstall the application from the original disks, or if necessary, go to the vendor for another copy of an application. You, however, are the only one who has a copy of the term paper that is due tomorrow. Forewarned is forearmed.

## Write Protection

A floppy disk is normally ***write-enabled*** (the square hole is covered) so that you can change the contents of the disk. Thus, you can create (save) new files to a write-enabled disk and/or edit or delete existing files. Occasionally, however, you may want to ***write-protect*** a floppy disk (by sliding the tab to expose the square hole) so that its contents cannot be modified. This is typically done with a backup disk when you want to prevent the accidental deletion of a file or the threat of virus infection.

## Our Last Exercise

As we have indicated throughout the appendix, the ability to move and copy files is of paramount importance. The only way to master these skills is through practice, and so we offer one last exercise in which you execute a variety of commands to reinforce the material.

The exercise begins with the floppy disk containing the five practice files in drive A. We ask you to create two folders on drive A (step 1) and to move the various files into these folders (step 2). Next, you copy a folder from drive A to drive C (step 3), modify one of the files in the folder on drive C (step 4), then copy the modified file back to drive A (step 5). We ask you to delete a file in step 6, then recover it from the Recycle Bin in step 7. There is a lot to do, so let's get started.

## HANDS-ON EXERCISE 4

### *The Windows Explorer*

**Objective:** To use the Windows Explorer to move, copy, and delete a file, then recover a deleted file from the Recycle Bin. Use Figure 12 as a guide in the exercise.

**STEP 1: Create a New Folder**

- Start the Windows Explorer and maximize its window. Place the floppy disk (from hands-on exercise 2 or 3) in drive A.
- Select (click) the icon for **drive A** in the left pane of the Explorer window. Drive A should contain the files shown in Figure 12a. It does not contain any folders.
- Point to a blank area anywhere in the **right pane,** then click the **right mouse button** to display a context-sensitive menu.
- Click (or point to) the **New command** in the menu, then click **Folder** to create a new Folder on drive A.
- The icon for a new folder will appear with the name of the folder (New Folder) highlighted. Type **Computing 101** to change the name of the folder. Press the **enter key.**
- Click the icon for **drive A** once again. Pull down the **File menu,** click (or point to) the **New command,** and click **Folder** as the type of object to create.
- Type **Other Files** to change the name of the folder. Press **enter.** The right pane should now contain five documents and two folders.
- Pull down the **View menu.** Click (or point to) the **Arrange icons command** to display a submenu, then click the **By Name command.** The folders are displayed in alphabetical order followed by the files in alphabetical order.

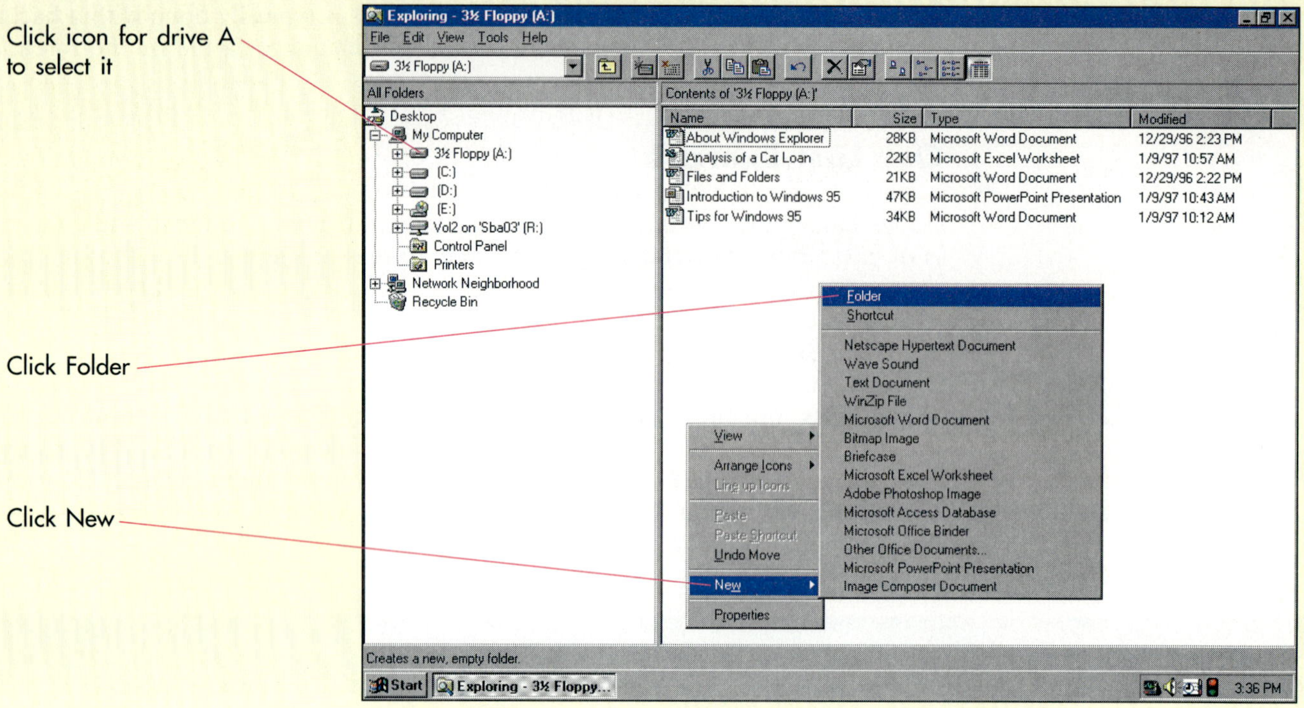


(a) Create a New Folder (step 1)

**FIGURE 12** Hands-on Exercise 4

## RENAME COMMAND

Point to a file or a folder, then click the right mouse button to display a menu with commands pertaining to the object. Click the Rename command. The name of the file or folder will be highlighted with the insertion point (a flashing vertical line) positioned at the end of the name. Enter a new name, to replace the selected name, or click anywhere within the name to change the insertion point and edit the name.

### STEP 2: Move a File

➤ Click the **plus sign** next to drive A to expand the drive as shown in Figure 12b. Note the following:

- Drive A is selected in the left pane. The right pane displays the contents of drive A (the selected object in the left pane). The folders are shown first and appear in alphabetical order. The file names are displayed after the folders and are also in alphabetical order.
- There is a minus sign next to the icon for drive A in the left pane, indicating that its folders have been expanded. Thus, the folder names also appear under drive A in the left pane.

➤ Click and drag the icon for the file **About Windows Explorer** from the right pane to the **Computing 101 folder** in the left pane. This moves the file into that folder.

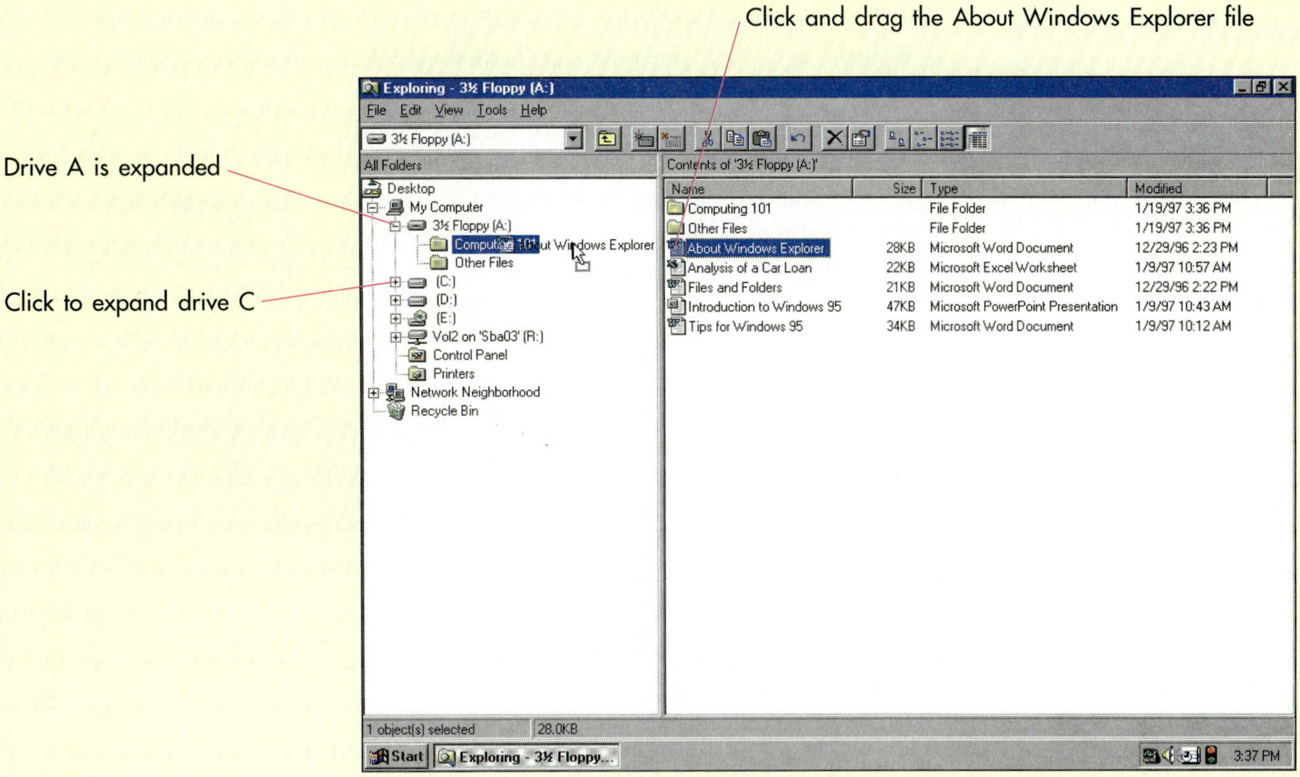


(b) Move the Files (step 2)

**FIGURE 12** Hands-on Exercise 4 (continued)

- Click and drag the **Tips for Windows 95 icon** and the **Files and Folders icon** to the **Computing 101 folder** to move these files into the folder.
- Click the **Computing 101 icon** in the left pane to select the folder and display its contents in the right pane. You should see the three files that were just moved.
- Click the icon for **drive A** in the left pane, then click and drag the remaining files, **Analysis of a Car Loan** and **Introduction to Windows 95** to the **Other Files folder.**

### USE THE RIGHT MOUSE BUTTON

The result of dragging a file with the left mouse button depends on whether the source and destination folders are on the same or different drives. Dragging a file to a folder on a different drive copies the file. Dragging the file to a folder on the same drive moves the file. If you find this hard to remember, and most people do, click and drag with the right mouse button to display a shortcut menu asking whether you want to copy or move the file. This simple tip can save you from making a careless (and potentially serious) error. Use it!

### STEP 3: Copy a Folder

- If necessary, click the **plus sign** next to the icon for drive C to expand the drive and display its folders as shown in Figure 12c.
- Do *not* click the folder icon for drive C, as drive A is to remain selected. (You can expand or collapse an object without selecting it.)
- Point to the **Computing 101 folder** in either pane, click the **right mouse button** and drag the folder to the icon for **drive C** in the left pane, then release the mouse to display a shortcut menu. Click the **Copy Here** command.
- You should see the Copy files dialog box as the individual files within the folder are copied from drive A to drive C.

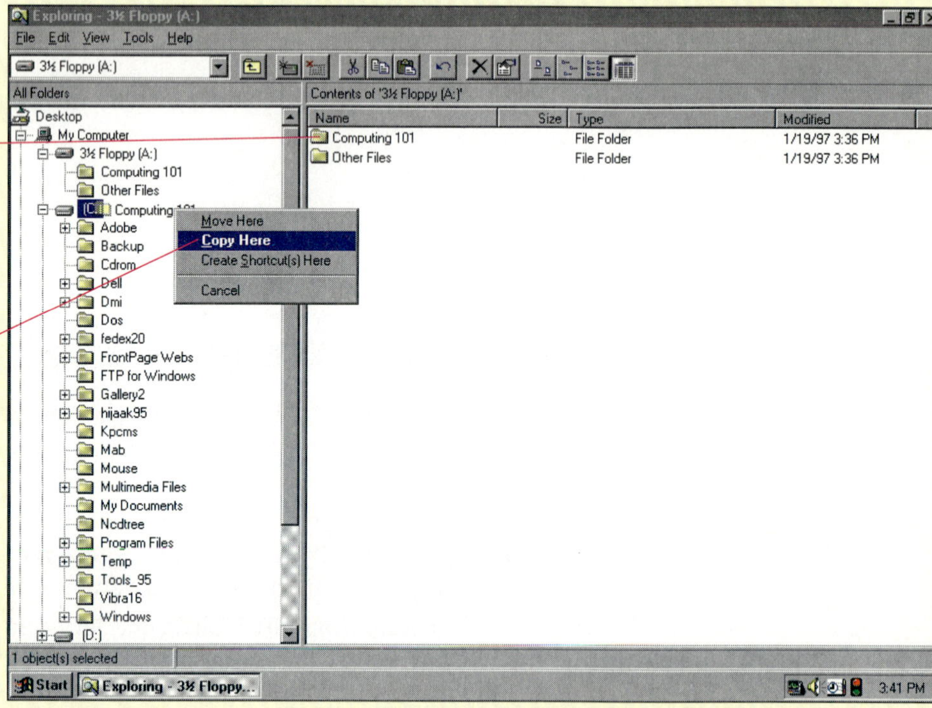


(c) Copy a Folder (step 3)

**FIGURE 12** Hands-on Exercise 4 (continued)

#### CUSTOMIZE THE EXPLORER WINDOW

Increase (or decrease) the size of the left pane within the Explorer Window by dragging the vertical line separating the left and right panes in the appropriate direction. You can also drag the right border of the various column headings (Name, Size, Tip, and Modified) in the right pane to increase (or decrease) the width of the column in order to see more (or less) information in that column. Double click the right border of a column heading to automatically adjust the column width to accommodate the widest entry in that column.

- ➤ If you see the Confirm Folder Replace dialog box, it means that the previous student forgot to delete the Computing 101 folder when he or she did this exercise. Click the **Yes to All button** so that the files on your floppy disk will replace the previous versions on drive C.
- ➤ Please remember to **delete** the Computing 101 folder on drive C, as described in step 8 at the end of the exercise.

**STEP 4: Modify a Document**

- ➤ Click (select) the **Computing 101 folder** on drive C to open the folder as shown in Figure 12d. The contents of this folder are shown in the right pane.
- ➤ Double click the **About Windows Explorer** file to open the file and edit the document. Press **Ctrl+End** to move to the end of the document. Add the sentence shown in Figure 12d followed by your name. (See boxed tip on page 46 if you are unable to read the document.)
- ➤ Pull down the **File menu** and click **Save** to save the modified file (or click the **Save button** on the Standard toolbar). Pull down the **File menu** and click **Exit** to exit from Microsoft Word.
- ➤ The entire Windows Explorer window is again visible. Pull down the **View menu** and click **Refresh** (or press the **F5 key**) to update the contents of the right pane. The date and time associated with the About Windows Explorer file has been changed to indicate that the file has just been modified.

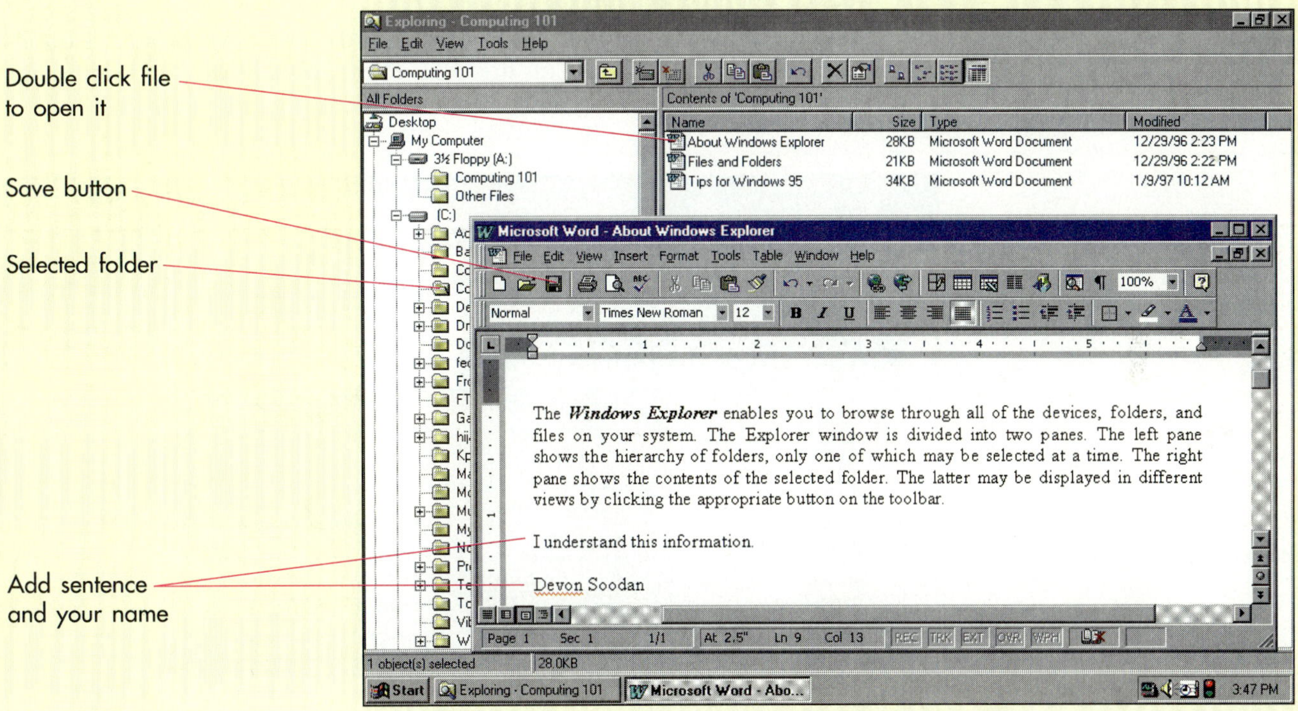


(d) Modify a Document (step 4)

**FIGURE 12** Hands-on Exercise 4 (continued)

## FILE FORMATS ARE INCOMPATIBLE

If you are unable to open the Word document in our exercise, it is because you are using Microsoft Word 7.0 (also known as Microsoft Word for Windows 95) rather than Word 97. The new release can read documents created in the earlier version, but the converse is not true—that is, Word 7.0 cannot read documents created by Word 97. (Our file was created in Word 97.) The incompatibility between Office 97 and its predecessor Office 95 is a potential problem for millions of users.

**STEP 5: Copy (Back Up) a File**

- Verify that the **Computing 101 folder** on drive C is the active folder as denoted by the open folder icon. Click and drag the icon for the **About Windows Explorer** file from the right pane to the **Computing 101 folder** on **drive A** in the left pane.
- You will see the message in Figure 12e, indicating that the folder (drive A) already contains a file called About Windows Explorer and asking whether you want to replace the existing file.
- Click **Yes** because you want to replace the previous version of the file on drive A with the updated version on drive C.
- You have just backed up the file; in other words, you have created a duplicate copy of a file on drive C on drive A. Thus, you can use the floppy disk to restore the file should anything happen to drive C.

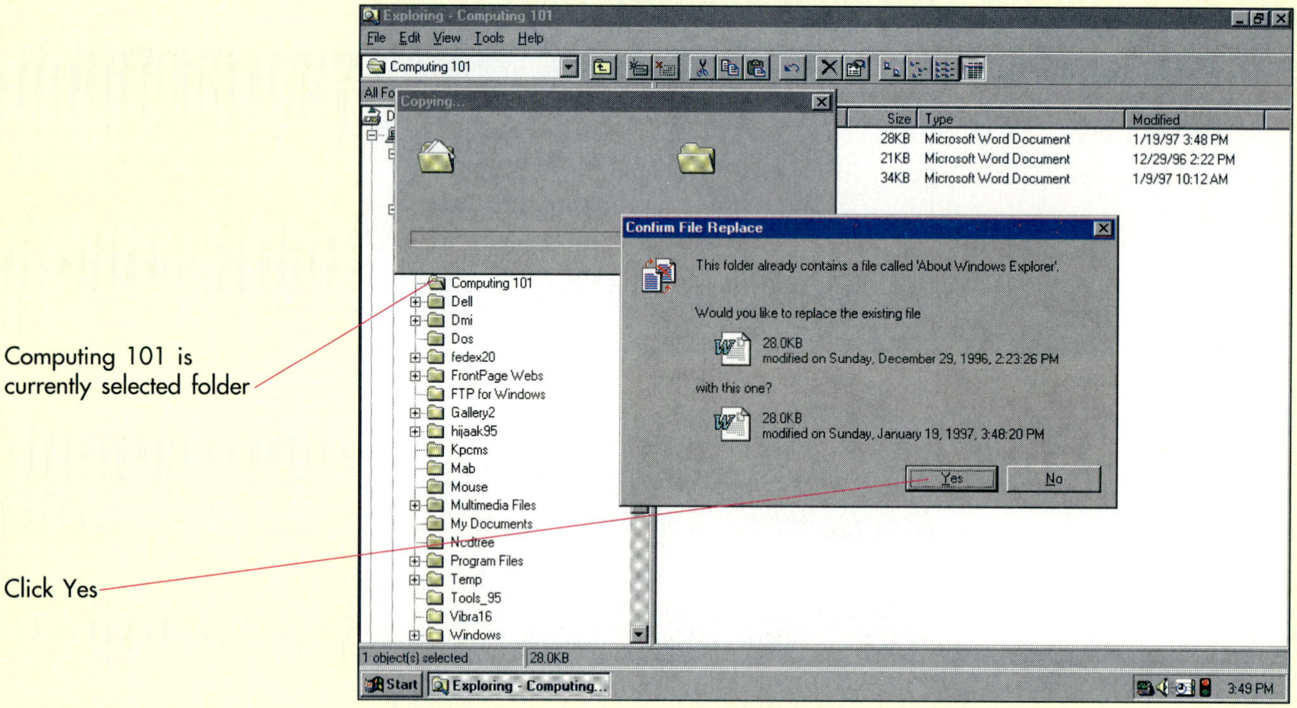


(e) Copy (Back Up) a File (step 5)

FIGURE 12 Hands-on Exercise 4 (continued)

## COPYING FROM ONE FLOPPY DISK TO ANOTHER

You've learned how to copy a file from drive C to drive A, or from drive A to drive C, but how do you copy a file from one floppy disk to another? It's easy when you know how. Place the first floppy disk in drive A, select drive A in the left pane of the Explorer windows, then copy the file(s) from the right pane to a temporary folder on drive C in the left pane. Remove the first floppy disk, and replace it with the second. Press the F5 key to refresh the display in the right pane. Select the temporary folder on drive C in the left pane, then click and drag the file(s) from the left pane to the floppy disk in the right pane.

**STEP 6: Delete a Folder**

- Select (click) the **Computing 101 folder** on drive C in the left pane. Pull down the **File menu** and click **Delete** (or press the **Del key**).
- You will see the dialog box in Figure 12f asking whether you are sure you want to delete the folder (that is, send the folder and its contents to the Recycle Bin). Note the green recycle logo within the box, which implies that you will be able to restore the file.
- Click **Yes** to delete the folder. The folder disappears from drive C. Pull down the **Edit menu.** Click **Undo Delete.** The deletion is cancelled and the folder reappears in the left pane.

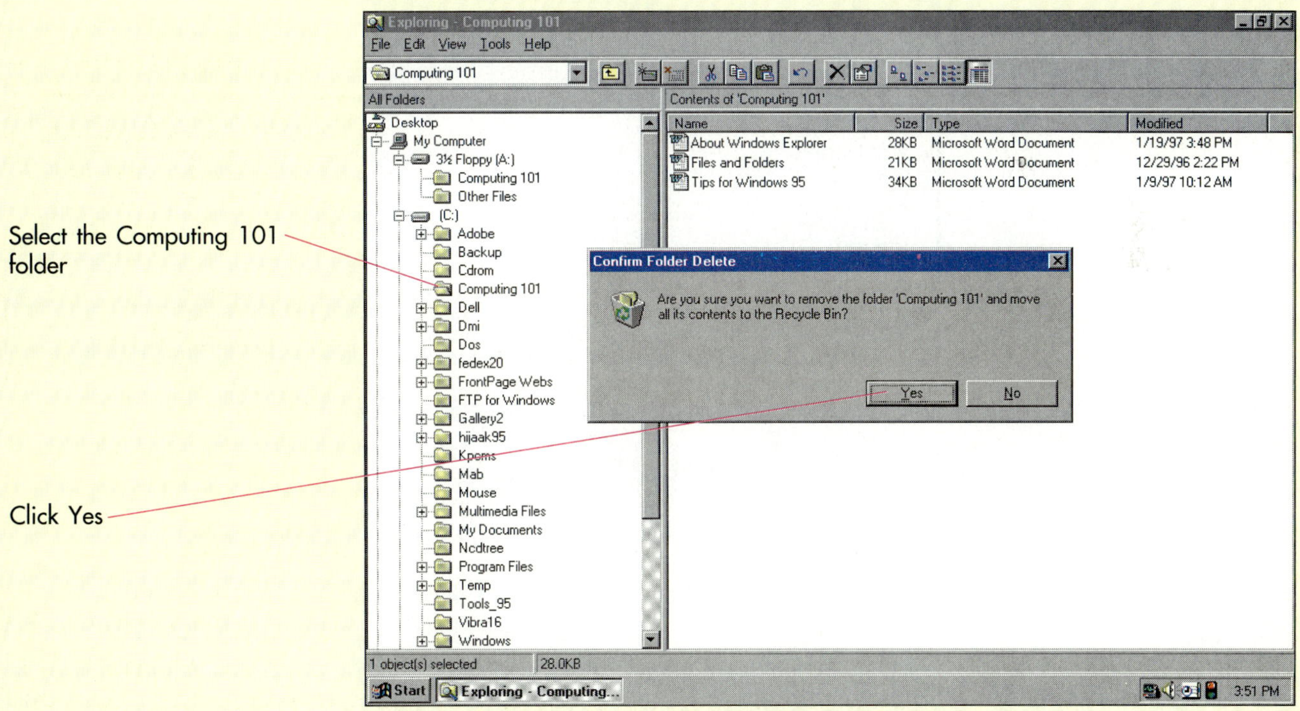


(f) Deleting a Folder (step 6)

**FIGURE 12** Hands-on Exercise 4 (continued)

**STEP 7: The Recycle Bin**

- If necessary, select the **Computing 101 folder** on drive C in the left pane. Select (click) the **About Windows Explorer** file in the right pane. Press the **Del key,** then click **Yes** when asked whether to delete the file.
- Double click the **Recycle Bin icon** on the desktop if you can see its icon, *or* Double click the **Recycled icon** within the window for drive C. (You may have to scroll in order to see the icon.)
- The Recycle Bin contains all files that have been previously deleted from drive C, and hence you may see a different number of files than those displayed in Figure 12g.
- Point to the **About Windows Explorer** file, click the **right mouse button** to display the shortcut menu in Figure 12g, then click **Restore.** The file disappears from the Recycle Bin because it has been returned to the Computing 101 folder. Select the folder and verify the file is back.

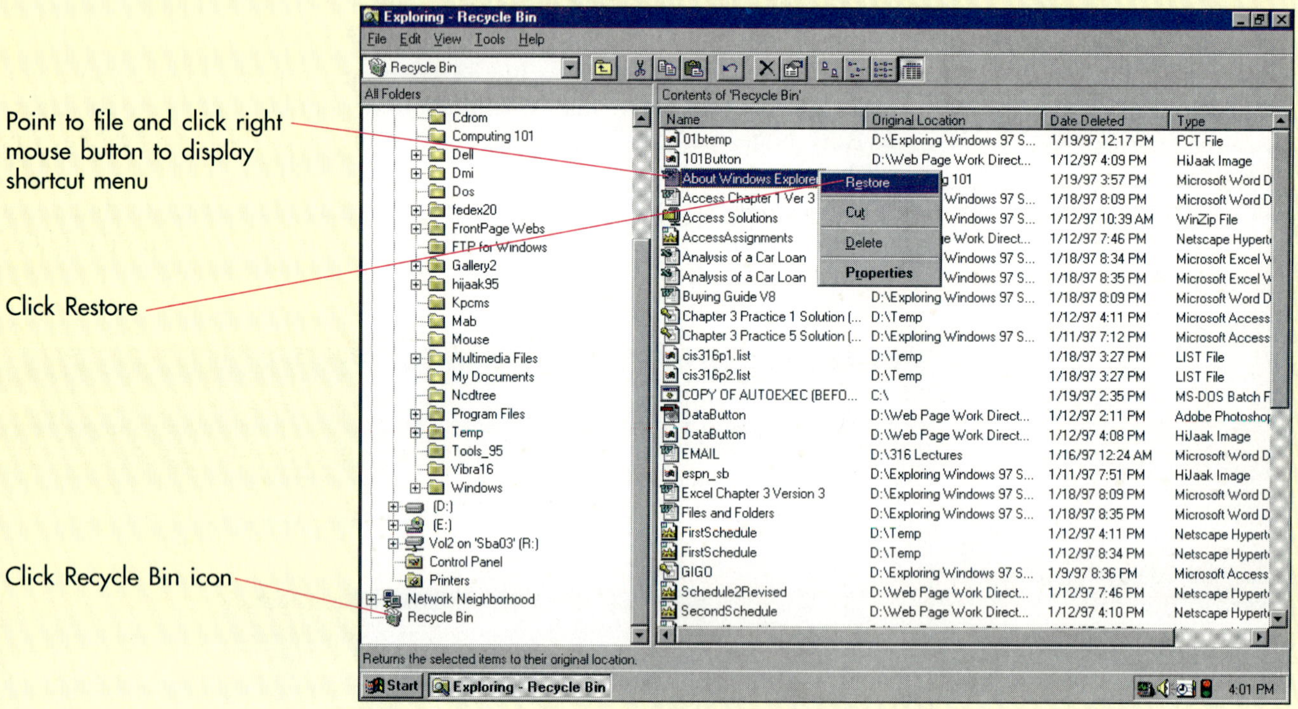


(g) Recover a File (step 7)

FIGURE 12 Hands-on Exercise 4 (continued)

**STEP 8: Complete the Exercise**

- Delete the **Computing 101 folder** on **drive C** as a courtesy to the next student.
- Click the **Computing 101 folder** on drive A in the left pane. Repeat the steps described on page 38 to capture the screen and prove to your instructor that you did the exercise.
- Exit Windows. Congratulations on a job well done. You have mastered the basics and are ready to begin working in Microsoft Office.

# INDEX